American Rhetoric from Roosevelt to Reagan

A Collection of Speeches and Critical Essays

Second Edition

Halford Ross Ryan

Washington & Lee University

WAVELAND PRESS, INC.

Prospect Heights, Illinois

For information about this book, write or call:

Waveland Press, Inc.
P.O. Box 400
Prospect Heights, Illinois 60070
(312) 634-0081

About the Editor

Halford Ryan graduated from Wabash College in 1966 and received the M.A. in 1968 and the Ph.D. in 1972 from the University of Illinois. He is professor of public speaking at Washington and Lee University, Lexington, Virginia. He teaches courses in American public address and presidential rhetoric.

Dr. Ryan has also authored/edited: *Persuasive Advocacy: Cases for Argumentation and Debate, American Orators of the Twentieth Century: Critical Studies and Sources* (co-edited with Bernard K. Duffy), and *American Orators Before 1900: Critical Studies and Sources* (co-edited with Bernard K. Duffy).

Contents

Contents

Acknowledgments

Along the way, one becomes obligated to certain people and institutions. I wish to acknowledge that debt here.

Professors Joseph O'Rourke and Victor Powell, Speech Department, Wabash College, taught a love and appreciation for public speaking and the study of speeches. Indeed, I gained from Wabash College a strong foundation in a liberal and humanistic education which leaves its vestiges in these pages. Prof. Eric Dean of the Religion Department encouraged me to undertake studies at Princeton Theological Seminary where, if only for a year, I further learned the principle of the text's being the *alpha* and *omega* of the critic's inquiry.

At the University of Illinois, the Speech and History Departments strongly influenced my perception of things rhetorical. Prof. Karl Wallace introduced me to Aristotle's *Rhetoric* where a knowledge of Greek proved invaluable, and Prof. Marie Nichols to rhetorical criticism and theory. Prof. Winton Solberg's American intellectual and cultural history courses and Prof. Robert Johannsen's history of the Civil War demonstrated the history of rhetoric's humanizing role in America.

The Washington and Lee University Glenn Grants have generously supported my original research in three presidential libraries, as has the Eleanor Roosevelt Institute.

Publisher Neil Rowe deserves the thanks of our discipline for his willingness to publish a very much needed anthology for a very small but significant market of scholars and students.

I wish to thank Nelson Keener, the Old Time Gospel Hour, for granting permission to print a text. I acknowledge the use of three speeches from the *New York Times*. The editors of *Vital Speeches of the Day* kindly cooperated in contributing to the core of the speech collection. Also, I wish to thank the various individuals who granted permission to use the journal essays: William Work for the Speech Communication Association, R. Gordon Hoxie for the Center for the Study of the Presidency, James

Weaver for the Central States Speech Association, Gary Keele for the Western Speech Communication Association, and John Sisco for the Southern Speech Communication Association.

Lastly, I thank my wife and good friend for always being there.

Halford Ryan
Lexington, Virginia

An Introduction to a Study of American Public Address

Waveland Press and I are grateful for the support of *American Rhetoric from Roosevelt to Reagan* and we offer a second edition to make it more responsive to the needs of its present and future patrons.

The student of contemporary American public address, rhetorical criticism, and persuasion needs two fundamental kinds of original materials upon which to build a successful mastery of these disciplines. I believe that the student can begin to study these disciplines by scrutinizing texts of speeches. But which speeches should one study? From many useful criteria, I chose two that somewhat overlap. First, I selected significant or standard political speakers. I make the word "political" go beyond mere party politics and use the word in its original and wider Greek sense of the *polis*: the concerns of the state. Second, I selected speeches which can be treated as examples of advocacy or debate on important issues of the American *polis*.

The genre of inaugural addresses is represented by Franklin Roosevelt's First and Fourth Inaugural Addresses and John Kennedy's Inaugural Address. FDR's First was one of the most persuasive inaugurals ever delivered, and JFK's was noted more for its accomplishments in style than for its attainments toward action. FDR's Fourth stands as one of his most personal and philosophical speeches.

The era of the New Deal produced rhetorical visions other than Roosevelt's. Father Charles Coughlin stridently attacked the president for allegedly double-crossing the American people. The appealing, but oversimplified, Share Our Wealth program trumpeted by Senator Huey Long also demonstrated that not everyone was beguiled by FDR's brand of persuasion. The New Deal may have ended on December 8, 1941 (Long was dead by an assassin's bullet and Coughlin was silenced by his ecclesiastical superiors), but the country then rallied around Roosevelt's war rhetoric with its anaphoristic accusations against the Japanese and its moral imperative that the American people "win through to absolute victory."

There have been eight First Ladies in the White House since the Roosevelt presidency, but there has only been one First Lady of the World. Eschewing designer clothes and "photo opportunities," Mrs. Eleanor Roosevelt turned her constructive energies toward helping the dispossessed after the death of her Franklin. "The Struggle for Human Rights" speech presents the good woman speaking well on behalf of humanity at a time when there were no human rights and it was not fashionable to speak on such subjects.

President Harry S Truman's "Far Eastern Policy" speech and General Douglas MacArthur's reply in "Don't Scuttle the Pacific" present an interesting study in who would be the rhetorical commander-in-chief during the Korean war. Against Truman's bald repetition and restatement of avoiding a third world war, MacArthur painted patriotic word pictures that caused Truman to be hung in effigy. Yet, when the dust of the patriotic pablum had settled, the plebian had triumphed over the patrician.

General Douglas MacArthur's "Duty, Honor, and Country" is an example of the Asian style, perhaps run amuck. Phrases, sentences, and even paragraphs were constructed in thirds to reinforce the trilogy slogan of West Point. The Attic style can be eloquent without being grandiloquent, understated without being obtrusive, and Adlai Stevenson's "Eulogy to Sir Winston Churchill" exhibits Stevenson's expertise in crafting epideictic oratory.

Richard Nixon's speeches must be reckoned with rhetorically. His "My Side of the Story" was probably the most successful political speech ever delivered. It cleverly cleared Nixon's path to the vice-presidency and yet concomitantly coalesced a conception of his character that haunted him throughout his oratorical career. "The War in Vietnam," through questionable rhetorical tactics, dalliance in political NewSpeak, and divisive language, pinpointed appeals that were acceptable to the silent majority but anathema to the vocal minority. "Cambodia" was the apotheosis, or nadir depending on one's perspective, of Nixon's scapegoating, polarizing, jingoistic justification for making public an already ongoing war in Cambodia.

Senator John Kennedy's *apologia* concerning his Catholicism was delivered in Houston, Texas, during the 1960 presidential campaign. The issue which had plagued presidential campaigner Alfred Smith a generation earlier was skillfully eliminated through the speech. Kennedy transcended the religious issue to the real issue concerning the kind of America he believed in and fought for. Such a strategy bolstered his political image, devalued the religious issue, and differentiated religious bigots from mainstream American politics. JFK's eagerness to confront the religious issue at the buckle of the Bible belt was repeated as the cold warrior went eyeball-to-eyeball with the Soviets over their missiles in Cuba. The "Arms Quarantine" speech (whose title is an instance of NewSpeak) was replete with devil-angel dichotomies, crisis rhetoric, and character-testing appeals.

Fortunately for the president and his people, the Russians blinked first as phrased by Secretary of State Dean Rusk.

Martin Luther King's "I Have a Dream" speech is *sui generis*. But the pragmatic possibilities of the dream had to be realized politically. The beginning of the end of racism in this country was set in motion by President Dwight Eisenhower over the situation in Little Rock, Arkansas. Although there is a hint in the speech of distaste for the task at hand, Ike spoke and acted to uphold the law of the land. Yet, it was a Southerner, Lyndon B. Johnson, who aroused the nation and the Congress to realize King's dream. LBJ's "The Right to Vote" speech to a joint session of the Congress was his most eloquent address on a right now taken for granted. This speech is a monument to LBJ's better nature.

1969 was an exceptional year for accusations and apologies. Senator Edward Kennedy's "Chappiquiddick" address was an *apologia* similar to Senator Nixon's televised "Checkers" speech. Although it answered the immediate accusations, lingering doubts persisted. Vice-President Spiro Agnew, standing in for his boss in 1969, accused the news media with a McCarthy-like rhetoric: guilt by association, character assassination, name-calling, and the appearance of "proof" in the form of statistical evidence. All of this was presented in Agnew's distinctive verbal style.

The role of women in American polity has been the concern of orators. Shirley Chisholm addressed the Equal Rights Amendment by noting its advantages for men as well as for women. Anita Taylor discussed the role communication and female communication can have for a woman as she decides *quo vadis*.

In recent memory, Democratic convention keynote addresses have had a remarkably salutary effect on their speakers' political careers. If the Watergate hearings capped Barbara Jordan's Congressional career, her 1976 keynote address secured her place in speech annals. Governor Mario Cuomo's much touted keynote address at the 1984 Democratic convention eloquently asked Americans to examine the differences between Reagan's rhetoric and reality. Only time will tell whether Cuomo's family-oriented rhetoric was a flash in the pan. Whatever the outcome, the speech substantiates the fact that oratory, even in the age of television, can still capture the American audience's attention and catapult a speaker to national status. At that same convention, the Rev. Jesse Jackson delivered his "Rainbow Coalition" address. Aside from the telling substance of his assessment of the American *polis*, the form of the speech might suggest an alternate title such as the "Rainbow Style" since almost every hue and shade of *elocutio* is refracted in Jackson's rhetoric.

On the other side of the aisle is the Rev. Jerry Falwell's "Strengthening Families in America." The speech is a hybrid of the Puritan jeremiad grounded in the twentieth-century cult of the personality. In both Jackson's and Falwell's speeches, one detects the sincere motivation of each man to "make straight paths of righteousness" in the United States and to urge Americans to fulfill the inscription on the Great Seal of the United States: *Novus Ordo Seculorum.*

President Jimmy Carter's rhetoric was often panned as being so languid as to be soporific. His address on the Panama Canal treaties was one of his best speeches. Carter's refutation of possible objections to the treaties was of particular interest. His rhetoric and policy ring true despite vehement objections from conservatives.

President Ronald Reagan's rhetoric closes this book. His "Free Enterprise" speech is an early harbinger of the Reagan revolution and signals the role anecdotes continue to serve in Reagan's speeches. America's first cowboy never sat taller in the saddle than in the Lebanon and Grenada address. Reagan wrapped failure in success and employed style that reflected Kate Smith's rendition of "God Bless America" to World War II audiences. Critics accused Reagan of reversing Teddy Roosevelt's famous dictum to speak loudly and carry a little stick when addressing the terrorist problem. The president responded to Kaddafi's measures in his speech on Libyan terrorism. Reagan's *apologia* on the arms sale to Iran could be an instance of the Teflon presidency gone awry. Hindsight will enable the student to assess whether the coating was worn too thin due to repeated usage.

Publishers Neil and Carol Rowe kindly consented to my personal wish that Oliver Wendell Holmes' ninetieth birthday speech be included. The diction is Brahmin, the values Puritan, and the eloquence understated: all from a man who fought in Mr. Lincoln's war as a young lieutenant.

In regard to the selection of the various speeches and speakers, I am aware of, and probably guilty of, "the irony of the artist: that a portrait is more often a reflection of the artist than of the sitter."[1]

Yet, a speech is something more than a text. A speaker delivered the speech to an audience in a particular time and place for some purpose and effect.[2] So, secondly, the student needs to have in hand essays about persuasive discourse written by rhetorical scholars. Again, from many criteria, I chose essays which focus on the case study approach.[3] Within that approach, and in order to acquaint the student with a range of practices in

[1]Conal Furay, *The Grass Roots Mind in America* (New York: New Viewpoints, 1977), p. 133.
[2]Marie Hochmuth, "The Criticism of Rhetoric," in *A History and Criticism of American Public Address* (3 vols.; New York: Russell and Russell, 1955), III, 1-23.
[3]See Waldo W. Braden, "III. Public Address and the Humanities," *Southern Speech Communication Journal,* 41 (1976), 151-157, and Theodore Otto Windt, Jr., "Hoyt H. Hudson: Spokesman for the Cornell School of Rhetoric," *Quarterly Journal of Speech,* 68 (1982), 186-200.

rhetorical criticism, I selected articles which illustrate different critical methodologies. The two essays on Roosevelt's inaugurals explicate three rhetorical techniques and trace the evolution of a rhetorical text. Prof. Gaske gives a fine framework for evaluating Long's demogogic discourse, and it can also be used to criticize some of the other speeches. Aside from a study of presidential interaction with his speech staff, the Truman piece offers an interesting analog to MacArthur's speech. Prof. Ling's penetrating essay demonstrates a Burkeian analysis of Senator Kennedy's Chappaquiddick speech. Prof. McGuckin treats the important role which values played in Senator Nixon's *apologia*, and Prof. Thompson analyzes values in Congresswoman Jordan's address. Prof. Ritter explicates public relations politics in the evolving role of an actor-turned-governor-turned-president. The essay on LBJ's voting rights address develops the speech in terms of the speech materials in the Johnson Library. Prof. Hahn demonstrates how JFK used his Inaugural Address to establish his presidential persona. As with my list of speeches, I wish that I were not constrained in my selection of essays because many other valuable ones could be included. I do not advocate any one methodology over another one because each stands on its own merits. Yet, having said that, I would find it salutary if, after assaying alternative methodologies, the student of rhetoric could conclude that one methodology—or some reasonable combination thereof—would more appropriately suit a particular rhetorical text. Methodologies were made for speeches and not speeches for methodologies. The student of rhetorical criticism and contemporary American public address should approach a speech with an informed but open mind. One should give careful consideration to Prof. Walter Fisher's admonition: "The essential stance of the critic must be *informed innocence.* Telling a useful 'truth' about a remarkable work requires that the critic...know as much as is possible about rhetorical things, especially history and theory. But however much information the critic brings to a work, it must not blind her or him to the information provided by the work itself."[4]

In closing, I acknowledge the shortcomings of any anthology of selected speeches and essays, and mine is perhaps an egregious example. If that is the case, I would apologize for my effort by recurring to a defense which Benjamin Franklin offered for adoption of the Constitution at the Constitutional Convention of 1787: "On the whole, sir, I can not help expressing a wish that every member of the convention who may still have objections to it, would, with me, on this occasion, doubt a little of his own infallibility, and, to make manifest our unanimity, put his name to this instrument."[5]

[4]Walter R. Fisher, "Genre: Concepts and Applications in Rhetorical Criticism," *Western Journal of Speech Communication,* 44 (1980), 299.

[5]Benjamin Franklin, "On the Faults of the Constitution," in *The World's Great Speeches,* ed. Lewis Copeland and Lawrence W. Lamm (3rd enlarged ed.; New York: Dover Publications, Inc., 1973), p. 237.

On His Ninetieth Birthday

Oliver Wendell Holmes, Jr.

Oliver Wendell Holmes, Jr. (March 8, 1841 - March 6, 1935) graduated from Harvard College in 1861; was a lieutenant in the Civil War; associate justice, 1882-99, and chief justice, 1899-1902, Supreme Judicial Court of Massachusetts; associate justice of Supreme Court of the United States, 1902-1932. He left the bulk of his estate to the United States of America. The speech was broadcast by radio on March 7, 1931. Published version: The Mind and Truth of Justice Holmes, *ed. Max Lerner (Boston: Little, Brown and Co., 1951).*

In this symposium my part is only to sit in silence. To express one's feelings as the end draws near is too intimate a task.

But I may mention one thought that comes to me as a listener-in. The riders in a race do not stop short when they reach the goal. There is a little finishing canter before coming to a standstill. There is time to hear the kind voice of friends and to say to oneself, "The work is done."

But just as one says that, the answer comes, "The race is over, but the work never is done while the power to work remains."

The canter that brings you to a standstill need not be only coming to rest. It cannot be, while you still live, for to live is to function. That is all there is in living.

And so I end with a line from a Latin poet who uttered the message more than fifteen hundred years ago: "Death, death, plucks my ear and says, 'Live—I am coming.'"

First Inaugural Address
Franklin Delano Roosevelt

Delivered in Washington, D.C., March 4, 1933. Franklin Roosevelt (January 30, 1882 - April 12, 1945) graduated from Harvard in 1904 and attended Columbia University Law School; practiced law, 1907-10; member of New York Senate, 1910-13; assistant Secretary of the Navy, 1913-20; Democratic vice president nominee, 1920; Governor of New York, 1929-33; 31st President of the United States, 1933-45. Published version: the following text is based on FDR's Reading Copy as corrected by a recording of the speech, and audience applause is bracketed. Acknowledgement is given to the Franklin D. Roosevelt Library.

President Hoover, Mr. Chief Justice, my friends. This is a day of national consecration, and I am certain that on this day my fellow Americans expect that on my induction into the Presidency I will address them with a candor and a decision which the present situation of our people impels. This is preeminently the time to speak the truth, the whole truth, frankly and boldly. Nor need we shrink from honestly facing conditions in our country today. This great nation will endure as it has endured, will revive, and will prosper. So, first of all, let me assert my firm belief that the only thing we have to fear is fear itself — nameless, unreasoning, unjustified terror which paralyzes needed efforts to convert retreat into advance.

In every dark hour of our national life, a leadership of frankness and of vigor has met with that understanding and support of the people themselves which is essential to victory. And I am convinced that you will again give that support to leadership in these critical days.

In such a spirit on my part and on yours we face our common difficulties. They concern, thank God, only material things. Values have shrunk to fantastic levels, taxes have risen, our ability to pay has fallen, government of all kinds is faced by serious curtailment of income, the means of exchange are frozen in the currents of trade, the withered leaves of industrial enterprise lie on every side, farmers find no markets for their produce, and the savings of many years in thousands of families are gone. More important, a host of unemployed citizens face the grim problem of existence, and an equally great number toil with little return. Only a foolish optimist can deny the dark realities of the moment.

And yet our distress comes from no failure of substance. We are stricken by no plague of locusts. Compared with the perils which our forefathers conquered, because they believed and were not afraid, we have still much to be thankful for. Nature still offers her bounty, and human efforts have multiplied it. Plenty is at our doorstep, but a generous use of it languishes in the very sight of the supply. Primarily, this is because the rulers of the exchange of mankind's goods have failed through their own stubbornness and their own incompetence, have admitted their failure, and have abdicated. Practices of the unscrupulous money-changers stand indicted in the court of public opinion, rejected by the hearts and minds of men.

True, they have tried, but their efforts have been cast in the pattern of an outworn tradition. Faced by failure of credit, they have proposed only the lending of more money. Stripped of the lure of profit by which to induce our people to follow their false leadership, they have resorted to exhortations, pleading tearfully for restored confidence. They only know the rules of a generation of self-seekers. They have no vision, and when there is no vision the people perish.

Yes, the money-changers have fled from their high seats in the temple of our civilization. We may now restore that temple to the ancient truths [applause]. The measure of that restoration lies in the extent to which we apply social values more noble than mere monetary profit. Happiness lies not in the mere possession of money; it lies in the joy of achievement, in the thrill of creative effort. The joy, the moral stimulation, of work no longer must be forgotten in the mad chase of evanescent profits. These dark days, my friends, will be worth all they cost us if they teach us that our true destiny is not to be ministered unto but to minister to ourselves, to our fellowmen [applause].

Recognition of that falsity of material wealth as the standard of success goes hand in hand with the abandonment of the false belief that public office and high political position are to be valued only by the standards of pride of place and personal profit. And there must be an end to conduct in banking and in business which too often has given to a sacred trust the likeness of callous and selfish wrongdoing [applause]. Small wonder that confidence languishes, for it thrives only on honesty, on honor, on the sacredness of obligations, on faithful protection, and on unselfish performance. Without them, it cannot live.

Restoration calls, however, not for changes in ethics alone. This nation is asking for action, and action now [applause].

Our greatest primary task is to put people to work [applause]. This is no unsolvable problem if we face it wisely and courageously. It can be accomplished in part by direct recruiting by the government itself, treating the task as we would treat the emergency of a war but at the same time, through this employment, accomplishing great—greatly needed projects to stimulate and reorganize the use of our great natural resources.

Hand in hand with that we must frankly recognize the overbalance of population in our industrial centers and by engaging on a national scale in a redistribution endeavor to provide a better use of the land for those best fitted for the land [applause]. Yes, the task can be helped by definite efforts to raise the values of agricultural products and with this the power to purchase the output of our cities. It can be helped by preventing realistically the tragedy of the growing loss through forecl—foreclosure of our small homes and our farms. It can be helped by insistence that the Federal, the state, and the local government act forthwith on the demand that their cost be drastically reduced [applause]. It can be helped by the unifying of relief activities which today are often scattered, uneconomical, unequal. It can be helped by national planning for and supervision of all forms of transportation and of communications and other utilities that have a definitely public character. There are many ways in which it can be helped, but it can never be helped by merely talking about it [applause].

We must act, and we must act quickly.

And finally, in our progress towards a resumption of work we require two safeguards against a return of the evils of the old order. There must be a strict supervision of all banking and credits and investments [applause]. There must be an end to speculation with other people's money [applause]. And there must be provision for an adequate but sound currency [applause].

These, my friends, are the lines of attack. I shall presently urge upon a new Congress, in special session, detailed measures for their fulfillment, and I shall seek the immediate assistance of the forty-eight states.

Through this program of action we address ourselves to putting our own national house in order and making income balance outgo. Our international trade relations, though vastly important, are in point of time and necessity secondary to the establishment of a sound national economy [applause]. I favor as a practical policy the putting of first things first. I shall spare no effort to restore world trade by international economic readjustment, but the emergency at home cannot wait on that accomplishment. The basic thought that guides these specific means of national recovery is not nationally—narrowly nationalistic. It is the insistence, as a first consideration, upon the interdependence of the various elements in and parts of the United States of America, a recognition of the old and permanently important manifestation of the American spirit of the pioneer. It is the way to recovery. It is the immediate way. It is the strongest assurance that recovery will endure.

In the field of world policy I would dedicate this nation to the policy of the "good neighbor"—the neighbor who resolutely respects himself and, because he does so, respects the rights of others—the neighbor who respects his obligations and respects the sanctity of his agreements in and with a world of neighbors [applause].

If I read the temper of our people correctly, we now realize as we have never realized before our interdependence on each other, that we cannot merely take but we must give as well, that if we are to go forward, we must move as a trained and loyal army, willing to sacrifice for the good of a common discipline, because without such discipline no progress can be made, no leadership becomes effective. We are, I know, ready and willing to submit our lives and our property to such discipline because it makes possible a leadership which aims at the larger good. This I propose to offer, pledging that the larger purposes will bind upon us, bind upon us all as a sacred obligation, with a unity of duty hitherto evoked only in times of armed strife.

With this pledge taken, I assume unhesitatingly the leadership of this great army of our people dedicated to a disciplined attack upon our common problems.

Action in this image, action to this end, is feasible under the form of government which we have inherited from our ancestors. Our constitution is so simple, so practical, that it is possible always to meet extraordinary needs by changes in emphasis and arrangement without loss of essential form. That is why our constitutional system has proved itself the most superbly enduring political mechanism the modern world has ever seen. It has met every stress of vast expansion of territory, of foreign wars, of bitter internal strife, of world relations. And it is to be hoped that the normal balance of executive and legislative authority may be wholly equal, wholly adequate, to meet the unprecedented task before us. But it may be that an unprecedented demand and need for undelayed action may call for temporary departure from that normal balance of public procedure. I am prepared under my constitutional duty to recommend the measures that a stricken nation in the midst of a stricken world may require. These measures, or such other measures as the Congress may build out of its experience and wisdom, I shall seek within my constitutional authority to bring to speedy adoption. But in the event that the Congress shall fail to take one of these two courses, in the event that the national emergency is still critical, I shall not evade the clear course of duty that will then confront me. I shall ask the Congress for the one remaining instrument to meet the crisis: broad executive power to wage a war against the emergency, as great as the power that would be given to me if we were in fact invaded by a foreign foe [applause].

For the trust reposed in me I return the courage and the devotion that befit the time. I can do no less.

We face the arduous days that lie before us in the warm courage of national unity, with the clear consciousness of seeking old and precious moral values, with the clean satisfaction that comes from the stern performance of duty by old and young alike. We aim at the assurance of a rounded, a permanent national life. We do not distrust the essen—the future of essential democracy. The people of the United States have not failed. In their need they have registered a mandate that they want direct, vigorous action. They have asked for discipline and direction under leadership. They have made me the present instrument of their wishes. In the spirit of the gift, I take it.

In this dedication [applause], in this dedication of a nation, we humbly ask the blessing of God. May he protect each and every one of us. May he guide me in the days to come.

Roosevelt's First Inaugural
A Study of Technique

Halford Ross Ryan

Historian David Potter's observation that, by historical hindsight, the critic might not perceive events as contemporaries comprehended them[1] is germane to a study of Franklin Delano Roosevelt's First Inaugural Address. Although Roosevelt had large majorities in the Congress, he could not know the "Hundred Days" legislation would pass without Congressional demurral or difficulty. To assume that FDR knew of his forthcoming legislative successes when he fashioned his first inaugural is mistaken, and such an assumption causes the critics to miss some valuable insights concerning FDR and his speech.

FDR's first inaugural is one of his best known and most important speeches. If for no other reason, it was a significant speech because FDR believed it contained all of the elements of his New Deal.[2] Samuel I. Rosenman ranked the speech among FDR's best: "This was one of the President's truly great speeches, not only in form and substance but in accomplishment."[3] And Harry Hopkins thought it was FDR's best speech: "For myself I think his first inaugural address was the best speech he ever made.... With that one speech, and in those few minutes, the appalling anxiety and fears were lifted, and the people of the United States knew that they were going into a safe harbor under the leadership of a man who never knew the meaning of fear."[4] But surprisingly little rhetorical attention has been paid the speech.[5]

[1]David M. Potter, *The Impending Crisis 1848-1861,* ed. Don E. Fehrenbacher (New York: Harper & Row, 1976), p. 145.

[2]*The Public Papers and Addresses of Franklin D. Roosevelt,* ed. Samuel I. Rosenman (1928-1936, 5 vols.; New York: Random House, 1938), II, 16.

[3]Samuel I. Rosenman, *Working with Roosevelt* (New York: Harper, 1952), p. 89.

[4]Harry L. Hopkins, "Foreword" in *Nothing to Fear,* ed. B.D. Zevin (Boston: Houghton Mifflin, 1946), p. viii.

[5]Although the following rhetorical works on FDR are helpful, they do not explicate FDR's first inaugural nor its significance: Earnest Brandenburg, "The Preparation of Franklin D. Roosevelt's Speeches," *Quarterly Journal of Speech,* 35 (1949), 214-21; Earnest Brandenburg

This article originally appeared in the *Quarterly Journal of Speech,* 65 (1979), 137-49, and is reprinted with the permission of the Speech Communication Association.

My primary purpose in this essay is to examine three rhetorical techniques that FDR used in his speech. Before discussing them, however, I wish to establish that they were indeed *his* techniques; and after discussing them I shall observe their similarity to Adolph Hitler's rhetorical techniques in response to the *zeitgeist* of March, 1933.

The Production of the Speech

In this section, I wish to examine three general areas: the nature of the texts, who was responsible for the original draft and the famous fear statement, and selected textual emendations by FDR.

The following extant drafts are in the Roosevelt Library, Hyde Park, New York: the first draft, which is in FDR's handwriting; the second draft, a typed copy of the first with a variety of emendations; the third draft, also typed, which includes the emendations from draft two and additional emendations; and a final typed reading copy from which FDR delivered his speech.[6]

The existence of Roosevelt's handwritten draft, in conjuction with a note which FDR had attached to this draft (the note stated that he wrote the first draft at Hyde Park on 27 February 1933), has led some to conclude that FDR authored his own inaugural address.[7] Although FDR wrote this first draft, he was not responsible for its authorship.

Rather, Raymond Moley composed the first draft. In fine, Moley has related how he prepared the first draft, how FDR copied his draft in longhand at Hyde Park, and how Moley tossed his own draft into the fire, with the words "This is your speech now," after FDR had finished copying his

and Waldo W. Braden, "Franklin D. Roosevelt's Voice and Pronunciation," *Quarterly Journal of Speech,* 38 (1952), 23-30; Harold P. Zelko, "Franklin D. Roosevelt's Rhythm in Rhetorical Style," *Quarterly Journal of Speech,* 28 (1942), 138-41; Hermann G. Stelzner, "'War Message,' December 8, 1941: An Approach to Language," *Speech Monographs,* 33 (1966), 419-37; Earnest Brandenburg and Waldo W. Braden, "Franklin Delano Roosevelt" in *A History and Criticism of American Public Address,* ed. Marie Kathryn Hochmuth, III (New York: Longmans, Green, 1955), 458-530.

[6]Inaugural Address, 1933, Master Speech File, Box 0610, Roosevelt Library. The first draft is on legal paper. The second draft was typed on Tuesday, February 28. The third draft was retyped on Wednesday, March 1. The reading copy was typed on March 3 in Washington. Hereafter, references to the Roosevelt Library holdings on the first inaugural will be cited as Master Speech File.

[7]James MacGregor Burns, *Roosevelt: The Lion and the Fox* (New York: Harcourt, Brace, 1956), p. 162. Edgar Eugene Robinson, *The Roosevelt Leadership 1933-1945* (Philadelphia: Lippincott, 1955), p. 104; Rosenman, *Working with Roosevelt,* p. 89; Ernest J. Wrage and Barnet Baskerville, eds., *Contemporary Forum: American Speeches on Twentieth-Century Issues* (New York: Harper, 1962), p. 136.

draft.[8] Moley's version is independently verified by an investigation of FDR's handwritten draft. Several of FDR's handwritten pages do suggest that he did copy them from another source. Instead of the speech text's filling each successive page, there are lacunae on pages three, five, and seven. These lacunae suggest that FDR took more pages to write than did Moley, or to put it another way, the ten pages of copy could be reduced to approximately eight pages if FDR had written his text seriatim on each page.[9]

As for the famous fear statement, "the only thing we have to fear is fear itself," a variety of sources have implied that it was somehow FDR's.[10] However, the phrase was undoubtedly Louis Howe's handiwork. Howe was FDR's personal secretary and Howe dictated a whole beginning paragraph for the third draft in which the phrase appears *de novo.*[11] If the phrase were not original with Howe, then his original source has eluded later researchers.[12]

I turn now to selected emendations made in the texts. But I shall deal only with FDR's revisions, and then only those revisions which are germane to my study.

Only one major relevant revision appears on the handwritten draft (FDR's copy from Moley's draft). In the second paragraph, Moley wrote of leadership in past national crises—the Revolution, the early emergence of the nation, and the Civil War—and how the people's support of that leadership "on every occasion has won through to." FDR crossed out the

[8]Raymond Moley, *The First New Deal* (New York: Harcourt, Brace & World, 1966), p. 114. Moley gives a general description of his composition of the address and discusses his and Louis Howe's role in subsequent drafts (pp. 99-115). Moley includes photographs of the handwritten draft, but he does not picture the other three critical drafts. Moley advises that in his earlier book, *After Seven Years* (New York: Harper, 1939), he made only casual reference to the authorship of the first inaugural because his "function as a collaborator was well known" and everyone knew he "would be involved in the preparation of this speech" (p. 116).

[9]Master Speech File, first handwritten draft, pp. 1-10.

[10]Gunther thought the phrase was uniquely FDR's, John Gunther, *Roosevelt in Retrospect* (New York: Harper, 1950), p. 124. Rosenman thought FDR read it in Thoreau: "Nothing is so much to be feared as fear," Rosenman, *Working with Roosevelt,* p. 91; Henry David Thoreau, *The Journal of Henry David Thoreau,* ed. Bradford Torrey and Francis H. Allen (New York: Dover, 1962), 7 Sept. 1851, p. 261. Wecter suggested it might have come from the *Ladies' Home Journal:* "There is nothing to fear—except fear." Dixon Wecter, *The Age of the Great Depression 1929-41* (New York: Macmillan, 1948), p. 44; "It's Up to the Women," editorial, *Ladies' Home Journal,* Jan. 1932, p. 3.

[11]Moley, *The First New Deal,* p. 115.

[12]Asbell believed that Howe filched the phrase from a newspaper department store advertisement, Bernard Asbell, *The F.D.R. Memoirs* (Garden City: Doubleday, 1973), p. 32; however, Freidel has complained that the piece has eluded later researchers: Frank Freidel, *Franklin D. Roosevelt Launching the New Deal* (Boston: Little, Brown, 1973), p. 203. My search of Howe's papers provided nothing.

quoted phrase and substituted "is an essential to victory."[13] Not only is FDR's phrase more concise, but it also links leadership with victory in a military-like sense, about which I shall note more later.

A variety of minor emendations are made in the second draft (the first typed one), but I pass them by because they are not in FDR's bold, print-like handwriting.

The third draft (the second typed one) is replete with FDR's handwriting and contains some significant alterations. In his paragraph that contained his fear statement, Howe had written, "nameless, unreasoning, unjustified terror which paralyzes the needed efforts to bring about prosperity once more." With a definite emphasis on military-like words, FDR produced, "which paralyzes *needed* efforts *to convert retreat into advance*" [hereafter, italicized words indicate FDR's emendations]. Later on, the text read: "The standards of the money-changers stand indicted"; however, FDR wished further to denigrate the bankers by writing: *"Practices* of the *unscrupulous* money-changers stand indicted." *Practices* somewhat sullies the loftiness of "standards" and *unscrupulous* quite speaks for itself. Treating the bankers in the same vein a bit later, FDR changed "They know of no other ways than the ancient rules" to "They know *only* the rules *of a generation of self-seekers."* A little later on, FDR further strengthened the text to cast additional ridicule on the bankers, "The moral stimulation of work must no longer be submerged in the sham of evanescent profit scouring" became "The moral stimulation of work *no longer* must be *forgotten* in *the mad chase of* evanescent profits."[14] All of these emendations demonstrate that FDR took particular pains (pleasure?) to denigrate and deprecate the bankers more than Moley's draft had done. Later, I shall demonstrate why.

In the latter part of his address, FDR turned to his personal leadership as President. In a number of places in this draft FDR strengthened or clarified Moley's language in order to enhance the positive nature and vigor of his intended leadership style. The following examples illustrate the point. "Because without such discipline no progress can be made, or any leadership really led" became "Because without such discipline no progress *is* made, *no* leadership *becomes effective."* The future tense of Moley's thought is brought into the present tense by FDR's change and stresses the immediacy of his leadership, and *effective* looks for immediate and tangible results. "I am prepared under my constitutional duty to indicate the measures" became "I am prepared under my constitutional duty to *recommend* the measures." *Recommend* has a stronger sense of positive advocacy than "indicate," which suggests merely pointing out. The point is

[13]Master Speech File, first handwritten draft, p. 1.
[14]Master Speech File, draft number three (typed), pp. 1-4.

that FDR wanted to stress his leadership role by taking the lead in recommending to Congress his measures rather than merely indicating to Congress what measures he thought were appropriate. But, interestingly, FDR deleted "sword of" in the following passage: "With this pledge taken, I assume unhesitatingly the sword of leadership of this great army of our people." Perhaps the term "sword" sounded too militaristic, and perhaps he wanted to stress his personal leadership rather than his assuming a symbolic sword of leadership. All of these emendations demonstrate that FDR wanted clearly to state and to show the active personal leadership with which he would assume the presidency, and that he wished to strengthen Moley's draft in those respects.[15]

The fourth draft, his actual reading copy, contained only one emendation. While waiting in the Senate Committee Room for the ceremonies to begin, FDR added in longhand an opening sentence: "This is a day of consecration." When he delivered the speech, he verbally inserted "national" before "consecration."[16]

In summary, one might have wished that FDR had authored his own first inaugural, but he did not; and that the famous fear statement, which is so intimately associated with him and his inaugural, was his also, but it was not. Nevertheless, FDR did make emendations on three of the four drafts, and most of those changes demonstrated his desire to use militaristic words to evoke military-like associations in his listeners. He paid special attention to the bankers by utilizing language which purposefully defamed them and their practices. Lastly, he managed his language to strengthen his leadership role. He would act immediately to lead the nation in its crisis. The philosophical significance of this textual investigation is that, although the forthcoming exegesis of FDR's rhetorical purposes is concerned with some of Moley's and Howe's ideas, FDR was satisfied with the text to make it his inaugural address, and many of the points I shall later make were expressly his word choices. What follows, then, is based on the assumption that "the President's speech is the President's speech."[17]

---

[15]*Ibid.,* pp. 10-11.

[16]Master Speech File, reading copy, pp. 1-2. Those sources, including government printings and Rosenman's edition of FDR's personal papers and speeches, which relied on the advanced text are thus in error.

[17]Arthur Larson, *Eisenhower: The President Knowbody Knew* (New York: Scribner's, 1968), p. 150. Although Larson said this of President Eisenhower, the statement probably can be generalized to all presidents, and it is specifically applicable to FDR. See Rosenman, *Working with Roosevelt,* for his analogous role as speech writer for FDR to Larson's for Eisenhower, and Rosenman's analogous conclusion: "the finished product was always the same — it was Roosevelt himself" (p. 12).

The Techniques

Before discussing FDR's three rhetorical techniques, I wish to comment briefly on his speech as one in the genre of inaugural addresses. Wolfarth has isolated four major issues on which presidents traditionally speak: Domestic Issues, International Issues, American Traditions, and Other.[18] FDR's first inaugural pays tribute to American Traditions. Some typical examples are "This great nation," "the American spirit of the pioneer," "seeking old and precious moral values," "essential democracy," and so forth. A handful of sentences centered around the "good neighbor" policy comprise his treatment of International Issues. But FDR's predominant theme was Domestic Issues. In an accompanying notation for his inaugural address, FDR wrote that in his speech he attempted primarily to allay the nation's fear: "I sought principally in the foregoing Inaugural Address to banish, so far as possible, the fear of the present and of the future which held the American people and the American spirit in its grasp."[19] Indeed, his famous fear statement made an indelible impression on the American mind. Yet, however popularized and catchy FDR's famous fear statement was, it was not the crux of his speech. Nor was it the solitary theme on which commentators based their evaluations of his speech's efficacy with his reading and listening audiences. A close examination of FDR's first inaugural reveals that he used three rhetorical techniques to aid him in announcing his implementation of his New Deal. In this section, I shall examine these techniques in relationship to the American people and the Congress within the inaugural context of March, 1933.

The Scapegoat Technique

In early 1933, America's preeminent concern was the banking crisis. Almost 5,000 banks had failed since 1929, and twenty-two states had closed their banks prior to March 4 of FDR's inaugural year.[20] The spiraling effects of margin and then more margin, stock losses, foreclosures, and, ultimately, bank failures probably had at their epicenter the bankers and the brokers. Tugwell specifically indicted them: "Wall Street was again the wicked place it had been during the progressive era. The financial establishment was being blamed for what had happened."[21] And Farr concurred with Tugwell's analysis: "It was true that most of the guilt belonged to the

---

[18]Donald L. Wolfarth, "John F. Kennedy in the Tradition of Inaugural Speeches," *Quarterly Journal of Speech,* 47 (1961), 130.

[19]*The Public Papers and Addresses of Franklin D. Roosevelt,* II, 16.

[20]Samuel Eliot Morison, *The Oxford History of the American People* (New York: Oxford University Press, 1965), p. 949.

[21]Rexford G. Tugwell, *Roosevelt's Revolution* (New York: Macmillan, 1977), p. 6.

money changers, who probably had something to do with the Stock Exchange."[22]

FDR's coup in his inaugural was to make the moneychangers the scapegoat[23] for the Depression. It has already been demonstrated, via the textual emendations, how FDR purposefully used language to denigrate the moneychangers. In his speech, he unflinchingly proclaimed what was believed by the average American—the moneychangers were culpable for the Depression. The efficacy of his using the scapegoat technique ensued from his ability to channel the American people's anxieties and frustrations from themselves to the moneychangers. The speech text leaves no doubt that FDR utilized the scapegoat technique to blame Wall Street for the Depression: "the rulers of the exchange of mankind's goods have failed through their own stubbornness and their own incompetence, have admitted their failure, and have abdicated. Practices of the unscrupulous money-changers stand indicted in the court of public opinion, rejected by the hearts and minds of men." And, again, "Yes, the money-changers have fled from their high seats in the temple of our civilization. We may now restore that temple to the ancient truths."[24] Leuchtenburg noted that FDR's delivery matched the mood of his language: "Grim, unsmiling, chin uplifted, his voice firm, almost angry, he lashed out at the bankers."[25] Having castigated Wall Street, FDR then indicated that he would direct his New Deal measures toward checking it and its practices. In order to stop a return to the "evils of the old order," FDR announced that there would be banking reform: "There must be a strict supervision of all banking and credits and investments. (Applause.) There must be an end to speculation with other people's money. (Applause). And there must be a provision for an adequate but sound currency. (Applause.)"[26] To this end, Congress passed FDR's Emergency Banking Act on March 9.[27] The task of putting "people to work" began with the Civilian Conservation Corps, March 31; the fear of foreclosure was alleviated by the Emergency Farm Mortgage Act, May 12, and the Home Owner's Loan Act, June 13.[28]

---

[22]Finis Farr, *FDR* (New Rochelle: Arlington House, 1972), p. 182.

[23]The scapegoat has its derivation in Jewish antiquity, when the people symbolically placed their sins on a goat's head and then allowed the goat to escape into the wilderness, thus relieving them of their guilt.

[24]Franklin D. Roosevelt, "First Inaugural Address," in *Great American Speeches 1898-1963*, ed. John Graham (New York: Meredith, 1970), pp. 51-52. I utilize this text because it is a verbatim printing from a recording of the inaugural address, Caedmon Record, TC 2033-A. Hereinafter the address is cited as First Inaugural.

[25]William E. Leuchtenburg, *Franklin D. Roosevelt and the New Deal: 1932-1940* (New York: Harper & Row, 1963), p. 41.

[26]First Inaugural, p. 53; Caedmon Record, TC 2033-A.

[27]Morison, p. 954.

[28]*Ibid.*

Various contemporary signs indicated that FDR struck a responsive rhetorical chord by utilizing his scapegoat technique. When he said that he would restore the "temple to the ancient truths," his inaugural audience applauded for the first time.[29] Editors from Universal Films and Pathe News included FDR's attack on the bankers in their news film.[30] Tugwell noted that FDR "tramped hard on those who were responsible."[31] Morison observed that FDR gave the moneychangers an "excoriation."[32] The newsprint media also supported FDR's use of the scapegoat technique. The *Christian Century* noted, "The 'false moneychangers' deserve all the condemnation that can be heaped upon them."[33] *The Nation* observed that Roosevelt dealt the moneychangers a "verbal scourging."[34] *Newsweek* stated, "It was an assault on the bankers, against whom the voices of the distressed are raised in an ever-swelling chorus as the depression endures."[35] The scapegoat technique also had FDR's desired effect on the business community. *The Times* (London) noted that FDR was "likely to rouse the opposition of a good many vested interests."[36] FDR used the scapegoat technique to blunt the expected opposition from those *laissez-faire* sympathizers who might attack his New Deal banking and investment measures.[37] Rauch observed that FDR was somewhat successful in disarming his banking critics: "The bankers were in a chastened mood....They had lost the cohesion of a vested group."[38]

FDR, then, used the scapegoat technique to blame Wall Street for the Depression and the banking crisis. Available evidence from the inaugural audience, from contemporary news-films and news-print media, and from later commentators suggests that FDR was successful in obtaining his end.

Military Metaphor

Although Americans had elected FDR and his New Deal, questions still remained about the nature of his personal leadership. Granted, FDR and the Democratic party platform had advocated reform and recovery through

---

[29]Caedmon Record, TC 2033-A.

[30]Universal Films, Film MP 77-5, Roosevelt Library; Pathe News, Film 201-29-1, Roosevelt Library. Complete news-film footage of FDR's first inaugural is not extant; therefore, what the news editors retained in their truncated versions is significant.

[31]Rexford G. Tugwell, *In Search of Roosevelt* (Cambridge: Harvard Univ. Press, 1972), p. 222.

[32]Morison, p. 950.

[33]"The Inaugural Address," *Christian Century*, 15 Mar. 1933, p. 351.

[34]"The Faith of Roosevelt," *The Nation*, 15 Mar. 1933, p. 278.

[35]"Roosevelt Takes Oath in Crisis," *Newsweek*, 11 Mar. 1933, p. 9.

[36]"The President's Speech," *The Times* (London), 6 Mar. 1933, p. 13, col. 2.

[37]Conkin has argued that the end of government *laissez-faire* was, in hindsight, actually a boon to business. Paul K. Conkin, *The New Deal* (New York: Crowell, 1967), p. 34.

[38]Basil Rauch, *The History of the New Deal: 1933-1938* (New York: Creative Age Press, 1944), p. 61.

lower tariffs, unemployment relief, the protection of investments and agriculture, the repeal of the Prohibition amendment, etc.; yet Americans avidly awaited his inaugural address, which should cue the nation to how he planned to lead the country out of the Depression.[39]

Knowing that his program would need mass support and that the New Deal would bring broad and at times radical departures from conducting government as it had been until 1933, Roosevelt endeavored to garner that support by using military metaphor. Osborn has argued that an examination of metaphor can "permit a more precise focusing upon whatever values and motives are salient in society at a given time."[40] Leuchtenburg studied the Depression era values and motives and concluded that FDR puposefully responded to the Depression crisis by using military metaphor: "Roosevelt's inaugural address...reflected the sense of wartime crisis,"[41] and "President Roosevelt sought to restore national confidence by evoking the mood of wartime."[42] The careful listener or reader would have noted that FDR had deployed an advance guard of military metaphor in the early parts of his address: "retreat into advance," "victory," "direct recruiting," and "emergency of war." But when FDR directly urged support for and acceptance of his New Deal leadership in the latter three-fourths of his speech, his language was replete with military metaphor:

> if we are to go forward, we must move as a trained and loyal army, willing to sacrifice for the good of a common discipline, because without such discipline no progress can be made, no leadership becomes effective. We are, I know, ready and willing to submit our lives and our property to such discipline because it makes possible a leadership which aims at the larger good. This I propose to offer, pledging that the larger purposes will bind upon us, bind upon us all a sacred obligation, with a unity of duty hitherto evoked only in times of armed strife. With this pledge taken, I assume unhesitatingly the leadership of this great army of our people dedicated to a disciplined attack upon our common problems.[43]

There can be little doubt that FDR purposefully used the military metaphor to create the symbol of a great American army. This army, organized under the personal leadership of its new Commander-in-Chief, would wage war

---

[39] Approximately 50,000,000 Americans listened to FDR's address on the radio, and the immediate inaugural audience numbered approximately 150,000.

[40] Michael Osborn, "Archetypal Metaphor in Rhetoric: The Light-Dark Family," *Quarterly Journal of Speech,* 53 (1967), 126.

[41] William E. Leuchtenburg, "The New Deal and the Analogue of War," in *Change and Continuity in Twentieth-Century America,* ed. John Braeman, Robert H. Bremner, and Everett Walters (n.p.: Ohio State Univ. Press, 1964), p. 104.

[42] *Ibid.,* p. 105.

[43] First Inaugural, pp. 53-54.

on the Depression. In fact, a certain Rev. Hicks from Yonkers, New York, had urged in a letter to FDR that he call for a "mobilization as if the United States were at war."[44] The repetition of "discipline" four times and of "leadership" three times, and other value laden words, such as "duty," "sacred obligation," and "armed strife," should reinforce those salient values and desires which yearned for action against the Depression. If Conkin was correct when he argued that "The situation invited a surrender of power to some leader,"[45] then FDR's military metaphor facilitated Americans' surrender of power and liberty, much as one does in the real Army, to their Commander-in-Chief.

The effect-oriented responses from private persons and the press were favorable to FDR's military metaphor appeals. From all quarters came support for FDR's bid for quasi-military leadership power, and that support was often couched in Roosevelt's infectious military metaphor. Republican Alfred M. Landon of Kansas affirmed, "If there is any way in which a Republican governor of a midwestern state can aid the President in the fight, I now enlist for the duration of the war."[46] Myron C. Taylor, chairman of United States Steel Corporation, declared, "I hasten to re-enlist to fight the depression to its end."[47] James Hagerty wrote in the *New York Times,* "In the phraseology which ran all through his speech he indicated that he regarded the United States as in an economic war."[48] The *New York Times* capsulized other leading newspapers' comments, parts of which are included here: The *Constitution* in Atlanta said Roosevelt gave a "straight-from-the-shoulder attack"; the *News-Age Herald* in Birmingham labeled the speech "a clarion call for nation unity in the face of a crisis"; the *Plain Dealer* in Cleveland responded to FDR's military metaphor and characterized the speech as "fighting words, fit for a time that calls for militant action"; in Des Moines, the *Register* believed "it is the rallying of the country to renewal of a courageous and sustained war on the depression."[49] The New York *Daily News* had not supported Roosevelt, but it pledged itself "to support the policies of FDR for a period of at least one year; longer if circumstances warrant."[50] In its inimitable manner, *The Times* (London) also took notice of Roosevelt's military metaphor: "What is important to note is the spirit which inspired it throughout. A high and

[44]Letter from the Rev. William C. Hicks, St. Andrew's Memorial Church, Yonkers, New York, 24 Feb. 1933, PPF 10, Box 1, Roosevelt Library.
[45]Conkin, p. 30.
[46]Quoted in Cabell Phillips, *From the Crash to the Blitz: 1929-1939* (London: Macmillan, 1969), p. 107.
[47]"Leaders Here Praise Address as 'Strong,'" *New York Times,* 5 Mar. 1933, p. 6, col. 6.
[48]James A. Hagerty, "Roosevelt Address Stirs Great Crowd," *ibid.,* p. 2, col. 2.
[49]"Comment of Press on Roosevelt's Inaugural Address," *ibid.,* p. 6, cols. 4-5.
[50]Quoted in Phillips, p. 107.

resolute militancy breathes in every line."[51]

But this successful use of military metaphor—as gauged by private and media reaction—could also hurt FDR if Americans misperceived his intent. Therefore, in what seems to be an effort to reassure Americans that they had little to fear of a nascent executive dictatorship in his New Deal, FDR hastened to allay the American people: "Action in this image, action to this end, is feasible under the form of government which we have inherited from our ancestors. Our constitution is so simple, so practical, that it is possible always to meet extraordinary needs by changes in emphasis and arrangement without the loss of essential form."[52] The critic might have challenged FDR's assertion that "changes in emphasis and arrangement" can ensue without a "loss of essential form," but Farr believed the assertion sounded fine to about 99 percent of FDR's listeners and, anyway, there was little time to raise that question because FDR's confident voice continued on.[53]

However, Adolph Hitler's Fuehrer-principle was fresh in some Americans' minds and they were not so easily beguiled. Partially indicative of this thinking was William Randolph Hearst's *New York Mirror* issue of 6 March, which headlines its story, **"Roosevelt Asks Dictator's Role."**[54] Edmund Wilson, editor of the *New Republic,* believed that FDR's military metaphor signaled a dire warning: "The thing that emerges most clearly is the warning of a dictatorship."[55] Rauch has written that, even among liberals, the military metaphor caused some concern: "Liberals were later to profess they found the germs of fascism in the First New Deal. Perhaps they found cause for suspicion in the evocation of the 'regimented' moods of wartime."[56]

Although some contemporary, and especially later, critics were less comfortable with FDR's military metaphor than were most of his contemporaries, Roosevelt's military metaphor successfully evoked in the American people a patriotic duty and discipline to support his quasi-military leadership in his symbolic war on the Depression. Lest this military metaphor might smack too much of an incipient executive dictatorship, FDR took pains to assure his audience that the Constitution would survive, that mere changes in emphasis would not affect its essential form.

Carrot-and-Stick Technique

During the interregnum (November 1932 to March 1933), Roosevelt

---

[51]"The President's Speech," *The Times* (London), 6 Mar. 1933, p. 13, col. 2.

[52]First Inaugural, p. 54.

[53]Farr, p. 182.

[54]Quoted in *ibid.,* p. 191.

[55]Quoted in William Manchester, *The Glory and the Dream* (Boston: Little, Brown, 1973), p. 77.

[56]Rauch, p. 59.

received advice from many quarters, including even President Herbert Hoover, on how he could help to stop the deepening Depression. Of particular concern here is the advice FDR received on how to cope with the new Congress, about which some predictions were not particularly encouraging. Rollins has given an accurate picture of Congress *before* FDR's inaugural was delivered: "The new Congress was already divided and confused. Some wanted inflation, some a sound gold dollar. Some wanted a 30-hour week, some employment guaranteed. Some looked for a new Mussolini, some for a new Jefferson."[57] Political commentator Walter Lippmann wrote that it would take a strong President to lead a boisterous Congress: "The new Congress will be an excitable and impetuous body, and it will respect only a President who knows his own mind and will not hesitate to employ the whole authority of his position."[58] FDR received from Senator Key Pittman of Nevada a letter (11 February 1933) in which Pittman warned FDR about the Congress: "your leadership...is going to be exceedingly difficult for a while. Democrats have grown...individualistic, they have lost the habit of cooperation, they have grown unaccustomed to discipline."[59] Of these typical warnings, Patterson has written, "Such predictions of an unruly Congress in a time of social and economic crisis were commonplace in the months prior to Roosevelt's inauguration."[60] FDR had enlisted the country in his symbolic army with the military metaphor; he had used the scapegoat technique to subdue Wall Street; he had a favorable press;[61] he had now only to deal with the Congress.

Accordingly, FDR resorted to the carrot-and-stick approach to move the Congress to follow his executive leadership. His carrot was a clever cajoling of Congress to act either on its own or in tandem with him:

> And it is to be hoped that the normal balance of executive and legislative authority may be wholly equal, wholly adequate, to meet the unprecedented task before us. But it may be that an unprecedented demand and need for undelayed action may call for temporary departure from that normal balance of public procedure. I am prepared under my constitutional duty to recommend the measures that a stricken nation in the midst of a stricken world may require. These measures, or such measures as the Congress may build out of its experience and wisdom, I shall seek within my constitutional authority to bring to speedy adoption.[62]

[57]Alfred B. Rollins, Jr., *Roosevelt and Howe* (New York: Knopf, 1962), p. 367.
[58]Quoted in James T. Patterson, *Congressional Conservatism and the New Deal* (Lexington: Univ. of Kentucky Press, 1967), p. 1.
[59]*Ibid.*
[60]*Ibid.,* pp. 1-2.
[61]Manchester, p. 81.
[62]First Inaugural, p. 54.

But if the carrot were not motivation enough, then the stick would be:

> But in the event that the Congress shall fail to take one of these two courses, in the event that the national emergency is still critical, I shall not evade the clear course of duty that will then confront me. I shall ask the Congress for the one remaining instrument to meet the crisis: broad executive power to wage a war against the emergency, as great as the power that would be given to me if we were in fact invaded by a foreign foe.[63]

The tumultuous applause which immediately followed, and it was the greatest applause of any passage in the speech,[64] could not have been mistaken by the listening members of Congress. Eleanor Roosevelt thought the applause was "a little terrifying. You felt that they would do *anything*—if only someone would tell them *what* to do."[65] The *News* in Dallas supported FDR's carrot-and-stick technique by suggesting that, "if Congress fails him, the country will strongly back him in his demands for virtual war powers."[66] The conservative Boston *Transcript* even agreed with FDR: "The President's program demands dictatorial authority. This is unprecedented in its implications, but such is the desperate temper of the people that it is welcome."[67]

In hindsight, the Congress was anything but intransigent, but FDR did not know that when he fashioned his speech. Conkin observed, "Almost any legislative proposal would pass."[68] Patterson believed that Congress' willingness to cooperate with FDR stemmed from its wish to delegate responsibility, its eagerness to spend, and because FDR was actually more conservative than was the Congress.[69] Although the carrot-and-stick technique admittedly did not directly cause Congress to cooperate, it did nevertheless serve a vital function. The carrot-and-stick's efficacy ensued from FDR's willingness to use the stick if it were necessary. Rollins believed that if FDR had not demonstrated his ability to act and to lead, he might have failed on inauguration day: "What Roosevelt did do, with monumental success, was to preserve the faith which vague commitment or partial action might have shattered."[70]

[63]*Ibid.*

[64]Caedmon Record TC 2033-A; Freidel, p. 205; Pathe News and Universal Films both included this important segment (see n.30).

[65]Joseph P. Lash, *Eleanor and Franklin* (New York: Norton, 1971), p. 360.

[66]"Comment of Press on Roosevelt's Inaugural Address," *New York Times,* 5 Mar. 1933, p. 6, col. 6.

[67]Quoted in Phillips, p. 107.

[68]Conkin, p. 30.

[69]Patterson, pp. 4-5.

[70]Rollins, p. 366.

Roosevelt and Hitler Compared

The *zeitgeist* of March, 1933, manifested some similar conditions in Germany and the United States,[71] and these conditions were utilized by their respective leaders. Humphrey has outlined the conditions and their causes:

> The same world-wide economic collapse which brought Hitler to power in Germany in 1933, brought Roosevelt and the New Deal to America. . . . [I]n the month of March, 1933, the positions of Roosevelt and Hitler were strangely similar. Both had risen to power on the crest of a wave of protest against things as they were. Both men and both nations faced problems of unemployment, financial collapse, and the task of inspiring a bewildered and despairing people.[72]

Toland believed that Hitler's *Weltanschauung* originated "in New York City's Wall Street."[73]

In reacting to similar conditions, the two leaders used similar language. Hitler blamed the Jews and other halfhearted lukewarm people (*die Halben*) for the Depression.[74] The historical originators of the scapegoat became under Hitler the very object of his attack. Hitler also used militaristic terms in his speeches. Words such as "blood, authority of personality, and a fighting spirit," as well as "victory" and "fight," interspersed his speeches.[75] On 23 March 1933, Hitler used the carrot-and-stick technique in opening the Reichstag. He offered the Reichstag an "opportunity for friendly co-operation"; but his stick was, "It is for you, gentlemen of the Reichstag, to decide between war and peace."[76] Chancellor Hitler demonstrated that he appreciated the efficacy of Roosevelt's various techniques in his inaugural address by the language Hitler chose to express his congratulatory cable:

> The Reich Chancellor is in accord with the President that the virtues of sense of duty, readiness for sacrifice, and discipline must be the supreme rule of the whole nation. This moral demand, which the President is addressing to every single citizen, is only the quintessence of German philosophy of the State, expressed in its motto "The Public Weal Before Private Gain."[77]

Mussolini's *Il Giornale d'Italia* saw in FDR's inaugural a reaffirmation of its views:

---

[71]Fred L. Casmir, "The Hitler I Heard," *Quarterly Journal of Speech,* 49 (1963), 9-10.

[72]Hubert H. Humphrey, *The Political Philosophy of the New Deal* (Baton Rouge: Louisiana State Univ. Press, 1970), pp. xx-xxi.

[73]John Toland, *Adolph Hitler* (Garden City: Doubleday, 1976), I, 239.

[74]Robert Payne, *The Life and Death of Adolph Hitler* (New York: Praeger, 1973), p. 232.

[75]*Ibid.,* p. 234.

[76]Toland, I, 322.

[77]Quoted in Toland, I, 340-41.

> President Roosevelt's words are clear and need no comment to make
> even the deaf hear that not only Europe but the whole world feels the
> need of executive authority capable of acting with full powers of cutting
> short the purposeless chatter of legislative assemblies. This method of
> government may well be defined as Fascist.[78]

With similar circumstances in which they came to power, with similar
reactions via their similar rhetorical techniques, would not one expect their
personal leadership to be similar? Under Hitler, Germany became a Nazi
dictatorship. The possibility certainly existed for FDR to become a dictator. Gunther has wisely observed that possibility: "We are apt to forget
nowadays the immense, unprecedented, overwhelming authority conferred
on FDR by an enthusiastically willing Congress during the first hundred
days of his first administration. The Reichstag did not give Hitler much
more."[79] Farr has observed that FDR's "proposed charter of authority, as
we read it today, was simplicity itself: the President was king."[80] And
Robinson noted, "Clearly, semi-dictatorial powers had been granted the
President."[81] Yet, the United States did not have a Mussolini or a Hitler in
Franklin Delano Roosevelt.

One reason was the nature of their respective countries. Halasz has
argued that the United States had a long history of constitutional democracy which Germany did not have; moreover, FDR was not asking for a
sacrifice of political freedom, as was Hitler; nor were the American people,
as were most Germans, convinced that the Depression demanded such a
sacrifice.[82] The Democratic party did not utilize intimidation and physical
force to bully others, as did the Nazis, and the Republican party could and
did oppose FDR, whereas Hitler stifled dissent and suppressed opposing
political parties.

Also, Hitler and Roosevelt had critical differences in their conceptions of
leadership and the framework in which it should be exercised. On the first
day he assumed the office of Reich Chancellor, Hitler said he would never
relinquish it: "No power in the world will ever get me out of here alive."[83]
Juxtaposed to that statement is an interesting FDR emendation of the third
draft, which suggests that FDR had a more reasonable and limited conception of his leadership tenure. On the draft, FDR added *present* to the

[78]Quoted in Freidel, p. 208.
[79]Quoted in Manchester, p. 80.
[80]Farr, p. 183.
[81]Robinson, p. 107.
[82]Nicholas Halasz, *Roosevelt Through Foreign Eyes* (Princeton: Van Nostrand, 1961), pp. 44-
55.
[83]Paul Preston, "The Burning of the Reichstag," in *Sunrise and Storm Clouds,* Vol. X of
Milestones of History, ed. Roger Morgan (New York: Newsweek Books, 1975), p. 137.

following sentence: "They have made me the *present* instrument of their wishes."[84] The term "present" implies the four-year term, and it does not preclude some other president four years later—nor is a permanent Roosevelt presidency thereby suggested. In the 1934 Nuremburg rallies, Hitler's minion Rudolph Hess proclaimed, "The party is Hitler. Hitler, however, is Germany just as Germany is Hitler. Heil Hitler!"[85] No such language has been adduced to FDR's most ardent supporters. While Hitler was the embodiment of Louis XIV's popularly ascribed dictum *l'etat c'est moi,* FDR clearly was not. By philosophy and practice, FDR preferred to work within accepted constitutional channels. Although he threatened Congress in his inaugural, he indicated that he would rather work with them. As Gunther wrote, "Roosevelt, it might be mentioned parenthetically, always strove to work *with* Congress; this is a point often forgotten these days, but it was vital."[86] Moreover, FDR had a respect for the Constitution and its essential democracy. Although Sherwood granted that "No President since Lincoln tested the elasticity of the Constitution as he [FDR] did," Sherwood also held that FDR did not equal "Lincoln's record in circumventing the Constitution."[87] Manchester opined that "Roosevelt preferred to work within the Constitution."[88] In the final evaluation, then, Freidel was probably correct in his conclusion that FDR did not intend to assume the role of a Hitler because that was too repugnant to his basic thinking."[89]

Conclusion

In his First Inaugural Address, FDR's main concern was Domestic Issues. An investigation of his textual emendations has demonstrated that he selected words to effect certain ends. He used the scapegoat technique to blame the bankers and brokers for the Depression, an efficacious technique because FDR used it to adapt to and to speak for the existing and prevalent attitudes against Wall Street. He marshaled a military metaphor to evoke in the American people a sense of duty and discipline—values salient and needed in a time of national crisis—to persuade the citizens of the nation to support his quasi-military leadership in his war on the Depression. For the members of Congress he used the carrot-and-stick technique to demonstrate to them and the country his desire to act either in tandem with the Congress or alone if it failed him. FDR successfully used these techniques because

[84]Master Speech File, draft number three (typed), p. 13.
[85]Quoted in Toland, I, 381.
[86]Gunther, p. 278.
[87]Robert E. Sherwood, *Roosevelt and Hopkins: An Intimate History* (New York: Harper, 1948), p. 41.
[88]Manchester, p. 81.
[89]Freidel, p. 205.

their potential efficacy was available in attitudes of the immediate inaugural audience, of most of the contemporary news media, and, perhaps most importantly, of the members of Congress and ultimately the American people. Rodgers realized the successful effect that FDR's address had on the American people, that it "first won for him the support of the great masses of people and put behind his efforts the full force of an overwhelming public opinion."[90]

The *zeitgeist* of March 1933 produced Hitler and Roosevelt, who utilized similar rhetorical techniques in reacting to the Depression. Although their rhetorical means were similar, basic dissimilarities in their respective countries, their leadership roles, and their expected tenure of rule accounted for their diametrically opposed ends as national leaders.

Closing remarks are perhaps best left to Roosevelt, himself. His three rhetorical techniques coalesce in his inaugural conclusion: "The people of the United States have not failed. In their need they have registered a mandate that they want direct, vigorous action. They have asked for discipline and direction under leadership. They have made me the present instrument of their wishes. In the spirit of the gift, I take it."[91]

---

[90]Cleveland Rodgers, *The Roosevelt Program* (New York: Putnam, 1933), p. 16.
[91]First Inaugural, p. 54.

War Address
Franklin Delano Roosevelt

To Joint Session of Congress of the United States at Washington, D.C. on December 8, 1941 at 12:30 P.M. The published version appeared in Vital Speeches of the Day, *December 15, 1941, p. 130.*

Yesterday, December 7, 1941—a date which will live in infamy—the United States of America was suddenly and deliberately attacked by naval and air forces of the Empire of Japan.

The United States was at peace with that nation and, at the solicitation of Japan, was still in conversation with its Government and its Emperor looking toward the maintenance of peace in the Pacific.

Indeed, one hour after Japanese air squadrons had commenced bombing Oahu, the Japanese Ambassador to the United States and his colleague delivered to the Secretary of State a formal reply to a recent American message. While this reply stated that it seemed useless to continue the existing diplomatic negotiations, it contained no threat or hint of war or armed attack.

It will be recorded that the distance of Hawaii from Japan makes it obvious that the attack was deliberately planned many days or even weeks ago. During the intervening time, the Japanese Government has deliberately sought to deceive the United States by false statements and expressions of hope for continued peace.

The attack yesterday on the Hawaiian Islands has caused severe damage to American naval and military forces. Very many American lives have been lost. In addition, American ships have been reported torpedoed on the high seas between San Francisco and Honolulu.

Yesterday the Japanese Government also launched an attack against Malaya.

Last night Japanese forces attacked Hongkong.

Last night Japanese forces attacked Guam.

Last night Japanese forces attacked the Philippine Islands.

Last night the Japanese attacked Wake Island.

This morning the Japanese attacked Midway Island.

Japan has, therefore, undertaken a surprise offensive extending through-out the Pacific area. The facts of yesterday speak for themselves. The people of the United States have already formed their opinions and well understand the implications to the very life and safety of our nation.

As Commander in Chief of the army and navy I have directed that all measures be taken for our defense.

Always will we remember the character of the onslaught against us.

No matter how long it may take us to overcome this premeditated invasion, the American people in their righteous might will win through to absolute victory.

I believe I interpret the will of the Congress and of the people when I assert that we will not only defend ourselves to the uttermost but will make very certain that this form of treachery shall never endanger us again.

Hostilities exist. There is no blinking at the fact that our people, our territory and our interests are in grave danger.

With confidence in our armed forces — with the unbounding determination of our people — we will gain the inevitable triumph — so help us God.

I ask that the Congress declare that since the unprovoked and dastardly attack by Japan on Sunday, December 7, a state of war has existed between the United States and the Japanese Empire.

Fourth Inaugural Address
Franklin Delano Roosevelt

*Delivered from The South Portico of the White House,
January 20, 1945, about 12:06 p.m., e.w.t., Broadcast Nationally. The speech is from the Reading Copy; Roosevelt's deletions are bracketed and his additions are italicized.*

Mr. Chief Justice, Mr. Vice President, My Friends: You will understand
and, I believe, agree with my wish that the form of this Inauguration be
simple and its words brief.

We Americans of today, together with our Allies are passing through a
period of supreme test. It is a test of our courage — of our resolve — of our
wisdom — of our essential [decency] *democracy.*

If we meet that test — successfully and honorably — we shall perform a
service of historic importance *of historic* importance which men and women
and children will honor throughout all time.

As I stand here today, having taken the solemn oath of office in the
presence of my fellow countrymen — in the presence of our God — I know
that it is America's purpose that we shall not fail.

In the days and [in] the years that are to come, we shall work for a just
and [durable] *honorable* peace, *a durable peace,* as today we work and fight
for total victory in war.

We can and we will achieve such a peace.

We shall strive for perfection. We shall not achieve it immediately — but
we still shall strive. We may make mistakes — but they must never be mistakes which result from faintness of heart or abandonment of moral principle.

I remember that my old schoolmaster, Dr. Peabody, said — in days that
seemed to us then to be secure and untroubled — *he said,* "Things in life will
not always run smoothly. Sometimes we will be rising toward the heights —

This speech appeared as footnote 48 in "Roosevelt's Fourth Inaugural address: A Study of Its
Composition," by Halford Ross Ryan in the *Quarterly Journal of Speech,* 67 (1981), 157-66.

then all will seem to reverse itself and start downward. The great fact to remember is that the trend of civilization itself is forever upward; that a line drawn through the middle of the peaks and the valleys of the centuries always has an upward trend.''

Our Constitution of 1787 was not a perfect instrument; it is not perfect yet. But it provided a firm base upon which all manner of men, of all races and colors and creeds, could build our solid structure of democracy.

And so today, in this year of war, 1945, we have learned lessons — at a fearful cost — and we shall profit by them.

We have learned that we cannot live alone, at peace; that our own well-being is dependent on the well-being of other nations, far away. We have learned that we must live as men *and* not as ostriches, nor as dogs in the manger.

We have learned to be citizens of the world, members of the human community.

We have learned the simple truth, as Emerson said, that, ''The only way to have a friend is to be one.''

We can gain no lasting peace if we approach it with suspicion and mistrust — [and] *or* with fear. We can gain it only if we proceed with the understanding and *the* confidence and *the* courage which flow from conviction.

The Almighty God has blessed our land in many ways. He has given our people stout hearts and strong arms with which to strike mighty blows for freedom and truth. He has given to our country a faith which has become the hope of all peoples in an anguished world.

So, we pray [now] to Him *now* for the vision to see our way clearly — to see the way that leads to a better life for ourselves and for all our fellow men — *and* to the achievement of His will to peace on earth.

Roosevelt's Fourth Inaugural Address:
A Study of Its Composition
Halford Ross Ryan

Research for this article was supported by a grant from the Eleanor Roosevelt Institute in the Franklin D. Roosevelt Library, Hyde Park, New York.

The exigencies of World War II impinged upon FDR's Fourth Inaugural Address in a variety of ways. In a press conference held in November, 1944, FDR indicated his decision to keep his fourth inaugural ceremony brief. A reporter asked him: "Are you going to parade any on inauguration day?" FDR replied: "No. Who is there here to parade?"[1] Consequently, the nation was alerted that "President Roosevelt's fourth inaugural will be one of the simplest and soberest in the nation's recent history."[2] The long standing tradition of holding the inaugural ceremony at the Capitol was suspended because Roosevelt believed that holding the inauguration at the White House was more in keeping with the war effort.[3] His inaugural audience was the smallest on record: fewer than five thousand persons were on the White House grounds for the ceremony and perhaps another three thousand persons were outside the gates.[4] After George Washington's

---

[1] *The Public Papers and Addresses of Franklin D. Roosevelt, 1944-45,* ed. Samuel I. Rosenman (New York: Harper and Brothers, 1950), p. 424.

[2] "Roosevelt Asks Simple Inaugural," *New York Times,* 15 Nov. 1944, p. 18.

[3] For the rationale "to save money, manpower and materials," see *The Public Papers of Franklin D. Roosevelt, 1944-45,* p. 525.

[4] "Roosevelt Takes Fourth-Term Oath," *New York Times,* 21 Jan. 1945, p. 26. See also William D. Hassett, *Off the Record with F.D.R. 1942-1945* (New Brunswick: Rutgers University Press, 1958), p. 312.

This article originally appeared in the *Quarterly Journal of Speech,* 67 (1981), 157-66, and is reprinted with the permission of the Speech Communication Association.

Second Inaugural Address, Roosevelt's Fourth Inaugural Address was the briefest.[5] Arthur Krock wrote that "The few hundred words to which he wisely confined his inaugural address yesterday were in keeping with the nature of the occasion."[6] Until Amendment XXII to the Constitution is repealed, a fourth inaugural occasion will not be repeated.

My purpose is to study the composition of FDR's Fourth Inaugural Address from its inception to its delivery on January 20, 1945.[7] I study the speech's composition for two reasons. First, I shall clarify the confusion that exists about the author of the speech. My thesis is that the speech ensued solely from Robert Sherwood's submitted draft. Second, I believe the rhetorical scholar should demonstrate, whenever possible, what thoughts in a speech were the President's and what thoughts were the speech writers', and why these thoughts were kept or rejected. A study of this speech can illuminate FDR's thoughts at a critical juncture in history by noting the salience of what he rejected as well as what he maintained. No one has studied the composition of this speech; moreover, the secondary works shed little light on what was maintained and no light at all on what was rejected. Hence, to reveal FDR's thoughts in the composition of his fourth inaugural, one must examine the speech drafts.[8]

The Composition of the Drafts

The original materials for this study are ten speech drafts, some significant carbon copies of these drafts, and the final reading copy of the address. I divide the ten primary drafts into five sets: (1) two drafts of random thoughts dictated by FDR, (2) one draft prepared by Archibald MacLeish, (3) two drafts prepared by Samuel Rosenman, (4) two drafts prepared by Robert Sherwood, and (5) three drafts from which the final reading copy ensued. The basic structure of the essay will be to discuss each set in its turn.

Rosenman shed some light on the composition of Roosevelt's speech, but part of his analysis is misleading. Rosenman recalled that: "Drafts had been submitted to the President by MacLeish, by Sherwood and by me....The President took all the drafts, including his own dictation, and combined

[5]Donald L. Wolfarth, "John F. Kennedy in the Tradition of Inaugural Speeches," *Quarterly Journal of Speech,* 47 (1961), 125.

[6]"The Fourth Inaugural," *New York Times,* 21 Jan. 1945, Section IV, p. 8.

[7]For the rationale that "Rhetorical scholars in particular have an obligation to illuminate the processes by which public discourse is originated, disseminated, and received," see Thomas W. Benson, "Inaugurating Peace: Franklin D. Roosevelt's Last Speech," *Speech Monographs,* 36 (1969), 147.

[8]Laura Crowell, "Building the 'Four Freedoms' Speech," *Speech Monographs,* 22 (1955), 266-83; Hermann G. Stelzner, " 'War Message,' December 8, 1941: An Approach to Language," *Speech Monographs,* 33 (1966), 419-37; Halford Ross Ryan, "Roosevelt's First Inaugural: A Study of Technique," *Quarterly Journal of Speech,* 65 (1979), 137-49.

them into a speech that was shorter than any of the three drafts."[9] Rosenman's recollection is supported by the fact that each writer's submitted draft had its pages fastened together with a blue ribbon. Roosevelt took these drafts plus his own blue-ribboned dictation under Presidential advisement. I believe Rosenman is misleading in implying that FDR himself combined all of the drafts into his own reading copy. First, there is no textual evidence to indicate that Roosevelt worked over the drafts via his emendations as he had done in his other speeches which have been studied, because, except for one minor emendation to be discussed later, Roosevelt's handwriting does not appear on any of the drafts.[10] Second, I shall argue that Roosevelt's final reading copy was developed in three stages solely from Sherwood's submitted draft. In the first stage, Roosevelt dictated his own thoughts as Rosenman recalled.[11] That fact is verified by the drafts. Roosevelt's initials (FDR), although not in his handwriting, appear on FDR's drafts so these thoughts are *his*. In the second stage, I believe Roosevelt directed each of his speech writers to use his dictated thoughts to write a draft. Accordingly, MacLeish, Rosenman, and Sherwood worked on their respective drafts with an eye toward submitting them to FDR. I believe FDR directed that a division of labor was to be maintained and that each writer was to be responsible for his own submission. I draw this inference from the drafts. Rosenman's initials (SIR) are on his drafts, Sherwood's initials (RES) are on his drafts, and MacLeish's abbreviation, A MacL, is on his draft. The third stage began when FDR selected Sherwood's submitted draft, and they fashioned the final speech. Grace Tully, FDR's secretary, supports my position that Sherwood "did considerable work" on the speech.[12]

FDR's Drafts

Two typewritten drafts represent Roosevelt's thoughts. The basis of FDR's address is on a one page, legal sized draft titled "Some Thoughts For Inaugural Speech," January 6, 1945.[13] Two thoughts are worth noting. The first was a quotation which Roosevelt remembered from his schoolmaster at

---

[9]Samuel I. Rosenman, *Working with Roosevelt* (New York: Harper and Brothers, 1952), pp. 516-17.

[10]See especially Crowell, "Building the 'Four Freedoms' Speech"; Stelzner, "'War Message,' December 8, 1941: An Approach to Language"; Ryan, "Roosevelt's First Inaugural: A Study of Technique."

[11]Rosenman, *Working with Roosevelt,* p. 517.

[12]Grace Tully, *F.D.R. My Boss* (New York: Charles Scribner's Sons, 1949), p. 351.

[13]"Some Thoughts for Inaugural Speech," January 6, 1945, Papers of Franklin D. Roosevelt, Master Speech File, No. 1570, Fourth Inaugural Address, January 20, 1945, Franklin D. Roosevelt Library, Hyde Park, New York, p. 1. Hereafter, citations for the various drafts will be given as Fourth Inaugural File.

Groton:[14] "I remember that my old schoolmaster said in the early days, 'Things in life will not always run smoothly—life is a series of ups and downs. Sometimes we will be rising toward the heights—then all will reverse itself and start downward. The great fact to remember is that the trend of civilization, like the trend of the individual, is on the average upward; that a line drawn through the middle of the peaks and valleys through the centuries always has been an upgrade trend!'"[15]

The second was: "At a time like this most of us need the confidence which flows from conviction."[16] FDR's mind was obviously on the war when he dictated these thoughts. He wished to reassure the American people that the trend of the war was positive and that America would eventually triumph. Looking beyond the war, he envisioned that the peace would place civilization on an upward trend once again. He also intimated that America's confidence that the war would be won would eventually be rewarded because of her conviction in her civilized war aims.

The second draft, consisting of three legal sized, typewritten pages, is titled "Other Thoughts for Inaugural Speech" and is dated January 13, 1945.[17] FDR's initials, although again not in his handwriting, appear on this draft and I concur with Robinson that it also reflects FDR's thinking.[18] This draft was fastened together with the blue ribbon. Carried over from the January 6th draft are the schoolmaster quotation and the confidence from conviction sentiment. Two additions are salient. The following thought was reminiscent of his famous fear statement from his First Inaugural Address: "Twelve years ago I said in a day of stress that this country had to fear fear itself."[19] He also made an observation about the Constitution: "The Constitution of 1787 was neither perfect nor complete. It was the best that could be obtained at that time."[20] These four thoughts—the schoolmaster quotation, the confidence from conviction thought, the fear statement, and the Constitutional thought—were FDR's and he wanted them included in his address.

MacLeish's Draft

This set consists of a five page typed original and a carbon copy. Both are dated in the same handwriting, 1/15/44 (*Sic*), and carry MacLeish's abbre-

---

[14]For an appraisal of Groton's and Dr. Endicott Peabody's influence on Roosevelt, see Laura Crowell, "Roosevelt the Grotonian," *Quarterly Journal of Speech,* 38 (1952), 31-36.

[15]"Some Thoughts For Inaugural Speech," Fourth Inaugural File, p. 1.

[16]*Ibid.*

[17]"Other Thoughts For Inaugural Speech," January 13, 1945, Fourth Inaugural File, pp. 1-3.

[18]Edgar Eugene Robinson, *The Roosevelt Leadership 1933-1945* (Philadelphia: J.B. Lippincott, 1955), p. 342.

[19]"Other Thoughts For Inaugural Speech," Fourth Inaugural File, p. 2.

[20]*Ibid.*

viation. The only difference between the original and the carbon copy is that MacLeish evidently forgot to make an addition on the carbon copy that he had made on the original.[21] MacLeish's original draft has a blue ribbon attached to it which signifies that it went to FDR for his consideration. For three pages, MacLeish discoursed in some detail on the military aspects of the war. His last two pages looked forward to the freedom of the future, which was communicated in militaristic terms. Except for one instance, there is no discernible trace of MacLeish's thoughts in FDR's final address. Some of MacLeish's language appears to have been used in the final address, but MacLeish's language is strikingly similar to Sherwood's. In a line by line comparison, one can perceive these similarities (Sherwood's handwritten draft is italicized):

> *"You will understand and, I believe, agree with my wish that the*
> "You will understand my wish that the
> *forms of this Inauguration should be simple and its words brief.*
> forms of this Inauguration should be simple and its words brief.
> *There is no need to say in words what [all] mankind has seen*
> There is no need to say in words what all the world has seen
> *and experienced in action. The meaning of our Republic has been*
> in action. The meaning of our Republic has been
> *declared upon every continent of the earth and on the seas and*
> declared upon every continent of the earth and on its seas and
> *on the islands."*[22]
> in the islands."[23]

Because Sherwood's drafts are not dated, it is impossible to tell whether his handwritten draft pre-dates MacLeish's and an equally plausible case could be made for one man "copying" from the other. What can be determined, as I shall later show, is that Sherwood's language from his handwritten draft was chosen by FDR. I believe FDR rejected MacLeish's draft because it stressed too much militarism at a time when FDR wanted to stress peace and because it did not include any of FDR's dictated thoughts.

Rosenman's Drafts

This set consists of two drafts, but neither is dated. The first, consisting of five pages, is handwritten and has on its upper-right-hand corner a notation of the number of words: 742.[24] This numerical notation indicates that

[21]Archibald MacLeish, draft for Fourth Inaugural, Fourth Inaugural File, original typewritten and carbon copy, pp. 1-5.
[22]Robert Sherwood, handwritten draft for Fourth Inaugural, Fourth Inaugural File, p. 1.
[23]Archibald MacLeish, draft for Fourth Inaugural, Fourth Inaugural File, p. 1.
[24]Samuel I. Rosenman, typewritten draft for Fourth Inaugural, Fourth Inaugural File, p. 1.

Rosenman was fulfilling FDR's desire that the inaugural address be brief. FDR insisted that the address would "not be more than five minutes in length."[25] From the original handwritten draft, a typed original and two carbon copies were produced and these carry Rosenman's initials (SIR). The typed original was fastened with a blue ribbon, indicating that it was sent to FDR.

The typed original illustrates how Rosenman relied on FDR's core thoughts. Rosenman used FDR's confidence from conviction thought, but he gave its skeletal frame some flesh and muscle by expanding it: "The assurance of that world peace will not come overnight—it will not come easily. It will take hard work, it will take patience, it will take tolerance and mutual understanding. Above all, it will take conviction—unshakeable conviction that it can be done and that it must be done."[26] If Rosenman's specific and concrete words improved FDR's basic thought, his terseness sacrificed the imagery of FDR's schoolmaster quotation: "We must remember the truths we learned from childhood on—the course of life is not always smooth and level. Mankind can attain great heights—and can sink to low depths. But through the centuries, the trend of civilization—like the trend of the individual—has been forward and upward."[27] Rosenman also improved FDR's Constitutional thought by enlarging it by giving it specificity: "Our Constitution itself was not a perfect instrument in 1787—nor a complete one. But in 1787 it was the best that human beings had up to that date been able to achieve. The framers of the Constitution knew that they had not achieved perfection—nor did they insist upon perfection before they signed."[28] Finally, Rosenman revised FDR's fear statement. He simplified FDR's awkward verb-noun construction ["had to fear fear itself"] and made the thought reminiscent of the actual First Inaugural fear statement: "As in every day of crisis, the principal thing to fear is fear itself—fear that we cannot accomplish the high objectives we seek."[29] Except for the schoolmaster quotation, the three instances in which Rosenman used and revised FDR's core thoughts were a general improvement of FDR's original dictation.

Two other points about Rosenman's draft are worth making. First, nowhere in his draft did Rosenman have the MacLeish-Sherwood thought about the form and words of the inaugural being brief and simple. One can assume either that Rosenman did not see MacLeish's or Sherwood's drafts or that he did see them but disagreed with them. Second, there is evidence to indicate that both Rosenman and Sherwood got the following thought from

[25]Hassett, p. 311.
[26]Samuel I. Rosenman, typewritten draft for Fourth Inaugural, Fourth Inaugural File, p. 1.
[27]*Ibid.*, p. 2.
[28]*Ibid.*
[29]*Ibid.*, p. 4.

FDR himself or that one of them "copied" the thought from the other. Although it is impossible to determine the thought's origin, the similarity of Rosenman's and Sherwood's sentence strongly indicates a common source [Sherwood's sentence is italicized]:

"The Almighty God has blessed our land in a thousand ways."[30]

"God Almighty   has blessed this land in a thousand ways."[31]

On one of the carbon copies of the typed original, Rosenman made numerous revisions. The perplexing fact is that none of Rosenman's revisions on this carbon copy were on the typed original which was submitted to FDR, nor, for that matter, is there extant a new draft which should have ensued from Rosenman's revisions on this carbon copy. The fact that Rosenman revised the carbon copy indicates that he intended to polish the text, but for some inexplicable reason, did not.

Very little of Rosenman's submitted draft is identifiable or recognizable in the final speech. FDR evidently did not like Rosenman's version of the fear statement. The Constitutional thought was so revised that it did not resemble Rosenman's writing. FDR apparently wanted the schoolmaster quotation to remain more similar to his original than to Rosenman's version. Likewise, the confidence from conviction thought was partially restored to its original form. I believe FDR rejected Rosenman's draft because it strayed too far from his dictated thoughts. He evidently liked Sherwood's submitted speech better.

Sherwood's Drafts

This set consists of a three page handwritten draft which is undated, and a three page typed original of the handwritten draft. The typed original has a blue ribbon fastened to it. There are also two carbon copies of the original. One is designated "**First Draft**" and will be discussed later.

In his handwritten draft, Sherwood utilized all of FDR's core thoughts. He took the Constitutional thought and reshaped and redirected it: "Our Constitution of 1787 was not a perfect instrument — it is not perfect yet. But it provided a firm base upon which all manner of men, of all races and colors and creeds, could build the great and powerful and eternal structure of democracy."[32] He also used the schoolmaster quotation. In fact, Sherwood pasted the quotation, which was excised from a carbon copy, to his handwritten draft, and then revised it [his deletions are bracketed; his additions are italicized]:

[30]Robert E. Sherwood, handwritten draft for Fourth Inaugural, Fourth Inaugural File, p. 3.
[31]Samuel I. Rosenman, typewritten draft for Fourth Inaugural, Fourth Inaugural File, p. 4.
[32]Robert E. Sherwood, handwritten draft for Fourth Inaugural, Fourth Inaugural File, p. 2.

I remember that my old schoolmaster said in [the early] days *that seemed to us then to be secure and untroubled*: 'Things in life will not always run smoothly—life is a series of ups and downs. Sometimes we will be rising toward the heights—then all will seem to reverse itself and start downward. The great fact to remember is that the trend of civilization *itself* [like the trend of the individual] is *forever* [on the average] upward; that a line drawn through the middle of the peaks and valleys through the centuries always *has* [had] an *upward* [upgrade] trend.''[33]

Sherwood's schoolmaster quotation more closely approximated FDR's dictated original than did Rosenman's. As for the fear statement, Sherwood retained only the word fear and hence FDR's original fear statement lost its impact from its First Inaugural sense: "Those goals cannot be achieved if we proceed with suspicion and mistrust and with fear."[34] Immediately following this sentence, Sherwood used FDR's confidence from conviction thought. I believe he inserted it as an afterthought because he squeezed two lines of writing into one ruled line and denoted his interlinear addition with a caret: "They can be achieved only if we proceed with understanding and confidence—and with courage."[35] Sherwood treated understanding and confidence and courage as separate with an emphasis on courage; hence, FDR's original dictation lost some of its meaning. Except for the schoolmaster quotation, Sherwood's choice of words changed the emphasis and meaning of FDR's core thoughts. Sherwood seemed to pay lip service to the thoughts by including them in his draft, but his renditions retained little fidelity to FDR's dictated thoughts. So why did FDR choose Sherwood's draft? I said earlier that Rosenman's draft strayed too far from FDR's dictation, and I believe it is moot whether Sherwood's draft approximated the dictation better than Rosenman's did. The answer to the question of what tipped the balance in Sherwood's favor is in the nature of the language in Sherwood's draft.

I believe FDR liked Sherwood's draft better for the following reaons. (1) Since FDR wanted a brief speech, he evidently appreciated Sherwood's introduction about the form and words being simple and brief. Rosenman did not include that sentence in his draft. (2) Since FDR liked anaphora,[36] and since Sherwood's draft was replete with anaphora and Rosenman's was not, FDR evidently preferred Sherwood's style. (3) Although Rosenman discussed the war in less militaristic terms than MacLeish did, FDR evidently selected Sherwood's draft because it was practically devoid of war language. (4) Of lesser significance was probably the fact that at 674 words, Sherwood's draft was shorter than Rosenman's draft at 702 words.

[33]*Ibid.*

[34]*Ibid.*, p. 3.

[35]*Ibid.*

[36]See Harold P. Zelko, "Franklin D. Roosevelt's Rhythm in Rhetorical Style," *Quarterly Journal of Speech,* 28 (1942), 138-41.

The Final Address

This set consists of three drafts from which the reading copy developed. Sherwood has written that FDR paid close attention to the speech's composition: "He worked it over with more care and more interest than he had shown in the preparation of any speech in two years."[37] It is difficult to distinguish FDR's dictated emendations from those of Sherwood because all of the changes appear in Sherwood's handwriting. Yet, the fact remains that FDR accepted all the emendations. I shall treat the emendations as if they were FDR's.

The foundation of the final speech began on a carbon copy of Sherwood's submitted draft. Sherwood crossed out his initials (RES) and printed instead "**First Draft.**" It is as if the speech draft ceased to be Sherwood's and instead became FDR's. Several emendations were made on this draft and I shall select two to discuss. FDR's confidence from conviction thought was substantially restored to its original intent [deletions are bracketed; additions are italicized]: "They can be achieved only if we proceed with *the* understanding and confidence [—] and [with] courage *which flows from conviction.*"[38] It is probable that FDR dictated this change to restore his stress on conviction. Two inserts were produced for this draft and one of them was in the final address. Sherwood's handwritten insert was further revised by his hand [deletions are bracketed; additions are italicized]: "We may and probably shall make mistakes—but they must [not] *never* be *the kind of* mistakes [that] *which* result from faintness of heart or [the] *from cynical* abandonment of moral principle."[39] Again, I imagine FDR dictated this insert to establish that mistakes were ineveitable, but that he believed action was preferable to inaction based on weak will or lack of moral fiber.

A new draft titled "First Draft" developed from the above; actually, this was the second draft of the final address, and it was worked over extensively. The following selected examples demonstrate a desire to achieve brevity [deletions are bracketed; additions are italicized]: "You will understand and, I believe, agree with my wish that the form of this Inauguration [should] be simple and its words brief"; "We Americans of today, [—and our brothers of many lands who fight at our side—] *together with our allies,* are passing through a period of supreme test"; "We can and [we must and] we will achieve such a peace [despite all the doubts that may dilute our confidence or all the formidable obstacles that may be placed in our path]";

[37]Robert E. Sherwood, *Roosevelt and Hopkins* (New York: Harper and Brothers, 1948), p. 846.
[38]"**First Draft,**" Fourth Inaugural File, p. 3.
[39]"**First Draft,**" Insert A,.Fourth Inaugural File, p. 2.

"The Almighty God has blessed our land in [a thousand] *many* ways."[40] Excess verbiage was also excised from the schoolmaster quotation without sacrificing its imagery: "Things in life will not always run smoothly [—life is a series of ups and downs].... that a line drawn through the middle of the peaks and *the* valleys [through the centuries] *of the centuries* always has an upward trend."[41] In the following selection, care was taken to delete pessimistic words and make the thought more optimistic: "We shall strive for perfection. We [may] *shall* not achieve it *immediately*—[not in this generation nor the next one—] but we still shall strive. We may [and probably shall] make mistakes—but they must never be [the kind of] mistakes which result from faintness of heart or from cynical abandnment of moral principle."[42] Notice that "immediately" effectively and concisely replaced its eight word counterpart. Although some words were added to make the thoughts more specific or optimistic, the effect of the emendations was an overall reduction of words to achieve brevity. Consistent with FDR's aim to be brief, this draft was reduced from 779 to 604 words.

From these emendations on the typed "First Draft" (actually the second draft), a new typed "Second Draft" (actually the third draft) was produced. The emendations on this draft were less extensive than those on the second draft. The main changes were the insertion of the formal handwritten salutation, the deletion for brevity of two paragraphs, and some minor word changes for better felicity of expression. These changes reduced the word count in this draft from 604 words to 560 words.

From this draft, a typed, triple-spaced Final Reading Copy was produced. President Roosevelt's handwriting appeared twice on the reading copy. In an exceedingly shaky hand,[43] FDR wrote his name and noted that the text was the "orig. [*sic*] reading copy."[44] The other instance was his insertion of the name of his schoolmaster who had such an influence on his youth: "I remember that my old schoolmaster *Dr. Peabody* said...."[45]

An Evaluation of the Fourth Inaugural Address

At Hyde Park, I viewed two films of FDR's delivery.[46] His vigor in delivery seemed still to be with him and he often gestured with his head. But

[40]First Draft, Fourth Inaugural Address of the President, January 20, 1945, Fourth Inaugural File, pp. 1-3.

[41]*Ibid.*, p. 2.

[42]*Ibid.*

[43]For a description of FDR's deteriorating health as seen at his Fourth Inauguration, see John Gunther, *Roosevelt in Retrospect* (New York: Harper and Brothers, 1950), p. 364.

[44]Final Reading Copy, Fourth Inaugural Address of the President, The White House, January 20, 1945, Fourth Inaugural File, p. 5.

[45]*Ibid.*, p. 2. Italics are in original.

[46]Film MP-78-1, no. 3 and Film MP 65-7-21, Franklin D. Roosevelt Library.

he looked very old and very tired. His reading of the speech still had his superb phrasing, but the rate was slower and more cumbersome than one might expect.[47] In delivering the speech, Roosevelt made numerous changes from his reading copy[48] and hence several texts of the speech are in error.[49]

The reaction to the speech was mixed. Roosevelt's close admirers reacted favorably. Perkins wrote that "it was short but good. It was in the Roosevelt style."[50] Tully believed that "in finished form it was simple, succinct and impressive in its philosophical sincerity."[51] Others saw in the address FDR's attempt to preview the peace that would follow World War II. Brogan believed that "the brief inaugural speech was devoted to the great problem of peace. It was also an appeal for the banishing of suspicion."[52] *Newsweek* noted that his address was "a promise and a prayer."[53] Others reacted less favorably. *Time* observed that "It would probably never be considered a great speech, but it indicated the President's mood and temper."[54] FDR's assistant and omnibudsman William Hassett believed it was "hardly a notable address,"[55] and Finis Farr flatly stated: "The Fourth Inaugural Address was labored and platitudinous."[56] The speech was labored, but not in Farr's pejorative sense.

Conclusion

It was my thesis that Robert Sherwood composed the draft from which the inaugural address evolved and it was not, as Rosenman stated, FDR's combining all the drafts into his own composition. Since Ryan has demonstrated that Rosenman (and others) has inaccurately attributed the authorship of the First Inaugural to FDR,[57] the rhetorical critic should investigate carefully who really composed FDR's speeches. As in the case of his First

---

[47]Franklin D. Roosevelt, Fourth Inaugural Address — 1945, Listening Library, CX 367/2, Side 3.

[48](In the article as published in the *Quarterly Journal of Speech,* the entire text of Roosevelt's speech as it appears in this book was in footnote 48.)

[49]See *Nothing to Fear,* ed. B.D. Zevin (Boston: Houghton Mifflin, 1946), pp. 438-39; Franklin Delano Roosevelt, "Fourth Inaugural Address," in *Contemporary Forum,* ed. Ernest J. Wrage and Barnet Baskerville (New York: Harper and Brothers, 1962), pp. 262-62; Franklin Delano Roosevelt, "A Just and Honorable Peace," *Vital Speeches of the Day,* 1 March, 1945, p. 290; *The Public Papers of Franklin D. Roosevelt, 1944-45,* pp. 523-25.

[50]Frances Perkins, *The Roosevelt I Knew* (New York: The Viking Press, 1946), p. 394.

[51]Tully, p. 351.

[52]Denis W. Brogan, *The Era of Franklin D. Roosevelt,* in *The Chronicles of America Series,* ed. Allan Nevins (New York: Yale University Press, 1950), p. 354.

[53]"Hail to the Chief," *Newsweek,* 29 Jan. 1945, p. 40.

[54]"For the Fourth Time," *Time,* 29 Jan. 1945, pp. 18-19.

[55]Hassett, p. 312.

[56]Finis Farr, *FDR* (New Rochelle: Arlington House, 1972), p. 411.

[57]See Ryan, "Roosevelt's First Inaugural: A Study of Technique," p. 138.

Inaugural, FDR did not compose his Fourth Inaugural.

I also stated my belief that the rhetorical critic should attempt to demonstrate what thoughts were the speech writers, and what thoughts were the President's. In the case of the Fourth Inaugural, some insights into FDR's thinking at a critical time in history are gained by examining what he kept in his address as well as what he rejected. The point is that FDR made a choice from among the submitted drafts.

I argued that FDR rejected MacLeish's submitted draft because MacLeish stressed militarism too much at a time when Roosevelt wished to focus on the future peace rather than the past glories of war. Although Rosenman wrote a good draft, I believe FDR rejected it because Rosenman strayed too far from FDR's dictated thoughts and because Rosenman included some militarism in his draft. The fact remains that FDR selected Sherwood's draft, probably because its thoughts and its style more closely resembled his original dictation, and because it was shorter and contained few allusions to the war.

Although much of the Final Reading Copy had developed from Sherwood's submitted draft, the final address nevertheless had FDR's imprint on it. Although his original fear statement had lost its impact from its First Inaugural sense, FDR retained the word itself. In 1933, Roosevelt's fear statement allayed the fears of a stricken people in the midst of a depression, but in 1945, he appropriately used it to remind Americans that the coming peace should not be approached, as it had been after World War I, "with suspicion and mistrust—and with fear." Although Sherwood had altered it on his draft, the dictated confidence from conviction thought was returned to a close approximation of FDR's original dictation. Given the enormous task of rebuilding a peaceful postwar world, Roosevelt communicated to the American people his belief that they should be sustained and motivated in that effort "with the understanding and confidence and courage which flow from conviction." Although the Constitutional thought was redirected and reshaped, it was unmistakably from FDR's original dictation. He communicated in his Constitutional thought his political belief that the Constitution was not perfect in 1787 or in 1945, but that it was a solid structure upon which he had attempted to build his essential democracy. Although there were a few minor changes in the schoolmaster quotation, they did not appreciably alter the imagery of FDR's original thought. He aptly used the schoolmaster quotation to summarize the progress of his administration and the prosecution of World War II. Franklin Delano Roosevelt had stated his belief that under his leadership the nation had achieved his goals.

Every Man a King
Huey Pierce Long

Huey Long (August 30, 1893 - September 10, 1935) was Governor of Louisiana, 1928-31, and a U.S. Senator, 1931-35. This speech was delivered on February 23, 1934. Published version: Congressional Record, *73rd Congress, 2nd session, 78, pt. 4: 3450-53.*

Is that a right of life, when the young children of this country are being reared into a sphere which is more owned by 12 men than it is by 120,000,000 people?

Ladies and gentlemen, I have only 30 minutes in which to speak to you this evening, and I, therefore, will not be able to discuss in detail so much as I can write when I have all of the time and space that is allowed me for the subjects, but I will undertake to sketch them very briefly without manuscript or preparation, so that you can understand them so well as I can tell them to you tonight.

I contend, my friends, that we have no difficult problem to solve in America, and that is the view of nearly everyone with whom I have discussed the matter here in Washington and elsewhere throughout the United States — that we have no very difficult problem to solve.

It is not the difficulty of the problem which we have; it is the fact that the rich people of this country — and by rich people I mean the super-rich — will not allow us to solve the problems, or rather the one little problem that is afflicting this country, because in order to cure all of our woes it is necessary to scale down the big fortunes, that we may scatter the wealth to be shared by all of the people.

We have a marvelous love for this Government of ours; in fact, it is almost a religion, and it is well that it should be, because we have a splendid form of government and we have a splendid set of laws. We have everything here that we need, except that we have neglected the fundamentals upon which the American Government was principally predicated.

How many of you remember the first thing that the Declaration of Independence said? It said, ''We hold these truths to be self-evident, that there are certain inalienable rights for the people, and among them are life, liberty, and the pursuit of happiness''; and it said, further, ''We hold the view that all men are created equal.''

Now, what did they mean by that? Did they mean, my friends, to say that all men were created equal and that that meant that any one man was born to inherit $10,000,000,000 and that another child was to be born to inherit nothing?

Did that mean, my friends, that someone would come into this world without having had an opportunity, of course, to have hit one lick of work, should be born with more than it and all of its children and children's children could ever dispose of, but that another one would have to be born into a life of starvation?

That was not the meaning of the Declaration of Independence when it said that all men are created equal or ''That we hold that all men are created equal.''

Now was it the meaning of the Declaration of Independence when it said that they held that there were certain rights that were inalienable—the right of life, liberty, and the pursuit of happiness.

Is that right of life, my friends, when the young children of this country are being reared into a sphere which is more owned by 12 men than it is by 120,000,000 people?

Is that, my friends, giving them a fair shake of the dice or anything like the inalienable right of life, liberty, and the pursuit of happiness, or anything resembling the fact that all people are created equal; when we have today in America thousands and hundreds of thousands and millions of children on the verge of starvation in a land that is overflowing with too much to eat and too much to wear?

I do not think you will contend that, and I do not think for a moment that they will contend it.

Now let us see if we cannot return this Government to the Declaration of Independence and see if we are going to do anything regarding it. Why should we hesitate or why should we quibble or why should we quarrel with one another to find out what the difficulty is, when we know what the Lord told us what the difficulty is, and Moses wrote it out so a blind man could see it, then Jesus told us all about it, and it was later written in the Book of James, where everyone could read it?

I refer to the Scriptures, now, my friends, and give you what it says not for the purpose of convincing you of the wisdom of myself, not for the purpose, ladies and gentlemen, of convincing you of the fact that I am quoting the Scripture means that I am to be more believed than someone else; but I quote you the Scripture, or rather refer you to the Scripture, because whatever you see there you may rely upon will never be disproved so long as you or your children or anyone may live; and you may further depend upon the fact that not one historical fact that the Bible has ever contained has ever yet been disproved by any scientific discovery or by reason of anything that has been disclosed to man through his own individual mind or through the wisdom of the Lord which the Lord has allowed him to have.

But the Scripture says, ladies and gentlemen, that no country can survive, or for a country to survive it is necessary that we keep the wealth scattered among the people, that nothing should be held permanently by any one person, and that 50 years seems to be the year of jubilee in which all property would be scattered about and returned to the sources from which it originally came, and every seventh year debt should be remitted.

Those two things the Almighty said to be necessary—I should say He knew to be necessary, or else He would not have so prescribed that the property would be kept among the general run of the people and that everyone would continue to share in it; so that no one man would get half of it and hand it down to a son, who takes half of what was left, and that son hand it down to another one, who would take half of what was left, until, like a snowball going downhill, all of the snow was off of the ground except what the snowball had.

I believe that was the judgment and the view and the law of the Lord, that we would have to distribute wealth ever so often, in order that there could not be people starving to death in a land of plenty, as there is in America today.

We have in America today more wealth, more goods, more food, more clothing, more houses than we have ever had. We have everything in abundance here.

We have the farm problem, my friends, because we have too much cotton, because we have too much wheat, and have too much corn, and too much potatoes.

We have a home-loan problem because we have too many houses, and yet nobody can buy them and live in them.

We have trouble, my friends, in the country, because we have too much money owing, the greatest indebtedness that has ever been given to civilization, where it has been shown that we are incapable of distributing the actual things that are here, because the people have not money enough to supply themselves with them, and because the greed of a few men is such that they think it is necessary that they own everything, and their pleasure consists in the starvation of the masses, and in their possessing things they cannot use, and their children cannot use, but who bask in the splendor of sunlight and wealth, casting darkness and despair and impressing it on everyone else.

"So, therefore," said the Lord, in effect, "if you see these things that now have occurred and exist in this and other countries, there must be a constant scattering of wealth in any country if this country is to survive."

"Then," said the Lord, in effect, "every seventh year there shall be a remission of debts; there will be no debts after 7 years." That was the law.

Now, let us take America today. We have in America today, ladies and gentlemen, $272,000,000,000 of debt. Two hundred and seventy-two thousand millions of dollars of debts are owed by the various people of this country today. Why, my friends, that cannot be paid. It is not possible for that kind of debt to be paid.

The entire currency of the United States is only $6,000,000,000. That is all of the money that we have got in America today. All the actual money you have got in all of your banks, all that you have got in the Government Treasury, is $6,000,000,000; and if you took all that money and paid it out today you would still owe $266,000,000,000; and if you took all that money and paid again you would still owe $260,000,000,000; and if you took it, my friends, 20 times and paid it you would still owe $150,000,000,000.

You would have to have 45 times the entire money supply of the United States today to pay the debts of the people of America and then they would just have to start out from scratch, without a dime to go on with.

So, my friends, it is impossible to pay all of these debts, and you might as well find out that it cannot be done. The United States Supreme Court has definitely found out that it could not be done, because, in a Minnesota case, it held that when a State has postponed the evil day of collecting a debt it was a valid and constitutional exercise of legislative power.

Now, ladies and gentlemen, if I may proceed to give you some other words that I think you can understand — I am not going to belabor you by quoting tonight — I am going to tell you what the wise men of all ages and all times, down even to the present day, have all said: That you must keep the wealth of the country scattered, and you must limit the amount that any one man can own. You cannot let any man own $300,000,000,000 or $400,000,000,000. If you do, one man can own all of the wealth that the United States has in it.

Now, my friends, if you were off on an island where there were 100 lunches, you could not let one man eat up the hundred lunches, or take the hundred lunches and not let anybody else eat any of them. If you did, there would not be anything else for the balance of the people to consume.

So, we have in America today, my friends, a condition by which about 10 men dominate the means of activity in at least 85 percent of the activities that you own. They either own directly everything or they have got some kind of mortgage on it, with a very small percentage to be excepted. They own the banks, they own the steel mills, they own the railroads, they own the bonds, they own the mortgages, they own the stores, and they have chained the country from one end to the other, until there is not any kind of business that a small, independent man could go into today and make a living, and there is not any kind of business that an independent man can go into and make any money to buy an automobile with; and they have finally and gradually and steadily eliminated everybody from the fields in which there is a living to be made, and still they have got little enough sense to think they ought to be able to get more business out of it anyway.

If you reduce a man to the point where he is starving to death and bleeding and dying, how do you expect that man to get hold of any money to spend with you? It is not possible.

Then, ladies and gentlemen, how do you expect people to live, when the wherewith cannot be had by the people?

In the beginning I quoted from the Scriptures. I hope you will understand that I am not quoting Scripture to you to convince you of my goodness personally, because that is a thing between me and my Maker, that is something as to how I stand with my Maker and as to how you stand with your Maker. That is not concerned with this issue, except and unless there are those of you who would be so good as to pray for the souls of some of us. But the Lord gave his law, and in the Book of James they said so, that the rich should weep and howl for the miseries that had come upon them; and, therefore, it was written that when the rich hold goods they could not use and could not consume, you will inflict punishment on them, and nothing but days of woe ahead of them.

Then we have heard of the great Greek philosopher, Socrates, and the greater Greek philosopher, Plato, and we have read the dialog between Plato and Socrates, in which one said that great riches brought on great poverty, and would be destructive of a country. Read what they said. Read what Plato said; that you must not let any one man be too poor, and you must not let any one man be too rich; that the same mill that grinds out the extra rich is the mill that will grind out the extra poor, because, in order that the extra rich can become so affluent, they must necessarily take more of what ordinarily would belong to the average man.

It is a very simple process of mathematics that you do not have to study, and that no one is going to discuss with you.

So that was the view of Socrates and Plato. That was the view of the English statesmen. That was the view of American statesmen. That was the view of American statesmen like Daniel Webster, Thomas Jefferson, Abraham Lincoln, William Jennings Bryan, and Theodore Roosevelt, and even as late as Herbert Hoover and Franklin D. Roosevelt.

Both of these men, Mr. Hoover and Mr. Roosevelt, came out and said there had to be a decentralization of wealth, but neither one of them did anything about it. But, nevertheless, they recognized the principle. The fact that neither one of them ever did anything about it is their own problem that I am not undertaking to criticize; but had Mr. Hoover carried out what he says ought to be done, he would be retiring from the President's office, very probably, 3 years from now, instead of 1 year ago; and had Mr. Roosevelt proceeded along the lines that he stated were necessary for the decentralization of wealth, he would have gone, my friends, a long way already, and within a few months he would have probably reached a solution of all of the problems that afflict this country today.

But I wish to warn you now that nothing that has been done up to this date has taken one dime away from these big-fortune holders; they own just as much as they did, and probably a little bit more; they hold just as many of the debts of the common people as they ever held, and probably a little bit more; and unless we, my friends, are going to give the people of this country a fair shake of the dice, by which they will all get something out of the funds of this land, there is not a chance on the topside of this God's eternal earth by which we can rescue this country and rescue the people of this country.

It is necessary to save the Government of the country, but is much more necessary to save the people of America. We love this country. We love this Government. It is a religion, I say. It is a kind of religion people have read of when women, in the name of religion, would take their infant babes and throw them into the burning flame, where they would be instantly devoured by the all-consuming fire, in days gone by; and there probably are some people of the world even today, who, in the name of religion, throw their own babes to destruction; but in the name of our good Government people today are seeing their own children hungry, tired, half-naked, lifting their tear-dimmed eyes into the sad faces of their fathers and mothers, who cannot give them food and clothing they both needed, and which is necessary to sustain them, and that goes on day after day, and night after night, when day gets into darkness and blackness, knowing those children would arise in the morning without being fed, and probably go to bed at night without being fed.

Yet in the name of our Government, and all alone, those people undertake and strive as hard as they can to keep a good government alive, and how long they can stand that no one knows. If I were in their place tonight, the place where millions are, I hope that I would have what I might say — I cannot give you the word to express the kind of fortitude they have; that is the word — I hope that I might have the fortitude to praise and honor my Government that had allowed me here in this land, where there is too much to eat and too much to wear, to starve in order that a handful of men can have so much more than they can ever eat or they can ever wear.

Now, we have organized a society, and we call it "Share Our Wealth Society," a society with the motto "every man a king."

Every man a king, so there would be no such thing as a man or woman who did not have the necessities of life, who would not be dependent upon the whims and caprices and ipsi dixit of the financial martyrs for a living. What do we propose by this society? We propose to limit the wealth of big men in the country. There is an average of $15,000 in wealth to every family in America. That is right here today.

We do not propose to divide it up equally. We do not propose a division of wealth, but we propose to limit poverty that we will allow to be inflicted upon any man's family. We will not say we are going to try to guarantee any equality, or $15,000 to families. No; but we do say that one third of the average is low enough for any one family to hold, that there should be a guaranty of a family wealth of around $5,000; enough for a home, an automobile, a radio, and the ordinary conveniences, and the opportunity to educate their children; a fair share of the income of this land thereafter to that family so there will be no such thing as merely the select to have those things, and so there will be no such thing as a family living in poverty and distress.

We have to limit fortunes. Our present plan is that we will allow no one man to own more than $50,000,000. We think that with that limit we will be able to carry out the balance of the program. It may be necessary that we limit it to less than $50,000,000. It may be necessary, in working out of the plans, that no man's fortune would be more than $10,000,000 or $15,000,000. But be that as it may, it will still be more than any one man, or any one man and his children and their children, will be able to spend in their lifetimes; and it is not necessary or reasonable to have wealth piled up beyond that point where we cannot prevent poverty among the masses.

Another thing we propose is old-age pension of $30 a month for everyone that is 60 years old. Now, we do not give this pension to a man making $1,000 a year, and we do not give it to him if he has $10,000 in property, but outside of that we do.

We will limit hours of work. There is not any necessity of having overproduction. I think all you have got to do, ladies and gentlemen, is just limit the hours of work to such an extent as people will work only so long as is necessary to produce enough for all of the people to have what they need. Why, ladies and gentlemen, let us say that all of these labor-saving devices reduce hours down to where you do not have to work but 4 hours a day; that is enough for these people, and then praise be the name of the Lord, if it gets that good. Let it be good and not a curse, and then we will have 5 hours a day and 5 days a week, or even less than that, and we might give a man a whole month off during a year, or give him 2 months; and we might do what other countries have seen fit to do, and what I did in Louisiana, by having schools by which adults could go back and learn the things that have been discovered since they went to school.

We will not have any trouble taking care of the agricultural situation. All you have to do is balance your production with your consumption. You simply have to abandon a particular crop that you have too much of, and all you have to do is store the surplus for the next year, and the Government will take it over. When you have good crops in the area in which the crops that have been planted are sufficient for another year, put in your public works in the particular year when you do not need to raise any more, and by that means you get everybody employed. When the Government has enough of any particular crop to take care of all of the people, that will be all that is necessary; and in order to do all of this, our taxation is going to be to take the billion-dollar fortunes and strip them down to frying size, not to exceed $50,000,000, and if it is necessary to come to $10,000,000, we will come to $10,000,000. We have worked the proposition out to guarantee a limit upon property (and no man will own less than one third the average), and guarantee a reduction of fortunes and a reduction of hours to spread wealth throughout this country. We would care for the old people above 60 and take them away from this thriving industry and give them a chance to enjoy the necessities and live in ease, and thereby lift from the market the labor which would probably create a surplus of commodities.

Those are the things we propose to do. "Every man a king." Every man to eat when there is something to eat; all to wear something when there is something to wear. That makes us all a sovereign.

You cannot solve these things through these various and sundry alphabetical codes. You can have the N.R.A. and P.W.A. and C.W.A. and the U.U.G. and G.I.N. and any other kind of "dadgummed" lettered code. You can wait until doomsday and see 25 more alphabets, but that is not going to solve this proposition. Why hide? Why quibble? You know what the trouble is. The man that says he does not know what the trouble is is just hiding his face to keep from seeing the sunlight.

God told you what the trouble was. The philosophers told you what the trouble was; and when you have a country where one man owns more than 100,000 people, or a million people, and when you have a country where there are four men, as in America, that have got more control over things than all the 120,000,000 people together, you know what the trouble is.

We had these great incomes in this country; but the farmer, who plowed from sunup to sundown, who labored here from sunup to sundown for 6 days a week, wound up at the end of the time with practically nothing.

And we ought to take care of the veterans of the wars in this program. That is a small matter. Suppose it does cost a billion dollars a year—that means that the money will be scattered throughout this country. We ought to pay them a bonus. We can do it. We ought to take care of every single one of the sick and disabled veterans. I do not care whether a man got sick on the battlefield or did not; every man that wore the uniform of this country is entitled to be taken care of, and there is money enough to do it; and we need to spread the wealth of the country, which you did not do in what you call the N.R.A.

If the N.R.A. has done any good, I can put it all in my eye without having it hurt. All I can see that the N.R.A. has done is to put the little man out of business — the little merchant in his store, the little Dago that is running a fruit stand, or the Greek shoe-shining stand, who has to take hold of a code of 275 pages and study it with a spirit level and compass and looking-glass; he has to hire a Philadelphia lawyer to tell him what is in the code; and by the time he learns what the code is, he is in jail or out of business; and they have got a chain code system that has already put him out of business. The N.R.A. is not worth anything, and I said so when they put it through.

Now, my friends, we have got to hit the root with the ax. Centralized power in the hands of a few, with centralized credit in the hands of a few, is the trouble.

Get together in your community tonight or tomorrow and organize one of our Share Our Wealth societies. If you do not understand it, write me and let me send you the platform; let me give you the proof of it.

This is **Huey P. Long** talking, United States Senator, Washington, D.C. Write me and let me send you the data on this proposition. Enroll with us. Let us make known to the people what we are going to do. I will send you a button, if I have got enough of them left. We have got a little button that some of our friends designed, with our message around the rim of the button, and in the center "Every man a king." Many thousands of them are meeting through the United States, and every day we are getting hundreds and hundreds of letters. Share Our Wealth societies are now being organized, and people have it within their power to relieve themselves from this terrible situation.

Look at what the Mayo brothers announced this week, these greatest scientists of all the world today, who are entitled to have more money than all the Morgans and the Rockefellers, or anyone else, and yet the Mayos turn back their big fortunes to be used for treating the sick, and said they did not want to lay up fortunes in this earth, but wanted to turn them back where they would do some good; but the other big capitalists are not willing to do that, are not willing to do what these men, 10 times more worthy, have already done, and it is going to take a law to require them to do it.

Organize your Share Our Wealth Society and get your people to meet with you, and make known your wishes to your Senators and Representatives in Congress.

Now, my friends, I am going to stop. I thank you for this opportunity to talk to you. I am having to talk under the auspices and by the grace and permission of the National Broadcasting System tonight, and they are letting me talk free. If I had the money, and I wish I had the money, I would like to talk to you more often on this line, but I have not got it, and I cannot expect these people to give it to me free except on some rare instance. But, my friends, I hope to have the opportunity to talk with you, and I am writing to you, and I hope that you will get up and help in the work, because the resolutions and bills are before Congress, and we hope to have your help in getting together and organizing your Share Our Wealth society.

Now, that I have but a minute left, I want to say that I suppose my family is listening in on the radio in New Orleans, and I will say to my wife and three children that I am entirely well and hope to be home before many more days, and I hope they have listened to my speech tonight, and I wish them and all of their neighbors and friends everything good that may be had.

I thank you, my friends, for your kind attention, and I hope you will enroll with us, take care of your own work in the work of this Government, and share or help in our Share Our Wealth society.

I thank you.

The Analysis of Demagogic Discourse
Huey Long's "Every Man a King" Address
Paul C. Gaske

Dr. Gaske is Assistant Professor of Speech Communication, San Diego State University, California. A version of this paper was presented at the Western Speech Communication Association Convention, Phoenix, Arizona, November 1977, and is reprinted with the permission of the author.

Kenneth Burke, commenting on the necessity for the thorough investigation and analysis of *Mein Kampf,* noted:

> Here is the testament of a man who swung a great people into his wake. Let us watch it carefully; and let us watch it, not merely to discover some grounds for prophesying what political move is to follow Munich, and what move to follow that move, etc.; let us try also to discover what kind of 'medicine' this medicine-man has concocted, that we may know, with greater accuracy, exactly what to guard against, if we are to forestall the concocting of similar medicine in America.[1]

Burke's remarks transcend the specific case of Adolph Hitler, even as powerful and fearsome as Hitler was. They express a compelling rationale for the investigation of the discourse of any individual who is a genuinely moving force in the affairs of humankind. Of particular interest, however, is that class of individuals who represent a threat to conventions and values of free and reasonable decision-making societal institutions.

While "demagoguery" in its broad sense has been investigated to some

---

[1] Kenneth Burke, "The Rhetoric of Hitler's 'Battle'," in Robert L. Scott and Bernard L. Brock, (eds.), *Methods of Rhetorical Criticism: A Twentieth Century Perspective* (New York: Harper and Row, 1972), p. 239.

extent, the character of the demagogue, the conditions that encourage demagoguery, and the specific rhetorical methods and tactics employed by the demagogue have received scant attention.[2] Moreover, those studies which deal with the analysis of demagogic discourse have been neo-Aristotelian in approach.[3] Neo-Aristotelian criticism fails to isolate or uncover many of demagogic rhetoric's essential attributes, since its emphasis on logical proof precludes truly valid criticism of "nonrational" rhetoric.[4]

This investigation is designed to accomplish two principal objectives. First, the study will attempt to provide a general profile of the demagogue, situational factors which give rise to demagoguery, and characteristics of demagogic discourse with a conceptual framework for its analysis. Second, the investigation will examine the character of Huey Long, the conditions which surrounded his rise to power, and supply a critical analysis of his "Every Man a King" address of February 23, 1934. This speech, his first national radio broadcast, dramatically introduced the "Share Our Wealth" program to the American public and announced the formation of Share Our Wealth societies.

Defining the Demagogue[5]

Currently, the term demagogue has regressed to the point where anyone who distorts truth, is involved in politics for personal gain, or represents a threat to the established political order may be considered a demagogue.[6] The overall attitude toward the demagogue taken in this paper is best summarized by T. Harry Williams in his Pulitzer Prize-winning biography, *Huey Long:*

> I believe that some men, men of power, can influence the course of history. They appear in response to conditions, but they may alter the conditions, may give a new direction to history. In the process they may do great good or evil or both, but whatever the case they leave a different kind of world behind them. Their accomplishment should be recognized. I believe Huey Long was this kind of man.[7]

---

[2]e.g., Charles W. Lomas, "The Rhetoric of Demagoguery," *Western Speech Journal,* 25 (Summer, 1961), 160-168; Charles W. Lomas, "The Agitator in American Politics," *Western Speech Journal,* 24 (Spring 1960), 76-83; Mary G. McEdwards, "Agitative Rhetoric: Its Nature and Effect," *Western Speech Journal,* 32 (Winter 1968), 36-43.

[3]e.g., Elton Abernathy, "Huey Long: Oratorical 'Wealth-Sharing'," *Southern Speech Journal,* 21 (Winter 1955), 87-102; Ernest G. Bormann, "A Rhetorical Analysis of the National Radio Broadcasts of Senator Huey Pierce Long," *Speech Monographs,* 24 (November 1957), 244-257.

[4]Edwin Black, *Rhetorical Criticism: A Study in Method* (New York, 1965), pp. 114-125.

[5]Much of this section is borrowed from a previous convention paper written by the author.

[6]Lomas, "Rhetoric," 159-168.

[7]T. Harry Williams, *Huey Long* (New York: Knopf, 1969), pp. ix-x.

Williams' statement clearly indicates that Huey Long and other demagogues are not figures to be dismissed lightly, for they share many of the characteristics of what may be termed the "revered public figure." Yet they differ in equally critical respects.

The demagogue possesses at least three major characteristics of the revered public figure. The first is that both are mass leaders. This criterion may rest in the legitimate authority of the leader, such as an American President, or in the man's founding of a popular movement.[8] Thus, local rabble-rousers who fail to gain national prominence or a widespread following are excluded from classification as demagogues. For example, Dennis Kearney achieved considerable short-term success in San Francisco, but was unable to expand his influence beyond that city.[9] It is interesting to note that a demagogue is a "mass leader," consistent with the original meaning of the term "demagogue," as it draws its roots from the Greek words *demos* ("the people") and *agogos* ("leader"), or "mass leader."

Huey Long was not a mass leader at the time of the "Every Man a King" address, but he became one shortly thereafter. Within a month of the address, eight hundred thousand had joined Share Our Wealth societies; by September 1935, there were an estimated seven million members.[10] Although Roosevelt won the 1936 election by an unprecedented margin, the outcome in 1935, the height of Long's popularity, was by no means assured. James Farley, Roosevelt's chief political strategist, revealed the results of a secret national poll conducted by the Democratic National Committee designed to measure Long's vote-pulling strength:

> It indicated that, running on a third party ticket, Long would be able to poll between 3,000,000 and 4,000,000 votes....His probable support was not confined to Louisiana and nearby states. On the contrary, he had about as much following in the North as in the South, and he had as strong an appeal in the industrial centers as he did in the rural areas. Even the rock-ribbed Republican state of Maine, where the voters are steeped in conservatism, was ready to contribute to Long's total vote in about the same percentage as other states....It was easy to conceive a situation whereby Long, by polling more than 3,000,000 votes, might have the balance of power in the 1936 election. For instance, the poll indicated that he would command upward of 100,000 votes in New York state, a pivotal state in any national election; and a vote of that size could easily mean the difference between victory or defeat for the Democratic or Republican candidate. Take that number of votes away from either major candidate, and they would come mostly from our side, and the result might spell disaster.[11]

[8]Williams, pp. 414-416.
[9]Lomas, "Agitator," 76-83.
[10]Burton J. Hotaling, "Huey P. Long as Journalist and Propagandist," *Journalism Quarterly*, XX (1943), 26.
[11]Harnett T. Kane, *Louisiana Hayride* (New York: William Morrow, 1941), p. 126.

Moreover, Long demonstrated the capability to influence election results outside his immediate political sphere. Raymond Moley noted:

> By late March [1935] the Kingfish was threatening to campaign in states other than Louisiana for 'Share-the-Wealth' candidates. By April the Democratic high command not only expected him to defeat Senator Joseph T. Robinson of Arkansas and Senator Pat Harrison of Mississippi, two of the party's elder statesmen, in 1936, but was chewing mustaches over statistics purporting to show that he could make himself political master of the whole, vast Lower Mississippi Valley—perhaps even of great hunks of the West. Who knew where Huey...would end?[12]

Huey Long's life ended in a Louisiana hospital room, the victim of an assassin's bullet and questionable medical care, on September 10, 1935. At the time of his death, though many bemoaned the fact, he was unquestionably a mass leader.

A second common characteristic of the revered public figure and the demagogue is charisma, or the attraction of followers on the basis of personal qualities of the leader.[13] Charisma is exhibited in political figures in two basic forms, which may occur separately or in combination: mastery and representation. The charismatic leader who possesses mastery "is in varying degrees the master of events—one who orders the future."[14] That is, he appears to his followers to be not only a master of destiny, but also a man capable of *controlling* destiny. This type of charisma can assume several forms. As Raymond E. Spencer explained:

> The charisma of the sage derives from the power of his intellect; the charisma of the general derives from his strategic insight and his willingness to take calculated risks; the charisma of the prince flows from his administrative skill and his ability to manipulate his image and the charisma of the revolutionary leader is a product of his unshakable vision and his persuasive powers.[15]

The charismatic figure may possess one or more of these forms of mastery.[16]

Huey Long's mastery took two forms. The first was the mastery of the sage, one who has the power to create order from chaos. As Spencer writes:

> He [the sage] resolves the existential chaos of reality. He structures a cosmos. He provides guides for action and a premise for the future....The mass of men, incapable of achieving order for themselves, are awed by the

[12]Kane, pp. 126-127.

[13]Martin E. Spencer, "What is Charisma?" *British Journal of Sociology,* 24 (September 1973), 341.

[14]Spencer, "Charisma," 345.

[15]Spencer, 347.

[16]For example, Long possessed the mastery of the sage and the revolutionary leader.

demonstrated capacity of a great mind to make sense of an incomprehensible reality. The man who can do such things acquires a nimbus of the sacred.[17]

There has scarcely been a more disquieting time in American history than the Great Depression. For literally millions of Americans, their world was disintegrating, whether in the dust bowls of Oklahoma or in the streets of New York. Huey Long reordered and restructured the present world for those oppressed people that they might share in the riches of their country. Whether or not Share Our Wealth was a viable plan is a moot point; Long's sense of divine order created a reverential faith in his followers and an immediate hope in the present.

Long also possessed the mastery of the revolutionary leader. The revolutionary leader generates charisma not with accomplishments of the past, or successes in the present, but "by convincing his followers that *his vision of the future will come to pass.*"[18] Spencer goes on to point out:

> He [the revolutionary leader] is constantly generating and sustaining a revolutionary reality for his followers by his writings and speeches. It is his own unshakeable conviction in that reality, his iron will, his demonic energy and the power of his intelligence that envelops his followers in a world-to-be of his own creation.... The will and faith of the others may falter, but they return again and again to the inexhaustible fountain of the leader's vision.[19]

Whether Long's conviction was genuine is open to question, but that his followers believed in his messianic powers is not.[20] Schlesinger wrote of the Share Our Wealth program:

> It was, in short, a hillbilly's paradise.... It was the Snopeses' dream come true. Long rested his case on rhetoric and the Scriptures. 'I never read a line of Marx or Henry George or any of them economists,' he once said. 'It's all in the law of God.'[21]

By contrast, representation, the second form of charisma, may be said to occur when "the leader structures a universe of values for his followers that satisfies deep-felt needs."[22] In other words, the leader brings a promise of salvation to a troubled people by creating or reinforcing a set of values which maximally meet their needs. He can do so in a variety of ways. The

[17]Spencer, 345.

[18]Spencer, 346.

[19]Spencer, 346-347.

[20]Long's brother Julius, for example, was quoted by Schlesinger (p. 60) as stating, "The only sincerity there was in him was for himself."

[21]Arthur M. Schlesinger, Jr., *The Age of Roosevelt,* Vol. III: *The Politics of Upheaval* (Boston: Houghton Mifflin, 1960), p. 60.

[22]Spencer, 347.

leader may be an *innovator,* where he creates values which "answer the needs or diffuse the tensions of his agitated following" by reaching "into the historical situation to create a value order that is ripe for the time."[23] The man is not merely a product of his times, though he does capitalize on them. The *articulator,* a relatively common figure in politics, says what people wish to hear, but cannot or do not know how to say for themselves.[24] The articulator is identified with but not the creator of the value structure. And the *symbolizer* simply stands for the values he represents, and is thus the perfect example of the group type.[25]

Huey Long was both an innovator and an articulator. Much like the great religious leader, Long brought the promise of hope, redemption, and salvation to those most adversely affected by the depression. He created an identity for his followers through their membership in Share Our Wealth societies. As an articulator, Long not only created an identity for his supporters, but was their mouthpiece, a person who voiced their frustrations, hopes, and fears. As Raymond Gram Swing wrote:

> For his supporting public, Long is the under-dog southern farmer and villager, the suppressed, ignored, unprivileged person. He is the personification of their aspirations and their prejudices. And his appeal will be the same wherever he can display himself to unprivileged people.[26]

The basic difference between mastery and representation is summarized by Spencer: "In the case of mastery the sentiments toward the leader are characterized by *awe*; in representation those sentiments run in the direction of *enthusiasm*."[27] Not all mass leaders are charismatic and all charismatic figures are not mass leaders (although in politics charismatic figures are sufficiently rare as to virtually make them mass leaders by default). All American Presidents are mass leaders, but their leadership often comes from the exercise of legitimate power and not their charismatic qualities.

The third characteristic shared by the demagogue and the revered public figure is the status of popular hero. This characteristic, while more superficial in substance than charisma, nevertheless provides an excellent set of criteria for recognizing political demagogues. Specifically, to qualify as a popular hero, an individual must be:

(1) a person of fame, as indicated by news-space devoted to him, rumor and legend concerning him, or the fact that everybody knows him;

[23]Spencer, 347.
[24]Spencer, 348.
[25]Spencer, 348.
[26]Raymond Gram Swing, *Forerunners of American Fascism* (New York: Julian Messner, 1935), p. 88.
[27]Spencer, 347.

(2) a person who is commonly called a hero (or some equivalent or marginal term such as idol, champion, patron saint, martyr); and

(3) a person who is the object of hero-worship. The criteria for hero-worship are as follows:

  (a) the hero is admired, eulogized, acclaimed, or otherwise honored by his society;

  (b) he is formally recognized or canonized;

  (c) he is commemorated; or

  (d) he has a following of devotees, "fans," or hero-worshippers.[28]

Huey Long was a public hero; he was famous, heroic, and enjoyed hero worship. Thanks to massive press coverage (albeit largely negative) and his national radio broadcasts, Long was certainly a well-known personality. To the poor and disenfranchised, he was a champion; when scourged by the press and the Administration, he became a symbolic martyr. And the tens of thousands of letters Long received daily requesting admission to Share Our Wealth societies was a powerful form of hero worship.[29] The impact of the popular hero is explained by Orrin E. Klapp:

> The special sentimentality of the public toward a popular hero includes a certain endearment, a tremendous loyalty, a reluctance to admit critical reflection, and a faith and veneration which verges upon superstition. Once a public figure acquires the status of a popular hero, he is to be specially reckoned with as a social force.[30]

Popular heroes assume many guises. One is the "conquering hero," who is characterized by the extraordinary feats he performs, the contests he wins, the tests he overcomes, and the quests he seeks.[31] Another type of popular hero is the "clever hero," who achieves heroic status by defeating a stronger opponent by some means of deception, by using brains over brawn, or wily idealism over crass oppression. In many respects, the clever hero verges upon being a villain, yet he retains the admiration of the people.[32] A third type of hero is a "Cinderella," who succeeds more by luck, hard work, or miraculous assistance than by his innate cleverness.[33] The "delivering hero" characteristically rescues a person or group from

---

[28]Orrin E. Klapp, "Hero Worship in America," *American Sociological Review,* XIV (February, 1949), 54, note 4.

[29]Williams, pp. 700-701.

[30]Klapp, "Hero Worship," 54.

[31]Orrin E. Klapp, "The Folk Hero," *Journal of American Folklore,* LXII (January, 1949), 19-20.

[32]Orrin E. Klapp, "The Clever Hero," *Journal of American Folklore,* LXVII (January 1954), 21.

[33]Klapp, "Folk Hero," 20.

danger or distress, as in the belief in a savior or messiah.[34] The "culture hero" is, as the name implies, an important legendary figure who has made an important contribution to culture or welfare, e.g., Joseph Smith to the Mormon Church.[35] Finally, there is the "martyr," an often-tragic figure who dies heroically, fighting for a cause, characteristically betrayed by his friends or overwhelmed by his enemies.[36]

Huey Long in death was a martyr; in substance he was a delivering hero, a messiah rescuing his followers from the depression, leading them to the promised land of Share Our Wealth. Above all, however, he was a clever hero, a hero in much the same manner that Robin Hood, Don Juan, and Pancho Villa were heroes. Even a cursory examination of Long's gubernatorial career in Louisiana or as a United States Senator reflects this atypical quality. Whether telling legislators that he could buy and sell them like "dime a dozen punks," or greeting German naval commanders in green silk pajamas, Long personified the clever hero.[37] The effect is explained by Orrin E. Klapp:

> He [the clever hero] is upstart, rebel, lawbreaker, liar, thief, and male-factor; and yet in spite of being so—perhaps because of this—he is a social force.[38]

In other words, Huey Long was a hero for the same behavior for which he was indicted as a demagogue—it depended on one's social standing which view of him was held. For the intellectual and the wealthy, he represented the extreme danger to democracy. To the poor and disenfranchised, he was their patron saint, championing their cause, symbolizing their struggle.

The most easily recognizable distinction between the public figure and the demagogue is that the demagogue elicits from the public tremendous emotional reactions—both positive and negative.[39] The revered public figure may generate tremendous feeling as well, but it generally is of the hero-worship type. Controversy surrounds the demagogue, usually centering around not the specific merits of his programs, but around his worth as an individual. The question of whether the demagogue is good or evil, a man to be loved or hated, feared or worshipped, is paramount; thus most rhetoric about a demagogue is epideictic in character.

That Huey Long shared many qualities of the revered public figure has just been documented. That he also possessed the distinguishing qualities of

[34]Klapp, "Folk Hero," 21.
[35]Klapp, "Folk Hero," 21-22.
[36]Klapp, "Folk Hero," 22.
[37]Schlesinger, *Upheaval,* p. 42.
[38]Klapp, "Clever Hero," 21.
[39]Williams, p. ix.

the demagogue is easy to demonstrate. Long inspired extreme emotions in the public through his actions and his words, a point that has been amply proven here and in other studies. Williams' words are worth remembering: "Long was obviously the type of leader who excites violent antithetical emotions in people, even in those not closely associated with him."[40]

Second, the demagogue champions a single cause, while the revered public figure is much more diversified. The communist menace was Joseph McCarthy's sole issue; when the issue died, he was finished as a political force. The identification of the demagogue with a single, simplified issue may explain why it is virtually impossible for a demagogue to attain the White House. He simply lacks the adaptability and flexibility necessary to attract a wide enough following to win that political office. In his rapid rise to national prominence, the demagogue is stereotyped as a one-issue candidate, and the public finds it difficult to accept him as an authority in other areas.

Long also championed a single cause. Although peripheral issues to the redistribution of wealth and the Share Our Wealth program were occasionally mentioned, they were either integrated into his redistribution of wealth program, or were later deemphasized or dropped entirely.

Third, the public figure may spearhead a movement; the demagogue *is* the movement. That is, the man and his issue are so inextricably woven together that they become synonymous; the demagogue is a symbolic figure. To illustrate, the name "Joseph McCarthy" probably would bring instantaneous identification with "Red menace." Yet the name "John Kennedy" probably would trigger a wide variety of phrases, none of which would adequately describe the man or his policies and programs. In this manner, the demagogue resembles the founder of a religion. As Spencer writes, "The leader brings forth...a universe of values that creates the group. He is thus simultaneously an articulator and himself the primary symbol of the existence of the group."[41] With this man-as-movement characteristic, the demagogue, rightly or wrongly, is often viewed as a unidimensional rather than as a multidimensional personality.

Long and Share Our Wealth became inextricably linked. As its founder and chief spokesman, Long turned the program into a crusade, hoping that the surge of pent up emotions resulting from the frustrations of the depression could sweep him into the White House. Williams, noting this fact, commented, "It was the promise in Share Our Wealth to abolish misery and poverty that drew people to its banner. Enough of them would come, Huey hoped, to elect him President."[42]

---

[40]Williams, p. ix.
[41]Spencer, 346.
[42]Williams, pp. 700-701.

In sum, the revered public figure and the demagogue are similar in at least three important respects — they are mass leaders, charismatic, and heroic. Their differences are more a matter of degree but nevertheless critical in distinguishing the two classes. The demagogue elicits powerful antithetical emotional responses, he champions a single cause, and he and his issue become symbolically one idea, one driving force.

The Rise of Demagoguery

Situation and audience characteristics are so interrelated that to separate them for purposes of analysis is, by and large, a fruitless and counterproductive endeavor. One situational factor, however, must be taken as a presumption for demagogic rhetoric and demagogues to emerge: the existence of a democratic state. As James Fenimore Cooper wrote in *The American Democrat,* "The true theatre of a demagogue is a democracy."[43] Even in the case of Adolph Hitler, the state of Germany was democratic during his rise to power. Only after his assuming control of the existing political structure did he create a dictatorship. In an authoritarian state, there are no viable enemies of the government. Imprisonment, exile, and execution curb dissent and make demagoguery nonexistent. Revolutionary movements, if there are such, are typically carried underground.

Dictators and demagogues, thus, cannot be equated. A dictator's authority stems from his legitimate or coercive power; the demagogue's power rests in his ability to win a following, a following that is determined by his rhetorical skill. Adolph Hitler was one of the few dictators with such awesome rhetorical power, and few would deny that this ability was a major source of his effectiveness. As Swing,[44] Burke,[45] and others have indicated, the experience of Adolph Hitler is a compelling reason why a demagogue must not hold high office, particularly the Presidency, for he can and does use "the institutions of democracy to crush democracy."[46]

The situational and audience factors necessary for the rise of demagoguery are subject to cyclical fluctuations. This fluctuation should be viewed metaphorically — as the push and pull of mind and heart, of intellect and emotion. This struggle within people and among people vacillates between the polarities, and the state of the conflict is an excellent predictor of the state of the society. At one end of the spectrum is the extreme empiricism of the logical positivists; at the other, the fundamental doctrines of the spiritualists. At one end, an emphasis on the individual and a value on heterogeneity; at the other, an emphasis on the group or community and a

---

[43]Cited in Richard H. Rovere, *Senator Joe McCarthy* (New York: Harcourt, 1959), p. 45.
[44]Swing, *Forerunners.*
[45]Burke, "Battle."
[46]Kane, p. 4.

value on homogeneity. At one end, a reverence for science and an affirmation of intellectualism; at the other, a reverence for the spirit and an affirmation of anti-intellectualism.[47] Most of the time a society fluctuates between these extremes, but the closer a society moves in the direction of heart—of fundamentalism, homogeneity, anti-intellectualism, and spiritualism—the greater the probability for the rise of the demagogue.

At the root, perhaps, of audience response to the demagogue is economic dislocation—a significant disruption in the accustomed lifestyle of a significant body of individuals. This dislocation is not limited to the lower strata of a society, and the dislocation can be real or imagined, or, in many cases, some of both. Overt signs of disenfranchisement from the economic system may be such factors as widespread unemployment, falling GNP, and malnourishment. But, as Kenneth Burke pointed out, the crux of any economic dislocation is a religious statement, and so too, the crux of any religious statement is an economic issue.[48]

When Huey Long delivered his "Every Man a King" address, the nation was in the throes of the Great Depression: currency was unstable, the national debt was ballooning, the GNP was declining, and unemployment was over 20% nationally. As the high unemployment figures and a concomitantly large number of small business bankruptcies indicate, the depression was not restricted to those who had little wealth to begin with; it cut a wide swath across the middle class as well. A general outrage existed against many large businesses and individuals who were seemingly taking advantage of the depression to increase their economic worth. And the overall economic situation in 1934 was rapidly worsening, not improving, and there appeared little chance of speedy recovery.[49]

People were afraid, angry, looking for someone or something to blame for their condition, yet were experiencing the religious revivalism started by Billy Sunday and continued by men such as Father Coughlin. The rhetorical situation and the audience were united by the dominance of heart over mind. Kenneth Burke explained the reason for this dominance when he observed, "A people in collapse, suffering under economic frustration and the defeat of nationalistic aspirations, with the very midrib of their integrative efforts...in a state of dispersion, have little other than 'spiritual' basis to which they could refer their nationalistic dignity."[50]

[47]Richard Hofstadter, *Anti-intellectualism in American Life* (New York: Knopf, 1963), pp. 1-80.

[48]Kenneth Burke, *The Rhetoric of Religion* (Boston: Beacon Press, 1961), p. 293.

[49]According to the Department of Labor, unemployment was projected to rise in 1934 at a faster rate than in previous years; estimates of total numbers out of work went as high as 43 million.

[50]Kenneth Burke, *Permanence and Change,* 2nd ed. (Indianapolis: Bobbs-Merrill, 1965), pp. 274-294.

Seizing upon an appropriately religious theme, Long, in the "Every Man a King" address, created an enemy in the very wealthy and proclaimed the Share Our Wealth program a panacea for economic ills and a method for conquering the demonic rich. The specific tactics employed in the speech and their psychological "shaping" effect on the audience will be discussed in the third section of this paper.

Analyzing Demagogic Discourse

Demagogic discourse typically follows a classic psychological/motivational pattern for persuasion, as outlined in Kenneth Burke's *Permanence and Change.*[51] Its four stage development is illustrated below:

$$Guilt \longrightarrow Victimization \longrightarrow Redemption \longrightarrow Salvation$$

Each of these four stages will be developed in terms of : (1) the rationale for each phase; (2) general themes that Huey Long employed to achieve each stage; (3) specific strategies utilized in the "Every Man a King" address to reinforce each stage.

Guilt. Any persuasive form presupposes some distance, be it intellectual or emotional, between the speaker and his audience. This distance is used by the speaker to create a sense of guilt on the part of his hearers. As Lowenthal and Guterman noted:

> The leader of a movement must first convince his audience that its ideas are inadequate for coping with the situation that produces its discontent. He cannot win adherents without in a sense humiliating them, that is, suggesting that they are inferior in knowledge, strength, or courage and that they need him more than he needs them.[52]

Generally, Long created guilt in his audience on two issues, both implicitly, not explicitly stated. First, Long capitalized on his audience's feelings of impotence and ignorance when compared with those in power, that they were inadequately equipped to provide answers to their own problems. Second, they were made to feel guilty for being poor, as if they should have material wealth and were responsible for their poverty. One of these feelings of guilt, anger and frustration naturally arose.

In the "Every Man a King" address, the audience experienced guilt for allowing their young children to be malnourished, to be needlessly denied the necessities of life. This image is consistent with the general religious attitude that the sins of the adult population are borne, not by the adults themselves, but by their offspring. The following excerpt from the speech illustrates how the image was developed:

[51] Burke, *Permanence,* pp. 274-294.
[52] Leo Lowenthal and Norbert Guterman, *Prophets of Deceit,* 2d ed. (Palo Alto, Calif.: Pacific Books, 1970), p. 20.

Is that right of life, my friends, when the young children of this country
are being reared into a sphere which is more owned by 12 men than it is by
120,000,000 people?

Is that, my friends, giving them a fair shake of the dice or anything like
the inalienable right of life, liberty and the pursuit of happiness, or anything resembling the fact that all people are created equal, when we have
today thousands and hundreds of thousands and millions of children on
the verge of starvation in a land that is overflowing with too much to eat
and too much to wear?[53]

Victimage. Once the audience feels sufficiently guilty, that guilt must be
cancelled or shifted to the selection of a "sacrificial offering;"[54] in essense,
an enemy. The relationship between guilt and victimization is developed by
Lowenthal and Guterman:

On the one hand the agitator brands his followers as suckers, harping on
the suffering they have endured in their unsuccessful lives and thereby satis-
fying their latent masochism. On the other hand, he transforms this very
humiliation into something to be proud of, a mark of the new *elite* he will
eventually elevate. By projecting the responsibility for it on an unscrupulous and immoral enemy, he offers his followers a means of warding off
in advance all future humiliations. The humiliation is simultaneously deepened and surrounded by a halo.[55]

As a rule, Huey Long selected two basic enemies on which the ills of the
poor could be blamed. One, obviously, was the rich—they had deprived the
poor of what they rightfully deserved. And the other was the man ultimately
responsible for decisions affecting the poor, Franklin Delano Roosevelt.

The method most suitable for realizing victimization is *conspiracy.* That
is, once the audience perceives the enemy as consciously scheming to deny
them what is rightfully theirs, the enemy becomes a demonic figure and the
struggle against the enemy becomes a religious crusade.[56] The speaker can
make effective use of stereotypes, or "devil terms," to reinforce the resentment already felt by the audience.[57] Additionally, the use of simple
"parables" to illustrate the evils of the enemy should serve to connect the
enemy with the guilt or resentment. The conspiracy must be kept
simple—an emotional issue must not be complex, or its intensity wanes.[58]

In the "Every Man a King" address, the guilt created in the "suffering
little children" image, far from causing gloom and despair, imparts a sense

[53]Huey P. Long, "Every Man a King," in *Congressional Record,* 78 (March 1, 1934), 3451.
[54]Burke, *Permanence,* p. 284.
[55]Lowenthal and Guterman, *Deceit,* p. 23.
[56]Richard Hofstadter, "The Paranoid Style in American Politics," in *The Paranoid Style in American Politics and Other Essays* (New York: Alfred A. Knopf, 1965), p. 32.
[57]McEdwards, "Rhetoric," 37.
[58]Lomas, "Demagoguery," 165.

of intense righteous indignation, driving one to seek a cause for one's feelings of guilt. In essence, Long created a desire for a scapegoat, an enemy, a devil-figure. Long satisfied this motivational desire for a victim in the image of the conspiratorial wealthy. The development of this image occurred in two stages. The first identified the wealthy as the cause of the economic ills of the country. Early in the speech, Long pointed out:

> It is not the difficulty of the problem which we have; it is the fact that the rich people of this country—and by rich people I mean the super-rich—will not allow us to solve the problems, or rather the one little problem that is afflicting this country, because in order to cure all of our woes it is necessary to scale down the big fortunes, that we may scatter the wealth to be shared by all of the people.[59]

Mere attribution of causality, however, was insufficient to evoke intense feelings of hatred toward the rich. It was, therefore, essential that Long portray the wealthy as sinister, evil, demonic, conspiratorial—consciously oppressing the masses and perpetuating the suffering of the litle children.[60] The following passage is illustrative of this second stage of the image's development:

> ...the greed of a few men is such that they think it is necessary that they own everything, and their pleasure consists in the starvation of the masses, and in their possessing things they cannot use, and their children cannot use, but who bask in the splendor of sunlight and wealth, casting darkness and despair and impressing it on everyone else.[61]

The language in this passage casts the wealthy in a sinister pose—basking in "sunlight and wealth" while "casting darkness and despair." This archetypal light/dark metaphor is used frequently to villify the rich, and is a representative use of stereotype and "devil terms" to reinforce the resentment already held by the audience.[62]

The effect of an archetypal metaphor on an audience is further explained by Michael Osborn who observed, "Arising from the fundamental interests of men, they in turn activate basic motivational energies within an audience, and if successful turn such energies into a powerful current running in favor of the speaker's recommendations."[63] Similarly, the ideal psychological effect of the "conspiratorial wealthy" image is explained by Lowenthal and Guterman. They write, "By projecting the responsibility for it [guilt] on an unscrupulous and immoral enemy, he offers his followers a means of

---

[59]Long, 3451.
[60]Hofstadter, "Paranoid," p. 32.
[61]Long, 3451.
[62]McEdwards, "Agitative Rhetoric," p. 37.
[63]Michael Osborn, "Archetypal Metaphor in Rhetoric: The Light/Dark Family," *Quarterly Journal of Speech,* 33 (1967), 116.

warding off in advance all future humiliations. The humiliation is simultaneously deepened and surrounded by a halo.''[64]

For this state to be maximally reached, however, the image must be ''perfected'' or ''purified.''[65] For the image to be purified, it had to be ''strong enough to account for the ubiquitousness and omnipotence of his conspiracy in destroying the world to become its master.''[66] Long demonstrated this demonic potential of the conspiratorial wealthy in a simple parable, illustrating the evils of the enemy, and serving to make the enemy responsible for the existing guilt and resentment felt by the audience:

> Now, my friends, if you were off on an island where there were 100 lunches, you could not let one man eat up the hundred lunches, or take the hundred lunches and not let anybody else eat any of them. If you did, there would not be anything else for the balance of the people to consume.
>
> So, we have in America today, my friends, a condition by which about 10 men dominate the means of activity in at least 85 per cent of the activities that you own....[67]

To fight this powerful, heartless enemy was an awesome task, one that required more than a strictly ''logical'' foundation. Long had to provide a spiritual basis for fighting the conspiratorial wealthy, and he did so in the form of scriptural justification. That is, Long sanctioned retribution against the wealthy not merely on economic or even humanitarian grounds, but also on philosophical and religious precedent. Citing the Bible and Greek philosophers, Long observed:

> But the Lord gave his law, and in the Book of James...it was written that when the rich hold goods they could not use and could not consume, you will inflict punishment on them, and nothing but days of woe ahead of them....
>
> ...Read what Plato said; that you must not let any one man be too poor, and you must not let any one man be too rich; that the same mill that grinds out the extra rich is the mill that will grind out the extra poor, because, in order that the extra rich can become so affluent, they must necessarily take more of what ordinarily would belong to the average man.[68]

To this point in the address, Long had capitalized on a sense of guilt in his audience, had articulated the basis of the evil, had created and perfected an enemy responsible for the guilt feelings, and had justified, theologically and philosophically, retribution against the enemy.

Redemption. Once the audience has been awakened to the conspiracy and

[64]Lowenthal and Guterman, *Deceit,* p. 23.
[65]Burke, ''Battle,'' p. 249.
[66]Burke, ''Battle,'' p. 250.
[67]Long, 3451.
[68]Long, 3451.

has sufficiently strong feelings against the enemy, the speaker must provide an alternative — i.e., supply the means to eliminate the enemy. Essentially, the audience must be redeemed. By accepting the speaker's alternatives, the audience is simultaneously cleansed of their guilt and vindicated in their persecution of the enemy.[69]

Huey Long's plan of redemption was his "Share Our Wealth" program. By redistributing wealth and guaranteeing an annual income to all, it purged the audience of their guilt feelings and justified their rejection of F.D.R. and the wealthy.

The preferable techniques for communicating the redemptive qualities of the proposal are the use of "god terms" and over-simplification. Whereas "devil terms" evoke strong emotional responses against the enemy, "god terms" evoke a positive response toward the advocated position. The use of oversimplification makes the proposal easy for the audience to understand, or to think they understand. The effectiveness of this strategy is grudgingly admitted by Charles Lomas:

> The demagogue also believes in simplicity, but he carries it to absurdity; he oversimplifies and, as a result, his audiences understand him well. He seems to be merely stating the obvious, but in reality he is substituting prejudice and half-truth for fact. In much the same way Huey Long could win votes by speaking in the homespun language of back country Louisiana and by proposing to "Share the Wealth" of the country among all the people. In a gross oversimplification, he treated wealth as if it consisted of idle dollars in the bank, requiring only simple arithmetic to secure an equitable distribution.[70]

In the "Every Man a King" address, the retribution against the wealthy was to take place in the *redemptive* promise of Share Our Wealth. Not only was Share Our Wealth a proposal to redistribute wealth, but in doing so it also provided a means to eliminate the rich, a means of redemption from guilt. By accepting Long's alternatives, the audience was both cleansed of their guilt and vindicated in their pursuit of the enemy.[71] Share Our Wealth provided the *means* of redemption, but the audience had to commit themselves to the means of grace to be redeemed. Thus, *joining* the Share Our Wealth society (with its promise of redemption) was a dominant theme in the speech. The cleansing qualities of the society are explicated in the following statement by Long:

> This is Huey P. Long talking, United States Senator, Washington, D.C. Write me and let me send you the data on this proposition. Let us make known to the people what we are going to do....Share Our Wealth soci-

[69]Burke, *Permanence,* pp. 284-286.
[70]Lomas, "Demagoguery," p. 163.
[71]Burke, *Permanence,* pp. 284-286.

eties are now being organized, and people have it within their power to relieve themselves from this terrible situation.[72]

Salvation. The final stage of persuasion is for the audience to be "saved." Since the redemption phase provides the *means* for salvation, it only remains for the speaker to ensure the successful implementation of the proposal. The speaker has already shown the audience the Way and the Truth; he now must show them the Light. In effect, for the movement to be successful, its leader must be accepted as not merely an authority figure, but as a god-figure. Gerald L.K. Smith, one of Long's chief campaigners, remarked:

> No great movement has ever succeeded unless it has deified some one man.
> The Share-the-Wealth movement consciously deified Huey P. Long.[73]

In creating this image, the leader must engage in discourse fitting that of a deity. He must be viewed as a man of uncompromising principle, of sound judgment, and of limitless wisdom. A favorite method of demonstrating the latter is the emulation of Jesus' parables—the wise son and the fool, the unforgiving servant, the Good Samaritan.[74]

In the "Every Man a King" address, Long had already demonstrated his uncompromising principle and his "sound' judgment in his program of Share Our Wealth (even though Schlesinger and others demonstrated its unworkability[75]). His limitless wisdom was illustrated in the many parables he narrated and Scriptural justifications he employed. In addition, Long demonstrated himself as a man of vision as he described the state of euphoria, the heaven-on-earth that would result from membership in Share Our Wealth. All free, all equal, every man a king:

> Every man a king, so there would be no such thing as a man or woman who did not have the necessities of life, who would not be dependent on the whims and caprices and ipsi dixit of the financial martyrs for a living.
>
> 'Every man a king.' Every man to eat when there is something to eat; all to wear something when there is something to wear. That makes us all a sovereign.[76]

Long's skill in leading the audience from guilt, to victimage, to redemption, to salvation, given the state of the economy and the relationship between mind and heart, must account at least in part for the overwhelming success of the address.

A final, overall characteristic of demagogic discourse warrants attention.

[72]Long, 3452.
[73]Schlesinger, *Upheaval,* p. 64.
[74]Klapp, "Clever Hero," 23-31.
[75]Schlesinger, *Upheaval,* p. 63.
[76]Long, 3452.

Ideally, demagogic rhetoric should develop a strong unification theme, a plea that encompasses both the spiritual and geographical unity of the movement. Any religious movement requires a spiritual bond between the leader and members; if the link is broken, the movement dies. Often overlooked, however, is the important role of unity within the movement. If internal identity is lacking, the movement may die from within.

Huey Long's predominant concern in the "Every Man a King" address was not to create a deified image of himself—that would come later.[77] Instead, he concentrated on creating a group identity for the Share Our Wealth members and prospective members.

Long created a spiritual identity by the use of identification by antithesis; that is, "by some opposition shared in common."[78] The opposition was the conspiratorial enemy, who served, as scapegoat, *"to deflect attention from possible malefactors within one's camp."*[79]

From another perspective, Long sought to create a "restricted code" within his program; that is, to create a gap between sharers and nonsharers of the code.[80] He accomplished this task by establishing a "we/they" dichotomy. "We" were the framers of the Share Our Wealth (although in reality Long was the only framer), the champions of the Declaration of Independence and the Constitution, and responsible citizens determined to rectify the inequitable distribution of wealth in the United States. "They" were the evildoers, the enemy, the "super-rich" who had consciously schemed to oppress the poor, to deny the people their inalienable rights of life, liberty, and the pursuit of happiness. Thus, the "I" of individual membership became subordinate to the "we" of group membership, and the value of homogeneity was affirmed. The tactic also had the quality of alienating "them," making the enemy even more hostile than before. The tactic was effective, for it gave Long an enemy of ever-increasing proportions, one capable of being "perfected."

Not only was there a need for spiritual unity, but for geographical unity as well. For Adolph Hitler, the geographic center was Munich; for Share Our Wealth is was Long's office in Washington, D.C. The importance of a mecca is explained by Kenneth Burke, who argued, "Every movement that would recruit its followers from among many discordant and divergent bands, must have some spot towards which all roads lead. Each man may get there in his own way, but it must be the one unifying center of research for all.[81]

---

[77]Schlesinger, *Upheaval,* p. 64.
[78]Burke, "Situation," p. 286.
[79]Burke, "Situation," p. 286.
[80]Basil Bernstein, *Class, Codes, and Control* (London: Schocken, 1971), p. 148.
[81]Burke, "Battle," p. 239.

Huey Long not only created a spot where all roads led, but heavily publicized its Washington, D.C. location. Near the close of the speech, Long
remarked:

> This is Huey P. Long talking, United States Senator, Washington, D.C.
> Write me and let me send you the data on this proposition. Enroll with us.
> Let us make known to the people what we are going to do. I will send you
> a button, if I have got enough of them left. We have got a little button that
> some of our friends designed, with a message around the rim of the button,
> and in the center, 'Every man a king.' Many thousands of them are meet-
> ing through the United States, and every day we are getting hundreds and
> hundreds of letters.....[82]

The significance of the identification between geographic locale and the
individual member is unmistakable. Adolph Hitler concluded, "Only the
presence of such a center...can at length give a movement that force which
is rooted in the inner unity and in the recognition of a hand that represents
this unity."[83] The dominance of the unification theme can be traced directly
to the we/they dichotomy and the geographical structure of the movement.

This paper has argued for a revamped look at demagogues and demagogic discourse. Greater attention must be paid to the character of the demagogue and the situational factors which surround his rise in order to better
understand his rhetoric. Moreover, this essay has attempted to describe the
characteristics of demagogic discourse and detail a methodology appropriate for its analysis in both general terms and in the specific case of Huey
Long's "Every Man a King" address.

[82]Long, 3452.
[83]Adolph Hitler, *Mein Kampf,* quoted in Burke, "Battle," p. 240.

A Third Party

Charles Edward Coughlin

Father Coughlin (October 25, 1891 - October 27, 1979) gradu-
ated from the University of Toronto in 1911; he was ordained
a priest, Basilian Order, 1916; he began radio broadcasting in
1926, and served as pastor of the Shrine of the Little Flower,
Royal Oak, Michigan 1926-66. He announced the National
Union for Social Justice in November, 1934. A Third Party
was delivered as a broadcast to the nation, June 19, 1936.
Published version: Vital Speeches of the Day, *July 1, 1936,*
pp. 613-16.

Ladies and gentlemen, may I gratefully acknowledge that these broad-casting facilities have been extended to me by the Columbia Broadcasting System?

It is my purpose to engage your attention as I discuss, first, why I do not find it morally possible to support either the Republicans and their platform or the Democrats and their promises. Second, I shall make plain where the National Union for Social Justice, including myself, will stand in relation to the forthcoming elections in November of this year.

To clarify both of these answers permit me to preface my remarks with a statement of economic fact which necessitated the establishment of a change in our progressive civilization.

In the Autumn of 1932 it was my privilege to address the American people on the causes of the so-called depression and upon the obvious remedies required to bring about a permanent recovery.

Those were days which witnessed a complete breakdown of the financial system under which our Western civilization had been developed. It was also evident that under this financial system there resulted a concentration of wealth and a multiplication of impoverished families. Unjust wages and unreasonable idleness were universally recognized as contradictions in an age of plenty. To my mind it was inconceivable that irrational and needless want should exist in an age of plenty.

Were there not plenty of raw materials in America? Were not our citizens and our countrysides inhabited by plenty of skilled inventors, engineers, executives, workmen and farmers? At no time in the history of civilization was it possible for man to produce such an abundant supply, thanks to the benedictions of mass production machinery. At no time within the last two centuries was there such a demand on the part of our population for the thousands of good things capable of being produced in our fields and in our factories.

What was the basic cause which closed factories, which created idleness, which permitted weeds to overrun our golden fields and plowshares to rust? There was and is but one answer. Some call it lack of purchasing power. Others, viewing the problem in a more philosophic light, recognize that the financial system which was able to function in an age of scarcity was totally inadequate to operate successfully in an age of plenty.

Let me explain this statement briefly: Before the nineteenth century the ox-cart, the spade and the crude instruments of production were handicaps to the rapid creation of real wealth.

By 1932 a new era of production had come into full bloom. It was represented by the motor car, the tractor and the power lathe, which enabled the laborer to produce wealth ten times more rapidly than was possible for his ancestors. Within the short expanse of 150 years the problem of production had been solved, due to the ingenuity of men like Arkwright and his loom, Fulton and his steam engine, and Edison and his dynamo. These and a thousand other benefactors of mankind made it possible for the teeming millions of people throughout the world to transfer speedily the raw materials into the thousand necessities and conveniences which fall under the common name of wealth.

Thus, with the advent of our scientific era, with its far-flung fields, its spacious factories, its humming motors, its thundering locomotives, its highly trained mechanics, it is inconceivable how such a thing as a so-called depression should blight the lives of an entire nation when there was a plentitude of everything surrounding us, only to be withheld from us because the so-called leaders of high finance persisted in clinging to an outworn theory of privately issued money, the medium through which wealth is distributed.

I challenged this private control and creation of money because it was alien to our Constitution, which says "Congress shall have the right to coin and regulate the value of money." I challenged this system of permitting a small group of private citizens to create money and credit out of nothing, to issue it into circulation through loans and to demand that borrowers repay them with money which represented real goods, real labor and real service. I advocated that it be replaced by the American system—namely, that the creation and control of money and credit are the rights of the people through their democratic government.

Has this American system of money creation and control been our practice?

Unfortunately, no. Our governments, through a policy of perversion and subterfuge, established, step by step, the Federal Reserve Banking System. Power was given to a handful of our fellow-citizens to create and control more than 90 per cent of all our money mostly by a mere stroke of the fountain pen; to issue it into circulation as real legal tender; and to exact of the hundred and twenty-five million citizens the obligation of paying it back with interest, not through a stroke of the fountain pen but through arduous hours of toil, of sweat and of heartaches. Before the year 1932 very few persons fully realized the existence of this financial bondage.

Millions of citizens began asking the obvious questions: "Why should the farmer be forced to follow his plow at a loss?" "Why should the citizens — at least 90 per cent of them — be imprisoned behind the cruel bars of want when, within their grasp, there are plenty of shoes, of clothing, of motor cars, of refrigerators, to which they are entitled?"

As a result of these and similar questions, my friends, an intellectual revolution was generated in America. The moral problems of foods, of clothing, of shelter demanded a solution. The solution in democratic America must come from democratic legislation under the leadership of a sympathetic President who will initiate, in part, legislation and append his signature to just laws.

At last, when the most brilliant minds amongst the industrialists, bankers and their kept politicians had failed to solve the cause of the needless depression, there appeared upon the scene of our national life a new champion of the people, Franklin Delano Roosevelt! He spoke golden words of hope. He intimated to the American people that the system of permitting a group of private citizens to create money, then to issue it to the government as if it were real money, then to exact payment from the entire nation through a system of taxation earned by real labor and service, was immoral. With the whip of his scorn he castigated these usurers who exploited the poor. With his eloquent tongue he lashed their financial system which devoured the homes of widows and orphans.

No man in modern times received such plaudits from the poor as did Franklin Roosevelt when he promised to drive the money changers from the temple — the money changers who had clipped the coins of wages, who had manufactured spurious money and who had brought proud America to her knees.

March 4, 1933! I shall never forget the inaugural address, which seemed to re-echo the very words employed by Christ Himself as He actually drove the money changers from the temple.

The thrill that was mine was yours. Through dim clouds of the depression this man Roosevelt was, as it were, a new savior of his people!

Oh, just a little longer shall there be needless poverty! Just another year shall there be naked backs! Just another moment shall there be dark thoughts of revolution! Never again will the chains of economic poverty bite into the hearts of simple folks, as they did in the past days of the Old Deal!

Such were our hopes in the springtime of 1933.

My friends, what have we witnessed as the finger of time turned the pages of the calendar? Nineteen hundred and thirty-three and the National Recovery Act which multiplied profits for the monopolists; 1934 and the AAA which raised the price of foodstuffs by throwing back God's best gifts into His face; 1935 and the Banking Act which rewarded the exploiters of the poor, the Federal Reserve bankers and their associates, by handing over to them the temple from which they were to have been cast!

In 1936, when our disillusionment is complete, we pause to take inventory of our predicament. You citizens have shackled about your limbs a tax bill of $35,000,000,000, most of which, I repeat, was created by a flourish of a fountain pen. Your erstwhile saviour, whose golden promises ring upon the counter of performance with the cheapness of tin, bargained with the money changers that, with seventy billion laboring hours in the ditch, or in the factory, or behind the plow, you and your children shall repay the debt which was created with a drop of ink in less than ten seconds.

Is that driving the money changers out of the temple?

Every crumb you eat, every stitch of clothing you wear, every menial purchase which you make is weighted down with an unseen tax as you work and slave for the debt merchants of America. But the $55,000,000,000 of debt bonds, held mostly by the debt merchants and the well circumstanced of this country, have been ably safeguarded from taxation by this peerless leader who sham battles his way along the avenue of popularity with his smile for the poor and his blindness for their plight. Is that driving the money changers from the temple?

You laborers of America who work no more than an average of 200 days a year at $5 a day are forced to contribute at least fifty days of your labor — to steal it from your wives and your children, to deprive them of the conveniences and the luxuries advertised in every paper and magazine — as tribute for the benefit of the sacrosanct bondholders.

Is that driving the money changers from the temple?

You farmers of America, of whom 3,000 every week are driven over the hill to the poorhouse through the ruthless confiscation which is still protected under the guise of friendship, are forced to bear the burden of $8,000,000,000 of mortgage debt on farms at 6 per cent — farms which have depreciated 50 per cent during these last five years, farms which cannot be operated at a profit except temporarily through the immoral Tugwellism of destruction.

Is that driving the money changers from the temple, or is it driving Americans from their homes?

For God's command of "increase and multiply," spoken to our first parents, the satanic principles of "decrease and devastate" has been substituted.

It is not pleasant for me who coined the phrase "Roosevelt or ruin" — a phrase fashioned upon promises — to voice such passionate words. But I am constrained to admit that "Roosevelt and ruin" is the order of the day because the money changers have not been driven from the temple.

My friends, I come before you tonight not to ask you to return to the Landons, to the Hoovers, to the Old Deal exploiters who honestly defended the dishonest system of gold standardism and rugged individualism. Their sun has set never to rise again.

America has turned its back definitely upon the platitudinous platforms of "rugged individualism." Who at Cleveland dared call into question the plutocratic privilege enjoyed by the Federal Reserve bankers? Who among these moribund New Deal critics dared campaign for an annual, decent wage for the laborer and production at a profit for the farmer? Alas! These Punch and Judy Republicans, whose actions and words were dominated by the ventriloquists of Wall Street, are so blind that they do not recognize, even in this perilous hour, that their gold basis and their private coinage of money have bred more radicals than did Karl Marx or Lenin. To their system or ox-cart financialism we must never return!

Review the Landon platform with its proposal to revive the gold standard which succeeded in prostrating civilization. Hypocritically, it proposes the restoration to Congress of the right to coin and regulate money now held by the President.

Pause to consider the colossal fraud that this insincere wording attempts to perpetrate upon the people of this country: "Restore to Congress the power of coining and regulating money by repealing the laws relative to such now held by the President!"

Why, every intelligent person must recognize that our objective is to restore to Congress its constitutional power to coin and regulate money, now held not by the President, not by the Secretary of the Treasury, but by the Federal Reserve Bank, a privately owned corporation.

On the other hand, the Democratic platform is discredited before it is published. Was there not a 1932 platform? By Mr. Roosevelt and its colleagues was it not regarded as a solemn pledge to the people? Certainly it was! And where is it today? Under the direction of Rexford Tugwell, the power and the brains behind the White House throne, it was plowed under like the cotton, slaughtered like the pigs.

What credence, therefore, can prudent citizens place in the poetic pledges to be pronounced at Philadelphia by the Democrats?

In the history of American literature it will take its place alongside Eugene O'Neill's "Strange Interlude." Its offstage remarks in 1936 are supposed to remain unheard by the American public. But, judging by the previous platform, we know that while security for the aged will be advocated aloud, prosperity for the poor-house will be the whispered order.

Therefore, the veracity of the future upstage pledges must be judged by the echoings of the golden voice of a lost leader.

Said he, when the flag of hope was proudly unfurled on March 4, 1933: "Plenty is at our doorsteps, but the generous use of it languished in the very sight of the supply.... Primarily, this is because the rulers of the exchange of mankind's goods have failed through their own stubbornness and their own incompetence—have admitted their failure and abdicated. Practices of the unscrupulous money changers stand indicted in the court of public opinion, rejected by the hearts and minds of men.

"True, they have tried, but their efforts have been cast in the pattern of an outworn tradition. Faced by failure of credit, they have proposed only the lending of more money."

These words, my friends, are not mine. These are the caustic, devastating words uttered by Franklin Delano Roosevelt on March 4, 1933, condemning Franklin Delano Roosevelt in November of 1936.

Alas! The temple still remains the private property of the money changers. The golden key has been handed over to them for safekeeping— the key which now is fashioned in the shape of a double cross.

Oh, would that another Milton could write the story of "Paradise Lost" to the people. Would that the blind bard could reconstruct the theme of "Paradise Regained" by the bankers!

Neither Old Dealer nor New Dealer, it appears, has courage to assail the international bankers, the Federal Reserve bankers. In common, both the leaders of the Republicans and the Democrats uphold the old money philosophy. Today in America there is only one political party—the banker's party. In common, both old parties are determined to sham battle their way through this November election with the hope that millions of American citizens will be driven into the no-man's land of financial bondage.

My friends, there is a way out, a way to freedom! There is an escape from the dole standard of Roosevelt, the gold standard of Landon. No longer need you be targets in non-man's land for the financial crossfire of the sham-battlers!

Six hours ago the birth of "the Union party" was officially announced to the newspapers of the nation, thereby confirming information which hiterto was mine unofficially. The new candidate for President, together with his sponsors, formally requested my support, as they handed to me his platform. I have studied it carefully. I find that it is in harmony substantially with the principles of social justice.

As presented to me, this platform reads as if it were born in the hearts of a group of rebels.

If you think so, you are right in thinking so, because this group rebels against the bankers' bonds, their tax-exempt bonds, their radicalism and their financial slavery.

Who is the candidate for President of the Union party? He is one who has left his mark for erudition in the halls of Yale University and who already has carved for himself a niche of fame in the industrial and agricultural temple of America. He is a man who has made promises in the past and has kept them. He is a battler who has entered into fights and has fought them. He is an American and not an internationalist, a liberty lover and not a slave trader, who will fight for financial freedom as did his prototype, Lincoln, who waged war for physical freedom.

I refer to Congressman William Lemke of North Dakota, who has thrown his "cap" into the Presidential ring at the request of thousands of independent friends. Now that he has taken the step and has officially asked the National Union for its support, we declare him, on the strength of his platform and of his splendid record, eligible for indorsation.

He has chosen as a running mate for the Vice-Presidency Thomas Charles O'Brien, eminent former District Attorney of Boston, counsel for the Brotherhood of Railroad Trainmen and firm exponent of social justice. For ten years before graduating from Harvard University Mr. O'Brien labored as a baggageman.

Lemke and Yale, Agriculture and Republican! O'Brien and Harvard, Labor and Democrat!

East and West!

Protestant and Catholic, possessing one program of driving the money changers from the temple, of permitting the wealth of America to flow freely into every home!

The National Union still adheres firmly to its policy of endorsing and supporting candidates for Congress in any political party who have pledged allegiance to our principles.

To night it does not depart from its policy in endorsing the Union party candidate for President of the United States — a poor man who has worked with his hands against the hostile forces of nature and with his soul against the destructive forces of private money control.

God speed William Lemke and his friends as they proceed to file in each State!

This is a new day for America with its new "Union Party." Lemke has raised a banner of liberty for you to follow as you carry it unsullied into the ranks of the money changers' servants now occupying the White House and the halls of Congress.

Behind it will rally agriculture, labor, the disappointed Republicans and the outraged Democrats, the independent merchant and industrialist and every lover of liberty who desires to eradicate the cancerous growths from decadent capitalism and avoid the treacherous pitfalls of red communism.

The Struggle for Human Rights

Eleanor Roosevelt

Eleanor Roosevelt (October 11, 1884 - November 7, 1962) was the wife of Franklin D. Roosevelt. She was appointed by President Harry Truman U.S. representative to the United Nations General Assembly in 1945; she served as the U.S. representative, in addition to important committee work, until 1952. This speech was delivered in French at the Sorbonne, Paris, September 28, 1948. It was translated in the published version: Human Rights and Genocide, *Department of State publication 3416 (Washington, D.C.: Government Printing Office, 1949), pp. 1-12.*

I have come this evening to talk with you on one of the greatest issues of our time—that is the preservation of human freedom. I have chosen to discuss it here in France, at the Sorbonne, because here in this soil the roots of human freedom have long ago struck deep and here they have been richly nourished. It was here the Declaration of the Rights of Man was proclaimed, and the great slogans of the French Revolution—liberty, equality, fraternity—fired the imagination of men. I have chosen to discuss this issue in Europe because this has been the scene of the greatest historic battles between freedom and tyranny. I have chosen to discuss it in the early days of the General Assembly because the issue of human liberty is decisive for the settlement of outstanding political differences and for the future of the United Nations.

The decisive importance of this issue was fully recognized by the founders of the United Nations at San Francisco. Concern for the preservation and promotion of human rights and fundamental freedoms stands at the heart of the United Nations. Its Charter is distinguished by its preoccupation with the rights and welfare of individual men and women. The United Nations has made it clear that it intends to uphold human rights and to protect the dignity of the human personality. In the preamble to the Charter the keynote is set when it declares: "We the people of the United Nations determined... to reaffirm faith in fundamental human rights, in the dignity and worth of the human person, in the equal rights of men and women and of nations large and small, and... to promote social progress and better standards of life in larger freedom." This reflects the basic premise of the Charter that the peace and security of mankind are dependent on mutual respect for the rights and freedoms of all.

One of the purposes of the United Nations is declared in article 1 to be: "to achieve international cooperation in solving international problems of an economic, social, cultural, or humanitarian character, and in promoting and encouraging respect for human rights and for fundamental freedoms for all without distinction as to race, sex, language, or religion."

This thought is repeated at several points and notably in articles 55 and 56 the Members pledge themselves to take joint and separate action in cooperation with the United Nations for the promotion of "universal respect for, and observance of, human rights and fundamental freedoms for all without distinction as to race, sex, language, or religion."

The Human Rights Commission was given as its first and most important task the preparation of an International Bill of Rights. The General Assembly which opened its third session here in Paris a few days ago will have before it the first fruit of the Commission's labors in this task, that is the International Declaration of Human Rights.

This Declaration was finally completed after much work during the last session of the Human Rights Commission in New York in the spring of 1948. The Economic and Social Council has sent it without recommendation to the General Assembly, together with other documents transmitted by the Human Rights Commission.

It was decided in our Commission that a Bill of Rights should contain two parts:

> 1. A Declaration which could be approved through action of the Member States of the United Nations in the General Assembly. This Declaration would have great moral force, and would say to the peoples of the world "this is what we hope human rights may mean to all people in the years to come." We have put down here the rights that we consider basic for individual human beings the world over to have. Without them, we feel that the full development of individual personality is impossible.

> 2. The second part of the bill, which the Human Rights Commission has not yet completed because of the lack of time, is a covenant which would be in the form of a treaty to be presented to the nations of the world. Each nation, as it is prepared to do so, would ratify this covenant and the covenant would then become binding on the nations which

adhere to it. Each nation ratifying would then be obligated to change its laws wherever they did not conform to the points contained in the covenant.

This covenant, of course, would have to be a simpler document. It could not state aspirations, which we feel to be permissible in the Declaration. It could only state rights which could be assured by law and it must contain methods of implementation, and no state ratifying the covenant could be allowed to disregard it. The methods of implementation have not yet been agreed upon, nor have they been given adequate consideration by the Commission at any of its meetings. There certainly should be discussion on the entire question of this world Bill of Human Rights and there may be acceptance by this Assembly of the Declaration if they come to agreement on it. The acceptance of the Declaration, I think, should encourage every nation in the coming months to discuss its meaning with its people so that they will be better prepared to accept the covenant with a deeper understanding of the problems involved when that is presented, we hope, a year from now and, we hope, accepted.

The Declaration has come from the Human Rights Commission with unanimous acceptance except for four abstentions—the U.S.S.R., Yugoslavia, Ukraine, and Byelorussia. The reason for this is a fundamental difference in the conception of human rights as they exist in these states and in certain other Member States in the United Nations.

In the discussion before the Assembly, I think it should be made crystal clear what these differences are and tonight I want to spend a little time making them clear to you. It seems to me there is a valid reason for taking the time today to think carefully and clearly on the subject of human rights, because in the acceptance and observance of these rights lies the root, I believe, of our chance for peace in the future, and for the strengthening of the United Nations organization to the point where it can maintain peace in the future.

We must not be confused about what freedom is. Basic human rights are simple and easily understood: freedom of speech and a free press; freedom of religion and worship; freedom of assembly and the right of petition; the right of men to be secure in their homes and free from unreasonable search and seizure and from arbitrary arrest and punishment.

We must not be deluded by the efforts of the forces of reaction to prostitute the great words of our free tradition and thereby to confuse the struggle. Democracy, freedom, human rights have come to have a definite meaning to the people of the world which we must not allow any nation to so change that they are made synonymous with suppression and dictatorship.

There are basic differences that show up even in the use of words between a democratic and a totalitarian country. For instance "democracy" means one thing to the U.S.S.R. and another to the U.S.A. and, I know, in France. I have served since the first meeting of the nuclear commission on the Human Rights Commission, and I think this point stands out clearly.

The U.S.S.R. Representatives assert that they already have achieved many things which we, in what they call the "bourgeois democracies" cannot achieve because their government controls the accomplishment of these things. Our government seems powerless to them because, in the last analysis, it is controlled by the people. They would not put it that way—they would say that the people in the U.S.S.R. control their government by allowing their government to have certain absolute rights. We, on the other hand, feel that certain rights can never be granted to the government, but must be kept in the hands of the people.

For instance, the U.S.S.R. will assert that their press is free because the state makes it free by providing the machinery, the paper, and even the money for salaries for the people who work on the paper. They state that there is no control over what is printed in the various papers that they subsidize in this manner, such, for instance, as a trade-union paper. But what would happen if a paper were to print ideas which were critical of the basic policies and beliefs of the Communist government? I am sure some good reason would be found for abolishing the paper.

It is true that there have been many cases where newspapers in the U.S.S.R. have criticized officials and their actions and have been responsible for the removal of those officials, but in doing so they did not criticize anything which was fundamental to Communist beliefs. They simply criticized methods of doing things, so one must differentiate between things which are permissible, such as criticism of any individual or of the manner of doing things, and the criticism of a belief which would be considered vital to the acceptance of Communism.

What are the differences, for instance, between trade-unions in the totalitarian states and in the democracies? In the totalitarian state a trade-union is an instrument used by the government to enforce duties, not to assert rights. Propaganda material which the government desires the workers to have is furnished to the trade-unions to be circulated to their members.

Our trade-unions, on the other hand, are solely the instrument of the workers themselves. They represent the workers in their relations with the government and with management and they are free to develop their own opinions without government help or interference. The concepts of our trade-unions and those in totalitarian countries are drastically different. There is little mutual understanding.

I think the best example one can give of this basic difference of the use of terms is "the right to work." The Soviet Union insists that this is a basic right which it alone can guarantee because it alone provides full employment by the government. But the right to work in the Soviet Union means the assignment of workers to do whatever task is given to them by the government without an opportunity for the people to participate in the decision that the government should do this. A society in which everyone works is not necessarily a free society and may indeed be a slave society; on the other hand, a society in which there is widespread economic insecurity can turn freedom into a barren and vapid right for millions of people. We in the United States have come to realize it means freedom to choose one's job, to work or not to work as one desires. We, in the United States, have come to realize, however, that people have a right to demand that their government will not allow them to starve because as individuals they cannot find work of the kind they are accustomed to doing and this is a decision brought about by public opinion which came as a result of the great depression in which many people were out of work, but we would not consider in the United States that we had gained any freedom if we were compelled to follow a dictatorial assignment to work where and when we were told. The right of choice would seem to us an important, fundamental freedom.

I have great sympathy with the Russian people. They love their country and have always defended it valiantly against invaders. They have been through a period of revolution, as a result of which they were for a time cut off from outside contact. They have not lost their resulting suspicion of other countries and the great difficulty is today that their government encourages this suspicion and seems to believe that force alone will bring them respect.

We, in the democracies, believe in a kind of international respect and action which is reciprocal. We do not think others should treat us differently from the way they wish to be treated. It is interference in other countries that especially stirs up antagonism against the Soviet Government. If it wishes to feel secure in developing its economic and political theories within its territory, then it should grant to others that same security. We believe in the freedom of people to make their own mistakes. We do not interfere with them and they should not interfere with others.

The basic problem confronting the world today, as I said in the beginning, is the preservation of human freedom for the individual and consequently for the society of which he is a part. We are fighting this battle again today as it was fought at the time of the French Revolution and at the time of the American Revolution. The issue of human liberty is as decisive now as it was then. I want to give you my conception of what is meant in my country by freedom of the individual.

Long ago in London during a discussion with Mr. Vyshinsky, he told me there was no such thing as freedom for the individual in the world. All freedom of the individual was conditioned by the rights of other individuals. That, of course, I granted. I said: "We approach the question from a different point of view; we here in the United Nations are trying to develop ideals which will be broader in outlook, which will consider first the rights of man, which will consider what makes man more free: not governments, but man."

The totalitarian state typically places the will of the people second to decrees promulgated by a few men at the top.

Naturally there must always be consideration of the rights of others; but in a democracy this is not a restriction. Indeed, in our democracies we make our freedoms secure because each of us is expected to respect the rights of others and we are free to make our own laws.

Freedom for our peoples is not only a right, but also a tool. Freedom of speech, freedom of the press, freedom of information, freedom of assembly — these are not just abstract ideals to us; they are tools with which we create a way of life, a way of life in which we can enjoy freedom.

Sometimes the processes of democracy are slow, and I have known some of our leaders to say that a benevolent dictatorship would accomplish the ends desired in a much shorter time than it takes to go through the democratic processes of discussion and the slow formation of public opinion. But there is no way of insuring that a dictatorship will remain benevolent or that power once in the hands of a few will be returned to the people without struggle or revolution. This we have learned by experience and we accept the slow processes of democracy because we know that short-cuts compromise principles on which no compromise is possible.

The final expression of the opinion of the people with us is through free and honest elections, with valid choices on basic issues and candidates. The secret ballot is an essential to free elections but you must have a choice before you. I have heard my husband say many times that a people need never lose their freedom if they kept their right to a secret ballot and if they used that secret ballot to the full.

Basic decisions of our society are made through the expressed will of the people. That is why when we see these liberties threatened, instead of falling apart, our nation becomes unified and our democracies come together as a unified group in spite of our varied backgrounds and many racial strains.

In the United States we have a capitalistic economy. That is because public opinion favors that type of economy under the conditions in which we live. But we have imposed certain restraints; for instance, we have anti-trust laws. These are the legal evidence of the determination of the American people to maintain an economy of free competition and not to allow monopolies to take away the people's freedom.

Our trade-unions grow stronger because the people come to believe that this is the proper way to guarantee the rights of the workers and that the right to organize and to bargain collectively keeps the balance between the actual producer and the investor of money and the manager in industry who watches over the man who works with his hands and who produces the materials which are our tangible wealth.

In the United States we are old enough not to claim perfection. We recognize that we have some problems of discrimination but we find steady progress being made in the solution of these problems. Through normal democratic processes we are coming to understand our needs and how we can attain full equality for all our people. Free discussion on the subject is permitted. Our Supreme Court has recently rendered decisions to clarify a number of our laws to guarantee the rights of all.

The U.S.S.R. claims it has reached a point where all races within her borders are officially considered equal and have equal rights and they insist they have no discrimination where minorities are concerned.

This is a laudable objective but there are other aspects of the development of freedom for the individual which are essential before the mere absence of discrimination is worth much, and these are lacking in the Soviet Union. Unless they are being denied freedoms which they want and which they see other people have, people do not usually complain of discrimination. It is these other freedoms—the basic freedoms of speech, of the press, of religion and conscience, of assembly, of fair trial and freedom from arbitrary arrest and punishment, which a totalitarian government cannot safely give its people and which give meaning to freedom from discrimination.

It is my belief, and I am sure it is also yours, that the struggle for democracy and freedom is a critical struggle, for their preservation is essential to the great objective of the United Nations to maintain international peace and security.

Among free men the end cannot justify the means. We know the patterns of totalitarianism—the single political party, the control of schools, press, radio, the arts, the sciences, and the church to support autocratic authority; these are the age-old patterns against which men have struggled for three thousand years. These are the signs of reaction, retreat, and retrogression.

The United Nations must hold fast to the heritage of freedom won by the struggle of its peoples; it must help us to pass it on to generations to come.

The development of the ideal of freedom and its translation into the everyday life of the people in great areas of the earth is the product of the efforts of many peoples. It is the fruit of a long tradition of vigorous thinking and courageous action. No one race and no one people can claim to have done all the work to achieve greater dignity for human beings and greater freedom to develop human personality. In each generation and in each country there must be a continuation of the struggle and new steps forward must be taken since this is preeminently a field in which to stand still is to retreat.

The field of human rights is not one in which compromise on fundamental principles are possible. The work of the Commission on Human Rights is illustrative. The Declaration of Human Rights provides: "Everyone has the right to leave any country, including his own." The Soviet Representative said he would agree to this right if a single phrase was added to it — "in accordance with the procedure laid down in the laws of that country." It is obvious that to accept this would be not only to compromise but to nullify the right stated. This case forcefully illustrates the importance of the proposition that we must ever be alert not to compromise fundamental human rights merely for the sake of reaching unanimity and thus lose them.

As I see it, it is not going to be easy to attain unanimity with respect to our different concepts of government and human rights. The struggle is bound to be difficult and one in which we must be firm but patient. If we adhere faithfully to our principles I think it is possible for us to maintain freedom and to do so peacefully and without recourse to force.

The future must see the broadening of human rights throughout the world. People who have glimpsed freedom will never be content until they have secured it for themselves. In a true sense, human rights are a fundamental object of law and government in a just society. Human rights exist to the degree that they are respected by people in relations with each other and by governments in relations with their citizens.

The world at large is aware of the tragic consequences for human beings ruled by totalitarian systems. If we examine Hitler's rise to power, we see how the chains are forged which keep the individual a slave and we can see many similarities in the way things are accomplished in other countries. Politically men must be free to discuss and to arrive at as many facts as possible and there must be at least a two-party system in a country because when there is only one political party, too many things can be subordinated to the interests of that one party and it becomes a tyrant and not an instrument of democratic government.

The propaganda we have witnessed in the recent past, like that we perceive in these days, seeks to impugn, to undermine, and to destroy the liberty and independence of peoples. Such propaganda poses to all peoples the issue whether to doubt their heritage of rights and therefore to compromise the principles by which they live, or try to accept the challenge, redouble their vigilance, and stand steadfast in the struggle to maintain and enlarge human freedoms.

People who continue to be denied the respect to which they are entitled as human beings will not acquiesce forever in such denial.

The Charter of the United Nations is a guiding beacon along the way to the achievement of human rights and fundamental freedoms throughout the world. The immediate test is not only the extent to which human rights and freedoms have already been achieved, but the direction in which the world is moving. Is there a faithful compliance with the objectives of the Charter if some countries continue to curtail human rights and freedoms instead of to promote the universal respect for an observance of human rights and freedoms for all as called for by the Charter?

The place to discuss the issue of human rights is in the forum of the United Nations. The United Nations has been set up as the common meeting ground for nations, where we can consider together our mutual problems and take advantage of our differences in experience. It is inherent in our firm attachment to democracy and freedom that we stand always ready to use the fundamental democratic procedures of honest discussion and negotiation. It is now as always our hope that despite the wide differences in approach we face in the world today, we can with mutual good faith in the principles of the United Nations Charter, arrive at a common basis of understanding.

We are here to join the meetings of this great international Assembly which meets in your beautiful capital city of Paris. Freedom for the individual is an inseparable part of the cherished traditions of France. As one of the Delegates from the United States I pray Almighty God that we may win another victory here for the rights and freedoms of all men.

Far Eastern Policy
Harry S Truman

This speech was delivered in a radio address to the nation, Washington, D.C., April 11, 1951. Published version: Vital Speeches of the Day, *May 1, 1951, pp. 418-20.*

I want to talk to you tonight about what we are doing in Korea and about our policy in the Far East. In the simplest terms what we are doing in Korea is this: We are trying to prevent a third world war.

I think most people in this country recognized that fact last June. And they warmly supported the decision of the Government to help the Republic of Korea against the Communist aggressors. Now, many persons, even some who applauded our decision to defend Korea, have forgotten the basic reasons for our action.

It is right for us to be in Korea now. It was right last June. It is right today.

I want to remind you why this is true.

The Communists in the Kremlin are engaged in a monstrous conspiracy to stamp out freedom all over the world. If they were to succeed, the United States would be numbered among their principal victims. It must be clear to everyone that the United States cannot — and will not — sit idly by and await foreign conquest. The only question is: When is the best time to meet the threat and how?

The best time to meet the threat is in the beginning. It is easier to put out a fire in the beginning when it is small than after it has become a roaring blaze.

And the best way to meet the threat of aggression is for the peace-loving nations to act together. If they don't act together, they are likely to be picked off, one by one.

If they had followed the right policies in the 1930's — if the free countries had acted together, to crush the aggression of the dictators, and if they had acted in the beginning, when the aggression was small — there probably

86

would have been no World War II.

If history has taught us anything, it is that aggression anywhere in the world is a threat to the peace everywhere in the world. When that aggression is supported by the cruel and selfish rulers of a powerful nation who are bent on conquest, it becomes a clear and present danger to the security and independence of every free nation.

This is a lesson that most people in this country have learned thoroughly. This is the basic reason why we have joined in creating the United Nations. And, since the end of World War II, we have been putting that lesson into practice—we're working with other free nations to check the aggressive designs of the Soviet Union before they can result in a third world war.

This is what we did in Greece, when that nation was threatened by the aggression of international Communists.

The attack against Greece could have led to a general war. But this country came to the aid of Greece. The United Nations supported Greek resistance. With our help, the determination and efforts of the Greek people defeated the attack on the spot.

Another big Communist threat to peace was the Berlin blockade. That, too, could have led to war. But again it was settled because free men would not back down in an emergency.

The aggression against Korea is the boldest and most dangerous move the Communists have yet made.

The attack on Korea was part of a greater plan for conquering all of Asia.

I would like to read to you from a secret intelligence report which came to us after the attack. I have that report right here. It is a report of a speech a Communist Army officer in North Korea gave to a group of spies and saboteurs last May, one month before South Korea was invaded. The report shows in great detail how this invasion was a part of a carefully prepared plot. Here is part of what the Communist officer, who had been trained in Moscow, told his men:

"Our forces," he said, "are scheduled to attack South Korean forces about the middle of June... The coming attack on South Korea marks the first step toward the liberation of Asia."

Notice that he used the word "liberation." This is Communist double-talk meaning "conquest."

I have another secret intelligence report here. This one tells what another Communist officer in the Far East told his men several months before the invasion of Korea. And here's what he said: "In order to successfully undertake the long awaited world revolution, we must first unify Asia.... Java, Indo-China, Malaya, India, Tibet, Thailand, Philippines, and Japan are our ultimate targets.... The United States is the only obstacle on our road for the liberation of all countries in Southeast Asia. In other words we must unify the people of Asia and crush the United States." Again, liberation in Commie language means conquest.

That's what the Communist leaders are telling their people, and that is what they've been trying to do.

They want to control all Asia from the Kremlin.

This plan of conquest is in flat contradiction to what we believe. We believe that Korea belongs to the Koreans. We believe that India belongs to the Indians. We believe all the nations of Asia should be free to work out their affairs in their own way. This is the basis of peace in the Far East and it is the basis of peace everywhere else.

The whole Communist imperialism is back of the attack on peace in the Far East. It was the Soviet Union that trained and equipped the North Koreans for aggression. The Chinese Communists massed forty-four well-trained and well-equipped divisions on the Korean frontier. These were the troops they threw into battle when the North Korean Communists were beaten.

The question we have had to face is whether the Communist plan of conquest can be stopped without a general war. Our Government and other countries associated with us in the United Nations believe that the best chance of stopping it without a general war is to meet the attack in Korea and defeat it there.

That is what we have been doing. It is a difficult and bitter task.

But so far it has been successful.

So far, we have prevented World War III.

So far, by fighting a limited war in Korea, we have prevented aggression from succeeding, and bringing on a general war. And the ability of the whole free world to resist Communist aggression has been greatly improved.

We have taught the enemy a lesson. He has found out that aggression is not cheap or easy. Moreover, men all over the world who want to remain free have been given new courage and new hope. They know now that the champions of freedom can stand up and fight and that they will stand up and fight.

Our resolute stand in Korea is helping the forces of freedom now fighting in Indo-China and other countries in that part of the world. It has already slowed down the time-table of conquest.

In Korea itself, there are signs that the enemy is building up his ground forces for a new mass offensive. We also know that there have been large increases in the enemy's available air forces.

If a new attack comes, I feel confident it will be turned back. The United Nations fighting forces are tough and able and well equipped. They are fighting for a just cause. They are proving to all the world that the principle of collective security will work. We are proud of all these forces for the magnificent job they have done against heavy odds. We pray that their efforts may succeed, for upon their success may hinge the peace of the world.

The Communist side must now choose its course of action. The Communist rulers may press the attack against us. They may take further action which will spread the conflict. They have that choice, and with it the awful responsibility for what may follow. The Communists also have the choice of a peaceful settlement which could lead to general relaxation of the tensions in the Far East. The decision is theirs, because the forces of the United Nations will strive to limit the conflict if possible.

We do not want to see the conflict in Korea extended. We are trying to prevent a world war — not to start one. And the best way to do that is to make it plain that we and the other free countries will continue to resist the attack.

But you may ask why can't we take other steps to punish the aggressor. Why don't we bomb Manchuria and China itself? Why don't we assist the Chinese Nationalist troops to land on the mainland of China?

If we were to do these things we would be running a very grave risk of starting a general war. If that were to happen, we would have brought about the exact situation we are trying to prevent.

If we were to do these things we would become entangled in a vast conflict on the Continent of Asia and our task would become immeasurably more difficult all over the world.

What would suit the ambitions of the Kremlin better than for our military forces to be committed to a full scale war with Red China?

It may well be that, in spite of our best efforts, the Communists may spread the war. But it would be wrong — tragically wrong — for us to take the initiative in extending the war.

The dangers are great. Make no mistake about it. Behind the North Koreans and Chinese Communists in the front lines stand additional millions of Chinese soldiers. And behind the Chinese stand the tanks, the planes, the submarines, the soldiers, and the scheming rulers of the Soviet Union.

Our aim is to avoid the spread of the conflict.

The course we have been following is the one best calculated to avoid an all out war. It is the course consistent with our obligation to do all we can to maintain international peace and security. Our experience in Greece and Berlin shows that it is the most effective course of action we can follow.

First of all, it is clear that our efforts in Korea can blunt the will of the Chinese Communists to continue the struggle. The United Nations forces have put up a tremendous fight in Korea and have inflicted very heavy casualties on the enemy. Our forces are stronger now than they have been before. These are plain facts which may discourage the Chinese Communists from continuing their attack.

Second, the free world as a whole is growing in military strength every day. In the United States, in Western Europe, and throughout the world, free men are alert to the Soviet threat and are building their defenses. This may discourage the Communists rulers from continuing the war in Korea—and from undertaking new acts of aggression elsewhere.

If the Communist authorities realize they cannot defeat us in Korea, if they realize it would be foolhardy to widen the hostilities beyond Korea, then they may recognize the folly of continuing their aggression. A peaceful settlement may then be possible. The door is always open.

Then we may achieve a settlement in Korea which will not compromise the principles and purposes of the United Nations.

I have thought long and hard about this question of extending the war in Asia. I have discussed it many times with the ablest military advisers in the country. I believe with all my heart that the course we are following is the best course.

I believe that we must try to limit the war to Korea for these vital reasons: To make sure that the precious lives of our fighting men are not wasted; to see that the security of our country and the free world is not needlessly jeopardized; and to prevent a third world war.

A number of events have made it evident that General MacArthur did not agree with that policy. I have therefore considered it essential to relieve General MacArthur so that there would be no doubt or confusion as to the real purpose and aim of our policy.

It was with the deepest personal regret that I found myself compelled to take this action. General MacArthur is one of our greatest military commanders. But the cause of world peace is more important than any individual.

The change in commands in the Far East means no change whatever in the policy of the United States. We will carry on the fight in Korea with vigor and determination in an effort to bring the war to a speedy and successful conclusion. The new commander, Lieut. Gen. Matthew Ridgway has already demonstrated that he has the good qualities of military leadership needed for the task.

We are ready, at any time, to negotiate for a restoration of peace in the area. But we will not engage in appeasement. We are only interested in real peace.

Real peace can be achieved through a settlement based on the following factors:

1. The fighting must stop.
2. Concrete steps must be taken to insure that the fighting will not break out again.
3. There must be an end of the aggression.

A settlement founded upon these elements would open the way for the unification of Korea and the withdrawal of all foreign forces.

In the meantime, I want to be clear about our military objective. We are fighting to resist an outrageous aggression in Korea. We are trying to keep the Korean conflict from spreading to other areas. But at the same time we must conduct our military activities so as to insure the security of our forces. This is essential if they are to continue the fight until the enemy abandons its ruthless attempts to destroy the Republic of Korea.

That is our military objective — to repel attack and to restore peace.

In the hard fighting in Korea, we are proving that collective action among nations is not only a high principle but a workable means of resisting aggression. Defeat of aggression in Korea may be the turning point in the world's search for a practical way of achieving peace and security.

The struggle of the United Nations in Korea is a struggle for peace.

The free nations have united their strength in an effort to prevent a third world war.

That war can come if the Communist rulers want it to come. But this nation and its allies will not be responsible for its coming.

We do not want to widen the conflict. We will use every effort to prevent that disaster. And in so doing, we know that we are following the great principles of peace, freedom, and justice.

Harry S Truman
A Misdirected Defense for MacArthur's Dismissal
Halford Ross Ryan

This article originally appeared in Presidential Studies Quarterly, *11 (1981), 576-82, and is reprinted with the permission of the Center for the Study of the Presidency. Research for the article was supported by a University Grant in the Harry S Truman Library, Independence, Missouri.*

At 10:30 p.m. on 11 April 1951, President Harry Truman delivered to the nation his "Preventing a New World War" speech to defend his dismissal of General Douglas MacArthur. Bernstein and Matusow observed that "The public outcry against Truman's action was immediate, emotional, and rancorous."[1] Republicans in Congress actively considered impeachment and Truman's effigy was hanged in San Gabriel, California.[2] Before Truman even delivered his speech, the White House received about 2,301 (67%) letters and telegrams against MacArthur's dismissal and only 1,126 (32%) for it.[3] Truman anticipated the attack because "he had thought for a long time and very heavily on the consequences of the action and determined that it was a necessary and proper action, and that he couldn't avoid the criticism that inevitably followed."[4] Since Truman was under

[1] *The Truman Administration,* ed. Barton J. Bernstein and Allen J. Matusow (New York: Harper Colophon Books, 1966), p. 455.
[2] "President on Radio," *New York Times,* 12 April 1951, p. 1, col. 8; "Dismissal Angers South California," *New York Times,* 12 April 1951, p. 7, col. 1.
[3] Merne Arthur Harris, "The MacArthur Dismissal—A Study of Political Mail" (Diss.: Univ. of Iowa, 1966), pp. 250, 203.
[4] Transcript, Irving Perlmeter, Oral History Interview, May 23 and 24, 1964, Harry S. Truman Library, Independence, Missouri, p. 55. Hereafter, citations for the Truman Library will be given as HST.

attack for firing MacArthur, one would reasonably expect Truman to defend the dismissal in his speech; yet, an examination of the production of the relevant speech drafts will demonstrate why that was not the case.

The study of this speech elucidates Truman's interaction with his speech staff and Secretary of State Dean Acheson in the preparation of this speech, and assesses the speech's success.[5] I contend Truman should have forthrightly defended MacArthur's dismissal but was partially dissuaded from doing so by Acheson. As delivered, the speech basically defended Acheson's Korean war policy and not Truman's dismissal of MacArthur. Truman would have been more persuasive if he allowed his speech staff to give specific reasons in his speech for firing MacArthur. The firing demanded from Truman a specific defense for that action and not a general defense for the Korean war policy. Accordingly, I shall trace the production of the speech with a special focus on the subject of mentioning MacArthur and how this problem was solved.

The Production of the Speech Drafts

The State Department Draft

Robert Walrath Tufts produced the first draft and it reached the White House on Tuesday morning, 10 April.[6] I infer this draft was prepared by Tufts at Acheson's request because Tufts was a member of the Policy Planning Staff in the State Department.[7] From his meeting with Truman, Acheson had ample time to direct Tufts to prepare the draft.[8] Tufts outlined the history and defended the rationale for the Administration's Korean war policy in a nineteen page legal-size draft, but he never mentioned nor defended MacArthur's firing. Acheson had also worked on this draft and he urged the President to accept it. David Bell, speech writer and Administrative Assistant to the President, recalled from a 9:30 a.m. Wednesday, 11 April, speech staff meeting with the President that Truman's reaction to the

[5]For the rationale for the critic to study Truman's significant addresses to determine "To what degree did he rely upon others to prepare his speeches? How did he decide what should be in them? . . . Which speeches were effective, and which were not," see *The Truman Period as a Research Field,* ed. Richard S. Kirkendall (Columbia: Univ. of Missouri Press, 1967), pp. 12-13.

[6]"Report on Korea, 4-10-51, R. Tufts," on which is written "1st State Dept Draft given us — 4-10-51, AM," Papers of George M. Elsey, Box 74, HST, pp. 1-19.

[7]*Biographic Register of the Department of State,* Department of State Publication 4131, p. 444.

[8]Acheson, General Marshall, General Bradley and Averell Harriman met with the President on Friday afternoon, 6 April, at the President's request to discuss the MacArthur matter. On Saturday morning, 7 April, they informed the President that MacArthur should be recalled. See "The MacArthur Dismissal," April 28, 1951, President's Secretary's Files, Box 129, HST, pp. 1-2.

Tufts-Acheson draft was not favorable and that Truman wanted his own speech staff to rework the Tufts-Acheson draft: "He said he had read it, and Mrs. Truman had read it, and then he read it again. As far as he could see, it was just a lot of words. Murphy mentioned that Acheson had worked on it himself, and felt it was in pretty good shape. The P. said yes, he knew that, but he told Acheson we'd have to work it over to suit ourselves. This was a considerable relief to us, as we had been afraid we'd have to battle Acheson down to the wire."[9]

Truman's reaction was unfavorable because Acheson did not justify the firing. Acheson wanted the speech to focus solely on his Korean war policy: "The decision to relieve MacArthur was Truman's alone; however, in terms of policy, the decision had for its prime consequence the removal of Acheson's only formidable opponent to keeping the war in Korea limited."[10] Acheson accordingly specifically advised the President not to mention MacArthur: "Murphy then brought up the subject of mentioning MacA — asking if the President had made up his mind, recalling that Acheson had recommended against it the previous afternoon, and the President had tentatively agreed to that course, and saying that he (Murphy) felt strongly enough about it that if it was felt MacA couldn't be mentioned, he would recommend that the Pres. not give the speech at all."[11]

The speech staff was correctly concerned over battling Acheson down to the wire over mentioning MacArthur. They sensed the need for the President to defend MacArthur's firing rather than his being the mouthpiece for defending Acheson's limited war policy in Acheson's own words. Accordingly, the speech staff had produced its own draft in the interim because they handed Truman their draft to read: "The President said he wasn't sure he should make the speech, and felt we should defer the question of mentioning MacA, till 3:15, when he would meet with us and settle the whole thing. In the meantime, he would read our draft (which Murphy had just handed him)."[12] One should note that the President would have to decide the extent to which he would mention MacArthur. I turn now to the difficult task of discerning what draft the speech staff handed Truman to read and what Truman decided on MacArthur.

The Speech Staff's Drafts

Truman was dissatisfied with Acheson's draft so he directed his speech staff to produce a draft. David Bell and Charles Murphy, speech writer and Special Counsel to the President, were the White House speech writers for

[9]Letter from David Bell to George Elsey, 16 April 1951, Elsey Papers, Box 74, HST, pp. 1-2.
[10]David S. McLellan, *Dean Acheson: The State Department Years* (New York: Dodd, Mead, 1976), p. 313.
[11]Letter from David Bell to George Elsey, p. 2.
[12]*Ibid.*

this speech. In overview, each wrote his own drafts and then they collaborated on some drafts to furnish Truman with the finished draft they handed him to read at their meeting.

Charles Murphy produced two drafts which had his initials on them. His first draft, dated 4-10-51, was based on the Tufts-Acheson draft, but Murphy added six pages of handwritten materials plus many emendations.[13] Even with these changes, Murphy still retained the basic history and rationale for the Korean war policy. Murphy did not mention MacArthur in this draft. On a clean typed copy of draft one, Murphy produced a second draft, dated 4-11-51.[14] Upon reflection, Murphy wrote an insert about MacArthur's dismissal to be placed at the very end of the speech. Murphy indicated that MacArthur was fired because he did not agree with the Administration's Korean war policy and because Truman did not want anyone to be confused about the Administration's Korean war policy:

> I have thought long and hard about this question of extending the war in Asia. I have discussed it many times with the ablest military advisors in the country. I believe with all my heart that the course we are following is the best course. I believe that we must try to limit the war to Korea for these vital purposes: To make sure that the precious lives of our fighting men are not wasted; to see that the security of our country and the free world is not needlessly jeopardized; and to prevent a third world war.
>
> A number of recent events have made it evident that General MacArthur did not agree with that policy. I have therefore considered it essential to relieve General MacArthur so that there would be no doubt or confusion in the minds of anyone what our high purpose is.
>
> I took the action with the greatest reluctance, but the cause of world peace is more important than any individual.[15]

Although Murphy made many changes in the Tufts-Acheson draft, he basically followed their theme on the history and rationale for the Korean war policy, and only at the end did Murphy mention MacArthur. It was better to mention MacArthur at the end than not at all; however, by placing the dismissal justification at the end, Murphy merely stressed the Korean war policy and minimized why MacArthur was fired. Murphy's language implied that MacArthur was dismissed only because he differed with Ad-

---

[13]"Draft, CSM, 4-10-51," Tab 3, Elsey Papers, Box 74, HST, pp. 1-20. A typed copy of this draft is in Tab 4.

[14]This draft has "Third Draft, CSM, 4-11-51" on it. I count this as the second draft because this is merely a smooth copy of draft one in Tab 3.

[15]"Third Draft [second], CSM, 4-11-51," Tab 7, Elsey Papers, Box 74, HST, p. 13.

ministration policy. A stronger case could have been made against MacArthur, and David Bell made it in his draft.

David Bell produced two drafts. He composed the first one on 10 April.[16] Bell based his draft on Murphy's first typed draft. But most significantly, Bell added an introduction which stated a detailed rationale for MacArthur's dismissal. His introduction immediately arrested audience attention in the context of the dismissal crisis by indicating that the President would explain why he fired MacArthur. Bell stressed MacArthur's insubordination to his Commander in Chief:

My Fellow Americans:

Two days ago, I relieved General of the Army Douglas MacArthur of his command in the Far East, and appointed Lieutenant General Matthew Ridgway to succeed him. I want to tell you why I did that.

General MacArthur is a very great soldier. If he had confined himself to his duties and responsibilities as a military commander, I would have been glad to have him in command as long as he would stay.

But General MacArthur did not confine himself to his job as a military commander. Instead, time and time again, in violation of direct orders, he made official pronouncements on foreign policy—pronouncements which, if carried out in my judgment would spread the conflict in Korea into a full-scale war in Asia. Such a course is in direct conflict with the policy of the United States and the United Nations. We are doing our utmost to prevent the Korean conflict from growing into a third world war. We will do everything we can to make that policy succeed. The issue of peace is far greater than any individual.

General MacArthur's place in history as one of our greatest commanders is fully established. The Nation owes him a debt of gratitude for the distinguished and exceptional services which he has rendered his country in posts of great responsibility. For that reason, I deeply regret the necessity for the action I felt compelled to take in his case.

Full and vigorous debate on matters of national policy is essential under the constitutional system of our free democracy. It is fundamental, however, that military commanders must be governed by the policies and directives issued to them in the manner provided by our laws and Constitution.[17]

[16]"Draft, 4-10-51, DEB," Tab 5, Elsey Papers, Box 74, HST, pp. 1-13.
[17]*Ibid.*, pp. 1-2.

Bell's justification for the dismissal was better than Murphy's. Bell's introduction stressed that MacArthur's policy was insubordinate and inimical to American interests. He then used Murphy's Korean war history and rationale to reinforce the wisdom and correctness of MacArthur's dismissal by starkly contrasting Truman's policy with MacArthur's policy in Korea. By placing the defense at the very beginning, Bell met the dismissal crisis forthrightly. His introduction justified MacArthur's dismissal on Constitutional grounds rather than on whether the Administration's Korean war policy was correct. Bell's discussion of the insubordination charge was also more direct than Murphy's watered-down version. Bell produced a second draft but the MacArthur paragraphs remained the same.[18]

From the Third Draft [actually the second draft] a Fourth Draft [actually the third draft] was produced on 11 April.[19] I believe this draft was a joint effort by Bell and Murphy because neither's initials are on this draft. One page is very interesting in terms of MacArthur. It is a typed insert to replace the original page. Several emendations on it are worth noting [deletions are bracketed and additions are italicized]:

> I have therefore considered it essential to relieve General MacArthur so that there would be no doubt or confusion in the mind of anyone as to [what our high purpose is] *the real purpose and aim of our policy.*
>
> [I took this action with the greatest reluctance.] *It was with the deepest personal regret that I found myself compelled to take this action.* General MacArthur is one of our greatest military commanders. But the cause of world peace is more important than any individual.
>
> [Now that he has been relieved from active duty, I wish the General well. He will, of course, be free to state his personal views on our foreign policy to whatever extent he desires.][20]

Bell produced this page because the paragraph beginning "Now that he has..." appears *de novo* in this draft and it comes from Bell's first draft but it was not used in his second draft. Bell's forthright speech introduction must have been vetoed by the speech staff because the staff wished to honor Truman's tentative agreement with Acheson on not mentioning MacArthur. Bell then attempted to work in the paragraph to show that as a civilian, MacArthur could state his foreign policy views without reprisal. But that paragraph was excised, too. With the spector of Acheson's being against mentioning MacArthur, and with the President in tentative agreement, the

[18]"Draft of 4-11-51, D Bell," Tab 6, Elsey Papers, Box 74, HST, pp. 1-2.
[19]"Fourth Draft, 4-11-51," Tab 9, Esley Papers, Box 74, HST, pp. 1-13.
[20]*Ibid.,* p. 11.

speech staff must have believed that Murphy's watered-down version would be more palatable than Bell's version. This draft was retyped as the Fourth Draft [actually the fourth draft].

The President was handed the smooth copy of the Fourth Draft. This is the only draft which he corrected in his own handwriting.[21] All of his corrections appear in the final reading copy and no other emendations were included in it.[22] The President was satisfied with the speech and its minimal mentioning of MacArthur because he accepted it: "You will recall that at the beginning of the afternoon conference the Pres. said he didn't see how we could make this speech—he had a date Thursday night, and Friday would be too close to the J-J dinner. When we all urged him to make it that night (Wed.) he laughed, and said something about us all ganging up on him, but put up no real argument. I don't recall whether he said anything about our draft, but obviously he wouldn't have agreed to make the speech if he hadn't felt fairly comfortable about it."[23]

Truman made several emendations on the draft and they are significant because they illustrate his thinking at a critical time in American history. He crossed out words and substituted new ones, he made punctuation changes, and he excised whole sentences. Several emendations are worth noting. The President underlined words and phrases which were important to him: "to meet the attack in Korea and defeat it *there*"; "*The door is always open*"; "*But the cause of world peace is more important than any individual*"; "*We are only interested in real peace*"; and "That war can come if the communist rulers want it to come. *But this Nation and its allies will not be responsible for its coming.*"[24] He also communicated to his audience that the communists were at fault [his deletions are bracketed and his additions are italicized]: "These were the troops they threw into battle when the North Korean [army was driven back] *communists were beaten*" and "The question we have to face is whether [this] *the communist* plan of conquest can be stopped without a general war."[25] The President simplified the meaning in the following phrase: "If we were to do these things, we would [be enmeshed] *become entangled*."[26] He tried to make the text more optimistic by changing certain words to a more positive statement: "that it is the most [hopeful] *effective* course of action we can follow"; "these vital [purposes] *reasons*"; "But we [are] *will* not [interested] *engage* in appeasement"; and "for a practical way of [maintaining] *achieving* peace and security."[27]

[21]"Fourth Draft, 4-11-51," Tab 10, Elsey Papers, Box 74, HST, pp. 1-13.
[22]The reading copy is in Tab 13, Elsey Papers, Box 74, HST, pp. 1-5.
[23]Letter from David Bell to George Elsey, p. 2.
[24]"Fourth Draft, 4-11-51," Tab 10, pp. 5, 10, 11, 12 and 13.
[25]*Ibid.*, p. 5.
[26]*Ibid.*, p. 8.
[27]*Ibid.*, pp. 9, 11, 12 and 13.

These changes demonstrated that Truman made his speech staff's draft his own text by his final emendations. The speech staff still had ample time to prepare the reading copy from Truman's corrected copy in time for the late evening radio broadcast. President Truman also paid some attention to the delivery of the speech because he practiced it at least once. George Elsey remembered that the President was alone in the Fish Room "reading the speech aloud to himself" before he went to the Oval Office to deliver the speech.[28]

In sum, the speech staff won a minor victory with Acheson over mentioning MacArthur at the end of the speech. Yet, the basic theme and rationale for the address derived from the Tufts-Acheson draft. Bell was thwarted in his attempt to focus the speech on defending the dismissal rather than defending the Korean war policy. As delivered, the speech accomplished the opposite effect.

The Speech's Effect

President Truman's dismissal of General MacArthur has been vindicated on Constitutional grounds.[29] Rovere wrote that "His recall of General MacArthur, probably the one larger piece of work in his entire Administration where the initiative was clearly his own . . . was one that took considerable courage."[30] Harriman praised Truman's decision in the crisis: "President Truman was the one man who had the courage to step up and deal with it. It was one of the most courageous acts that any president did."[31]

Yet, contemporary support for the President's speech was weak. White House reaction mail was often caustic:

> "Who are you trying to kid?"
> "And I use the 'dear' only as a form of salutation."
> "Your speeches stink and you stink."
> "I cannot help but feel you are 100% wrong."
> "Your lousy speech over the radio trying to clear yourself of the blundering mistakes you made at the expense of General MacArthur are as stupid and dumb as your daughter's sand paper singing voice."[32]

[28]Memorandum Re Reference to General Ridgway, April 17, 1951, George M. Elsey, Tab 14, Elsey Papers, Box 74, HST, p. 1.

[29]For an excellent analysis of the negative political-military outcome of MacArthur's "Grand Design," see Matthew B. Ridgway, *The Korean War* (Garden City: Doubleday and Co., 1967), pp. 145-148.

[30]Richard H. Rovere, "Truman after Seven Years," *Harpers,* May, 1952, p. 29.

[31]W. Averell Harriman, "Mr. Truman's Way with Crisis," in *The Korean War: A 25-Year Perspective,* ed. Francis H. Heller (Lawrence: The Regents Press of Kansas, 1977), p. 235.

[32]Selected letters from President's Personal Files, Box 340, HST.

The mail statistics showed some favorable movement from the initial pro-con ratio of 32% - 67%, but the final figures were not reassuring: pro, 37,708 (45%) and con, 46,389 (55%).[33] Harris concluded the speech was not a success: "The speech did not produce a great volume of personal mail for the President nor did it create a wave of protest against MacArthur."[34] Although MacArthur's dismissal was received quite favorably by the allies,[35] Rees observed that "the President was unable to project the historical necessity of his policy in political terms that would appeal to the public."[36]

By Truman's own standards, this speech was not successful. Irving Perlmeter, Assistant Press Secretary to the President, indicated that Truman and his speech staff were cognizant of how they might best address the American listener: "He spoke for a purpose; to get some idea across; to get some result to occur and the impact of the speech, whether it would be understood, how it would be understood and by whom it would be understood, were always central in the discussions."[37] Truman observed that the speaker should accomplish his persuasive goal: "I would say that the effective speaker is one who accomplishes what he sets out to do" and he believed Cicero's method was efficacious to do that: "I believe an audience approves of Cicero's method, which was to state his case and then prove it."[38] Yet, no one has attempted to explain how the speech might have been more successful.

The explanation for Truman's relative failure as a Presidential persuader in this instance is attributable to his misdirected defense for firing MacArthur. Truman should have stated and proved his case against MacArthur. The defense should have primarily justified MacArthur's dismissal on Constitutional grounds. Bell's speech draft rightly emphasized the primacy of the Constitutional crisis. Truman later wrote that he fired MacArthur "because he wouldn't respect the authority of the President."[39] That was the case which Bell knew had to be communicated to the American public in the context of the dismissal crisis. Smith wisely perceived this when he wrote that Truman's best defense for firing

---

[33]Memorandum, William J. Hopkins to the President, May 8, 1951, President's Secretary's Files, Truman Papers, HST.

[34]Harris, p. 207.

[35]See Memo to Sec. of State, April 14, 1951, Selected Records Relating to the Korean War, Dept. of State, Box 10, Folder 37, HST, and "Relief Felt in U.N. on the Dismissal," *New York Times,* 12 April 1951, p. 1, col. 7.

[36]David Rees, *Korea: The Limited War* (New York: St. Martin's Press, 1964), p. 223.

[37]Transcript, Irving Perlmeter, p. 53.

[38]Eugene E. White and Clair R. Henderlider, "What Harry S Truman Told Us About Speaking," *Quarterly Journal of Speech,* 40 (1954), 39.

[39]Merle Miller, *Plain Speaking: An Oral Biography of Harry S Truman* (New York: G.P. Putnam's Sons, 1973), p. 287.

MacArthur depended on who was to be Commander-in-Chief: "But if he sticks doggedly to the point—do his opponents favor altering the basis of American government from Republicanism to Bonapartism—and reiterates it each time his enemies shift the conflict to other grounds, no honest American can do anything but admit that Mr. Truman's decision was right."[40] But the persuasive problem was intensified when Truman defended Acheson's limited war policy first and his firing of MacArthur second.

Truman later assessed the salience of topics in his speech: "I went on the air on the evening of April 11 to restate the government's policy to the American people. I explained why we were in Korea and why we could not allow the Korean affair to become a general all-out war. . . . I explained why it had become necessary to relieve General MacArthur."[41] Since the speech stressed Acheson's limited war policy, it was construed by the public to be a defense for that strategy rather than as a primary defense for dismissing MacArthur: "Harry Truman went on the air with the best defense that Lawyer Acheson could give him. Truman's argument gets its appeal from the fact that all sane men prefer peace to war and a small war to a big war. Truman's speech was constructed to give the impression that MacArthur was in favor of unlimited war while Truman was for limited war."[42]

In the context of the dismissal controversy, Americans listened to their radios to learn why Truman fired MacArthur. That context demanded a defense for the dismisal and not a broader defense for the limited war policy. Truman's speech would have been better received by his American audience if Bell's rather than Murphy's version of Acheson's draft would have been accepted. But it was not. Truman delivered Acheson's speech which stressed the limited war concept and secondarily mentioned in a few lines late in the speech why MacArthur was fired. Truman should have listened more to his speech staff's advice and less to Acheson's.

[40]Howard K. Smith, "Thou Art Soldier Only," *The Nation,* 21 April 1951, p. 363.

[41]Harry S Truman, *Memoirs by Harry S Truman,* Vol. Two: *Years of Trial and Hope* (Garden City: Doubleday and Co., 1956), p. 450.

[42]MacArthur vs. Truman," *Time,* 23 April 1951, p. 32.

Don't Scuttle the Pacific

Douglas MacArthur

*General MacArthur (January 26, 1880 - April 5, 1964) gradu-
ated from the United States Military Academy in 1903; he rose
from second lieutenant in 1903 to General in 1930 (and General of the Army in 1944); commander of U.S. and allied
forces in the Pacific and Japan, 1945-51; Commander-in-Chief
of United Nations forces in Korea, 1950-51. The speech was
delivered before a joint meeting of the United States Congress,
Washington, D.C., April 19, 1951. Published version:* Vital
Speeches of the Day, *May 1, 1951, pp. 430-33.*

Mr. President, Mr. Speaker and distinguished members of the Congress:
I stand on this rostrum with a sense of deep humility and great pride—
humility in the wake of those great American architects of our history who
have stood here before me, pride in the reflection that this home of legislative debate represents human liberty in the purest form yet devised.

Here are centered the hopes and aspirations and faith of the entire human
race.

I do not stand here as advocate for any partisan cause, for the issues are
fundamental and reach quite beyond the realm of partisan considerations.
They must be resolved on the highest plane of national interest if our course
is to prove sound and our future protected.

I trust, therefore, that you will do me the justice of receiving that which I
have to say as solely expressing the considered viewpoint of a fellow
American.

I address you with neither rancor nor bitterness in the fading twilight of
life, with but one purpose in mind: To serve my country.

The issues are global, and so interlocked that to consider the problems of
one sector oblivious to those of another is to court disaster for the whole.
While Asia is commonly referred to as the gateway to Europe, it is no less
true that Europe is the gateway to Asia, and the broad influence of the one

cannot fail to have its impact upon the other.

There are those who claim our strength is inadequate to protect on both fronts, that we cannot divide our effort. I can think of no greater expression of defeatism.

If a potential enemy can divide his strength on two fronts, it is for us to counter his efforts. The Communist threat is a global one. Its successful advance in one sector threatens the destruction of every other sector. You cannot appease or otherwise surrender to communism in Asia without simultaneously undermining our efforts to halt its advance in Europe.

Beyond pointing out these general truisms, I shall confine my discussion to the general areas of Asia.

Before one may objectively assess the situation now existing there, he must comprehend something of Asia's past and the revolutionary changes which have marked her course up to the present.

Long exploited by the so-called colonial powers, with little opportunity to achieve any degree of social justice, individual dignity or a higher standard of life such as guided our own noble administration in the Philippines, the peoples of Asia found their opportunity in the war just past to throw off the shackles of colonialism and now see the dawn of new opportunity, a heretofore unfelt dignity, and the self-respect of political freedom.

Mustering half of the earth's population, and 60 per cent of its natural resources, these peoples are rapidly consolidating a new force, both moral and material, with which to raise the living standard and erect adaptions of the design of modern progress to their own distinct cultural environments.

Whether one adheres to the concept of colonizations or not, this is the direction of Asian progress and it may not be stopped. It is a corollary to the shift of the world economic frontiers as the whole epicenter of world affairs rotates back toward the area whence it started.

In this situation, it becomes vital that our own country orient its policies in consonance with this basic evolutionary condition rather than pursue a course blind to reality that the colonial era is now past and the Asian peoples covet the right to shape their own free destiny.

What they seek now is friendly guidance, understanding and support, not imperious direction; the dignity of equality and not the shame of subjugation.

Their pre-war standard of life, pitifully low, is infinitely lower now in the devastation left in war's wake. World ideologies play little part in Asian thinking and are little understood.

What the people strive for is the opportunity for a little more food in their stomachs, a little better clothing on their backs; a little firmer roof over their heads, and the realization of the normal nationalist urge for political freedom.

These political-social conditions have but an indirect bearing upon our own national security, but do form a backdrop to contemporary planning which must be thoughtfully considered if we are to avoid the pitfalls of unrealism.

Of more direct and immediate bearing upon our national security are the changes wrought in the strategic potential of the Pacific Ocean in the course of the past war.

Prior thereto, the western strategic frontier of the United States lay on the littoral line of the Americas, with an exposed island salient extending out through Hawaii, Midway and Guam to the Philippines. That salient proved not an outpost of strength but an avenue of weakness along which the enemy could, and did, attack. The Pacific was a potential area of advance for any predatory force intent upon striking at the bordering land areas.

All this was changed by our Pacific victory. Our strategic frontier then shifted to embrace the entire Pacific Ocean, which became a vast moat to protect us as long as we held it. Indeed, it acts as a protective shield for all of the Americas and all free lands of the Pacific Ocean area. We control it to the shores of Asia by a chain of islands extending in an arc from the Aleutians to the Marianas, held by us and our free Allies.

From this island chain we can dominate with sea and air power every Asiatic port from Vladivostok to Singapore — with sea and air power, every port, as I said, from Vladivostock to Singapore — and prevent any hostile movement into the Pacific.

Any predatory attack from Asia must be an amphibious effort. No amphibious force can be successful without control of the sea lanes and the air over those lanes in its avenue of advance. With naval and air supremacy and modest ground elements to defend bases, any major attack from continental Asia toward us or our friends in the Pacific would be doomed to failure.

Under such conditions, the Pacific no longer represents menacing avenues of approach for a prospective invader. It assumes, instead, the friendly aspect of a peaceful lake.

Our line of defense is a natural one and can be maintained with a minimum of military effort and expense. It envisions no attack against anyone, nor does it provide the bastions essential for offensive operations, but properly maintained, would be an invincible defense against aggression.

The holding of this littoral defense line in the western Pacific is entirely dependent upon holding all segments thereof, for any major breach of that line by an unfriendly power would render vulnerable to determined attack every other major segment. This is a military estimate as to which I have yet to find a military leader who will take exception.

For that reason, I have strongly recommended in the past, as a matter of military urgency, that under no circumstances must Formosa fall under Communist control. Such an eventuality would at once threaten the freedom of the Philippines and the loss of Japan and might well force our western frontier back to the coast of California, Oregon and Washington.

To understand the changes which now appear upon the Chinese mainland, one must understand the changes in Chinese character and culture over the past fifty years. China up to fifty years ago was completely nonhomogeneous, being compartmented into groups divided against each other. The war-making tendency was almost non-existent as they still followed the tenets of the Confucian ideal pacifist culture.

At the turn of the century under the regime of Chang Tso-Lin efforts toward greater homogeneity produced the spark of a nationalist urge. This was further and more successfully developed under the leadership of Chiang Kai-shek, but has been brought to its great fruition under the present regime to the point that it has now taken on the character of a united nationalism of increasingly dominant aggressive tendencies.

Through these past fifty years the Chinese people have thus become militarized in their concepts and in their ideals. They now constitute excellent soldiers, with competent staffs and commanders. This has produced a new and dominant power in Asia, which, for its own purposes, is allied with Soviet Russia but which in its own concepts and methods has become aggressively imperialistic, with a lust for expansion and increased power normal to this type of imperialism.

There is little of the ideological concept either one way or another in the Chinese make-up. The standard of living is so low and the capital accumulation has been so thoroughly dissipated by war that the masses are desperate and eager to follow any leadership which seems to promise the alleviation of local stringencies.

I have from the beginning believed that the Chinese Communists' support of the North Koreans was the dominant one. Their interests are at present parallel with those of the Soviet, but I believe that the aggressiveness recently displayed not only in Korea but also in Indo-China and Tibet and pointing potentially toward the South reflects predominantly the same lust for the expansion of power which has animated every would-be conqueror since the beginning of time.

The Japanese people since the war have undergone the greatest reformation recorded in modern history. With a commendable will, eagerness to learn, and marked capacity to understand, they have from the ashes left in war's wake erected in Japan an edifice dedicated to the primacy of individual liberty and personal dignity, and in the ensuing process there has been created a truly representative government committed to the advance of political morality, freedom of economic enterprise and social justice.

Politically, economically, and socially, Japan is now abreast of many free nations of the earth and will not again fail the universal trust. That it may be counted upon to wield a profoundly beneficial influence over the course of events in Asia is attested by the magnificent manner in which the Japanese people have met the recent challenge of war, unrest and confusion surrounding them from the outside, and checked communism within their own frontiers without the slightest slackening in their forward progress.

I sent all four of our occupation divisions to the Korean battlefront without the slightest qualms as to the effect of the resulting power vacuum upon Japan. The results fully justified my faith.

I know of no nation more serene, orderly and industrious, nor in which higher hopes can be entertained for future constructive service in the advance of the human race.

Of our former ward, the Philippines, we can look forward in confidence that the existing unrest will be corrected and a strong and healthy nation will grow in the longer aftermath of war's terrible destructiveness. We must be patient and understanding and never fail them, as in our hour of need they did not fail us.

A Christian nation, the Philippines stands as a mighty bulwark of Christianity in the Far East, and its capacity for high moral leadership in Asia is unlimited.

On Formosa, the government of the Republic of China has had the opportunity.to refute by action much of the malicious gossip which so undermined the strength of its leadership on the Chinese mainland. The Formosan people are receiving a just and enlightened administration with majority representation on the organs of government, and politically, economically and socially they appear to be advancing along sound and constructive lines.

With this brief insight into the surrounding areas, I now turn to the Korean conflict.

While I was not consulted prior to the President's decision to intervene in support of the Republic of Korea, that decision, from a military standpoint, proved a sound one. As I say, it proved a sound one, as we hurled back the invader and decimated his forces. Our victory was complete, and our objectives within reach, when Red China intervened with numerically superior ground forces.

This created a new war and an entirely new situation, a situation not contemplated when our forces were committed against the North Korean invaders; a situation which called for new decisions in the diplomatic sphere to permit the realistic adjustment of military strategy. Such decisions have not been forthcoming.

While no man in his right mind would advocate sending our ground forces into continental China, and such was never given a thought, the new situation did urgently demand a drastic revision of strategic planning if our political aim was to defeat this new enemy as we had defeated the old.

Apart from the military need, as I saw it, to neutralize the sanctuary protection given the enemy north of the Yalu, I felt that military necessity in the conduct of the war made necessary—

(1) The intensification of our economic blockade against China.

(2) The imposition of a naval blockade against the China coast.

(3) Removal of restrictions on air reconnaissance of China's coastal area and of Manchuria.

(4) Removal of restrictions on the forces of the Republic of China on Formosa, with logistical support to contribute to their effective operations against the Chinese mainland.

For entertaining these views, all professionally designed to support our forces committed to Korea and bring hostilities to an end with the least possible delay and at a saving of countless American and Allied lives, I have been severely criticized in lay circles, principally abroad, despite my understanding that from a military standpoint the above views have been fully shared in the past by practically every military leader concerned with the Korean campaign, including our own Joint Chiefs of Staff.

I called for reinforcements, but was informed that reinforcements were not available. I made clear that if not permitted to destroy the enemy built-up bases north of the Yalu, if not permitted to utilize the friendly Chinese force of some 600,000 men on Formosa, if not permitted to blockade the China coast to prevent the Chinese Reds from getting succor from without, and if there were to be no hope of major reinforcements, the position of the command from the military standpoint forbade victory.

We could hold in Korea by constant maneuver and at an approximate area where our supply line advantages were in balance with the supply line disadvantages of the enemy, but we could hope at best for only an indecisive campaign with its terrible and constant attrition upon our forces if the enemy utilized his full military potential.

I have constantly called for the new political decisions essential to a solution.

Efforts have been made to distort my position. It has been said in effect that I was a warmonger. Nothing could be further from the truth.

I know war as few other men now living know it, and nothing to me is more revolting. I have long advocated its complete abolition, as its very destructiveness on both friend and foe has rendered it useless as a means of settling international disputes.

Indeed, on the second day of September, 1945, just following the surrender of the Japanese nation on the battleship Missouri, I formally cautioned as follows:

"Men since the beginning of time have sought peace. Various methods through the ages have been attempted to devise an international process to prevent or settle disputes between nations. From the very start workable methods were found in so far as individual citizens were concerned, but the mechanics of an instrumentality of larger international scope have never been successful.

"Military alliances, balances of power, leagues of nations, all in turn failed, leaving the only path to be by way of the crucible of war. The utter destructiveness of war now blocks out this alternative. We have had our last chance. If we will not devise some greater and more equitable system, our Armageddon will be at our door. The problem basically is theological and involves a spiritual recrudescence, an improvement of human character that will synchronize with our almost matchless advances in science, art, literature and all material and cultural developments of the past 2,000 years. It must be of the spirit if we are to save the flesh."*

But once war is forced upon us, there is no other alternative than to apply every available means to bring it to a swift end. War's very object is victory not prolonged indecision.

In war there is no substitute for victory.

There are some who for varying reasons would appease Red China. They are blind to history's clear lesson, for history teaches with unmistakable emphasis that appeasement but begets new and bloodier war. It points to no single instance where this end has justified that means, where appeasement has led to more than a sham peace.

Like blackmail, it lays the basis for new and successively greater demands until, as in blackmail, violence becomes the only other alternative. Why, my soldiers asked of me, surrender military advantages to an enemy in the field? I could not answer.

Some may say to avoid spread of the conflict into an all-out war with China. Others, to avoid Soviet intervention. Neither explanation seems valid, for China is already engaging with the maximum power it can commit, and the Soviet will not necessarily mesh its actions with our moves. Like a cobra, any new enemy will more likely strike whenever it feels that the relativity in military or other potential is in its favor on a world-wide basis.

The tragedy of Korea is further heightened by the fact that its military action is confined to its territorial limits. It condemns that nation, which it is our purpose to save, to suffer the devastating impact of full naval and air bombardment while the enemy's sanctuaries are fully protected from such attack and devastation.

Of the nations of the world, Korea alone, up to now, is the sole one which has risked its all against communism. The magnificence of the courage and fortitude of the Korean people defies description. They have chosen to risk

*Vital Speeches, Vol. II, No. 23, page 707.

death rather than slavery. Their last words to me were: "Don't scuttle the Pacific."

I have just left your fighting sons in Korea. They have met all tests there, and I can report to you without reservation that they are splendid in every way.

It was my constant effort to preserve them and end this savage conflict honorably and with the least loss of time and a minimum sacrifice of life. Its growing bloodshed has caused me the deepest anguish and anxiety. Those gallant men will remain often in my thoughts and in my prayers always.

I am closing my fifty-two years of military service. When I joined the Army, even before the turn of the century, it was the fulfillment of all of my boyish hopes and dreams.

The world has turned over many times since I took the oath on the plain at West Point, and the hopes and dreams have long since vanished, but I still remember the refrain of one of the most popular barrack ballads of that day which proclaimed most proudly that old soldiers never die; they just fade away.

And like the old soldier of that ballad, I now close my military career and just fade away, an old soldier who tried to do his duty as God gave him the light to see that duty. Good bye.

Duty, Honor and Country

Douglas MacArthur

This speech was delivered upon acceptance of the Sylvanus Thayer Award, U.S. Military Academy, West Point, N.Y., May 12, 1962. Published version: Vital Speeches of the Day, *June 15, 1962, pp. 519-21.*

No human being could fail to be deeply moved by such a tribute as this, coming from a profession I have served so long and a people I have loved so well. It fills me with an emotion I cannot express. But this award is not intended primarily for a personality, but to symbolize a great moral code — the code of conduct and chivalry of those who guard this beloved land of culture and ancient descent.

"Duty," "honor," "country" — those three hallowed words reverently dictate what you want to be, what you can be, what you will be. They are your rallying point to build courage when courage seems to fail, to regain faith when there seems to be little cause for faith, to create hope when hope becomes forlorn.

Unhappily, I possess neither that eloquence of diction, that poetry of imagination, nor that brilliance of metaphor to tell you all that they mean.

The unbelievers will say they are but words, but a slogan, but a flamboyant phrase. Every pedant, every demagog, every cynic, every hypocrite, every troublemaker, and, I am sorry to say, some others of an entirely different character, will try to downgrade them even to the extent of mockery and ridicule.

But these are some of the things they build. They build your basic character. They mold you for your future roles as the custodians of the Nation's defense. They make you strong enough to know when you are weak, and brave enough to face yourself when you are afraid.

They teach you to be proud and unbending in honest failure, but humble and gentle in success; not to substitute words for action; not to seek the path of comfort, but to face the stress and spur of difficulty and challenge; to learn to stand up in the storm, but to have compassion on those who fall; to master yourself before you seek to master others; to have a heart that is clean, a goal that is high; to learn to laugh, yet never forget how to weep; to reach into the future, yet never neglect the past; to be serious, yet never take yourself too seriously; to be modest so that you will remember the simplicity of true greatness; the open mind of true wisdom, the meekness of true strength.

They give you a temperate will, a quality of imagination, a vigor of the emotions, a freshness of the deep springs of life, a temperamental predominance of courage over timidity, an appetite for adventure over love of ease.

They create in your heart the sense of wonder, the unfailing hope of what next, and the joy and inspiration of life. They teach you in this way to be an officer and a gentleman.

And what sort of soldiers are those you are to lead? Are they reliable? Are they brave? Are they capable of victory?

Their story is known to all of you. It is the story of the American man at arms. My estimate of him was formed on the battlefields many many years ago, and has never changed. I regarded him then, as I regard him now, as one of the world's noblest figures; not only as one of the finest military characters, but also as one of the most stainless.

His name and fame are the birthright of every American citizen. In his youth and strength, his love and loyalty, he gave all that mortality can give. He needs no eulogy from me, or from any other man. He has written his own history and written it in red on his enemy's breast.

In 20 campaigns, on a hundred battlefields, around a thousand camp-fires, I have witnessed that enduring fortitude, that patriotic self-abnegation, and that invincible determination which have carved his statue in the hearts of his people.

From one end of the world to the other, he has drained deep the chalice of courage. As I listened to those songs in memory's eye I could see those staggering columns of the First World War, bending under soggy packs on many a weary march, from dripping dusk to drizzling dawn, slogging ankle deep through mire of shell-pocked roads; to form grimly for the attack, blue-lipped, covered with sludge and mud, chilled by the wind and rain, driving home to their objective, and for many, the the judgment seat of God.

I do not know the dignity of their birth, but I do know the glory of their death. They died unquestioning, uncomplaining, with faith in their hearts, and on their lips the hope that we would go on to victory.

Always for them: Duty, honor, country. Always their blood, and sweat, and tears, as they saw the way and the light. And 20 years later, on the other side of the globe, again the filth of dirty foxholes, the stench of ghostly trenches, the slime of dripping dugouts, those boiling suns of the relentless heat, those torrential rains of devastating storms, the loneliness and utter desolation of jungle trails, the bitterness of long separation of those they loved and cherished, the deadly pestilence of tropical disease, the horror of stricken areas of war.

Their resolute and determined defense, their swift and sure attack, their indomitable purpose, their complete and decisive victory—always victory, always through the bloody haze of their last reverberating shot, the vision of gaunt, ghastly men, reverently following your password of duty, honor, country.

You now face a new world, a world of change. The thrust into outer space of the satellite spheres and missiles marks a beginning of another epoch in the long story of mankind. In the five or more billions of years the scientists tell us it has taken to form the earth, in the three or more billion years of development of the human race, there has never been a more abrupt or staggering evolution.

We deal now, not with things of this world alone, but with the illimitable distances and yet unfathomed mysteries of the universe. We are reaching out for a new and boundless frontier. We speak in strange terms of harnessing the cosmic energy, of making winds and tides work for us, of the primary target in war, no longer limited to the armed forces of an enemy, but instead to include his civil population; of ultimate conflicts between a united human race and the sinister forces of some other planetary galaxy; such dreams and fantasies as to make life the most exciting of all times.

And through all this welter of change and development your mission remains fixed, determined, inviolable. It is to win our wars. Everything else in your professional career is but corollary to this vital dedication. All other public purpose, all other public projects, all other public needs, great or small, will find others for their accomplishments; but you are the ones who are trained to fight.

Yours is the profession of arms, the will to win, the sure knowledge that in war there is no substitute for victory, that if you lose, the Nation will be destroyed, that the very obsession of your public service must be duty, honor, country.

Others will debate the controversial issues, national and international, which divide men's minds. But serene, calm, aloof, you stand as the Nation's war guardians, as its lifeguards from the raging tides of international conflict, as its gladiators in the arena of battle. For a century and a half you have defended, guarded, and protected its hallowed traditions of liberty and freedom, of right and justice.

Let civilian voices argue the merits or demerits of our processes of government: Whether our strength is being sapped by deficit financing indulged in too long, by Federal paternalism grown too mighty, by power groups grown too arrogant, by politics grown too corrupt, by crime grown too rampant, by morals grown too low, by taxes grown too high, by extremists grown too violent; whether our personal liberties are as firm and complete as they should be.

These great national problems are not for your professional participation or military solution. Your guidepost stands out like a tenfold beacon in the night: Duty, honor, country.

You are the lever which binds together the entire fabric of our national system of defense. From your ranks come the great captains who hold the Nation's destiny in their hands the moment the war tocsin sounds.

The long, gray line has never failed us. Were you to do so, a million ghosts in olive drab, in brown khaki, in blue and gray, would rise from their white crosses, thundering those magic words: Duty, honor, country.

This does not mean that you are warmongers. On the contrary, the soldier above all other people prays for peace, for he must suffer and bear the deepest wounds and scars of war. But always in our ears ring the ominous words of Plato, that wisest of all philosophers: "Only the dead have seen the end of war."

The shadows are lengthening for me. The twilight is here. My days of old have vanished—tone and tints. They have gone glimmering through the dreams of things that were. Their memory is one of wondrous beauty, watered by tears and coaxed and caressed by the smiles of yesterday. I listen then, but with thirsty ear, for the witching melody of faint bugles blowing reveille, of far drums beating the long roll.

In my dreams I hear again the crash of guns, the rattle of musketry, the strange, mournful mutter of the battlefield. But in the evening of my memory I come back to West Point. Always there echoes and re-echoes: Duty, honor, country.

Today marks my final roll call with you. But I want you to know that when I cross the river, my last conscious thoughts will be of the corps, and the corps, and the corps.

I bid you farewell.

My Side of the Story

Richard Milhous Nixon

Richard Nixon (January 9, 1913 -   ) graduated from Whittier College in 1934 and received his law degree from Duke University in 1937, member of 80th-81st Congress; U.S. Senator, 1950-53; Vice-President of the United States, 1953-61; Republican candidate for president, 1960; 37th President of the United States, 1969-74. This speech was delivered as a nationwide broadcast, Los Angeles, California, September 23, 1952. Published version: Vital Speeches of the Day, *October 15, 1952, pp. 11-15.*

My Fellow Americans: I come before you tonight as a candidate for the Vice Presidency and as a man whose honesty and integrity have been questioned.

The usual political thing to do when charges are made against you is to either ignore them or to deny them without giving details.

I believe we've had enough of that in the United States, particularly with the present Administration in Washington, D.C. To me the office of the Vice Presidency of the United States is a great office, and I feel that the people have got to have confidence in the integrity of the men who run for that office and who might obtain it.

I have a theory, too, that the best and only answer to a smear or to an honest misunderstanding of the facts is to tell the truth. And that's why I'm here tonight. I want to tell you my side of the case.

I am sure that you have read the charge and you've heard that I, Senator Nixon, took $18,000 from a group of my supporters.

Now, was that wrong? And let me say that it was wrong—I'm saying, incidentally, that it was wrong and not just illegal. Because it isn't a question of whether it was legal or illegal, that isn't enough. The question is, was it morally wrong?

I say that it was morally wrong if any of that $18,000 went to Senator Nixon for my personal use. I say that it was morally wrong if it was secretly given and secretly handled. And I say that it was morally wrong if any of the contributors got special favors for the contributions that they made.

And now to answer those questions let me say this:

Not one cent of the $18,000 or any other money of that type ever went to me for my personal use. Every penny of it was used to pay for political expenses that I did not think should be charged to the taxpayers of the United States.

It was not a secret fund. As a matter of fact, when I was on "Meet the Press," some of you may have seen it last Sunday — Peter Edson came up to me after the program and he said, "Dick, what about this fund we hear about?" And I said, "Well, there's no secret about it. Go out and see Dana Smith, who was the administrator of the fund." And I gave him his address, and I said that you will find that the purpose of the fund simply was to defray political expenses that I did not feel should be charged to the Government.

And third, let me point out, and I want to make this particularly clear, that no contributor to this fund, no contributor to any of my campaign, has ever received any consideration that he would not have received as an ordinary constituent.

I just don't believe in that and I can say that never, while I have been in the Senate of the United States, as far as the people that contributed to this fund are concerned, have I made a telephone call for them to an agency, or have I gone down to an agency in their behalf. And the record will show that, the records which are in the hands of the Administration.

But then some of you will say and rightly, "Well, what did you use the fund for, Senator? Why did you have to have it?"

Let me tell you in just a word how a Senate office operates. First of all, a Senator gets $15,000 a year in salary. He gets enough money to pay for one trip a year, a round trip that is, for himself and his family between his home and Washington, D.C.

And then he gets an allowance to handle the people that work in his office, to handle his mail. And the allowance for my State of California is enough to hire thirteen people.

And let me say, incidentally, that that allowance is not paid to the Senator — it's paid directly to the individuals that the Senator puts on his payroll, that all of these people and all of these allowances are for strictly official business. Business, for example, when a constituent writes in and wants you to go down to the Veterans Administration and get some information about his GI policy. Items of that type for example.

But there are other expenses which are not covered by the Government. And I think I can best discuss those expenses by asking you some questions.

Do you think that when I or any other Senator makes a political speech, has it printed, should charge the printing of that speech and the mailing of that speech to the taxpayers?

Do you think, for example, when I or any other Senator makes a trip to his home state to make a purely political speech that the cost of that trip should be charged to the taxpayers?

Do you think when a Senator makes political broadcasts or political television broadcasts, radio or television, that the expense of those broadcasts should be charged to the taxpayers?

Well, I know what your answer is. The same answer that audiences give me whenever I discuss this particular problem. The answer is, "no." The taxpayers shouldn't be required to finance items which are not official business but which are primarily political business.

But then the question arises, you say, "Well, how do you pay for these and how can you do it legally?"

And there are several ways that it can be done, incidentally, and that it is done legally in the United States Senate and in the Congress.

The first way is to be a rich man. I don't happen to be a rich man so I couldn't use that.

Another way that is used is to put your wife on the payroll. Let me say, incidentally, my opponent, my opposite number for the Vice Presidency on the Democratic ticket, does have his wife on the payroll. And has had her on his payroll for the ten years—the past ten years.

Now just let me say this. That's his business and I'm not critical of him for doing that. You will have to pass judgment on that particular point. But I have never done that for this reason. I have found that there are so many deserving stenographers and secretaries in Washington that needed the work that I just didn't feel it was right to put my wife on the payroll.

My wife's sitting over here. She's a wonderful stenographer. She used to teach stenography and she used to teach shorthand in high school. That was when I met her. And I can tell you folks that she's worked many hours at night and many hours on Saturdays and Sundays in my office and she's done a fine job. And I'm proud to say tonight that in the six years I've been in the House and the Senate of the United States, Pat Nixon has never been on the Government payroll.

There are other ways that these finances can be taken care of. Some who are lawyers, and I happen to be a lawyer, continue to practice law. But I haven't been able to do that. I'm so far away from California that I've been so busy with my Senatorial work that I have not engaged in any legal practice.

And also as far as law practice is concerned, it seemed to me that the relationship between an attorney and the client was so personal that you couldn't possibly represent a man as an attorney and then have an unbiased view when he presented his case to you in the event that he had one before the Government.

And so I felt that the best way to handle these necessary political expenses of getting my message to the American people and the speeches I made, the speeches that I had printed, for the most part, concerned this one message — of exposing this Administration, the communism in it, the corruption in it — the only way that I could do that was to accept the aid which people in my home state of California who contributed to my campaign and who continued to make these contributions after I was elected were glad to make.

And let me say I am proud of the fact that not one of them has ever asked me for a special favor. I'm proud of the fact that not one of them has ever asked me to vote on a bill other than as my own conscience would dictate. And I am proud of the fact that the taxpayers by subterfuge or otherwise have never paid one dime for expenses which I thought were political and shouldn't be charged to the taxpayers.

Let me say, incidentally, that some of you may say, "Well, that's all right, Senator; that's your explanation, but have you got any proof?"

And I'd like to tell you this evening that just about an hour ago we received an independent audit of this entire fund.

I suggested to Gov. Sherman Adams, who is the chief of staff of the Dwight Eisenhower campaign, that an independent audit and legal report be obtained. And I have that audit here in my hand.

It's an audit made by the Price, Waterhouse & Co. firm, and the legal opinion of Gibson, Dunn & Crutcher, lawyers in Los Angeles, the biggest law firm and incidentally one of the best ones in Los Angeles.

I'm proud to be able to report to you tonight that this audit and this legal opinion is being forwarded to General Eisenhower. And I'd like to read to you the opinion that was prepared by Gibson, Dunn & Crutcher and based on all the pertinent laws and statutes, together with the audit report prepared by the certified public accountants.

"It is our conclusion that Senator Nixon did not obtain any financial gain from the collection and disbursement of the fund by Dana Smith; that Senator Nixon did not violate any Federal or state law by reason of the operation of the fund, and that neither the portion of the fund paid by Dana Smith directly to third persons nor the portion paid to Senator Nixon to reimburse him for designated office expenses constituted income to the Senator which was either reportable or taxable as income under applicable tax laws. (signed) Gibson, Dunn & Crutcher by Alma H. Conway."

Now that, my friends, is not Nixon speaking, but that's an independent audit which was requested because I want the American people to know all the facts and I'm not afraid of having independent people go in and check the facts, and that is exactly what they did.

But then I realize that there are still some who may say, and rightly so, and let me say that I recognize that some will continue to smear regardless of what the truth may be, but that there has been understandably some honest misunderstanding on this matter, and there's some that will say:

"Well, maybe you were able, Senator, to fake this thing. How can we believe what you say? After all, is there a possibility that maybe you got some sums in cash? Is there a possibility that you may have feathered your own nest?"

And so now what I am going to do—and incidentally this is unprecedented in the history of American politics—I am going at this time to give this television and radio audience a complete financial history; everything I've earned; everything I've spent; everything I owe. And I want you to know the facts. I'll have to start early.

I was born in 1913. Our family was one of modest circumstances and most of my early life was spent in a store out in East Whittier. It was a grocery store—one of those family enterprises. The only reason we were able to make it go was because my mother and dad had five boys and we all worked in the store.

I worked my way through college and to a great extent through law school. And then, in 1940, probably the best thing that ever happened to me happened, I married Pat—sitting over here. We had a rather difficult time after we were married, like so many of the young couples who may be listening to us. I practiced law; she continued to teach School. I went into the service.

Let me say that my service record was not a particularly unusual one. I went to the South Pacific. I guess I'm entitled to a couple of battle stars. I got a couple of letters of commendation but I was just there when the bombs were falling and then I returned. I returned to the United States and in 1946 I ran for the Congress.

When we came out of the war, Pat and I—Pat during the war had worked as a stenographer and in a bank and as an economist for a Government agency—and when we came out the total of our savings from both my law practice, her teaching and all the time that I was in the war—the total for that entire period was just a little less than $10,000. Every cent of that, incidentally, was in Government bonds.

Well, that's where we start when I go into politics. Now what have I earned since I went into politics? Well, here it is—I jotted it down, let me read the notes. First of all I've had my salary as a Congressman and as a Senator. Second, I have received a total in this past six years of $1,600 from estates which were in my law firm at the time that I severed my connection with it.

And, incidentally, as I said before, I have not engaged in any legal practice and have not accepted any fees from business that came into the firm after I went into politics. I have made an average of approximately $1,500 a year from nonpolitical speaking engagements and lectures. And then, fortunately, we've inherited a little money. Pat sold her interest in her father's estate for $3,000 and I inherited $1,500 from my grandfather.

We live rather modestly. For four years we lived in an apartment in Park Fairfax, in Alexandria, Va. The rent was $80 a month. And we saved for the time that we could buy a house.

Now, that was what we took in. What did we do with this money? What do we have today to show for it? This will surprise you, because it is so little, I suppose, as standards generally go, of people in public life. First of all, we've got a house in Washington which cost $41,000 and on which we owe $20,000.

We have a house in Whittier, Calif., which cost $13,000 and on which we owe $10,000. My folks are living there at the present time.

I have just $4,000 in life insurance, plus my G.I. policy which I've never been able to convert and which will run out in two years. I have no insurance whatever on Pat. I have no life insurance on our two youngsters, Patricia and Julie. I own a 1950 Oldsmobile car. We have our furniture. We have no stocks and bonds of any type. We have no interest of any kind, direct or indirect, in any business.

Now, that's what we have. What do we owe? Well, in addition to the mortgage, the $20,000 mortgage on the house in Washington, the $10,000 one on the house in Whittier, I owe $4,500 to the Riggs Bank in Washington, D.C. with interest 4½ per cent.

I owe $3,500 to my parents and the interest on that loan which I pay regularly, because it's the part of the savings they made through the years they were working so hard, I pay regularly 4 per cent interest. And then I have a $500 loan which I have on my life insurance.

Well, that's about it. That's what we have and that's what we owe. It isn't very much but Pat and I have the satisfaction that every dime that we've got is honestly ours. I should say this—that Pat doesn't have a mink coat. But she does have a respectable Republican cloth coat. And I always tell her that she'd look good in anything.

One other thing I probably should tell you because if we don't they'll probably be saying this about me too, we did get something—a gift—after the election. A man down in Texas heard Pat on the radio mention the fact that our two youngsters would like to have a dog. And, believe it or not, the day before we left on this campaign trip we got a message from Union Station in Baltimore saying they had a package for us. We went down to get it. You know what it was.

It was a little cocker spaniel dog in a crate that he sent all the way from Texas. Black and white spotted. And our little girl—Tricia, the 6-year-old—named it Checkers. And you know, the kids love the dog and I just want to say this right now, that regardless of what they say about it, we're gonna keep it.

It isn't easy to come before a nation-wide audience and air your life as I've done. But I want to say some things before I conclude that I think most of you will agree on. Mr. Mitchell, the chairman of the Democratic National Committee, made the statement that if a man couldn't afford to be in the United States Senate he shouldn't run for the Senate.

And I just want to make my position clear. I don't agree with Mr. Mitchell when he says that only a rich man should serve his Government in the United States Senate or in the Congress.

I don't believe that represents the thinking of the Democratic party, and I know that it doesn't represent the thinking of the Republican Party.

I believe that it's fine that a man like Governor Stevenson who inherited a fortune from his father can run for President. But I also feel that it's essential in this country of ours that a man of modest means can also run for President. Because, you know, remember Abraham Lincoln, you remember what he said: "God must have loved the common people—he made so many of them."

And now I'm going to suggest some courses of conduct.

First of all, you have read in the papers about other funds now. Mr. Stevenson, apparently, had a couple. One of them in which a group of business people paid and helped to supplement the salaries of state employees. Here is where the money went directly into their pockets.

And I think that what Mr. Stevenson should do should be to come before the American people as I have, give the names of the people that have contributed to that fund; give the names of the people who put this money into their pockets at the same time that they were receiving money from their state government, and see what favors, if any, they gave out for that.

I don't condemn Mr. Stevenson for what he did. But until the facts are in there is a doubt that will be raised.

And as far as Mr. Sparkman is concerned, I would suggest the same thing. He's had his wife on the payroll. I don't condemn him for that. But I think that he should come before the American people and indicate what outside sources of income he has had.

I would suggest that under the circumstances both Mr. Sparkman and Mr. Stevenson should come before the American people as I have and make a complete financial statement as to their financial history. And if they don't it will be an admission that they have something to hide. And I think that you will agree with me.

Because, folks, remember, a man that's to be President of the United States, a man that's to be Vice President of the United States must have the confidence of all the people. And that's why I'm doing what I'm doing, and that's why I suggest that Mr. Stevenson and Mr. Sparkman since they are under attack should do what I am doing.

Now, let me say this: I know that this is not the last of the smears. In spite of my explanation tonight other smears will be made; others have been made in the past. And the purpose of the smears, I know, is this—to silence me, to make me let up.

Well, they just don't know who they're dealing with. I'm going to tell you this: I remember in the dark days of the Hiss case some of the same columnists, some of the same radio commentators who are attacking me now and misrepresenting my position were violently opposing me at the time I was after Alger Hiss.

But I continued the fight because I knew I was right. And I can say to this great television and radio audience that I have no apologies to the American people for my part in putting Alger Hiss where he is today.

And as far as this is concerned, I intend to continue the fight.

Why do I feel so deeply? Why do I feel that in spite of the smears, the misunderstandings, the necessities for a man to come up here and bare his soul as I have? Why is it necessary for me to continue this fight?

And I want to tell you why. Because, you see, I love my country. And I think my country is in danger. And I think that the only man that can save America at this time is the man that's running for President on my ticket—Dwight Eisenhower.

You say, "Why do I think it's in danger?" and I say look at the record. Seven years of the Truman-Acheson Administration and what's happened? Six hundred million people lost to the Communists, and a war in Korea in which we have lost 117,000 American casualties.

And I say to all of you that a policy that results in a loss of 600,000,000 to the Communists and a war which costs us 117,000 American casualties isn't good enough for America.

And I say that those in the State Department that made the mistakes which caused that war and which resulted in those losses should be kicked out of the State Department just as fast as we can get 'em out of there.

And let me say that I know Mr. Stevenson won't do that. Because he defends the Truman policy and I know that Dwight Eisenhower will do that, and that he will give America the leadership that it needs.

Take the problem of corruption. You've read about the mess in Washington. Mr. Stevenson can't clean it up because he was picked by the man, Truman, under whose Administration the mess was made. You wouldn't trust a man who made the mess to clean it up—that's Truman. And by the same token you can't trust the man who was picked by the man that made the mess to clean it up—and that's Stevenson.

And so I say, Eisenhower, who owes nothing to Truman, nothing to the big city bosses, he is the man that can clean up the mess in Washington.

Take Communism. I say that as far as that subject is concerned, the danger is great to America. In the Hiss case they got the secrets which enabled them to break the American secret State Department code. They got secrets in the atomic bomb case which enabled 'em to get the secret of the atomic bomb, five years before they would have gotten it by their own devices.

And I say that any man who called the Alger Hiss case a "red herring" isn't fit to be President of the United States. I say that a man who like Mr. Stevenson has pooh-poohed and ridiculed the Communist threat in the United States—he said that they are phantoms among ourselves; he's accused us that have attempted to expose the Communists of looking for Communists in the Bureau of Fisheries and Wildlife—I say that a man who says that isn't qualified to be President of the United States.

And I say that the only man who can lead us in this fight to rid the Government of both those who are Communists and those who have corrupted this Government is Eisenhower, because Eisenhower, you can be sure, recognizes the problem and he knows how to deal with it.

Now let me say that, finally, this evening I want to read to you just briefly excerpts from a letter which I received, a letter which, after all this is over, no one can take away from me. It reads as follows:

"Dear Senator Nixon,

"Since I'm only 19 years of age I can't vote in the Presidential election but believe me if I could you and General Eisenhower would certainly get my vote. My husband is in the Fleet Marines in Korea. He's a corpsman on the front lines and we have a two-month-old son he's never seen. And I feel confident that with great Americans like you and General Eisenhower in the White House, lonely Americans like myself will be united with their loved ones now in Korea.

"I only pray to God that you won't be too late. Enclosed is a small check to help you in your campaign. Living on $85 a month it is all I can afford at present. But let me know what else I can do."

Folks, it's a check for $10, and it's one that I will never cash.

And just let me say this. We hear a lot about prosperity these days but I say, why can't we have prosperity built on peace rather than prosperity built on war? Why can't we have prosperity and an honest government in Washington, D.C., at the same time. Believe me, we can. And Eisenhower is the man that can lead this crusade to bring us that kind of prosperity.

And, now, finally, I know that you wonder whether or not I am going to stay on the Republican ticket or resign.

Let me say this: I don't believe that I ought to quit because I'm not a quitter. And, incidentally, Pat's not a quitter. After all, her name was Patricia Ryan and she was born on St. Patrick's Day, and you know the Irish never quit.

But the decision, my friends, is not mine. I would do nothing that would harm the possibilities of Dwight Eisenhower to become President of the United States. And for that reason I am submitting to the Republican National Committee tonight through this television broadcast the decision which it is theirs to make.

Let them decide whether my position on the ticket will help or hurt. And I am going to ask you to help them decide. Wire and write the Republican National Committee whether you think I should stay on or whether I should get off. And whatever their decision is, I will abide by it.

But just let me say this last word. Regardless of what happens I'm going to continue this fight. I'm going to campaign up and down America until we drive the crooks and the Communists and those that defend them out of Washington. And remember, folks, Eisenhower is a great man. Believe me. He's a great man. And a vote for Eisenhower is a vote for what's good for America.

A Value Analysis of Richard Nixon's 1952 Campaign-Fund Speech

Henry E. McGuckin, Jr.

Dr. McGuckin is Professor of Speech, San Francisco State University, California. This article originally appeared in Southern Speech Communication Journal, *33 (1968), 259-69, and is reprinted with permission from the Southern Speech Communication Association.*

Perhaps critically minded listeners were not impressed, but the mass audience that heard Nixon defend his personal integrity in a radio and televised speech in 1952 clearly was convinced by what he said. The means he used are analytically pointed out in this article.

The 1952 Republican march on Washington was temporarily halted when, on September 18, the front page of the *New York Post* announced: **"Millionaires' Club Finances Comfort of Nixon."** The *Post* story concerned a fund of eighteen thousand dollars donated by seventy-six prominent Californians supposedly to assist Nixon in his office and travel expenses. The question of the fund's legality was never seriously raised, but the political ethics of accepting eighteen thousand dollars from what was possibly a special-interest group caused serious concern. There were charges that the fund was not for campaign expenses but for Nixon's personal use. A movement began, primarily among the Citizens for Eisenhower committees, to have Nixon removed from the ticket. The movement rapidly gained support, and on September 20 the Eisenhower-supporting *Boston Post* carried the page-one headline **"Ousting of Nixon Demanded by Some of Ike's Advisors."** Similar headlines were read throughout the country.

Three days after the story broke, Republican leaders met in St. Louis to consider ways and means of handling the campaign-fund issue. They decided to ask Nixon for a public accounting of his personal budget. On September 23 Nixon spoke to a vast radio and television audience, presenting "My Side of the Story," and the famous "Checkers Speech" was born.

The effectiveness of the speech is documented. More than two million favorable telegrams and letters were received at Republican National Head-quarters within a week.[1] This response was historically unprecedented. That even Democrats were convinced of Nixon's effectiveness may be inferred from the fact that they dropped the fund as an issue. Furthermore, there is a modicum of experimental evidence that the speech remained reasonably effective for years after the campaign. This writer conducted an attitude-shift experiment with a random college audience (N = 62), using a kinescope of the television broadcast, and found a statistically significant (P = .05) shift of opinion in the direction of more favorable evaluations of Nixon's character.[2]

From the foregoing evidence, historical and experimental, we can conclude that Nixon was reasonably successful in persuading a significant portion of his audience of his desirable personal attributes. The question to be considered here is: How did he achieve this success? Nixon successfully identified with basic American cultural values to establish his apparent good sense, good will, and good moral character with his American audience — to establish, in short, his *ethos.*

Nixon's speech affords an excellent opportunity for an analysis of ethical proof in that it is perhaps the most widely heard speech in which ethos was the end object as well as persuasive means. Nixon set out to convince his listeners that, contrary to some reports, he was a good, honest, sincere American — in short, a credible man. Since he entered the speaking situation with his credibility challenged, his honesty questioned, his primary task was to establish credibility for his claim to credibility. This aspect of the speech is unusual and affords a rare opportunity for analysis of the ethical mode.

Ethos and Shared Values

Since Aristotle, rhetoricians have recognized ethos — the appearance of good will, good sense, and good moral character — as perhaps the most

[1]John Mason Brown, *Through These Men: Some Aspects of Our Passing History* (New York: Harper and Brothers, 1956), p. 102.
[2]Henry E. McGuckin, Jr., "A Study of Ethos in a Persuasive Speech where the Character of the Speaker is the Issue," unpublished master's thesis, San Francisco State College, 1959.

important mode of persuasion. But Aristotle, although he carefully described the phenomenon, was less than complete regarding the *means* by which a speaker achieves such appearances.

Modern critics have offered some intuitive suggestions for the enhancement of ethos. According to Brembeck and Howell, for example, ethos is strengthened when a speaker (1) associates himself with that which is virtuous and elevated, (2) bestows praise on himself and his cause, (3) creates an impression of sincerity, (4) identifies himself with his audience, and (5) offsets any personal reasons for the speech.[3] Thonssen and Baird offer a similar method for achieving ethos.[4]

Unfortunately the means to this achievement are not as simple as these criteria imply. The important questions remain: What is the nature of the virtue with which the speaker is to associate himself? What kinds of praise is he to bestow on himself and his cause? How is sincerity communicated? In what terms should the speaker identify himself with his audience, and how does he offset "any personal reasons" for the speech? Answers to these questions are likely to depend on the particular norms of particular groups addressed. "Virtue," for example, varies from group to group, and the speaker must choose among the virtues of his specific audience in order to be effective. He will base his choices, consciously or unconsciously, on the values of his audience; and if he would establish his ethos before a national *mass* audience, he must base his choices on the values common to most of the listeners. He must, in short, utilize a basic cultural-value system; and if his is an American audience, he must utilize American values.

The basic value of orientation of the American culture has been termed by Steele and Redding "The American Value System." These writers examined the works of American social psychologists and social anthropologists and extracted the following values as most representative of our culture: the individual, Puritan and pioneer morality, effort and optimism, science and secular rationality, efficiency and practicality, achievement and success, quantification, material comfort, generosity and considerateness, rejection of authority, equality (of opportunity), external conformity, sociality, humor, and patriotism.[5] Steele and Redding suggest "...that it is feasible to cast many cultural values in a form precise enough to be perceived within the 'content' of a speech, and that a reasonably quantitative 'content-analysis' can be executed."[6]

---

[3]Winston Brembeck and William S. Howell, *Persuasion: A Means of Social Control* (New York: Prentice-Hall, 1952), p. 387.

[4]Lester Thonssen and A. Craig Baird, *Speech Criticism* (New York: Ronald Press, 1948), p. 378.

[5]Edward D. Steele and W. Charles Redding, "The American Value System: Premises for Persuasion," *Western Speech*, XXVI (Spring, 1962), 83-91.

[6]Steele, 91.

In the following analysis (an application of Steele's and Redding's suggestion) the American value system will be conceived as a set of distinct categories for the description of Nixon's identification with common notions of values shared among his audience. American values are italicized as they appear in the analysis. Identifications with other values, common to his audience but less peculiarly American (such as courage and modesty), will also be indicated. A kinescope of the complete television broadcast was the source utilized in this analysis.[7]

Value Analysis of Nixon's Address

Nixon's ethos was probably related to more than the verbal strategies of his speech. It was aided by the television setting of a home library or study with a desk—symbols of *success*. His dress in an ordinary business suit demonstrated *equality* and *external conformity*. The presence of his wife, also simply attired, attested to his *sociality*—family togetherness in this case.[8] The conversational, plain-folks language in which Nixon phrased his speech probably tended to establish a sense of *equality* between him and his listeners. Thus, Nixon began affirming American values from his first appearance on the television screen. His language choices contributed to this process even before his first argument was completed.

The speech opened with Nixon's affirmation of one facet of *Puritan morality*—personal honesty:

> My Fellow Americans: I come before you tonight...as a man whose honesty and integrity have been questioned.
>
> The usual political thing to do when charges are made against you is either to ignore them or to deny them without giving details.
>
> I believe we've had enough of that...particularly with the present administration....
>
> I have a theory...that the best and only answer to a smear or to an honest misunderstanding of the facts is to tell the truth.

Nixon then introduced his discussion of the eighteen thousand dollar fund with: "...it isn't a question of whether it was legal or illegal, that isn't enough. The question is, was it morally wrong?" Here Nixon amplified his affirmation of *Puritan morality* by making the propriety of the fund a basically moral question.

Nixon next discussed the financial allowances for meeting senatorial

[7]For the published text see Richard Nixon, "My Side of the Story," *Vital Speeches,* XIX (October 15, 1952), 11-15.

[8]The growing political importance of contemporary candidate's wives is indicative of the changing role of women and correspondingly changing American values. One can imagine the electorate's reaction to the candidate of a few decades back who utilized his wife as a public campaign asset to the degree that Nixon and Kennedy utilized theirs.

office expenses and chose an interesting example of the uses that are made of these allowances:

> ...All of these allowances are for strictly official business. Business, for example, when a constituent writes in and wants you to go down to the Veterans Administration and get some information about his GI policy. Items of that type for example.

The image of the busy senator going down to the Veterans Administration offices to get information for a perplexed GI is probably unrealistic, but it adds to Nixon's morality; for one aspect of *Puritan morality* is that service is the only moral purpose of political power. Nixon has here described himself as a public servant who is evidently not too busy to extend his service to individuals among his constituents. This statement also attests to Nixon's concern for *the individual.*

Nixon touched upon the American value of *equality* when he considered the means by which a senator might meet purely political expenses. He said: "The first way is to be a rich man. I don't happen to be a rich man, so I couldn't use that way."

His next point concerned the reasons why he did not put his wife upon the government pay roll: "I have found that there are so many deserving stenographers and secretaries in Washington that needed the work that I just didn't feel it was right to put my wife on the pay roll." Nixon's concern for *the individual* is here reemphasized.

Nixon said that he could not meet political expenses by continuing his law practice, because he was too far from California, too busy with senatorial duties, and because:

> ...It seemed to me that the relationship between an attorney and the client was so personal that you couldn't possibly represent a man as an attorney and then have an unbiased view when he presented his case to you in the event that he had one before the government.

Here, again, Nixon sought to establish his honesty and integrity *(Puritan morality).*

Other means being unavailable to him (for *moral* reasons), Nixon had to rely on contributions from his supporters to help him in his cause of:

> ...getting my message to the American people, and the speeches I made, the speeches I had printed, for the most part, concerned this one message—of exposing this Administration, the Communists in it, the corruption in it....

Here Nixon briefly touched the American value of *rejection of authority* ("exposing this Administration") and announced himself as a crusading opponent of those who reject American values—the Communists and the corrupt.

Nixon described the legal firm of Gibson, Dunn & Crutcher, which delivered a legal opinion regarding the fund, as "...the biggest law firm and incidentally one of the best ones in Los Angeles," and thus utilized *quantification* to support his claim to honesty. Not only was he found to be honest, but he was found so by "the biggest law firm."

Nixon concluded the audit report with another affirmation of his openness and honestly—his *Puritan morality*:

> ...And that, my friends, is not Nixon speaking, that's an independent audit which was requested because I want the American people to know all the facts and I'm not afraid of having independent people go in and check the facts, and that is exactly what they did.

Nixon then began his "complete financial history...everything I've made, everything I've spent, everything I owe." He opened with an autobiographical sketch:

> I was born in 1913. Our family was one of modest circumstances and most of my early life was spent in a store out in East Whittier. It was a grocery store—one of those family enterprises. The only reason we were able to make it go was because my mother and dad had five boys and we all worked in the store.

The primary American value here is *success* (from family grocery store to the United States Senate and Vice-Presidential candidacy). Other values alluded to are *Puritan morality* (hard work) and *sociality* (family cooperation). Nixon continued in the same vein:

> I worked my way through college and to a great extent through law school [*Puritan morality*]. And then, in 1940, probably the best thing that ever happened to me happened, I married Pat—sitting over there [*sociality* (togetherness)]. We had a rather difficult time after we were married like so many of the young couples who may be listening to us [*equality*]. I practiced law; she continued to teach. I went into the service [*patriotism*].

> Let me say that my service record is not a particularly unusual one [*modesty*]. I went to the South Pacific. I guess I'm entitled to a couple of battle stars. I got a couple of letters of commendation, but I was just there when the bombs were falling and then I returned [*courage, modesty*]. I returned to the United States and in 1946 I ran for the Congress [*success*].

Nixon discussed actual finances for a few paragraphs and then resumed:

> We live rather modestly. For four years we lived in an apartment in Park Fairfax. In Alexandria, Virgina. The rent was $80 a month [*equality*]. And we saved for the time that we could buy a house [*Puritan morality* (thrift)].

> Now, that was what we took in...What do we have today to show for it? This will surprise you, because it is so little, I suppose, as standards generally go, of people in public life [*equality*]. First of all, we've got a house in Washington which cost $41,000 and on which we owe $20,000.

We have a house in Whittier, California, which cost $13,000 and on which we owe $10,000. My folks are living there at the present time [*sociality, generosity*].

...I owe $3,500 to my parents and the interest on that loan which I pay regularly, because it's the part of the savings they made through the years they were working so hard [*Puritan morality*]....

Well that's about it. That's what we have and that's what we owe. It isn't very much but Pat and I have the satisfaction that every dime that we've got is honestly ours. I should say this—that Pat doesn't have a mink coat. But she does have a respectable Republican cloth coat. And I always tell her she'd look good in anything [*equality, sociality, Puritan morality*].

To complete his financial history Nixon told of a gift he received from "a man down in Texas":

...It was a little cocker spaniel dog in a crate that he sent all the way from Texas. Black and white spotted. And our little girl—Trisha, the 6-year-old —named it Checkers. And you know, the kids love that dog and I just want to say this right now, that regardless of what they say about it, we're gonna keep it.

Perhaps Nixon's original purpose in the reference to the dog was to ridicule his detractors; however, we must assume that the argument was serious; and we must note Nixon's identification with the values of *courage* and *sociality* (love and concern for his children and, indeed, for dogs— which, while not a value discussed by social psychologists, would seem to merit at least a small niche in the American system.)

Nixon introduced the more specifically political section of his speech with a strong affirmation of *equality* (of opportunity) and cited God and Abraham Lincoln as two others who affirm that value:

...Mr. Mitchell, the Chairman of the Democratic National Committee, made the statement that if a man couldn't afford to be in the United States Senate he shouldn't run for the Senate.

And I just want to make my position clear. I don't agree with Mr. Mitchell when he says that only a rich man should serve his government....

I believe that it's fine that a man like Governor Stevenson who inherited a fortune from his father can run for President. But I also feel it's essential in this country of ours that a man of modest means can also run for President. Because, you know, remember Abraham Lincoln; you remember what he said: 'God must have loved the common people—he made so many of them.'

Nixon challenged his Democratic opponents to come before the public, as he was doing, and explain their campaign finances. Then he implied his *courage* and *patriotism* by saying:

...Why do I feel so deeply? Why do I feel that in spite of the smears, the misunderstandings, the necessities for a man to come up here and bare his soul as I have? Why is it necessary for me to continue this fight? And I want to tell you why. Because, you see, I love my country....

Nixon then shifted the discussion from himself to Eisenhower. In praising Eisenhower, however, Nixon did not neglect his own ethos. It is interesting to note the proximity of a first-person singular pronoun to references to Eisenhower: "...the man that's running for President on *my* ticket — *Dwight Eisenhower.*" "...*I* know that *Dwight Eisenhower.*" "And so *I* say, *Eisenhower.*" "Believe *me,* we can. And *Eisenhower...*" "...*Eisenhower* is a great man. Believe *me. He's* a great man."

Nixon next read a letter from the wife of a Korean combat soldier, which, besides suggesting his concern for *the individual,* linked his name closely with Eisenhower's: "...if I could vote, *you and General Eisenhower* [italics mine] would certainly get my vote...and I feel confident that with *great Americans like you and General Eisenhower* in the White House..."

Nixon's strategy regarding Eisenhower was an almost circular process, since he first attempted to establish his own ethos, which tended to give credence to his praise of Eisenhower, with whom he then identified to gain further ethos. Of course, Eisenhower, the much-admired presidential candidate of the Republican Party, was already a symbol of virtue and morality to most Americans before this speech, but Nixon probably gained from the use of Eisenhower's name by waiting until he had partly established his own ethos. Had he begun by immediately identifying with Eisenhower, his identification probably would have been less credible and less effective.

Near his conclusion Nixon again demonstrated his sociality (conformity to group opinion here) and also his *practicality*:

> ...I would do nothing to harm the possibilities of Dwight Eisenhower to become President of the United States. And for that reason I am submitting to the Republican National Committee tonight through this television broadcast the decision which is theirs to make.

> ...And I am going to ask you to help them decide. Wire or write the Republican National Committee whether you think I should stay on or whether I should get off. And whatever their decision is, I will abide by it.

Nixon's last words affirmed his *courage* and his concern for America (*patriotism*) as opposed to "Communists" and "crooks," and made a parting identification with Eisenhower and America's welfare:

> But just let me say this last word. Regardless of what happens I'm going to continue this fight. I'm going to campaign up and down America until we drive the crooks and Communists and those that defend them out of Washington. And remember, folks, a vote for Eisenhower is a vote for what's good for America.

Below is the sum of identifications by Nixon with particular American values:

Nixon's Sincerity

Nixon's apparent sincerity throughout the speech was probably crucial to his success in building ethos. Possibly Nixon's greatest asset here was the stress and strain of the speaking situation. Merton reported in his study of the Kate Smith war-bond drive that "...the presumed stress and strain of the eighteen-hour series of broadcasts seemed to her listeners to validate her sincerity."[9] Nixon probably had the same advantage as Smith. Interested citizens knew of the great importance of the speech to Nixon's personal political aspirations and to Republican hopes generally, and Nixon himself left no doubt as to the strain he was under. His speaking pitch, the occasional break in his voice, and his facial expression all revealed emotional stress. Furthermore, he directly referred to this stress in the text of his speech: "I come before you...as a man whose honesty and integrity have been questioned...it isn't easy to come before a nation-wide audience and air your life as I've done...to bare his soul as I have..."

Conclusions

It has been shown that Nixon's campaign-fund speech was effective in convincing a significant portion of his mass American audience of his

[9]Robert Merton, *Mass Persuasion* (New York: Harper and Brothers, 1946), p. 90.

"good sense, good will, and good moral character"—the Aristotelian constituents of ethos. A value analysis of the speech demonstrates the probability that an important means of achieving this conviction was Nixon's indentification with the American value system.

Many of Nixon's identifications were almost blatantly obvious, and it may be that among more critical listeners such appeals are ineffective at best. Among the less critical, however, and perhaps especially among those predisposed to react favorably, it would seem that even the most transparent identifications with basic values are effective. Such, apparently, is the potency of our value system that many will reward with esteem, with *ethos,* the man who espouses it, however, obviously.

The War in Vietnam

Richard Milhous Nixon

*This speech was delivered as a nationwide broadcast from the
White House, May 14, 1969. Published version:* Vital Speeches
of the Day, *June 1, 1969, pp. 482-84.*

Good evening, my fellow Americans. I have asked for this television time
tonight to report to you on our most difficult and urgent problem, the war
in Vietnam.

Since I took office four months ago nothing has taken so much of my
time and energy as the search for a way to bring lasting peace to Vietnam.

I know that some believe that I should have ended the war immediately
after the Inauguration by simply ordering our forces home from Vietnam.
This would have been an easy thing to do. It might have been a popular
thing to do.

But I would have betrayed my solemn responsibility as President of the
United States if I had done so. I want to end this war. The American people
want to end this war. The people of South Vietnam want to end this war.

But we want to end it permanently so that the younger brothers of our
soldiers in Vietnam will not have to fight in the future in another Vietnam
someplace else in the world.

The fact that there is no easy way to end the war does not mean that we
have no choice but to let the war drag on with no end in sight. For four
years American boys have been fighting and dying in Vietnam. For 12
months our negotiators have been talking with the other side in Paris. And
yet the fighting goes on. The destruction continues. Brave men still die.

The time has come for some new initiatives. Repeating the old formulas
and the tired rhetoric of the past is not enough. When Americans are risking their lives in war it is the responsibility of their leaders to take some risks
for peace.

I would like to report to you tonight on some of the things we have been doing in the past four months to bring true peace. And then I would like to make some concrete proposals to speed that day.

Our first step began before Inauguration. This was to launch an intensive review of every aspect of the nation's Vietnam policy. We accepted nothing on faith. We challenged every assumption and every statistic. We made a systematic, serious examination of all the alternatives open to us. We carefully considered recommendations offered both by critics and supporters of past policies.

From the review it became clear at once that the new Administration faced a set of immediate operational problems. The other side was preparing for a new offensive. There was a wide gulf of distrust between Washington and Saigon. In eight months of talks in Paris there had been no negotiations directly concerned with a final settlement.

And therefore, we moved on several fronts at once. We frustrated the attack which was launched in late February. As a result the North Vietnamese and the Vietcong failed to achieve their military objective.

We restored a close working relationship with Saigon. And in the resulting atmosphere of mutual confidence President Thieu and his government have taken important initiatives in the search for a settlement.

We speeded up the strengthening of the South Vietnamese forces. And I am glad to report tonight that as a result General Abrams told me on Monday that progress in the training program had been excellent and that apart from any developments that may occur in the negotiations in Paris the time is approaching when South Vietnamese forces will be able to take over some of the fighting fronts now being manned by Americans.

In weighing alternate courses, we have had to recognize that the situation as it exists today is far different from what it was two years ago, or four years ago, or 10 years ago. One difference is that we no longer have the choice of not intervening. We've crossed that bridge. There are now more than half a million American troops in Vietnam and 35,000 Americans have lost their lives.

We can have honest debate about whether we should have entered the war in Vietnam. We can have honest debate about how the war has been conducted. But the urgent question today is what to do now that we are there. And against that background let me discuss first what we have rejected and second, what we are prepared to accept.

We have ruled out attempting to impose a purely military solution on the battlefield. We have also ruled out either a one-sided withdrawal from Vietnam, or the acceptance in Paris of terms that would amount to a disguised American defeat.

When we assumed the burden of helping defend South Vietnam, millions of South Vietnamese men, women and children placed their trust in us. To abandon them now would mean a massacre that would shock and dismay everyone in the world who values human life.

Abandoning the South Vietnamese people, however, would jeopardize more than lives in South Vietnam. It would threaten our long-term hopes for peace in the world. A great nation cannot renege on its pledges. A great nation must be worthy of trust.

When it comes to maintaining peace, "prestige" is not an empty word. I am not speaking of false pride or bravado—they should have no place in our policies. I speak rather of the respect that one nation has for another's integrity in defending its principles and meeting its obligations.

If we simply abandon our effort in Vietnam, the cause of peace might not survive the damage that would be done to other nations' confidence in our reliability.

Another reason for not withdrawing unilaterally stems from debates within the Communist world between those who argue for a policy of containment or confrontation with the United States and those who argue against it. If Hanoi were to succeed in taking over South Vietnam by force—even after the power of the United States has been engaged, it would greatly strengthen those leaders who scorn negotiation, who advocate aggression and who minimize the risk of confrontation with the United States. It would bring peace now but it would enormously increase the danger of a bigger war later.

If we are to move successfully from an era of confrontation to an era of negotiation, then we have to demonstrate—at the point at which confrontation is being tested—that confrontation with the United States is costly and unrewarding.

Almost without exception, the leaders of non-Communist Asia have told me that they would consider a one-sided American withdrawal from Vietnam to be a threat to the security of their own nations.

In determining what choices would be acceptable, we have to understand our essential objective in Vietnam. What we want is very little but very fundamental. We seek the opportunity for the South Vietnamese people to determine their own political future without outside interference.

Let me put it plainly: What the United States wants for South Vietnam is not the important thing. What North Vietnam wants for South Vietnam is not the important thing. What is important is what the people of South Vietnam want for South Vietnam.

The United States has suffered over a million casualties in four wars in this century. Whatever faults we may have as a nation, we have asked nothing for ourselves in return for those sacrifices. We have been generous toward those whom we have fought. We've helped our former foes as well as our friends in the task of reconstruction. We are proud of this record and we bring the same attitude in our search for a settlement in Vietnam.

In this spirit let me be explicit about several points:

We seek no bases in Vietnam.

We seek no military ties.

We are willing to agree to neutrality for South Vietnam if that is what the South Vietnamese people freely choose.

We believe that there should be an opportunity for full participation in the political life of South Vietnam by all political elements that are prepared to do so without the use of force or intimidation.

We are prepared to accept any government in South Vietnam that results from the free choice of the South Vietnamese people themselves.

We have no intention of imposing any form of government upon the people of South Vietnam, nor will we be a party to such coercion.

In pursuing our limited objective we insist on no rigid diplomatic formula. Peace could be achieved by an informal understanding, provided that the understanding is clear and that there were adequate assurances that it would be observed.

Peace on paper is not as important as peace in fact. And so this brings us to the matter of negotiations.

We must recognize that peace in Vietnam cannot be achieved overnight. A war that has raged for many years will require detailed negotiations and cannot be settled by a single stroke.

What kind of a settlement will permit the South Vietnamese people to determine freely their own political future? Such a settlement will require the withdrawal of all non-South Vietnamese forces, including our own, in South Vietnam, and procedures for political choice that give each significant groups in South Vietnam a real opportunity to participate in the political life of the nation.

To implement these principles I reaffirm now our willingness to withdraw our forces on a specified timetable. We ask only that North Vietnam withdraw its forces from South Vietnam, Cambodia and Laos into North Vietnam also in accordance with a timetable.

We include Cambodia and Laos to insure that these countries would not be used as bases for a renewed war. Our offer provides for a simultaneous start on withdrawal by both sides, for agreement on a mutually acceptable timetable and for the withdrawal to be accomplished quickly.

The North Vietnamese delegates have been saying in Paris that political issues should be discussed along with military issues and that there must be a political settlement in the South. We do not dispute this but the military withdrawal involves outside forces and can therefore be properly negotiated by North Vietnam and the United States, with the concurrence of its allies.

The political settlement is an internal matter which ought to be decided among the South Vietnamese themselves and not imposed by outsiders.

However, if our presence at these political negotiations would be helpful and if the South Vietnamese concerned agreed, we would be willing to participate along with the representatives of Hanoi, if that, also, were desired.

Recent statements by President Thieu have gone far toward opening the way to a political settlement. He has publicly declared his government's willingness to discuss a political solution with the National Liberation Front and has offered free elections.

This was a dramatic step forward. A reasonable offer that could lead to a settlement.

The South Vietnamese Government has offered to talk without preconditions. I believe the other side should also be willing to talk without preconditions. The South Vietnam Government recognizes as we do that a settlement must permit all persons and groups that are prepared to renounce the use of force to participate freely in the political life of South Vietnam.

To be effective, such a settlement would require two things. First, a process that would allow the South Vietnamese people to express their choice and second, a guarantee that this process would be a fair one.

We do not insist on a particular form of guarantee, but the important thing is that the guarantee should have the confidence of the South Vietnamese people and that they should be broad enough to protect the interests of all major South Vietnamese groups.

This, then, is the outline of the settlement that we seek to negotiate in Paris. Its basic terms are very simple. Mutual withdrawal of non-South Vietnamese forces from South Vietnam and free choice for the people of South Vietnam. I believe that the long-term interests of peace require that we insist on no less and that the realities of the situation require that we seek no more.

And now, to make very concrete what I have said, I propose the following specific measures which seem to me consistent with the principles of all parties. These proposals are made on the basis of full consultation with President Thieu:

As soon as agreement can be reached, all non-South Vietnamese forces would begin withdrawals from South Vietnam. Over a period of 12 months, by agreed-upon stages, the major portions of all U.S., allied and other non-South Vietnamese forces would be withdrawn.

At the end of this 12-month period the remaining United States, allied and other non-South Vietnamese forces would move into designated base areas and would not engage in combat operations.

The remaining U.S. and allied forces would complete their withdrawal as the remaining North Vietnamese forces were withdrawn and returned to North Vietnam.

An international supervisory body, acceptable to both sides, would be created for the purpose of verifying withdrawal, and for any other purpose agreed upon between the two sides.

This international body would begin operating in accordance with an agreed timetable and would participate in arranging supervised cease-fire in Vietnam.

As soon as possible after the international body was functioning, elections would be held under agreed procedures and under the supervision of the international body.

Arrangements would be made for the release of prisoners of war on both sides at the earliest possible time.

All parties would agree to observe the Geneva accords of 1954 regarding South Vietnam and Cambodia and the Laos accords of 1962.

I believe this proposal for peace is realistic and takes account of the legitimate interests of all concerned. It is consistent with President Thieu's six points and it can accommodate the various programs put forth by the other side.

We and the government of South Vietnam are prepared to discuss the details with the other side. Secretary Rogers is now in Saigon and he will be discussing with President Thieu how together we may put forward these proposed measures most usefully in Paris.

He will, as well, be consulting with our other Asian allies about these measures while on his Asian trip. However, I would stress that these proposals are not offered on a take-it-or-leave-it basis. We are quite willing to consider other approaches consistent with our principles.

We are willing to talk about anybody's program — Hanoi's four-point, the N.L.F.'s 10 points, provided it can be made consistent with the very few basic principles I have set forth here tonight.

Despite our agreement with several of its points, we welcome the fact that the N.L.F. has put forward its first comprehensive program. We are studying that program carefully.

However, we cannot ignore the fact that immediately after the offer the scale of enemy attacks stepped up and American casualties in Vietnam increased.

Let me make one point clear: If the enemy wants peace with the United States that is not the way to get it.

I have set forth a peace program tonight which is generous in its terms. I have indicated our willingness to consider other proposals. But no greater mistake could be made than to confuse flexibility with weakness, of being reasonable with lack of resolution.

I must also make clear in all candor that if the needless suffering continues this will affect other decisions. Nobody has anything to gain by delaying.

Reports from Hanoi indicate that the enemy has given up hope for a military victory in South Vietnam but is counting on a collapse of American will in the United States. There could be no greater error in judgment.

Let me be quite blunt. Our fighting men are not going to be worn down. Our mediators are not going to be talked down. And our allies are not going to be let down.

My fellow Americans, I have seen the ugly face of war in Vietnam. I've seen the wounded in field hospitals, American boys, South Vietnamese boys, North Vietnamese boys. They were different in many ways—the color of their skins, their religions, their races. Some were enemies, some were friends.

But the differences were small compared with how they were alike. They were brave men. And they were so young. Their lives, their dreams for the future had been shattered by a war over which they had no control.

With all the moral authority of the office which I hold, I say that America could have no greater and prouder role than to help to end this war in a way which will bring nearer that day in which we can have a world order in which people can live together in peace and friendship.

I do not criticize those who disagree with me on the conduct of our peace negotiations. And I do not ask unlimited patience from a people whose hopes for peace have too often been raised and then cruelly dashed over the past four years.

I have tried to present the facts about Vietnam with complete honesty. And I shall continue to do so in my reports to the American people.

Tonight, all I ask is that you consider these facts. And whatever our differences that you support a program which can lead to a peace we can live with and a peace we can be proud of.

Nothing could have a greater effect in convincing the enemy that he should negotiate in good faith than to see the American people united behind a generous and reasonable peace offer.

In my campaign for the Presidency, I pledged to end this war in a way that would increase our chances to win true and lasting peace in Vietnam, in the Pacific and in the world.

I am determined to keep that pledge. If I fail to do so, I expect the American people to hold me accountable for that failure.

But while I will never raise false expectations, my deepest hope, as I speak to you tonight, is that we shall be able to look back on this day as that critical turning point when American initiative moved us off dead center and forward to the time when this war will be brought to an end, and when we shall be able to devote the unlimited energies and dedication of the American people to the exciting challenges of peace.

Thank you.

Cambodia

Richard Milhous Nixon

This speech was delivered as a nationwide broadcast from the White House, April 31, 1970. Published version: Vital Speeches of the Day, *May 15, 1970, pp. 450-52.*

Good evening my fellow Americans. Ten days ago in my report to the nation on Vietnam I announced a decision to withdraw an additional 150,000 Americans from Vietnam over the next year. I said then that I was making that decision despite our concern over increased enemy activity in Laos, in Cambodia and in South Vietnam.

And at that time I warned that if I concluded that increased enemy activity in any of these areas endangered the lives of Americans remaining in Vietnam, I would not hesitate to take strong and effective measures to deal with that situation.

Despite that warning, North Vietnam has increased its military aggression in all these areas, and particularly in Cambodia.

After full consultation with the National Security Council, Ambassador Bunker, General Abrams and my other advisors, I have concluded that the actions of the enemy in the last 10 days clearly endanger the lives of Americans who are in Vietnam now and would constitute an unacceptable risk to those who will be there after withdrawal of another 150,000.

To protect our men who are in Vietnam, and to guarantee the continued success of our withdrawal and Vietnamization program, I have concluded that the time has come for action.

Tonight, I shall describe the actions of the enemy, the actions I have ordered to deal with that situation, and the reasons for my decision.

Cambodia — a small country of seven million people — has been a neutral nation since the Geneva Agreement of 1954, an agreement, incidentally, which was signed by the government of North Vietnam.

American policy since then has been to scrupulously respect the neutrality of the Cambodian people. We have maintained a skeleton diplomatic mission of fewer than 15 in Cambodia's capital, and that only since last August.

For the previous four years, from 1965 to 1969 we did not have any diplomatic mission whatever in Cambodia, and for the past five years we have provided no military assistance whatever and no economic assistance to Cambodia.

North Vietnam, however, has not respected that neutrality. For the past five years, as indicated on this map, as you see here, North Vietnam has occupied military sanctuaries all along the Cambodian frontier with South Vietnam. Some of these extend up to 20 miles into Cambodia.

The sanctuaries are in red, and as you note they are on both sides of the border.

They are used for hit-and-run attacks on American and South Vietnamese forces in South Vietnam. These Communist-occupied territories contain major base camps, training sites, logistics facilities, weapons and ammunition factories, airstrips and prisoner of war compounds.

And for five years neither the United States nor South Vietnam has moved against these enemy sanctuaries because we did not with to violate the territory of a neutral nation.

Even after the Vietnamese Communists began to expand these sanctuaries four weeks ago, we counseled patience to our South Vietnamese allies and imposed restraints on our own commanders.

In contrast to our policy the enemy in the past two weeks has stepped up his guerrilla actions and he is concentrating his main force in these sanctuaries that you see in this map, where they are building up the large massive attacks on our forces and those of South Vietnam.

North Vietnam in the last two weeks has stripped away all pretense of respecting the sovereignty or the neutrality of Cambodia. Thousands of their soldiers are invading the country from the sanctuaries. They are encircling the capital of Pnompenh. Coming from these sanctuaries as you see here, they had moved into Cambodia and are encircling the capital.

Cambodia, as a result of this, has sent out a call to the United States, to a number of other nations, for assistance. Because if this enemy effort succeeds, Cambodia would become a vast enemy staging area and a springboard for attacks on South Vietnam along 600 miles of frontier: a refuge where enemy troops could return from combat without fear of retaliation.

North Vietnamese men and supplies could then be poured into that country, jeopardizing not only the lives of our men but the people of South Vietnam as well.

Now confronted with this situation we had three options:

First, we can do nothing. Now, the ultimate result of that course of action is clear. Unless we indulge in wishful thinking, the lives of Americans remaining in Vietnam after our next withdrawal of 150,000 would be gravely threatened.

Let us go to the map again.

Here is South Vietnam. Here is North Vietnam. North Vietnam already occupies this part of Laos. If North Vietnam also occupied this whole band in Cambodia or the entire country, it would mean that South Vietnam was completely outflanked and the forces of Americans in this area as well as the South Vietnamese would be in an untenable military position.

Our second choice is to provide massive military assistance to Cambodia itself and, unfortunately, while we deeply sympathize with the plight of seven million Cambodians whose country has been invaded, massive amounts of military assistance could not be rapidly and effectively utilized by this small Cambodian Army against the immediate trap.

With other nations we shall do our best to provide the small arms and other equipment which the Cambodian Army of 40,000 needs and can use for its defense.

But the aid we will provide will be limited for the purpose of enabling Cambodia to defend its neutrality and not for the purpose of making it an active belligerent on one side or the other.

Our third choice is to go to the heart of the trouble.

And that means cleaning out major North Vietnamese- and Vietcong-occupied territories, these sanctuaries which serve as bases for attacks on both Cambodia and American and South Vietnamese forces in South Vietnam.

Some of these, incidentally are as close to Saigon as Baltimore is to Washington. This one, for example, is called the Parrots' Beak — it's only 33 miles from Saigon.

Now faced with these three options, this is the decision I have made. In co-operation with the armed forces of South Vietnam, attacks are being launched this week to clean out major enemy sanctuaries on the Cambodian-Vietnam border. A major responsibility for the ground operation is being assumed by South Vietnamese forces.

For example, the attacks in several areas, including the parrot's beak, that I referred to a moment ago, are exclusively South Vietnamese ground operations, under South Vietnamese command, with the United States providing air and logistical support.

There is one area however, immediately above the parrot's beak where I have concluded that a combined American and South Vietnamese operation is necessary.

And now, let me give you the reasons for my decision.

A majority of the American people, a majority of you listening to me are for the withdrawal of our forces from Vietnam. The action I have taken tonight is indispensable for the continuing success of that withdrawal program.

A majority of the American people want to end this war rather than to have it drag on interminably.

The action I have taken tonight will serve that purpose.

A majority of the American people want to keep the casualties of our brave men in Vietnam at an absolute minimum.

Tonight, American and South Vietnamese units will attack the headquarters for the entire Communist military operation in South Vietnam. This key control center has been occupied by the North Vietnemese and Vietcong for five years in blatant violation of Cambodia's neutrality.

This is not an invasion of Cambodia. The areas in which these attacks will be launched are completely occupied and controlled by North Vietnamese forces.

Our purpose is not to occupy the areas. Once enemy forces are driven out of these sanctuaries and once their military supplies are destroyed, we will withdraw.

These actions are in no way directed to security interests of any nation. Any government that chooses to use these actions as a pretext for harming relations with the United States will be doing so on its own responsibility and on its own initiative and we will draw the appropriate conclusions.

The action I take tonight is essential if we are to accomplish that goal.

We take this action not for the purpose of expanding the war into Cambodia but for the purpose of ending the war in Vietnam, and winning the just peace we all desire.

We have made and will continue to make every possible effort to end this war through negotiation at the conference table rather than through more fighting in the battlefield.

Let's look again at the record.

We stopped the bombing of North Vietnam. We have cut air operations by over 20 per cent. We've announced the withdrawal of over 250,000 of our men. We've offered to withdraw all of our men if they will withdraw theirs. We've offered to negotiate all issues with only one condition: and that is that the future of South Vietnam be determined, not by North Vietnam, and not by the United States, but by the people of South Vietnam themselves.

The answer of the enemy has been intransigence at the conference table, belligerence at Hanoi, massive military aggression in Laos and Cambodia and stepped-up attacks in South Vietnam designed to increase American casualties.

This attitude has become intolerable.

We will not react to this threat to American lives merely by plaintive diplomatic protests.

If we did, credibility of the United States would be destroyed in every area of the world where only the power of the United States deters aggression.

Tonight, I again warn the North Vietnamese that if they continue to escalate the fighting when the United States is withdrawing its forces, I shall meet my responsibility as commander in chief of our armed forces to take the action I consider necessary to defend the security of our American men.

The action I have announced tonight puts the leaders of North Vietnam on notice that we will be patient in working for peace. We will be conciliatory at the conference table, but we will not be humiliated. We will not be defeated.

We will not allow American men by the thousands to be killed by an enemy from privileged sanctuary.

The time came long ago to end this war through peaceful negotiations. We stand ready for those negotiations. We've made major efforts many of which must remain secret.

I say tonight all the offers and approaches made previously remain on the conference table whenever Hanoi is ready to negotiate seriously.

But if the enemy response to our most conciliatory offers for peaceful negotiation continues to be to increase its attacks and humiliate and defeat us, we shall react accordingly.

My fellow Americans, we live in an age of anarchy, both abroad and at home. We see mindless attacks on all the great institutions which have been created by free civilizations in the last 500 years. Even here in the United States, great universities are being systematically destroyed.

Small nations all over the world find themselves under attack from within and from without. If when the chips are down the world's most powerful nation—the United States of America—acts like a pitiful, helpless giant, the forces of totalitarianism and anarchy will threaten free nations and free institutions throughout the world.

It is not our power but our will and character that is being tested tonight.

The question all Americans must ask and answer tonight is this:

Does the richest and strongest nation in the history of the world have the character to meet a direct challenge by a group which rejects every effort to win a just peace, ignores our warning, tramples on solemn agreements, violates the neutrality of an unarmed people and uses our prisoners as hostages?

If we fail to meet this challenge all other nations will be on notice that despite its overwhelming power the United States when a real crisis comes will be found wanting.

During my campaign for the Presidency, I pledged to bring Americans home from Vietnam. They are coming home. I promised to end this war. I shall keep that promise. I promised to win a just peace. I shall keep that promise.

We shall avoid a wider war, but we are also determined to put an end to this war.

In this room, Woodrow Wilson made the great decision which led to victory in World War I.

Franklin Roosevelt made the decisions which led to our victory in World War II.

Dwight D. Eisenhower made decisions which ended the war in Korea and avoided war in the Middle East.

John F. Kennedy in his finest hour made the great decision which removed Soviet nuclear missiles from Cuba and the western hemisphere.

I have noted that there's been a great deal of discussion with regard to this decision I have made. And I should point out that I do not contend that it is in the same magnitude as these decisions that I have just mentioned.

But between those decisions and this decision, there is a difference that is very fundamental. In those decisions the American people were not assailed by counsels of doubt and defeat from some of the most widely known opinion leaders of the nation.

I have noted, for example, that a Republican Senator has said that this action I have taken means that my party has lost all chance of winning the November elections, and others are saying today that this move against enemy sanctuaries will make me a one-term President.

No one is more aware than I am of the political consequences of the action I've taken. It is tempting to take the easy political path, to blame this war on previous Administrations, and to bring all of our men home immediately — regardless of the consequences, even though that would mean defeat for the United States; to desert 18 million South Vietnamese people who have put their trust in us; to expose them to the same slaughter and savagery which the leaders of North Vietnam inflicted on hundreds of thousands of North Vietnamese who chose freedom when the Communists took over North Vietnam in 1954.

To get peace at any price now, even though I know that a peace of humiliation for the United States would lead to a bigger war or surrender later.

I have rejected all political considerations in making this decision. Whether my party gains in November is nothing compared to the lives of 400,000 brave Americans fighting for our country and for the cause of peace and freedom in Vietnam.

Whether I may be a one-term President is insignificant compared to whether by our failure to act in this crisis the United States proves itself to be unworthy to lead the forces of freedom in this critical period in world history.

I would rather be a one-term president and do what I believe was right than to be a two-term President at the cost of seeing America become a second-rate power and to see this nation accept the first defeat in its proud 190-year history.

I realize in this war there are honest, deep differences in this country about whether we should have become involved, that there are differences to how the war should have been conducted.

But the decision I announce tonight transcends those differences, for the lives of American men are involved. The opportunity for 150,000 Americans to come home in the next 12 months is involved. The future of 18-million people in South Vietnam and 7-million people in Cambodia is involved, the possibility of winning a just peace in Vietnam and in the Pacific is at stake.

It is customary to conclude a speech from the White House by asking support for the President of the United States.

Tonight, I depart from that precedent. What I ask is far more important. I ask for your support for our brave men fighting tonight halfway around the world, not for territory, not for glory but so that their younger brothers and their sons and your sons can have a chance to grow up in a world of peace and freedom, and justice.

Thank you, and good night.

The Serious Situation in Little Rock

Dwight David Eisenhower

General Eisenhower (October 14, 1890 - March 29, 1969) was graduated from the United States Military Academy in 1915; he rose from second lieutenant in 1915 to General of the Army, 1944; Army Chief of Staff, 1945-48; president of Columbia University, 1948-52; 34th President of the United States, 1953-61. The speech was delivered from the White House, Washington, D.C., September 24, 1957. Published version: Vital Speeches of the Day, *October 15, 1957, pp. 11-12.*

Good evening, My Fellow Citizens: For a few minutes this evening I want to talk to you about the serious situation that has arisen in Little Rock. To make this talk I have come to the President't office in the White House. I could have spoken from Rhode Island, where I have been staying recently, but I felt that, in speaking from the house of Lincoln, of Jackson and of Wilson, my words would better convey both the sadness I feel in the action I was compelled today to take and the firmness with which I intend to pursue this course until the orders of the Federal Court at Little Rock can be executed without unlawful interference.

In that city, under the leadership of demagogic extremists, disorderly mobs have deliberately prevented the carrying out of proper orders from a Federal Court. Local authorities have not eliminated that violent opposition and, under the law, I yesterday issued a Proclamation calling upon the mob to disperse.

This morning the mob again gathered in front of the Central High School of Little Rock, obviously for the purpose of again preventing the carrying out of the Court's order relating to the admission of Negro children to that school.

Whenever normal agencies prove inadequate to the task and it becomes necessary for the Executive Branch of the Federal Government to use its powers and authority to uphold Federal Courts, the President's responsibility is inescapable.

In accordance with that responsibility, I have today issued an Executive Order directing the use of troops under Federal authority to aid in the execution of Federal law at Little Rock, Arkansas. This became necessary when my Proclamation of yesterday was not observed, and the obstruction of justice still continues.

It is important that the reasons for my action be understood by all our citizens.

As you know, the Supreme Court of the United States has decided that separate public educational facilities for the races are inherently unequal and therefore compulsory school segregation laws are unconstitutional.

Our personal opinions about the decision have no bearing on the matter of enforcement; the responsibility and authority of the Supreme Court to interpret the Constitution are very clear. Local Federal Courts were instructed by the Supreme Court to issue such orders and decrees as might be necessary to achieve admission to public schools without regard to race—and with all deliberate speed.

During the past several years, many communities in our Southern States have instituted public school plans for gradual progress in the enrollment and attendance of school children of all races in order to bring themselves into compliance with the law of the land.

They thus demonstrated to the world that we are a nation in which laws, not men, are supreme.

I regret to say that this truth—the cornerstone of our liberties—was not observed in this instance.

It was my hope that this localized situation would be brought under control by city and State authorities. If the use of local police powers had been sufficient, our traditional method of leaving the problem in those hands would have been pursued. But when large gatherings of obstructionists made it impossible for the decrees of the Court to be carried out, both the law and the national interest demanded that the President take action.

Here is the sequence of events in the development of the Little Rock school case.

In May of 1955, the Little Rock School Board approved a moderate plan for the gradual desegregation of the public schools in that city. It provided that a start toward integration would be made at the present term in the high school, and that the plan would be in full operation by 1963. Here I might say that in a number of communities in Arkansas integration in the schools has already started and without violence of any kind. Now this Little Rock plan was challenged in the courts by some who believed that the period of time as proposed in the plan was too long.

The United States Court at Little Rock, which has supervisory responsibility under the law for the plan of desegregation in the public schools, dismissed the challenge, thus approving a gradual rather than an abrupt change from the existing system. The court found that the school board had acted in good faith in planning for a public school system free from racial discrimination.

Since that time, the court has on three separate occasions issued orders directing that the plan be carried out. All persons were instructed to refrain from interfering with the efforts of the school board to comply with the law.

Proper and sensible observance of the law then demanded the respectful obedience which the nation has a right to expect from all its people. This, unfortunately, has not been the case at Little Rock. Certain misguided persons, many of them imported into Little Rock by agitators, have insisted upon defying the law and have sought to bring it into disrepute. The orders of the court have thus been frustrated.

The very basis of our individual rights and freedoms rests upon the certainty that the President and the Executive Branch of Government will support and insure the carrying out of the decisions of the Federal Courts, even, when necessary, with all the means at the President's command.

Unless the President did so, anarchy would result.

There would be no security for any except that which each one of us could provide for himself.

The interest of the nation in the proper fulfillment of the law's requirements cannot yield to opposition and demonstrations by some few persons.

Mob rule cannot be allowed to override the decisions of our courts.

Now, let me make it very clear that Federal troops are not being used to relieve local and state authorities of their primary duty to preserve the peace and order of the community. Nor are the troops there for the purpose of taking over the responsibility of the School Board and the other responsible local officials in running Central High School. The running of our school system and the maintenance of peace and order in each of our states are strictly local affairs and the Federal Government does not interfere except in a very few special cases and when requested by one of the several states. In the present case the troops are there, pursuant to law, solely for the purpose of preventing interference with the orders of the Court.

The proper use of the powers of the Executive Branch to enforce the orders of a Federal Court is limited to extraordinary and compelling circumstances. Manifestly, such an extreme situation has been created in Little Rock. This challenge must be met and with such measures as will preserve to the people as a whole their lawfully-protected rights in a climate permitting their free and fair exercise.

The overwhelming majority of our people in every section of the country are united in their respect for observance of the law—even in those cases where they may disagree with that law.

They deplore the call of extremists to violence.

The decision of the Supreme Court concerning school integration, of course, affects the South more seriously than it does other sections of the country. In that region I have many warm friends, some of them in the city of Little Rock. I have deemed it a great personal privilege to spend in our Southland tours of duty while in the military service and enjoyable recreational periods since that time.

So from intimate personal knowledge, I know that the overwhelming majority of the people in the South—including those of Arkansas and of Little Rock—are of good will, united in their efforts to preserve and respect the law even when they disagree with it.

They do not sympathize with mob rule. They, like the rest of our nation, have proved in two great wars their readiness to sacrifice for America.

A foundation of our American way of life is our national respect for law.

In the South, as elsewhere, citizens are keenly aware of the tremendous disservice that has been done to the people of Arkansas in the eyes of the nation, and that has been done to the nation in the eyes of the world.

At a time when we face grave situations abroad because of the hatred that Communism bears toward a system of government based on human rights, it would be difficult to exaggerate the harm that is being done to the prestige and influence, and indeed to the safety, of our nation and the world.

Our enemies are gloating over this incident and using it everywhere to misrepresent our whole nation. We are portrayed as a violator of those standards of conduct which the peoples of the world united to proclaim in the Charter of the United Nations. There they affirmed "faith in fundamental human rights" and "in the dignity and worth of the human person" and they did so "without distinction as to race, sex, language or religion."

And so, with deep confidence, I call upon the citizens of the State of Arkansas to assist in bringing to an immediate end all interference with the law and its processes. If resistance to the Federal Court orders ceases at once, the further presence of Federal troops will be unnecessary and the City of Little Rock will return to its normal habits of peace and order and a blot upon the fair name and high honor of our nation will be removed.

Thus will be restored the image of America and of all its parts as one nation, indivisible, with liberty and justice for all.

Good night, and thank you very much.

Speech to Greater Houston Ministerial Association

John Fitzgerald Kennedy

John Kennedy (May 29, 1917 - November 22, 1963) graduated from Harvard in 1940; he was a member of Congress, 1947 - 53; United States Senator [Massachusetts] 1953 - 61; 35th President of the United States, 1961-63. Published version: New York Times, September 13, 1960, p. 22. The speech was delivered in Houston, Texas, September 12, 1960.

I am grateful for your generous invitation to state my views.

While the so-called religious issue is necessarily and properly the chief topic here tonight, I want to emphasize from the outset that I believe that we have far more critical issues in the 1960 election: the spread of Communist influence, until it now festers only ninety miles off the coast of Florida —the humiliating treatment of our President and Vice President by those who no longer respect our power—the hungry children I saw in West Virginia, the old people who cannot pay their doctor's bills, the families forced to give up their farms—an America with too many slums, with too few schools, and too late to the moon and outer space.

These are the real issues which should decide this campaign. And they are not religious issues—for war and hunger and ignorance and despair know no religious barrier.

But because I am a Catholic, and no Catholic has ever been elected President, the real issues in this campaign have been obscured—perhaps deliberately. In some quarters less responsible than this. So it is apparently necessary for me to state once again—not what kind of church I believe in, for that should be important only to me, but what kind of America I believe in.

I believe in an America where the separation of church and state is absolute—where no Catholic prelate would tell the President (should he be a Catholic) how to act and no Protestant minister would tell his parishioners for whom to vote—where no church or church school is granted any public funds or political preference—and where no man is denied public office merely because his religion differs from the President who might appoint him or the people who might elect him.

I believe in an America that is officially neither Catholic, Protestant nor Jewish—where no public official either requests or accepts instructions on public policy from the Pope, the National Council of Churches or any other ecclesiastical source—where no religious body seeks to impose its will directly or indirectly upon the general populace or the public acts of its officials—and where religious liberty is so indivisible that an act against one church is treated as an act against all.

For, while this year it may be a Catholic against whom the finger of suspicion is pointed, in other years it has been, and may someday be again, a Jew—or a Quaker—or a Unitarian—or a Baptist. It was Virginia's harassment of Baptist preachers, for example, that led to Jefferson's statute of religious freedom. Today, I may be the victim—but tomorrow it may be you—until the whole fabric of our harmonious society is ripped apart at a time of great national peril.

Finally, I believe in an America where religious intolerance will someday end—where all men and all churches are treated as equal—where every man has the same right to attend or not to attend the church of his choice—where there is no Catholic vote, no anti-Catholic vote, no bloc voting of any kind—and where Catholics, Protestants and Jews, both the lay and the pastoral level, will refrain from those attitudes of disdain and division which have so often marred their works in the past, and promote instead the American ideal of brotherhood.

That is the kind of America in which I believe. And it represents the kind of Presidency in which I believe—a great office that must be neither humbled by making it the instrument of any religious group, nor tarnished by arbitrarily withholding it, its occupancy from the members of any religious group. I believe in a President whose views on religion are his own private affair, neither imposed upon him by the nation or imposed by the nation upon him as a condition to holding that office.

I would not look with favor upon a President working to subvert the First Amendment's guarantees of religious liberty (nor would our system of checks and balances permit him to do so). And neither do I look with favor upon those who would work to subvert Article VI of the Constitution by requiring a religious test—even by indirection—for if they disagree with that safeguard, they should be openly working to repeal it.

I want a chief executive whose public acts are responsible to all and obligated to none—who can attend any ceremony, service or dinner his office may appropriately require him to fulfill—and whose fulfillment of his Presidential office is not limited or conditioned by any religious oath, ritual or obligation.

This is the kind of America I believe in—and this is the kind of America I fought for in the South Pacific and the kind my brother died for in Europe. No one suggested then that we might have a "divided loyalty," that we did "not believe in liberty" or that we belonged to a disloyal group that threatened "the freedoms for which our forefathers died."

And in fact this is the kind of America for which our forefathers did die when they fled here to escape religious test oaths, that denied office to members of less favored churches, when they fought for the Constitution, the Bill of Rights, the Virginia Statute of Religious Freedom—and when they fought at the shrine I visited today—the Alamo. For side by side with Bowie and Crockett died Fuentes and McCafferty and Bailey and Bedillio and Carey—but no one knows whether they were Catholics or not. For there was no religious test there.

I ask you tonight to follow in that tradition, to judge me on the basis of fourteen years in the Congress—on my declared stands against an ambassador to the Vatican, against unconstitutional aid to parochial schools, and against any boycott of the public schools (which I attended myself)—and instead of doing this do not judge me on the basis of these pamphlets and publications we have all seen that carefully select quotations out of context from the statements of Catholic Church leaders, usually in other countries, frequently in other centuries, and rarely relevant to any situation here—and always omitting, of course, that statement of the American bishops in 1948 which strongly endorsed church-state separation.

I do not consider these other quotations binding upon my public acts—why should you? But let me say, with respect to other countries, that I am wholly opposed to the state being used by any religious group, Catholic or Protestant, to compel, prohibit or prosecute the free exercise of any other religion. And that goes for any persecution at any time, by anyone, in any country.

And I hope that you and I condemn with equal fervor those nations which deny their Presidency to Protestants and those which deny it to Catholics. And rather than cite the misdeeds of those who differ, I would also cite the record of the Catholic Church in such nations as France and Ireland—and the independence of such statesmen as de Gaulle and Adenauer.

But let me stress again that these are my views—for, contrary to common newspaper usage, I am not the Catholic candidate for President. I am the Democratic party's candidate for President who happens also to be a Catholic.

I do not speak for my church on public matters—and the church does not speak for me.

Whatever issue may come before me as President, if I should be elected—on birth control, divorce, censorship, gambling, or any other subject—I will make my decision in accordance with these views, in accordance with what my conscience tells me to be in the national interest, and without regard to outside religious pressure or dictate. And no power or threat of punishment could cause me to decide otherwise.

But if the time should ever come—and I do not concede any conflict to be remotely possible—when my office would require me to either violate my conscience, or violate the national interest, then I would resign the office, and I hope any other conscientious public servant would do likewise.

But I do not intend to apologize for these views to my critics of either Catholic or Protestant faith, nor do I intend to disavow either my views or my church in order to win this election. If I should lose on the real issues, I shall return to my seat in the Senate satisfied that I tried my best and was fairly judged.

But if this election is decided on the basis that 40,000,000 Americans lost their chance of being President on the day they were baptized, that it is the whole nation that will be the loser in the eyes of Catholics and non-Catholics around the world, in the eyes of history, and in the eyes of our own people.

But if, on the other hand, I should win this election, I shall devote every effort of mind and spirit to fulfilling the oath of the Presidency—practically identical, I might add, with the oath I have taken for fourteen years in the Congress. For, without reservation, I can, and I quote "solemnly swear that I will faithfully execute the office of President of the United States and will to the best of my ability preserve, protect and defend the Constitution, so help me God."

Inaugural Address
John Fitzgerald Kennedy

Published version: Vital Speeches of the Day, *February 1, 1961, pp. 226-227. The speech was delivered in Washington, D.C. on January 20, 1961.*

Vice President Johnson, Mr. Speaker, Mr. Chief Justice, President Eisenhower, Vice President Nixon, President Truman, Reverend Clergy, fellow citizens: We observe today not a victory of party but a celebration of freedom — symbolizing an end as well as a beginning — signifying renewal as well as change. For I have sworn before you and Almighty God the same solemn oath our forebears prescribed nearly a century and three-quarters ago.

The world is very different now. For man holds in his mortal hands the power to abolish all forms of human poverty and all forms of human life. And yet the same revolutionary beliefs for which our forebears fought are still at issue around the globe — the belief that the rights of man come not from the generosity of the state but from the hand of God.

We dare not forget today that we are the heirs of that first revolution. Let the word go forth from this time and place, to friend and foe alike, that the torch has been passed to a new generation of Americans — born in this century, tempered by war, disciplined by a hard and bitter peace, proud of our ancient heritage — and unwilling to witness or permit the slow undoing of those human rights to which this nation has always been committed, and to which we are committed today at home and around the world.

Let every nation know, whether it wishes us well or ill, that we shall pay any price, bear any burden, meet any hardship, support any friend, oppose any foe to assure the survival and the success of liberty.

This much we pledge — and more.

To those old allies whose cultural and spiritual origins we share, we pledge the loyalty of faithful friends. United, there is little we cannot do in a

156

host of new cooperative ventures. Divided, there is little we can do—for we dare not meet a powerful challenge at odds and split asunder.

To those new states whom we welcome to the ranks of the free, we pledge our word that one form of colonial control shall not have passed away merely to be replaced by a far more iron tyranny. We shall not always expect to find them supporting our view. But we shall always hope to find them strongly supporting their own freedom—and to remember that, in the past, those who foolishly sought power by riding the back of the tiger ended up inside.

To those peoples in the huts and villages of half the globe struggling to break the bonds of mass misery, we pledge our best efforts to help them help themselves, for whatever period is required—not because the Communists may be doing it, not because we seek their votes, but because it is right. If a free society cannot help the many who are poor, it can not save the few who are rich.

To our sister republics south of our border, we offer a special pledge—to convert our good words into good deeds—in a new alliance for progress—to assist free men and free governments in casting off the chains of poverty. But this peaceful revolution of hope cannot become the prey of hostile powers. Let all our neighbors know that we shall join with them to oppose aggression or subversion anywhere in the Americas. And let every other power know that this hemisphere intends to remain the master of its own house.

To that world assembly of sovereign states, the United Nations, our last best hope in an age where the instruments of war have far outpaced the instruments of peace, we renew our pledge of support—to prevent it from becoming merely a forum for invective—to strengthen its shield of the new and the weak—and to enlarge the area in which its writ may run.

Finally, to those nations who would make themselves our adversary, we offer not a pledge but a request: that both sides begin anew the quest for peace, before the dark powers of destruction unleashed by science engulf all humanity in planned or accidental self-destruction.

We dare not tempt them with weakness. For only when our arms are sufficient beyond doubt can we be certain beyond doubt that they will never be employed.

But neither can two great and powerful groups of nations take comfort from our present course—both sides overburdened by the cost of modern weapons, both rightly alarmed by the steady spread of the deadly atom, yet both racing to alter that uncertain balance of terror that stays the hand of mankinds final war.

So let us begin anew—remembering on both sides that civility is not a sign of weakness, and sincerity is always subject to proof. Let us never negotiate out of fear. But let us never fear to negotiate.

Let both sides explore what problems unite us instead of belaboring those problems which divide us.

Let both sides, for the first time, formulate serious and precise proposals for the inspection and control of arms—and bring the absolute power to destroy other nations under the absolute control of all nations.

Let both sides seek to invoke the wonders of science instead of its terrors. Together let us explore the stars, conquer the deserts, eradicate disease, tap the ocean depths and encourage the arts and commerce.

Let both sides unite to heed in all corners of the earth the command of Isaiah—to "undo the heavy burdens...[and] let the oppressed go free."

And if a beach-head of co-operation may push back the jungles of suspicion, let both sides join in creating a new endeavor not a new balance of power, but a new world of law, where the strong are just and the weak secure and the peace preserved.

All this will not be finished in the first 100 days. Nor will it be finished in the first 1,000 days, nor in the life of this Administration, nor even perhaps in our lifetime on this planet. But let us begin.

In your hands, my fellow citizens, more than mine, will rest the final success or failure of our course. Since this country was founded, each generation of Americans has been summoned to give testimony to its national loyalty. The graves of young Americans who answered the call to service surround the globe.

Now the trumpet summons us again—not as a call to bear arms, though arms we need—not as a call to battle, though embattled we are—but a call to bear the burden of a long twilight struggle year in and year out, "rejoicing in hope, patient in tribulation"—a struggle against the common enemies of man: tyranny, poverty, disease and war itself.

Can we forge against these enemies a grand and global alliance, north and south, east and west, that can assure a more fruitful life for all mankind? Will you join in that historic effort?

In the long history of the world, only a few generations have been granted the role of defending freedom in its hour of maximum danger. I do not shrink from this responsibility—I welcome it. I do not believe that any of us would exchange places with any other people or any other generation. The energy, the faith, the devotion which we bring to this endeavor will light our country and all who serve it—and the glow from that fire can truly light the world.

And so, my fellow Americans: ask not what your country can do for you—ask what you can do for your country.

My fellow citizens of the world: ask not what America will do for you, but what together we can do for the freedom of man.

Finally, whether you are citizens of America or citizens of the world, ask of us here the same high standards of strength and sacrifice which we ask of you. With a good conscience our only sure reward, with history the final judge of our deeds, let us go forth to lead the land we love, asking His blessing and His help, but knowing that here on earth God's work must truly be our own.

Ask Not What a Youngster Can Do For You: Kennedy's Inaugural Address

Dan F. Hahn

Dr. Hahn is Professor of Communication, Queens College of City University of New York. This essay originally appeared in Presidential Studies Quarterly, *12 (1982), 610-14, and is reprinted with permission of the Center for the Study of the Presidency.*

On January 20, 1961 the youngest man ever to be elected to the White House was sworn in as President of the United States. Notable, in addition to the conspicuousness of his youth, was the fact that he had been elected by one of the narrowest margins in the history of the presidency. These two facts were not unrelated, for one of the suspicions about him during the campaign, thus one of the possible causes for the slimness of his victory margin, had been the question of whether he was old enough, mature enough, wise enough for the office.

Consequently, one of the problems facing the young President on his inaugural day was the need to improve his ethos with the American public—specifically, by demonstrating his maturity. But such a demonstration was not without its drawbacks, for he could not afford to sacrifice the image of youthful vigor which had impressed another element of the public. And the two elements, maturity and youthfulness, had to be connected in such a natural way that they could mold into a single unified speech. What follows is an analysis of how John Kennedy accomplished these diverse goals in his Inaugural Address.

Maturity

In demonstrating that he was old enough for the office, Mr. Kennedy exhibited (1) his rationality, (2) what Professor Kenny has called "antiquing by association,"[1] and (3) his reverence.

Rationality

Stylistically, Kennedy's inaugural is best remembered for its abundance of antitheses. The most famous quotation from the speech, "ask not what your country can do for you; ask what you can do for your country,"[2] and the second most famous, "Let us never negotiate out of fear. But let us never fear to negotiate," are both examples of antithesis. There are another twenty-eight examples of antithesis in the speech.

Edward Kennedy has traced the relation of this reliance upon antithesis to Kennedy's establishment of rationality in this speech:

> antithesis is ideally suited to a problem-solution posture.... It is rational because it reduces contention [to] a struggle between *only* two forces. It creates the illusion of a sifting, elimination process in which reason can cut through to the central core of problems.
>
> ...Antithesis places issues and forces in contrast. But in doing so it suggests "we should do this" only *after* a consideration of the consequences of "doing that." The result of such repeated use of antithesis is a consolidation of the suggestion that innovation would be proposed only *after* thoughtfulness. Decision would come *after* debate.[3]

In short, young Kennedy's use of antithesis proved that he would be judicious, would weigh all alternatives before acting; his employment of antithesis demonstrated his rationality.

Additionally, it should be noted that antithesis present dualities, thus one who utilizes them demonstrates his allegiance to the dualism which epitomizes Western thought. Furthermore, the specific contents of the

---

[1] Edward J. Kenny, "Another Look at Kennedy's Inaugural Address," *Today's Speech,* 13 (November, 1965) p. 18.

[2] All quotations from the speech are from John F. Kennedy, "For the Freedom of Man; We Must All Work Together," *Vital Speeches of the Day,* 27 (February 1, 1961) 226-227.

[3] Kenny, *op. cit.*

dualities found in this speech reinforced the American thought of that day, specifically the contemporary orientation toward Communism. When Kennedy pitted friends versus foes, nations that wish us well versus those that wish us ill, and instruments of war versus instruments of peace, he was demonstrating his understanding of the East-West, Communism-Capitalism dichotomy—an understanding which perfectly paralleled the understanding of his audience, hence proved to that audience his rationality. Thus did President Kennedy prove his maturity by demonstrating his rationality through employment of the stylistic trope of antithesis.

Antiquing by Association

When Professor Kenny coined the phrase, "antiquing by association," he had reference to the fact that Kennedy was preceded in the inaugural festivities by the octogenerian poet, Robert Frost, and that Kennedy's presentation took on, by association, some of the wisdom of Frost's age.

Without denying that possibility, I want to suggest that more significant examples of "antiquing by association" can be found in the speech itself. Most obvious, perhaps, are the many references in the speech to the revered American forefathers. In the first paragraph, Kennedy points out that the oath of office he had just sworn was "the same solemn oath our forebears prescribed nearly a century and three quarters ago."

On a more substantive level, in the next paragraph he argued that "the same revolutionary beliefs for which our forebears fought are still at issue around the globe." Then, to demonstrate that he understood the nature of that revolutionary dispute, he identified it as "the belief that the rights of man come not from the generosity of the state, but from the hand of God." Hence, not only did Kennedy identify with the forefathers, he demonstrated that he understood that their revolution centered upon what the Declaration of Independence called the "self-evident" truth that all beings "are endowed by their Creator with certain unalienable rights." And in the next paragraph he identified himself with those who are "proud of our ancient heritage."

Later in the speech, in a much more oblique reference, he spoke of how energy, faith and devotion could "light our country," and argued, "the glow from that fire can truly light the world." To those attuned to such historical parallels, the fire seen round the world brings to mind the "shot heard round the world" from Lexington, Concord, the totality of the American revolution and the forefathers who fought it.

Additional "antiquing by association" can be found in the style of the speech. Again, the use of antitheses is significant, for antithesis is "an archaic language form'''[4] and the use of it insinuates an association with an older rhetoric.

But Kennedy's use of archaic language was not limited to antitheses, for words archaic, or at least long out of use, were sprinkled liberally throughout the speech. The passing of "the torch" suggests the ancient olympics, "split asunder" recalls the language of the Bible, "writ" implies ancient, perhaps Latin, legalities, "the quest" reminds us of the Middle Ages and "the trumpet" calls forth visions of the tumbling walls of Jericho.

A speaker armed with such linguistic and referential associations with antiquity could go far toward dispelling a youthful image.

Reverence

But Kennedy's efforts at demonstrating maturity did not stop there, for he also dissolved fears about his youth with his reverence. The popular assumption about youth is that they are irreverent—to the religion of their parents, to the ideas of their country, to the history of their people. In each of these realms Kennedy demonstrated reverence, thus maturity.

"God" has been defined as a word in the last sentence of a political speech. But Kennedy did not limit himself to such a formulaic reference to religious belief. In the first paragraph he pointed out that his oath of office was sworn before not only the citizenry but also "Almighty God." As already indicated, later he identified himself with those who believe that "the rights of man" come from "the hand of God."

He also referred to the "spiritual origins" we share with our "old allies," quoted Isiah's command to "undo the heavy burdens and let the oppressed go free," and ended with the thought that "here on earth God's work must truly be our own." Thus the religious references, without being oppressively heavy-handed, were scattered throughout the speech.

Kennedy also demonstrated his reverence for the pantheon of American values, chiefly peace and freedom.[5] Of the twenty-seven paragraphs in the speech, eleven were devoted to peace, eight to freedom and two linked these dual concerns. When it is realized that the remaining six paragraphs included the introduction, the conclusion and the transitions, it becomes more apparent to what degree the speech was centered on those two values.

An additional element of Kennedy's appeal in the realm of values was his use of phraseology reminding the audience of Lincoln. Most notably, his "united, there is little we cannot do... divided, there is little we can do"

[4]*Ibid.*
[5]In a broader context, Carol A. Berthold found that freedom and peace were always the key positive terms in President Kennedy's rhetoric. See "Kenneth Burke's Cluster-Agon Method: Its Development and an Application," *Central States Speech Journal,* 27 (Winter, 1976) 302-309.

and the reference to the hemispheric intention to be "the master of its own house" called to mind similar phraseology of Lincoln's. Many politicians, of course, employ Lincoln's phrases, but Kennedy's utilization, in addition to showing reverence for a highly venerated past president, seemed especially appropriate for the young man elected to that office on the centennial of Lincoln's election, and who had demonstrated exceptional concern for the plight of American Blacks in the course of his campaign.

A corollary of Kennedy's reverence for the values of his audience was his exhibition that he had learned the lessons of history. Specifically, that care must be taken that the overthrow of colonialism not bring to power another set of tyrannical leaders, that tyrants are sometimes tempted by weakness, that the battle against tyranny, poverty, disease and war is never won easily but requires a "long twilight struggle," that history is the final judge of our deeds.

In all of these ways, then, Kennedy asserted his maturity, his wisdom, his denial that "youth is the season of credulity."[6]

However, Kennedy also had to demonstrate that this maturity was accompanied with the youthful vigor which had been so important in his campaign.

Youth

Just as every generation must face the same old problems and fight the same old fights, so it must take into consideration the new. And Kennedy did so early in the address when he pointed out, "The world is very different now. For man holds in his mortal hands the power to abolish all forms of human poverty and all forms of human life." Would the new generation of Americans, epitomized by the new president, have the required rigor?" Yes, said Kennedy, for they were "born in this century, tempered by war, disciplined by a hard and bitter peace [and] proud of [their] ancient heritage."

Strength

One key to that youthful vitality was strength. Here, again, the visual comparison with Robert Frost was valuable, as was the visual contradiction between Kennedy and others on the dais—Chief Justice Warren, President Eisenhower, President Truman, etc.

But the essence of youth summarized in the presence of John Kennedy was not dilettantish, for this generation would "pay any price, bear any

[6]William Pitt, Earl of Chatham. Speech in the House of Commons. January 14, 1766.

burden, meet any hardship, support any friend, oppose any foe.'' Yet this new generation was not made up of warmongers; they preferred cooperation to enmity, peace to war, and wanted to ''explore what problems unite us instead of laboring those problems which divide us.'' Throughout, nonetheless, they were realists, knowing that the agenda could not be completed in a hundred days nor a thousand days but would require a ''year in and year out'' struggle.

Commitment

Despite the difficulty of the tasks, this new generation, ''the heirs of that first revolution,'' were committed to defending human rights and freedom throughout the globe, ''casting off the chains of poverty,'' supporting the United Nations, bringing nuclear weapons under control, eradicating disease and building a world ''where the strong are just and the weak secure and the peace preserved.''

All this, of course, was to be undertaken while continuing the commitment to all the old American values, to continuing old national friendships even as new lines were drawn to the emerging nations, to continuing to guard against ''those nations who would make themselves our adversary'' even as we explored with them ways to replace the ''balance of power'' with ''a new world of law.''

It will be noted that passionate commitment is, while not the exclusive province of youth, at least an assumed characteristic of those years. Thus, asserting commitment implies youthfulness, but doing so in an address which also establishes maturity suggests that the passion would be moderated by wisdom.

Unafraid

Another presumed characteristic of youth is fearlessness. This strong and committed new generation, suggested Kennedy, was not afraid of assuming the burdens he had described. None of them would have ''exchange[d] places with any other people or any other generation.'' As for Kennedy himself, ''I do not shrink from this responsibility—I welcome it.'' So ''let us begin.''

The ''torch'' had ''been passed to a new generation''—strong and committed and unafraid. They were, like Kennedy, young and tough— eager for the challenge and the responsibility.

The Connection

To this point we have seen how Kennedy established his maturity yet simultaneously reinforced his image of youthful vigor. It remains to be demonstrated how he integrated the two images without offending any portion of his audience.

On the surface it would seem that there is nothing more natural than age giving way to youth. It is a father and son custom as old as civilization.

Yet Kennedy did face a ticklish situation. For he was the youngest elected president yet... and he was taking the reins from the oldest. Further, the elder (Eisenhower) had been a highly popular president, reelected by a landslide in '56, whereas Kennedy had slipped in with the tiniest of margins. Hence, this was not a transition based on the "throw the rascals out" tradition. His inaugural could not take as its point of departure the failures of the previous administration.

In a sense, Kennedy faced what many sons have faced—the question of how to ease out the old without accusation; how to introduce change without condemnation. In families, that often is accomplished by transcending any father-son enmity and focusing upon a larger frame—the good of the family or the good of the business.

Kennedy also adopted this strategem of transcendence, pointing out that the inauguration was not a celebration of the victory of youth over age, not a celebration of one party over another, "but a celebration of freedom." The triumph was not his, nor his party's, but the American system's.

True, the old administration was ending. True, the new was beginning. True, there would be changes. But, significantly, there would also be renewal. For the old was inherent in the new—in the inaugural oath "prescribed" by the founders; in the continuation of faith in the revolutionary beliefs and the "human rights to which this Nation has always been committed"; in the continuation of the old national friendships; in the continuation of concern for the values of freedom and peace; in the continuation of loyalty and service to the country, and continuing reverence for those countrymen who had sacrificed their lives around the globe; and in the continuation of the American purpose of fulfilling God's work on earth.

To underline the sense that many of his projects were continuations of traditional concerns, Kennedy utilized phrases like "renew our pledge" and "begin anew." And other linguistic configurations suggested continuity. For instance, if he had wanted merely to call the nation to arms, he could have said "Now the trumpet summons us..." but, having the additional purpose of connecting the old and the young, within his own image and within the nation, he chose to say, "Now the trumpet summons us *again*."

Conclusion

I conclude that Kennedy, faced with the need both to overcome the liabilities and build on the strengths of his youthfulness did so by stressing his rationality, relation to antiquity and reverence while reinforcing his strength, commitment and fearlessness. His mastery of each was reinforced by connecting the two images through a transcendence to the national image of democracy and a demonstration of the continuity of his administration with those that had gone before. The young president thereby proved his mastery of the oldest legal profession on earth.

Arms Quarantine of Cuba

John Fitzgerald Kennedy

Published version: Vital Speeches of the Day, *November 15, 1962, pp. 66-68. This speech was delivered as a nationwide broadcast from the White House, October 22, 1962.*

This government as promised has maintained the closest surveillance of the Soviet military build-up on the island of Cuba.

Within the past week unmistakable evidence has established the fact that a series of offensive missile sites is now in preparation on that imprisoned island.

The purpose of these bases can be none other than to provide a nuclear strike capability against the Western Hemisphere.

Upon receiving the first preliminary hard information of this nature last Tuesday morning at 9 A.M., I directed that our surveillance be stepped up. And having now confirmed and completed our evaluation of the evidence and our decision on a course of action, this Government feels obliged to report this new crisis to you in fullest detail.

The characteristics of these new missile sites indicate two distinct types of installations. Several of them include medium-range ballistic missiles capable of carrying a nuclear warhead for a distance of more than 1,000 nautical miles.

Each of these missiles, in short, is capable of striking Washington, D.C., the Panama Canal, Cape Canaveral, Mexico City or any other city in the southeastern part of the United States, in Central America or in the Caribbean area.

Additional sites not yet completed appear to be designed for intermediate-range ballistic missiles capable of traveling more than twice as far, and thus capable of striking most of the major cities in the Western Hemisphere ranging as far north as Hudson's Bay, Canada, and as far south as Lima, Peru.

In addition, jet bombers, capable of carrying nuclear weapons, are now being uncrated and assembled in Cuba while the necessary air bases are being prepared.

This urgent transformation of Cuba into an important strategic base by the presence of these large long-range and clearly offensive weapons of sudden mass destruction constitutes an explicit threat to the peace and security of all the Americas in flagrant and deliberate defiance of the Rio Pact of 1947, the traditions of this nation and hemisphere, the joint resolution of the 87th Congress, the Charter of the United Nations and my own public warnings to the Soviets on Sept. 4 and 13.

This action also contradicts the repeated assurances of Soviet spokesmen both publicly and privately delivered that the arms build-up in Cuba would retain its original defensive character and that the Soviet Union had no need or desire to station strategic missiles on the territory of any other nation.

The size of this undertaking makes clear that it had been planned for some months.

Yet only last month after I had made clear the distinction between any introduction of ground-to-ground missiles and the existence of defensive antiaircraft missiles, the Soviet Government, publicly stated on Sept. 11 that, and I quote, the armaments and military equipment sent to Cuba are designed exclusively for defensive purposes, unquote, that there is—and I quote the Soviet Government—there is no need for the Soviet Government to shift its weapons for a retaliatory blow to any other country, for instance, Cuba, unquote, and that—and I quote the Government—the Soviet Union has so powerful rockets to carry these nuclear warheads that there is no need to search for sites for them beyond the boundaries of the Soviet Union, unquote.

That statement was false.

Only last Thursday, as evidence of this rapid offensive buildup was already in my hand, Soviet Foreign Minister Gromyko told me in my office that he was instructed to make it clear once again, as he said his Government had already done, that Soviet assistance to Cuba, and I quote, pursued solely the purpose of contributing to the defense capabilities of Cuba, unquote.

That, and I quote him, "training by Soviet specialists of Cuban nationals in handling defensive armaments was by no means offensive," and that if it were otherwise, Mr. Gromyko went on, "the Soviet Government would never become involved in rendering such assistance."

That statement was also false.

Neither the United States of America nor the world community of nations can tolerate deliberate deception and offensive threats on the part of any nation, large or small. We no longer live in a world where only the actual firing of weapons represents a sufficient challenge to a nation's security to constitute maximum peril.

Nuclear weapons are so destructive and ballistic missiles are so swift that any substantially increased possibility of their use or any sudden change in their deployment may well be regarded as a definite threat to peace.

For many years both the Soviet Union and the United States, recognizing this fact, have deployed strategic nuclear weapons with great care, never upsetting the precarious status quo which insured that these weapons would not be used in the absence of some vital challenge.

Our own strategic missiles have never been transferred to the territory of any other nation under a cloak of secrecy and deception and our history, unlike that of the Soviets since the end of World War II, demonstrates that we have no desire to dominate or conquer any other nation or impose our system upon its people.

Nevertheless, American citizens have become adjusted to living daily on the bull's-eye of Soviet missiles located inside the U.S.S.R. or in submarines.

In that sense missiles in Cuba add to an already clear and present danger — although it should be noted the nations of Latin America have never previously been subjected to a potential nuclear threat.

But this secret, swift, extraordinary build-up of Communist missiles in an area well-known to have a special and historical relationship to the United States and the nations of the Western Hemisphere, in violation of Soviet assurances and in defiance of American and hemispheric policy — this sudden, clandestine decision to station strategic weapons for the first time outside of Soviet soil — is a deliberately provocative and unjustified change in the status quo which cannot be accepted by this country if our courage and our commitments are ever to be trusted again, by either friend or foe.

The nineteen thirties taught us a clear lesson. Aggressive conduct, if allowed to go unchecked and unchallenged, ultimately leads to war.

This nation is opposed to war. We are also true to our word.

Our unswerving objective, therefore, must be to prevent the use of these missiles against this or any other country; and to secure their withdrawal or elimination from the Western Hemisphere.

Our policy has been one of patience and restraint, as befits a peaceful and powerful nation which leads a worldwide alliance.

We have been determined not to be diverted from our central concerns by mere irritants, and fanatics. But now further action is required. And it is underway. And these actions may only be the beginning.

We will not prematurely or unnecessarily risk the course of worldwide nuclear war in which even the fruits of victory would be ashes in our mouth, but neither will we shrink from that risk at any time it must be faced.

Acting, therefore, in the defense of our own security and of the entire Western Hemisphere and under the authority entrusted to my by the Constitution as endorsed by the resolution of the Congress, I have directed that that the following initial steps be taken immediately:

First, to halt this offensive build-up, a strict quarantine on all offensive military equipment under shipment to Cuba is being initiated. All ships of any kind bound for Cuba from whatever nation or port will, where they are found to contain cargoes of offensive weapons, be turned back. This quarantine will be extended if needed to other types of cargo and carriers.

We are not at this time, however, denying the necessities of life as the Soviets attempted to do in their Berlin blockade of 1948.

Second, I have directed the continued and increased close surveillance of Cuba and its military build-up.

The foreign ministers of the O.A.S. in their communiqué of Oct. 6 rejected secrecy on such matters in this hemisphere. Should these offensive military preparations continue, thus increasing the threat to the hemisphere, further action will be justified.

I have directed the armed forces to prepare for any eventualities, and I trust that in the interests of both the Cuban people and the Soviet technicians at the sites, the hazards to all concerned of continuing this threat will be recognized.

Third, it shall be the policy of this nation to regard any nuclear missile launched from Cuba against any nation in the Western Hemisphere as an attack by the Soviet Union on the United States requiring a full retaliatory response upon the Soviet Union.

Fourth, as a necessary military precaution, I have reinforced our base at Guantanamo, evacuated today the dependents of our personnel there and ordered additional military units to be on a stand-by alert basis.

Fifth, we are calling tonight for an immediate meeting of the organization of consultation under the Organization of American States to consider this threat to hemispheric security and to invoke Articles 6 and 8 of the Rio Treaty in support of all necessary action.

The United Nations Charter allows for regional security arrangements and the nations of this hemisphere decided long ago against the military presence of outside powers.

Our other allies around the world have also been alerted.

Sixth, under the Charter of the United Nations we are asking tonight that an emergency meeting of the Security Council be convoked without delay to take action against this latest Soviet threat to world peace.

Our resolution will call for the prompt dismantling and withdrawal of all offensive weapons in Cuba under the supervision of U.N. observers before the quarantine can be lifted.

Seventh, and finally, I call upon Chairman Khrushchev to halt and eliminate this clandestine, reckless and provocative threat to world peace and to stable relations between our two nations.

I call upon him further to abandon this course of world domination and to join in an historic effort to end the perilous arms race and to transform the history of man.

He has an opportunity now to move the world back from the abyss of destruction by returning to his Government's own words that it had no need to station missiles outside its own territory, and withdrawing these weapons from Cuba; by refraining from any action which will widen or deepen the present crisis, and then by participating in a search for peaceful and permanent solutions.

This nation is prepared to present its case against the Soviet threat to peace and our own proposals for a peaceful world at any time and in any forum—in the O.A.S., in the United Nations, or in any other meeting that could be useful without limiting our freedom of action.

We have, in the past, made strenuous efforts to limit the spread of nuclear weapons. We have proposed the elimination of all arms and military bases in a fair and effective disarmament treaty. We are prepared to discuss new proposals for the removal of tensions on both sides including the possibilities of a genuinely independent Cuba free to determine its own destiny.

We have no wish to war with the Soviet Union for we are a peaceful people who desire to live in peace with all other peoples.

But it is difficult to settle or even discuss these problems in an atmosphere of intimidation.

That is why this latest Soviet threat or any other threat which is made either independently or in response to our actions this week must and will be met with determination.

Any hostile move anywhere in the world against the safety and freedom of peoples to whom we are committed including in particular the brave people of West Berlin will be met by whatever action is needed.

Finally, I want to say a few words to the captive people of Cuba to whom this speech is being directly carried by special radio facilities.

I speak to you as a friend, as one who knows of your deep attachment to your fatherland, as one who shares your aspirations for liberty and justice for all.

And I have watched and the American people have watched with deep sorrow how your nationalist revolution was betrayed and how your fatherland fell under foreign domination.

Now your leaders are no longer Cuban leaders inspired by Cuban ideals. They are puppets and agents of an international conspiracy which has turned Cuba against your friends and neighbors in the Americas and turned it into the first Latin-American country to become a target for nuclear war, the first Latin-American country to have these weapons on its soil.

These new weapons are not in your interests. They contribute nothing to your peace and well being; they can only undermine it.

But this country has no wish to cause you to suffer or to impose any system upon you. We know that your lives and land are being used as pawns by those who deny your freedom. Many times in the past the Cuban people have risen to throw out tyrants who destroyed their liberty.

And I have no doubt that most Cubans today look forward to the time when they will be truly free, free from foreign domination, free to choose their own leaders, free to select their own system, free to own their own land, free to speak and write and worship without fear or degradation.

And then shall Cuba be welcomed back to the society of free nations and to the associations of this hemisphere.

My fellow citizens, let no one doubt that this is a difficult and dangerous effort on which we have set out. No one can foresee precisely what course it will take, or what course or casualties will be incurred.

Many months of sacrifice and self-discipline lie ahead, months in which both our patience and our will will be tested. Months in which many threats and denunciations will keep us aware of our dangers. But the greatest danger of all would be to do nothing.

The path we have chosen for the present is full of hazards, as all paths are. But it is the one most consistent with our character and courage as a nation and our commitments around the world.

The cost of freedom is always high, but Americans have always paid it.

And one path we shall never choose, and that is the path of surrender, or submission.

Our goal is not the victory of might, but the vindication of right; not peace at the expense of freedom, but both peace and freedom here in this hemisphere, and, we hope around the world.

God willing, that goal will be achieved.

I Have a Dream
Martin Luther King, Jr.

*Martin Luther King (January 15, 1929 - April 4, 1968) gradu-
ated from Morehouse College in 1948, and he received the
B.D. degree from Crozer Theological Seminary in 1951 and
the PH.D. from Boston University in 1955. He was president
of the Southern Christian Leadership Conference, and he
received a Nobel Peace Prize in 1964. This speech is consistently placed among the great speeches in American history. The
speech was delivered in Washington, D.C., August 28, 1963.*

I am happy to join with you today in what will go down in history as the
greatest demonstration for freedom in the history of our nation.

Five score years ago, a great American, in whose symbolic shadow we
stand today, signed the Emancipation Proclamation. This momentous de-
cree came as a great beacon light of hope to millions of Negro slaves, who
had been seared in the flames of withering injustice. It came as a joyous
daybreak to end the long night of their captivity.

But one hundred years later, the Negro still is not free. One hundred years
later, the life of the Negro is still sadly crippled by the manacles of segregation and the chains of discrimination. One hundred years later, the Negro
lives on a lonely island of poverty in the midst of a vast ocean of material
prosperity. One hundred years later, the Negro still languishes in the corners of American society and finds himself an exile in his own land.

So we've come here today to dramatize a shameful condition. In a sense
we've come to our nation's capital to cash a check. When the architects of
our Republic wrote the magnificent words of the Constitution and the
Declaration of Independence, they were signing a promissory note to which
every American was to fall heir. This note was a promise that all men—yes,
black men as well as white men—would be guaranteed the unalienable
rights of life, liberty, and the pursuit of happiness.

It is obvious today that America has defaulted on this promissory note insofar as her citizens of color are concerned. Instead of honoring this sacred obligation, America has given the Negro people a bad check, a check which has come back marked "insufficient funds." But we refuse to believe that the bank of justice is bankrupt. We refuse to believe that there are insufficient funds in the great vaults of opportunity of this nation. So we've come to cash this check — a check that will give us upon demand the riches of freedom and the security of justice.

We have also come to this hallowed spot to remind America of the fierce urgency of now. This is no time to engage in the luxury of cooling off or to take the tranquilizing drug of gradualism. Now is the time to make real the promises of democracy. Now is the time to rise from the dark and desolate valley of segregation to the sunlit path of racial justice. Now is the time to lift our nation from the quicksand of racial injustice to the solid rock of brotherhood. Now is the time to make justice a reality for all God's children.

It would be fatal for the nation to overlook the urgency of the moment. This sweltering summer of the Negro's legitimate discontent will not pass until there is an invigorating autumn of freedom and equality. Nineteen sixty-three is not an end, but a beginning. Those who hope that the Negro needed to blow off steam and will now be content will have a rude awakening if the nation returns to business as usual. There will be neither rest nor tranquillity in America until the Negro is granted his citizenship rights. The whirlwinds of revolt will continue to shake the foundations of our nation until the bright day of justice emerges.

But that is something that I must say to my people who stand on the warm threshold which leads into the palace of justice. In the process of gaining our rightful place we must not be guilty of wrongful deeds. Let us not seek to satisfy our thirst for freedom by drinking from the cup of bitterness and hatred.

We must forever conduct our struggle on the high plane of dignity and discipline. We must not allow our creative protest to degenerate into physical violence. Again and again we must rise to the majestic heights of meeting physical force with soul force. The marvelous new militancy which has engulfed the Negro community must not lead us to a distrust of all white people, for many of our white brothers, as evidenced by their presence here today, have come to realize that their destiny is tied up with our destiny. And they have come to realize that their freedom is inextricably bound to our freedom. We cannot walk alone.

As we walk, we must make the pledge that we shall always march ahead. We cannot turn back. There are those who ask the devotees of civil rights, "When will you be satisfied?" We can never be satisfied as long as the Negro is the victim of the unspeakable horrors of police brutality. We can never be satisfied as long as our bodies, heavy with the fatigue of travel, cannot gain lodging in the motels of the highways and the hotels of the cities. We cannot be satisfied as long as the Negro's basic mobility is from a smaller ghetto to a larger one. We can never be satisfied as long as our children are stripped of their selfhood and robbed of their dignity by signs stating "For Whites Only." We cannot be satisfied as long as a Negro in Mississippi cannot vote and a Negro in New York believes he has nothing for which to vote. No, no, we are not satisfied, and we will not be satisfied until justice rolls down like waters and righteousness like a mighty stream.

I am not unmindful that some of you have come here out of great trials and tribulations. Some of you have come fresh from narrow jail cells. Some of you have come from areas where your crest — quest for freedom left you battered by the storms of persecution and staggered by the winds of police brutality. You have been the veterans of creative suffering. Continue to work with the faith that unearned suffering is redemptive.

Go back to Mississippi, go back to Alabama, go back to South Carolina, go back to Georgia, go back to Louisiana, go back to the slums and ghettos of our Northern cities, knowing that somehow this situation can and will be changed. Let us not wallow in the valley of despair.

I say to you today, my friends, so even though we face the difficulties of today and tomorrow, I still have a dream. It is a dream deeply rooted in the American dream.

I have a dream that one day this nation will rise up and live out the true meaning of its creed: "We hold these truths to be self-evident; that all men are created equal."

I have a dream that one day on the red hills of Georgia the sons of former slaves and the sons of former slaveowners will be able to sit down together at the table of brotherhood.

I have a dream that one day even the state of Mississippi, a state sweltering with the heat of injustice, sweltering with the heat of oppression, will be transformed into an oasis of freedom and justice.

I have a dream that my four little children will one day live in a nation where they will not be judged by the color of their skin but by the content of their character.

I have a dream today.

I have a dream that one day, down in Alabama, with its vicious racists, with its governor having his lips dripping with the words of interposition and nullification, one day right there in Alabama little black boys and black girls will be able to join hands with little white boys and white girls as sisters and brothers.

I have a dream today.

I have a dream that one day every valley shall be exalted, every hill and mountain shall be made low, the rough places will be made plain and the crooked places will be made straight, and the glory of the Lord shall be revealed, and all flesh shall see it together.

This is our hope. This is the faith that I go back to the South with. With this faith we will be able to hew out of the mountain of despair a stone of hope. With this faith we will be able to transform the jangling discords of our nation into a beautiful symphony of brotherhood. With this faith we will be able to work together, to pray together, to struggle together, to go to jail together, to stand up for freedom together, knowing that we will be free one day.

This will be the day...this will be the day when all of God's children will be able to sing with new meaning: "My country 'tis of thee, sweet land of liberty, of thee I sing. Land where my fathers died, land of the Pilgrims' pride, from every mountainside, let freedom ring," and if America is to be a great nation, this must become true.

So let freedom ring. From the prodigious hilltops of New Hampshire, let freedom ring. From the mighty mountains of New York, let freedom ring, from the heightening Alleghenies of Pennsylvania!

Let freedom ring from the snowcapped Rockies of Colorado!

Let freedom ring from the curvaceous slopes of California!

But not only that.

Let freedom ring from Stone Mountain of Georgia!

Let freedom ring from Lookout Mountain of Tennessee!

Let freedom ring from every hill and mole hill of Mississippi.

From every mountainside, let freedom ring, and when this happens... when we allow freedom to ring, when we let it ring from every village and every hamlet, from every state and every city, we will be able to speed up that day when all of God's children, black men and white men, Jews and Gentiles, Protestants and Catholics, will be able to join hands and sing in the words of the old Negro spiritual, "Free at last! Free at last! Thank God Almighty, we are free at last!"

Eulogy on
Sir Winston Churchill
Adlai Ewing Stevenson

*Adlai Stevenson (February 5, 1900 - July 14, 1965) gradu-
ated from Princeton in 1922 and received his law degree from
Northwestern in 1926; he held various government posts from
1941-47; Governor of Illinois, 1949-53; Democratic candidate
for president, 1952, 1956; Ambassador to the United Nations,
1961-65. The eulogy was delivered at a memorial service for Sir
Winston Churchill at the National Cathedral, Washington,
D.C., January 28, 1965. Published version:* The Times
(London), January 29, 1965, p. 15.

Today we meet in sadness to mourn one of the world's greatest citizens.
Sir Winston Churchill is dead. The voice that led nations, raised armies,
inspired victories and blew fresh courage into the hearts of men is silenced.
We shall hear no longer the remembered eloquence and wit, the old courage
and defiance, the robust serenity of indomitable faith. Our world is thus
poorer, our political dialogue is diminished and the sources of public
inspiration run more thinly for all of us. There is a lonesome place against
the sky.

So we are right to mourn. Yet, in contemplating the life and the spirit of
Winston Churchill, regrets for the past seem singularly insufficient. One
rather feels a sense of thankfulness and of encouragement that throughout
so long a life, such a full measure of power, virtuosity, mastery and zest
played over our human scene.

Contemplating this completed career, we feel a sense of enlargement and
exhilaration. Like the grandeur and the power of the masterpieces of art
and music, Churchill's life uplifts our hearts and fills us with fresh

178

revelation of the scale and the reach of human achievement. We may be sad; but we rejoice as well, as all must rejoice when they "now praise famous men" and see in their lives the full splendor of our human estate.

And regrets for the past are insufficient for another reason. Churchill, the historian, felt the continuity of past and present, the contribution which mighty men and great events make to future experience; history's "flickering flame" lights up the past and sends its gleams into the future. So to the truth of Santayanas dictum, "Those who will not learn from the past are destined to repeat it," Churchill's whole life was witness.

It was his lonely voice that in the Thirties warned Britain and Europe of the follies of playing all over again the tragedy of disbelief and of unpreparedness. And in the time of Britain's greatest trial he mobilized the English language to inspire his people to historic valor. It was his voice again that helped assemble the great coalition that has kept peace steady throughout the last decades.

He once said: "We cannot say the past is past without surrendering the future." So today the "past" of his life and his achievements are a guide and light to the future. And we can only properly mourn and celebrate this mighty man by heeding him as a living influence in the unfolding dramas of our days ahead.

What does he tell us of this obscure future whose outlines we but dimly perceive? First, I believe, he would have us reaffirm his serene faith in human freedom and dignity. The love of freedom was not for him an abstract thing but a deep conviction that the uniqueness of man demands a society that gives his capacities full scope. It was, if you like, an aristocratic sense of the fullness and the value of life. But he was a profound democrat, and the cornerstone of his political faith, inherited from his beloved father, was the simple maxim "Trust the people." Throughout his long career, he sustained his profound concern for the well-being of his fellow citizens.

Instinctively, profoundly, the people trusted "good old Winnie," the peer's son. He could lead them in war because he had respected them in peace. He could call for their greatest sacrifices for he knew how to express their deepest dignity—citizens of equal value and responsibility in a free and democratic state.

His crucial part in the founding of the United Nations expressed his conviction that the Atlantic Charter so audaciously proclaimed by Roosevelt and Churchill at the height of Hitler's victories would have to be protected by institutions embodying the ideal of the rule of law and international cooperation.

For him, humanity, its freedom, its survival, towered above pettier interests—national rivalries, old enmities, the bitter disputes of race and creed. "In victory—magnanimity; in peace—good will" were more than slogans. His determination to continue in politics after his defeat in 1945 and to toil on in the 1950's to the limit of health and of endurance sprang from his belief that he could still "bring nearer that lasting peace which the masses of people of every race and in every land so fervently desire." The great soldier and strategist was first of all a man of peace—and for perhaps the most simple reason—his respect, his faith, his compassion for the family of man.

His career saw headlong success and headlong catastrophe. He was at the height. He was flung to the depths. He saw his worst prophecies realized, his worst forebodings surpassed. Yet throughout it all his zest for living, gallantry of spirit, wry humor and compassion for human frailty took all grimness out of his fortitude and all pomposity out of his dedication.

Churchill's sense of the incomparable value and worth of human existence never faltered, for the robust courage with which he lived to the very full never faltered. In the darkest hour, the land could still be bright, and for him hopes were not deceivers. It was forever fear that was the dupe. Victory at last would always lie with life and faith, for Churchill saw beyond the repeated miseries of human frailty the larger vision of mankind's "upward ascent towards his distant goal."

He used to say that he was half American and all English. But we put that right when the Congress made him an honorary citizen of his mother's native land and we shall always claim a part of him. I remember once years ago during a long visit at his country house he talked proudly of his American Revolutionary ancestors and happily of his boyhood visits to the United States. As I took my leave I said I was going back to London to speak to the English Speaking Union and asked if he had any message for them. "Yes," he said, "tell them that you bring greetings from an English-speaking Union." And I think that perhaps it was to the relations of the United Kingdom and the United States that he made his finest contribution.

In the last analysis, all the zest and life and confidence of this incomparable man sprang, I believe, not only from the rich endowment of his nature, but also from a profound and simple faith in God. In the prime of his powers, confronted with the apocalyptic risks of annihilation, he said serenely: "I do not believe that God has despaired of his children." In old age, as the honors and excitements faded, his resignation had a touching simplicity: "Only faith in a life after death in a brighter world where dear ones will meet again—only that and the measured tramp of time can give consolation."

The great aristocrat, the beloved leader, the profound historian, the gifted painter, the superb politician, the lord of language, the orator, the wit—yes, and the dedicated bricklayer—behind all of them was the man of simple faith, steadfast in defeat, generous in victory, resigned in age, trusting in a loving providence and committing his achievements and his triumphs to a higher power.

Like the patriarchs of old, he waited on God's judgment and it could be said of him—as of the immortals that went before him—that God "magnified him in the fear of his enemies and with his words he made prodigies to cease. He glorified him in the sight of kings and gave him commandments in the sight of his people. He showed him his Glory and sanctified him in his faith...."

The Right to Vote

Lyndon Baines Johnson

*Lyndon Johnson (August 27, 1908 - January 22, 1973) gradu-
ated from Southwest Texas College in 1930; he was a member
of Congress, 1937-48; U.S. Senator from 1949 - 61; Vice-
President, 1961-63; 36th President of the United States, 1963-
69. Published version:* Vital Speeches of the Day, *April 1,
1965, pp. 354-57. The speech was delivered before the Joint
Session of Congress, March 15, 1965.*

Mr. Speaker, Mr. President, members of the Congress, I speak tonight
for the dignity of man and the destiny of democracy. I urge every member
of both parties, Americans of all religions and of all colors, from every
section of this country, to join me in that cause.

At times, history and fate meet at a single time in a single place to shape a
turning point in man's unending search for freedom.

So it was at Lexington and Concord. So it was a century ago at Appomat-
tox. So it was last week in Selma, Ala.

There, long suffering men and women peacefully protested the denial of
their rights as Americans. Many were brutally assaulted. One good man—a
man of God—was killed.

There is no cause for pride in what has happened in Selma. There is no
cause for self-satisfaction in the long denial of equal rights of millions of
Americans. But there is cause for hope and for faith in our democracy in
what is happening here tonight.

For the cries of pain and the hymns and protests of oppressed people have
summoned into convocation all the majesty of this great Government—the
Government of the greatest nation on earth.

Our mission is at once the oldest and the most basic of this country—to
right wrong, to do justice, to serve man.

In our time we have come to live with the moments of great crisis. Our lives have been marked with debate about great issues, issues of war and peace, issues of prosperity and depression.

But rarely in any time does an issue lay bare the secret heart of America itself. Rarely are we met with a challenge, not to our growth or abundance, or our welfare or our security, but rather to the values and the purposes and the meaning of our beloved nation.

The issue of equal rights for American Negroes is such an issue.

And should we defeat every enemy, and should we double our wealth and conquer the stars, and still be unequal to this issue, then we will have failed as a people and as a nation.

For, with a country as with a person, "What is a man profited if he shall gain the whole world, and lose his own soul?"

There is no Negro problem. There is no Southern problem. There is no Northern problem. There is only an American problem.

And we are met here tonight as Americans — not as Democrats or Republicans; we're met here as Americans to solve that problem.

This was the first nation in the history of the world to be founded with a purpose. The great phrases of that purpose still sound in every American heart, North and South:

"All men are created equal." "Government by consent of the governed." "Give me liberty or give me death."

And those are not just clever words, and those are not just empty theories.

In their name Americans have fought and died for two centuries and tonight around the world they stand there as guardians of our liberty risking their lives.

Those words are promised to every citizen that he shall share in the dignity of man. This dignity cannot be found in a man's possessions. It cannot be found in his power or in his position. It really rests on his right to be treated as a man equal in opportunity to all others.

It says that he shall share in freedom. He shall choose his leaders, educate his children, provide for his family according to his ability and his merits as a human being.

To apply any other test, to deny a man his hopes because of his color or race or his religion or the place of his birth is not only to do injustice, it is to deny America and to dishonor the dead who gave their lives for American freedom.

Our fathers believed that if this noble view of the rights of man was to flourish it must be rooted in democracy. The most basic right of all was the right to choose your own leaders.

The history of this country in large measure is the history of expansion of that right to all of our people. Many of the issues of civil rights are very complex and most difficult. But about this there can and should be no argument: every American citizen must have an equal right to vote.

There is no reason which can excuse the denial of that right. There is no duty which weighs more heavily on us than the duty we have to insure that right. Yet the harsh fact is that in many places in this country men and women are kept from voting simply because they are Negroes.

Every device of which human ingenuity is capable has been used to deny this right. The Negro citizen may go to register only to be told that the day is wrong, or the hour is late, or the official in charge is absent.

And if he persists and, if he manages to present himself to the registrar, he may be disqualified because he did not spell out his middle name, or because he abbreviated a word on the application. And if he manages to fill out an application, he is given a test.

The registrar is the sole judge of whether he passes this test. He may be asked to recite the entire Constitution, or explain the most complex provisions of state law.

And even a college degree cannot be used to prove that he can read and write. For the fact is that the only way to pass these barriers is to show a white skin.

Experience has clearly shown that the existing process of law cannot overcome systematic and ingenious discrimination. No law that we now have on the books, and I have helped to put three of them there, can insure the right to vote when local officials are determined to deny it. In such a case, our duty must be clear to all of us.

The Constitution says that no person shall be kept from voting because of his race or his color. We have all sworn an oath before God to support and to defend that Constitution. We must now act in obedience to that oath.

Wednesday, I will send to Congress a law designed to eliminate illegal barriers to the right to vote.

The broad principles of that bill will be in the hands of the Democratic and Republican leaders tomorrow. After they have reviewed it, it will come here formally as a bill.

I am grateful for this opportunity to come here tonight at the invitation of the leadership to reason with my friends, to give them my views and to visit with my former colleagues.

I have had prepared a more comprehensive analysis of the legislation which I intended to submit to the clerk tomorrow, but which I will submit to the clerks tonight. But I want to really discuss the main proposals of this legislation.

This bill will strike down restrictions to voting in all elections, Federal, state and local, which have been used to deny Negroes the right to vote.

The bill will establish a simple, uniform standard which cannot be used, however ingenious the effort, to flout our Constitution. It will provide for citizens to be registered by officials of the United States Government, if the state officials refuse to register them.

It will eliminate tedious, unnecessary lawsuits which delay the right to vote.

Finally, this legislation will insure that properly registered individuals are not prohibited from voting.

I will welcome the suggestions from all the members of Congress — I have no doubt that I will get some — on ways and means to strengthen this law and to make it effective.

But experience has plainly shown that this is the only path to carry out the command of the Constitution. To those who seek to avoid action by their national Government in their home communities, who want to and' who seek to maintain purely local control over elections, the answer is simple: Open your polling places to all your people.

Allow men and women to register and vote whatever the color of their skin.

Extend the rights of citizenship to every citizen of this land.

There is no constitutional issue here. The command of the Constitution is plain. There is no moral issue. It is wrong — deadly wrong — to deny any of your fellow Americans the right to vote in this country.

There is no issue of state's rights or national rights. There is only the struggle for human rights.

I have not the slightest doubt what will be your answer. But the last time a President sent a civil rights bill to the Congress it contained a provision to protect voting rights in Federal elections. That civil rights bill was passed after eight long months of debate. And when that bill came to my desk from the Congress for signature, the heart of the voting provision had been eliminated.

This time, on this issue, there must be no delay, or no hesitation, or no compromise with our purpose.

We cannot, we must not, refuse to protect the right of every American to vote in every election that he may desire to participate in.

And we ought not, and we cannot, and we must not wait another eight months before we get a bill.

We have already waited 100 years and more and the time for waiting is gone.

So I ask you to join me in working long hours and nights and weekends, if necessary, to pass this bill.

And I don't make that request lightly, for from the window where I sit with the problems of our country I recognize that from outside this chamber is the outraged conscience of a nation, the grave concern of many nations and the harsh judgment of history on our acts.

But even if we pass this bill the battle will not be over.

What happened in Selma is part of a far larger movement which reaches into every section and state of America. It is the effort of American Negroes to secure for themselves the full blessings of American life.

Their cause must be our cause too. Because it's not just Negroes, but really it's all of us, who must overcome the crippling legacy of bigotry and injustice.

And we shall overcome.

As a man whose roots go deeply into Southern soil, I know how agonizing racial feelings are. I know how difficult it is to reshape the attitudes and the structure of our society. But a century has passed—more than 100 years —since the Negro was freed.

And he is not fully free tonight.

It was more than 100 years ago that Abraham Lincoln—a great President of another party—signed the Emancipation Proclamation. But emancipation is a proclamation and not a fact.

A century has passed—more than 100 years—since equality was promised, and yet the Negro is not equal.

A century has passed since the day of promise, and the promise is unkept. The time of justice has now come, and I tell you that I believe sincerely that no force can hold it back. It is right in the eyes of man and God that it should come, and when it does, I think that day will brighten the lives of every American.

For Negroes are not the only victims. How many white children have gone uneducated? How many white families have lived in stark poverty? How many white lives have been scarred by fear, because we wasted energy and our substance to maintain the barriers of hatred and terror?

And so I say to all of you here and to all in the nation tonight that those who appeal to you to hold on to the past do so at the cost of denying you your future. This great rich, restless country can offer opportunity and education and hope to all—all, black and white, all, North and South, sharecropper and city dweller.

These are the enemies: poverty, ignorance, disease. They are our enemies, not our fellow man, not our neighbor. And these enemies too—poverty, disease and ignorance—we shall overcome.

Now let none of us in any section look with prideful righteousness on the troubles in another section or the problems of our neighbors.

There is really no part of America where the promise of equality has been fully kept. In Buffalo as well as in Birmingham, in Philadelphia as well as Selma, Americans are struggling for the fruits of freedom. This is one nation. What happens in Selma and Cincinnati is a matter of legitimate concern to every American.

But let each of us look within our own hearts and our own communities and let each of us put our shoulder to the wheel to root out injustice wherever it exists.

As we meet here in this peaceful historic chamber tonight, men from the South, some of whom were at Iwo Jima, men from the North who have carried Old Glory to the far corners of the world and who brought it back without a stain on it, men from the East and from the West are all fighting together without regard to religion or color or region in Vietnam. Men from every region fought for us across the world 20 years ago. And now in these common dangers, in these common sacrifices, the South made its contribution in honor and gallantry no less than any other region in the Great Republic. And in some instances, a great many of them, more.

And I have not the slightest doubt that good men from everywhere in this country, from the Great Lakes to the Gulf of Mexico, from the Golden Gate to the harbors along the Atlantic, will rally now together in this cause to vindicate the freedom of all Americans.

For all of us owe this duty and I believe that all of us will respond to it. Your President makes that request of every American.

The real hero of this struggle is the American Negro. His actions and protests, his courage to risk safety, and even to risk his life, have awakened the conscience of this nation. His demonstrations have been designed to call attention to injustice, designed to provoke change; designed to stir reform.

He has called upon us to make good the promise of America. And who among us can say that we would have made the same progress were it not for his persistent bravery and his faith in American democracy?

For at the real heart of battle for equality is a deep-seated belief in the democratic process. Equality depends, not on the force of arms or tear gas, but depends upon the force of moral right—not on recourse to violence, but on respect for law and order.

There have been many pressures upon your President and there will be others as the days come and go. But I pledge you tonight that we intend to fight this battle where it should be fought—in the courts, and in the Congress, and in the hearts of men.

We must preserve the right of free speech and the right of free assembly.

But the right of free speech does not carry with it—as has been said—the right to holler fire in a crowded theatre.

We must preserve the right to free assembly. But free assembly does not carry with it the right to block public thoroughfares to traffic.

We do have a right to protest. And a right to march under conditions that do not infringe the constitutional rights of our neighbors. And I intend to protect all those rights as long as I am permitted to serve in this office.

We will guard against violence, knowing it strikes from our hands the very weapons which we seek—progress, obedience to law, and belief in American values.

In Selma, as elsewhere, we seek and pray for peace. We seek order, we seek unity, but we will not accept the peace of stifled rights or the order imposed by fear, or the unity that stifles protest — for peace cannot be purchased at the cost of liberty.

In Selma tonight as in every — and we had a good day there — as in every city we are working for a just and peaceful settlement. We must all remember after this speech I'm making tonight, after the police and the F.B.I. and the marshals have all gone, and after you have promptly passed this bill, the people of Selma and the other cities of the nation must still live and work together.

And when the attention of the nation has gone elsewhere they must try to heal the wounds and to build a new community. This cannot be easily done on a battleground of violence as the history of the South itself shows. It is in recognition of this that men of both races have shown such an outstandingly impressive responsibility in recent days — last Tuesday and again today.

The bill I am presenting to you will be known as a civil rights bill.

But in a larger sense, most of the program I am recommending is a civil rights program. Its object is to open the city of hope to all people of all races, because all Americans just must have the right to vote, and we are going to give them that right.

All Americans must have the privileges of citizenship, regardless of race, and they are going to have those privileges of citizenship regardless of race.

But I would like to caution you and remind you that to exercise these privileges takes much more than just legal right. It requires a trained mind and a healthy body. It requires a decent home and the chance to find a job and the opportunity to escape from the clutches of poverty.

Of course people cannot contribute to the nation if they are never taught to read or write; if their bodies are stunted from hunger; if their sickness goes untended; if their life is spent in hopeless poverty, just drawing a welfare check.

So we want to open the gates to opportunity. But we're also going to give all our people, black and white, the help that they need to walk through those gates.

My first job after college was as a teacher in Cotulla, Texas, in a small Mexican-American school. Few of them could speak English and I couldn't speak much Spanish.

My students were poor and they often came to class without breakfast and hungry. And they knew even in their youth the pain of prejudice. They never seemed to know why people disliked them, but they knew it was so because I saw it in their eyes.

I often walked home late in the afternoon after the classes were finished wishing there was more that I could do. But all I knew was to teach them the little that I knew, hoping that it might help them against the hardships that lay ahead.

And somehow you never forget what poverty and hatred can do when you see its scars on the hopeful face of a young child.

I never thought then, in 1928, that I would be standing here in 1965. It never even occurred to me in my fondest dreams that I might have the chance to help the sons and daughters of those students, and to help people like them all over this country.

But now I do have that chance. And I'll let you in on a secret—I mean to use it.

And I hope that you will use it with me. This is the richest, most powerful country which ever occupied this globe. The might of past empires is little compared to ours. But I do not want to be the President who built empires, or sought grandeur, or extended dominion. I want to be the President who educated young children to the wonders of their world.

I want to be the President who helped to feed the hungry and to prepare them to be taxpayers instead of tax eaters.

I want to be the President who helped the poor to find their own way and who protected the right of every citizen to vote in every election.

I want to be the President who helped to end hatred among his fellow men and who promoted love among the people of all races, all regions and all parties.

I want to be the President who helped to end war among the brothers of this earth.

And so at the request of your beloved Speaker and the Senator from Montana, the majority leader, the Senator from Illinois, the minority leader, Mr. McCulloch and other members of both parties, I came here tonight, not as President Roosevelt came down one time in person to veto a bonus bill; not as President Truman came down one time to urge the passage of a railroad bill, but I came down here to ask you to share this task with me. And to share it with the people that we both work for.

I want this to be the Congress—Republicans and Democrats alike—which did all these things for all these people.

Beyond this great chamber—out yonder—in 50 states are the people that we serve. Who can tell what deep and unspoken hopes are in their hearts tonight as they sit there and listen?

We all can guess, from our own lives, how difficult they often find their own pursuit of happiness.

How many problems each little family has. They look most of all to themselves for their future, but I think that they also look to each of us.

Above the pyramid on the great seal of the United States it says in Latin, "God has favored our undertaking." God will not favor everything that we do. It is rather our duty to divine his will. But I cannot help believe that He truly understands and that He really favors the undertaking that we begin here tonight.

LBJ'S Voting Rights Address: Adjusting Civil Rights to the Congress and the Congress to Civil Rights

Halford Ross Ryan

Steven Lawson observed that "most appraisals of the Johnson presidency and civil rights have been written without the benefit of research at the Lyndon B. Johnson Library."[1] His observation applies to LBJ's Voting Rights Address before a Joint Session of Congress on March 15, 1965. Research in the Johnson Library can shed new light, which is unobtainable from other sources, on the president's and his speech staff's rhetorical activities for this speech. Accordingly, three points can be explicated: (1) how speech writer Richard Goodwin produced the speech; (2) how President Johnson's version of his obtaining an "invitation" to address the Joint Session is misleading; and (3) how Horace Busby's memorandum helped the speech staff and the president to adjust the voting rights law to the Congress and the Congress to the real voting rights issue.

The Speech's Production

President Johnson discussed in *The Vantage Point* the events surrounding the composition of his speech, yet his version is misleading.

[1]Steven F. Lawson, "Civil Rights," in *Exploring the Johnson Years*, ed. Robert A. Divine (Austin: University of Texas Press, 1981), p. 94

The research in the Lyndon Baines Johnson Library was supported by a grant from the Maurice L. Mednick Memorial Fund.

LBJ recounted how the speech drafts were continually rewritten until the speech was actually delivered.[2] Although I made a thorough attempt to locate these drafts that should have ensued from such a revision process, I was unable to find them. What I did find was an original draft, a revised draft, and a large typewritten draft that served as the Reading Copy.

The first draft was composed by Richard Goodwin, Special Assistant to the President, 4/1/64-9/20/65, on March 15, 1965.[3] Goodwin's first draft accounted for almost seventy per cent of Johnson's address as delivered. The other thirty per cent was added in the revised draft, but, except as later noted, it was unclear who made those additions. LBJ evidently selected Goodwin to write the speech because "the President had great admiration for sort of a spare eloquence that Goodwin was very good at."[4] The second or revised draft was actually Goodwin's first draft with some minor changes and dictated [perhaps by LBJ?] inserts. On the cover sheet of this revised draft is a note, dated 3/16/65, which states that the President's Reading Copy was typed from this second draft.

The Reading Copy, or teleprompter text, demonstrates that the president did give the text some last minute attention. Although his changes were not extensive, he made some emendations on the text which he subsequently delivered in the speech. Examples of these emendations in LBJ's handwriting are [his additions are italicized]: "Equality depends not on the force of arms *or tear gas,*" "But the right of free speech does not carry with *it the right to holler fire in a crowded theatre,*" and "My first job after college was a teacher in a small Mexican-*American* school."[5] He also underlined certain words for vocal emphasis, as in the following passages: "*All* American *must* have the right to vote. And we are going to *give* them that right. *All* Americans must have the *privileges of citizenship regardless* of race. And they are going to *have* those privileges."[6] Since the large typewritten Reading Copy exists, and even has the president's emendations and underlinings on it, LBJ's recollection that "I had to deliver most of the speech from a rough copy lying on the rostrum" is interesting because it was not a rough but a finished text from which he read.[7]

---

[2]Lyndon Baines Johnson, *The Vantage Point* (New York: Holt, Rinehart and Winston, 1971), pp. 164-65.

[3]Goodwin's last name appears on the first draft of the speech, see Voting Rights Message, Box 7, Office Files of Bill Moyers, Lyndon Baines Johnson Library, Austin, Texas.

[4]Transcript, Jack Valenti, Oral History Interview, II, 37, LBJ Library.

[5]Statements, 3-15-65, Special Message to Congress, teleprompter text, pp. 10-12, LBJ Library.

[6]Ibid, p. 12.

[7]Johnson, *The Vantage Point*, p. 165.

Another example of the kind of materials the speech critic can find only in the Johnson Library is a document that reveals an interesting handling of information about the speech writing process. In response to queries about the production of the speech, Jack Valenti issued a memorandum to all staff members to indicate the line which all were to follow in regard to questions about who wrote the speech:

> The President wrote the speech. He talked out what he wanted to say—and as drafts were prepared in response to his dictation, the President personally edited and revised.
>
> I have refused (even to Marianne) to tell who of the staff even took down the President's notes, saying that secretaries and staffers worked in teams to respond to the President's requirements.
>
> The President kept revising the speech, even until the final minutes (the STAR carried a photo today showing handwritten sentences in the typed text and I called attention to that photo to show that the President was making last minute revisions).
>
> I mention this to point up the interest—and to caution our people NOT to mention the names of anyone who had anything to do with the speech else they will take that as evidence of someone doing the principal creative work.[8]

Speech writer Richard Goodwin was responsible for two-thirds of the "principal creative work," and the speech drafts are not compatible with the impression one gains from Johnson's book nor from Valenti's protestation.[9]

LBJ's "Invitation" to Address the Congress

Presidential legislation is normally accompanied by a written message to Congress, but Johnson realized that "the cold words of a written message" would not accomplish his momentous task of persuading the Congress to pass the voting rights act.[10] Exercising a tenet of the rhetorical presidency, LBJ wanted to take his case directly to the people and to the Congress. As the *vox populi*, his physical presence before the Congress would communicate to it that LBJ spoke for all of the people. Concomitantly, by addressing a joint session of the Congress, LBJ could communicate to the

---

[8]Memorandum, Jack Valenti to the President and the staff, March 16, 1965, SP 2-3/1965/HU 2-7, LBJ Library.

[9]Valenti later identified Goodwin as the principal writer. See Jack Valenti, *A Very Human President* (New York: W.W. Norton, 1975), p. 85.

[10]Johnson, *The Vantage Point*, p. 164.

people that the Congress was receptive to his message. This dual strategy was necessary because of the passions the civil rights issue stirred in certain citizens and in Congressmen and Senators from some sections of the country. LBJ realized his words, coupled with the symbolic action of his addressing a joint session, could overwhelm his opponents. At a meeting on Sunday, March 14, the president inveigled the Congressional leadership into persuading him to address a joint session of Congress despite objections by Senators Everett Dirksen and Mike Mansfield. Johnson knew that bipartisan support for a joint session speech would signal critically necessary Senatorial support for the address and hence the Voting Rights Act. A symbolic imprimatur would thus be given Johnson's speech. To support this contention, I employ Valenti's original notes of the meeting. LBJ obviously used these same notes for the basis of his book, but he disordered and deleted certain important facts in the flow of the meeting. (Valenti's original notes are so critical to the case that they are included in Appendix I, and I arbitrarily numbered each entry in brackets to aid in identifying the points.)

Johnson's version in *The Vantage Point* differs from Valenti's original notes of the gathering. First, it was Speaker John McCormack who suggested that the President address a Joint Session (did the president prompt him?); it was not, as LBJ wrote, McCormack who spoke against Dirksen and Mansfield, but quite the reverse, see [1] to [5] in Appendix I. It is not unreasonable to postulate that LBJ assumed that Dirksen and Mansfield were against a speech. It is clear that Johnson placed them in a defensive posture at the meeting. Second, LBJ deleted that he next spoke against the two senators. He wanted to refute their objections during the meeting, but the deletion from the book suggests that he did not want his later readers to infer that he was applying his famous "Texas twist" on Mansfield and Dirksen,[11] see [6]. Third, LBJ completely overlooked Vice President Hubert Humphrey's helpful support for the speech, see [8], and inexplicably Johnson did not place Humphrey at the meeting. Fourth, Johnson deleted his presidential threat: he would either use the television, or the Congress, or the newspapers to communicate his message, see [9]. The threat was evidently effective. If Johnson used the television and/or the newspapers alone, this could cast the Congress as not being responsive to the wishes of *vox populi*. However, the Congress could signal its intent to work with the president by inviting him to address a bill on which both would legislate in tandem. This was the opening for Representatives Carl Albert and McCormack to urge the president to address the Congress, see [10-11], and for McCormack and Attorney General Nicholas Katzenbach—

---

[11]Neil MacNeil, *Dirksen: Portrait of a Public Man* (Cleveland: World Publishing Co., 1970), p. 229.

(LBJ also failed to mention that Katzenbach was at the meeting) to urge the president to speak, see [17-18]. LBJ used this meeting to orchestrate the leadership to ask him to do what he had already intended to do. Moreover, he, and the leadership including the Vice President and the Attorney General, countered Dirksen's and Mansfield's objections by obtaining overriding support from other prominent Congressional and administration figures for a joint session speech. Perhaps Johnson himself best supports that interpretation: "Dirksen, you started this arm-twisting label—I don't arm-twist anybody," see [19].

The President's Rhetorical Strategy

The basis for LBJ's persuasive appeal can be found in a letter dated February 27, 1965, from Horace Busby, Special Assistant to the President, to Bill Moyers. Busby perceived deficiencies in the Voting Rights message which, at that time, was the "cold print" that would accompany the bill. His objections not only found their way into the legislation, but they also made Johnson's speech more persuasive.

Busby believed that the Voting Rights message addressed the wrong issue. He asserted that by trying to solve the problems of literacy tests, the good faith standard, and employing Federal registrars, the message stressed the wrong points and unnecessarily invoked the image of a return to Reconstruction in the South.[12] As the message stood, it attempted to adjust the wrong civil rights issue to the Congress and hence it would be difficult to adjust the Congress to a bad bill. Busby perceptively stated the crux of the real voting rights issue that the president should address:

> The right to register should be placed on a par with the right to vote. Thus far, this has not been done. The poll tax amendment to the Constitution is a first step, and a firm precedent for this approach.... To reach the real problem in the south, the need is for legislation making it a Federal criminal offense to obstruct, intimidate or prevent citizens from registering to vote. Corollary with this, it is perfectly logical and justifiable to define "obstruction" or "intimidation" the inequitable administration of qualifying tests prescribed for the residents of a State by that State's governing body. Politically and morally, such a position seems to me stronger and more defensible.[13]

Moyers sent Busby's letter on to the President with the note "I thought you

---

[12]Memorandum, Horace Busby to Bill Moyers, February 27, 1965, Voting Rights Message, Box 7, Office Files of Bill Moyers, LBJ Library.
[13]Ibid.

would be interested in Buzz's remarks on the Voting Rights message."[14] Moyers also sent the letter to Attorney General Katzenbach.

In a reply to Moyers, dated March 1, 1965, Katzenbach communicated how the Justice Department was "redrafting the message in order to emphasize" Busby's points, and Katzenbach concluded his letter by admonishing that "the real task will be to explain the need as persuasively as possible in favor of the approach contained in the message."[15] It is significant to observe that the president saw, and that the Attorney General and Mr. Moyers understood, Busby's insight.

In order to be a successful persuader, the president knew that he must present good reasons in his address:[16]

> He knew that in order to get a congressman to vote for something you've got to put it on such a basis that the congressman can vote for it and explain his vote back home. Now there's no problem in the northern states, but in the border states and in some of the western states and the Southwest, he had to put all of these great bills that he wanted to pass and fashion them in such a way and give rational reasons for voting that a congressman could go back and say, "Well, I voted for this, but let me tell you why I did." And by emphasizing the fact that the voting rights was the most important right that anybody could have, he was able to convince a lot of congressmen that they ought to vote for it.[17]

President Johnson's Joint Session speech was a superb example of adjusting voting rights to the Congress and the Congress to voting rights.[18] The persuasiveness of Johnson's argument appealed to the moral and legal good reason that all Americans must have the right to register in order to exercise the right to vote. Mrs. Johnson was correct when she observed the true essence of her husband's appeal: "The gist of the speech to me was concentrated in one sentence, calling on those communities who wished to avoid action by their national government, to 'open your polling places to all your people.' The solution for them would lie therein."[19] Busby's advice

---

[14]Ibid.

[15]Memorandum, Nicholas Katzenbach to Bill Moyers and Lee White, March 1, 1965, Voting Rights Message, Box 7, Office Files of Bill Moyers, LBJ Library.

[16]I acknowledge a direct paraphrase from a timeless essay, see Karl R. Wallace, "The Substance of Rhetoric: Good Reasons," *Quarterly Journal of Speech* 49 (1963): 239-59.

[17]Valenti, Oral History, p. 37.

[18]I am indebted to Professor Donald Bryant's famous dictum that rhetoric's function is *"adjusting ideas to people and of people to ideas,"* see Donald C. Bryant, "Rhetoric: Its Function and Its Scope," *Quarterly Journal of Speech* 39 (1953): 413. Italics are in the original.

[19]Lady Bird Johnson, *A White House Diary* (New York: Holt, Rinehart and Winston, 1970), p. 253.

enabled the president to present a cogent and a convincing argument for a bill by linking all Americans' right to vote to their right to register:

> But about this there can and should be no argument. Every American citizen must have an equal right to vote. There is no reason which can excuse the denial of that right. There is no duty which weighs more heavily on us than the duty we have to ensure that right.
>
> Open your polling places to all your people. Allow men and women to register and vote whatever the color of their skin. Extend the rights of citizenship to every citizen of this land.
>
> It is wrong—deadly wrong—to deny any of your fellow Americans the right to vote in this country.
>
> We cannot, we must not refuse to protect the right of every American to vote in every election that he may desire to participate in.[20]

LBJ tried as best he could to be an effective presidential communicator.[21] Although he relied heavily upon the teleprompter, he often looked directly at the camera to reinforce his points. He often emphasized salient arguments by tightening his lips and jaw. At other times, he stressed his language by leaning his head and whole body forward as if to menace the Congress. His speaking rate, while slow, did communicate a dignity and gravity that befitted the occasion. Rowland Evans and Robert Novak believed "it was by all odds the best, more genuinely moving speech Johnson had made as President."[22]

Letters and telegrams to the White House gauged the president's persuasiveness. The pro-letters filled two and one-half boxes whereas the con-letters filled only one-fourth of a box. Some selected letters indicate that the president successfully adjusted his voting rights speech to the American audience: Frank Mankiewicz, "I have not seen or heard an address which moved me as much since the days of FDR, and I was a very young and impressionable fellow then"; Eugene Carson Blake, "I feel you have more than fulfilled anything that any of us could have asked or expected in articulating...the strong position of your administration with regard to the greatest moral issue in our land"; Supreme Court Justice William O. Douglas, "You were absolutely superb last night—the best ever"; Senator Edmund Muskie, "a truly great State paper"; James C. Hagerty, "There have been a few times in my life that I have been so deeply

[20] *Public Papers of the Presidents: Lyndon B. Johnson, 1965,* (Washington: United States Government Printing Office, 1968), I, 281-87.

[21] "LBJ Addresses a Joint Session of Congress About Civil Rights, 3-15-65," Motion Picture 506, LBJ Library.

[22] Rowland Evans and Robert Novak, *Lyndon B. Johnson: The Exercise of Power* (New York: New American Library, 1966), p. 497.

moved''; and Mexican President Dias Ordaz noted LBJ's ''poignant reference'' to the Mexican-Americans in Cotulla, Texas (one will recall that Johnson wrote in ''American'' on his teleprompter text) and Ordaz was ''deeply touched.''[23] As one might expect, the negative reaction mail was often caustic. A woman from Richmond, Virginia telegraphed the president:''Think you need and could receive help from any good qualified and competent doctor suggest you make appointment with nearest good psychiatrist stop Results would 'overcome' many problems facing America today''; another woman from Anderson, South Carolina opined: ''I think it's the worse thing I have even seen to slay the South''; and a woman from Eastlake, Ohio thought ''Use of communist slogan 'We shall overcome' in your speech last night regrettable.''[24]

National newspapers indicated in their editorials and columns positive reception of the president's persuasion. Many commented directly on Johnson's rhetorical strategy of linking the right to register to the right to vote: the Cleveland *Plain Dealer*, ''Mr. Johnson will send to Congress legislation designed to eliminate illegal barriers to the right to vote''; the Houston *Post*, ''the right to vote hardly could have been stated more forcefully—or more fervently''; the Dallas *Morning News*, ''Full judgment on the President's voting message is impossible without a study of the bill itself. But there can be little quarrel with the generalities of his talk to the joint session: voting is a right. It cannot be abridged grossly and unfairly''; the Atlanta *Constitution*, ''A voting rights bill should be passed and the President explained in unanswerable detail why this is so''; the Washington *Post*, ''He asked Congress to pass legislation that will strike down restrictions to voting in all elections''; and the *Wall Street Journal,* ''When President Johnson said that a Negro's right to vote on a parity with his neighbor is the most fundamental of his rights he spoke only the simple truth.''[25]

Congress also responded favorably to the president. Lady Bird Johnson and Evans and Novak had noted that the address was rather long.[26] However, Congressional applause—including two standing ovations—accounted for 8 minutes and 40 seconds, which meant that although the delivery time was 45 minutes and 20 seconds, LBJ actually spoke for 36 minutes and 40 seconds.[27] Lyndon Johnson signed the Voting Rights Act of 1965 on August 6.

---

[23]See SP 2-3/1965/HU 2-7, Boxes 68-70, LBJ Library.

[24]SP 2-3/1965/HU 2-7, Boxes 68-70, LBJ Library.

[25]Editors' News Service, Voting Rights Message, Box 7, Office Files of Bill Moyers, LBJ Library.

[26]See Johnson, *A White House Diary,* p. 253, and Evans and Novak, p. 497.

[27]Memorandum to the President from Jack Valenti, April 6, 1965, SP 2-3/1965/ HU 2-7, LBJ Library.

Conclusion

The research materials in the Johnson Library elucidated the production and rhetorical strategy for LBJ's joint session speech on voting rights. He orchestrated the leadership into overcoming Dirksen's and Mansfield's objections against a speech to Congress, rather than a written message; thus, LBJ signaled the country that Congress, and especially the Senate, was behind the joint session speech and hence behind the voting rights bill. Speechwriter Goodwin produced the major part of the speech and Johnson personalized the text with his emendations. Busby's memorandum was used to provide the speech's basic rhetorical strategy: the right to vote must be linked to the right to register. Since all Americans had the right to vote, on which there could be no meaningful contention or debate, LBJ adjusted the real need issue to the Congress. Insidious impediments to blacks' registering had to bow to their greater right to vote. Concomitantly, the audience was adjusted appropriately by this linkage because no moral or logical argument could be adduced against the right to vote, hence not against the right to register to vote. The Voting Rights Act of 1965 was a need whose time was long overdue and as gauged from a variety of sources, Lyndon B. Johnson was a successful presidential persuader.

Appendix I

The following handwritten notes were made by Jack Valenti of the President's meeting with the Congressional leadership on Sunday, March 14, 1965. See Mr. Valenti's notes, March 14, 1965, President's Appointment File [Diary Backup], LBJ Library.

[1] *Mansfield*   Make one suggestion — send up bill Tuesday.
[2] *Dirksen*   Send up Monday afternoon. Policy meetings Demo and Repub on Tuesday. Better to have those people go over it.
[3] *McCullough*   Join others these suggestions.
[4] *McCormack*   Suggested that Pres. go over to Joint Session — tell about the bill — also bring statement on Viet Nam. Have you thought about this?
[5] *Dirksen*   Don't panic now. This is deliberate govt. Don't let these people say "We scared him into it." Don't circumvent the Congress.
[6] *Pres*   I wouldn't think about that. People do not know the facts — that we are doing everything we can to solve this. We must tell the people to give us time to work this out.
[7] (Dirksen and Mansfield are against joint session speech).
[8] *Humphrey*   Logic in what you are saying. But emotions are running high. A message of what this govt. is doing — simply — is what is needed. I told my crowd they had to go on record with their views. They believed unamiously [sic] in your going on TV.

[9] *Pres* I intend to tell the country what we recommend. Either I do it on TV or newspapers—or the Congress.

[10] *Albert* I don't think your coming before Congress would be a sign of panic. *I think it would help.* [Italics in original.]

[11] *McCormack* It would show bipartisanship—also show the world.

[12] *Pres* Probably come down Mon or Tues night—about 9:00—and send the bill up Wednesday.

[13] *Kuchel* Repub leader—Dem leader—Atty Gen—work together—Wallace is giving himself a trapdoor—"all eligible voters."

[14] *Pres* I put my stamp of approval on a voting bill in my state of the union speech. We intend to minimize the eligibility-age, for example is alright. We suggested the word "eligible" rather than "qualified."

[15] *McCollough* Next 48 hours gives us to study bill—Pres. go before Congress—then have the bill on Wednesday.

[16] *Pres* I've had two girls sleeping with me—you made WH fireproof but not soundproof.

[17] *McCormack* Do you want to address a Joint Session?

[18] *Katzenb* This would put the problem and the solution before the country.

[19] *Pres* Let's say TUES nite and send the bill up Wednesday. Dirksen, you started this arm-twisting label—I don't arm-twist anybody.

Television Statement to the People of Massachusetts

Edward Moore Kennedy

Edward Kennedy (February 22, 1932 -) graduated from Harvard in 1956, and received his law degree from the University of Virginia, 1959; United States Senator [Massachusetts] since 1962. Published version: The New York Times, *July 26, 1969, p. 10. The speech was broadcast nationally from Joseph P. Kennedy's home, July 25, 1969.*

My fellow citizens:

I have requested this opportunity to talk to the people of Massachusetts about the tragedy which happened last Friday evening.

This morning I entered a plea of guilty to the charge of leaving the scene of an accident. Prior to my appearance in court it would have been improper for me to comment on these matters.

But tonight I am free to tell you what happened and to say what it means to me.

On the weekend of July 18 I was on Martha's Vineyard Island participating with my nephew, Joe Kennedy — as for 30 years my family has participated — in the annual Edgartown Sailing Regatta.

Only reasons of health prevented my wife from accompanying me.

On Chappiquiddick Island, off Martha's Vineyard, I attended, on Friday evening, July 18, a cook-out, I had encouraged and helped sponsor for a devoted group of Kennedy campaign secretaries.

When I left the party, around 11:15 P.M., I was accompanied by one of these girls, Miss Mary Jo Kopechne, Mary Jo was one of the most devoted members of the staff of Senator Robert Kennedy. She worked for him for four years and was broken up over his death. For this reason, and because she was such a gentle, kind and idealistic person, all of us tried to help her

200

feel that she still had a home with the Kennedy family.

There is no truth, no truth whatever, to the widely circulated suspicions of immoral conduct that have been leveled at my behavior and hers regarding that evening. There has never been a private relationship between us of any kind.

I know of nothing in Mary Jo's conduct on that or any other occasion—the same is true of the other girls at that party—that would lend any substance to such ugly speculation about their character.

Nor was I driving under the influence of liquor.

Little over one mile away, the car that I was driving on the unlit road went off a narrow bridge which had no guard rails and was built on a left angle to the road.

The car overturned in a deep pond and immediately filled with water. I remember thinking as the cold water rushed in around my head that I was for certain drowning.

Then water entered my lungs and I actually felt the sensation of drowning. But somehow I struggled to the surface alive. I made immediate and repeated efforts to save Mary Jo by diving into strong and murky current but succeeded only in increasing my state of utter exhaustion and alarm.

My conduct and conversations during the next several hours to the extent that I can remember them make no sense to me at all.

Although my doctors informed me that I suffered a cerebral concussion as well as shock, I do not seek to escape responsibility for my actions by placing the blame either in the physical, emotional trauma brought on by the accident or on anyone else.

I regard as indefensible the fact that I did not report the accident to the police immediately.

Instead of looking directly for a telephone after lying exhausted in the grass for an undetermined time, I walked back to the cottage where the party was being held and requested the help of two friends, my cousin, Joseph Gargan, and Phil Markham, and directed them to return immediately to the scene with me—this was sometime after midnight—in order to undertake a new effort to dive down and locate Miss Kopechne.

Their strenuous efforts, undertaken at some risk to their own lives also proved futile.

All kinds of scrambled thoughts—all of them confused, some of them irrational, many of them which I cannot recall and some of which I would not have seriously entertained under normal circumstances—went through my mind during this period.

They were reflected in the various inexplicable, inconsistent, and inconclusive things I said and did, including such questions as whether the girl might still be alive somewhere out of that immediate area, whether some awful curse did actually hang over all the Kennedys, whether there was some justifiable reason for me to doubt what had happened and to delay my report, whether somehow the awful weight of this incredible incident might in some way pass from my shoulders.

I was overcome, I'm frank to say, by a jumble of emotions, grief, fear, doubt, exhaustion, panic, confusion and shock.

Instructing Gargan and Markham not to alarm Mary Jo's friends that night, I had them take me to the ferry crossing. The ferry having shut down for the night, I suddenly jumped into the water and impulsively swam across, nearly drowning once again in the effort, and returned to my hotel about 2 A.M. and collapsed in my room.

I remember going out at one point and saying something to the room clerk.

In the morning, with my mind somewhat more lucid, I made an effort to call a family legal adviser, Burke Marshall, from a public telephone on the Chappaquiddick side of the ferry and belatedly reported the accident to the Martha's Vineyard police.

Today, as I mentioned, I felt morally obligated to plead guilty to the charge of leaving the scene of an accident. No words on my part can possibly express the terrible pain and suffering I feel over this tragic incident.

This last week has been an agonizing one for me and the members of my family, and the grief we feel over the loss of a wonderful friend will remain with us the rest of our lives.

These events, the publicity, innuendo and whispers which have surrounded them and my admission of guilt this morning — raises the question in my mind of whether my standing among the people of my state has been so impaired that I should resign my seat in the United States Senate.

If at any time the citizens of Massachusetts should lack confidence in their Senator's character or his ability, with or without justification, he could not in my opinion adequately perform his duty and should not continue in office.

The people of this state, the state which sent John Quincy Adams and Daniel Webster and Charles Sumner and Henry Cabot Lodge and John Kennedy to the United States Senate are entitled to representation in that body by men who inspire their utmost confidence.

For this reason, I would understand full well why some might think it right for me to resign. For me this will be a difficult decision to make.

It has been seven years since my first election to the Senate. You and I share many memories — some of them have been glorious, some have been very sad. The opportunity to work with you and serve Massachusetts has made my life worthwhile.

And so I ask you tonight, people of Massachusetts, to think this through with me. In facing this decision, I seek your advice and opinion. In making it, I seek your prayers for this is a decision that I will have finally to make on my own.

It has been written a man does what he must in spite of personal consequences, in spite of obstacles and dangers and pressures, and that is the basis of all human morality.

Whatever may be the sacrifices he faces, if he follows his conscience — the loss of his friends, his fortune, his contentment, even the esteem of his fellow man — each man must decide for himself the course he will follow.

The stories of the past courage cannot supply courage itself. For this, each man must look into his own soul.

I pray that I can have the courage to make the right decision. Whatever is decided and whatever the future holds for me, I hope that I shall have, be able to put this most recent tragedy behind me and make some further contribution to our state and mankind, whether it be in public or private life.

Thank you and good night.

A Pentadic Analysis of Senator Edward Kennedy's Address to the People of Massachusetts
July 25, 1969

David A. Ling

Dr. Ling is Associate Professor, Department of Speech, Central Michigan University, Mt. Pleasant, Michigan. This *article originally appeared in* Central States Speech Journal, *21 (1970), 81-86, and is reprinted with permission from the* Central States Speech Association.

On July 25, 1969 Senator Edward Kennedy addressed the people of the state of Massachusetts for the purpose of describing the events surrounding the death of Miss Mary Jo Kopechne. The broadcasting networks provided prime time coverage of Senator Kennedy's address, and a national audience listened as Kennedy recounted the events of the previous week. The impact of that incident and Kennedy's subsequent explanation have been a subject of continuing comment ever since.

This paper will examine some of the rhetorical choices Kennedy made either consciously or unconsciously in his address of July 25th. It will then speculate on the possible impact that those choices may have on audience response to the speech. The principle tool used for this investigation will be the "Dramatistic Pentad" found in the writings of Kenneth Burke.

The Pentad and Human Motivation

The pentad evolved out of Burke's attempts to understand the bases of human conduct and motivation. Burke argues that "human conduct being in the realm of action and end...is most directly discussible in dramatistic terms."[1] He maintains that, in a broad sense, history can be viewed as a play, and, just as there are a limited number of basic plots available to the author, so also there are a limited number of situations that occur to man. It, therefore, seems appropriate to talk about situations that occur to man in the language of the stage. As man sees these similar situations (or dramas) occurring, he develops strategies to explain what is happening. When man uses language, according to Burke, he indicates his strategies for dealing with these situations. That is, as man speaks he indicates how he perceives the world around him.

Burke argues that whenever a man describes a situation he provides answers to five questions: "What was done (act), when or where it was done (scene), who did it (agent), how he did it (agency), and why (purpose)."[2] Act, scene, agent, agency, and purpose are the five terms that constitute the "Dramatistic Pentad." As man describes the situation around him, he orders these five elements to reflect his view of that situation.

Perhaps the clearest way to explain how the pentad functions is to examine Burke's own use of the concept in *The Grammar of Motives*.[3] In that work, Burke argues that various philosophical schools feature different elements of the human situation. For example, the materialist school adopts a vocabulary that focuses on the scene as the central element in any situation. The agent, act, agency and purpose are viewed as functions of the scene. On the other hand, the idealist school views the agent (or individual) as central and subordinates the other elements to the agent. Thus, both the materialist and the idealist, looking at the same situation, would describe the same five elements as existing in that situation. However, each views a different element as central and controlling. In Burke's own analysis he further suggests philosophical schools that relate to the other three elements of the pentad: the act, agency and purpose. What is important in this analysis is not which philosophical schools are related to the featuring of each element. What is important is that as one describes a situation his ordering of the five elements will suggest which of the several different views of that situation he has, depending on which element he describes as controlling.

This use of the pentad suggests two conclusions. First, the pentad functions as a tool for content analysis. The five terms provide a method of determining how a speaker views the world. Indeed, this is what Burke means when he says that the pentad provides "a synoptic way to talk about their

[1]Kenneth Burke, *Permanence and Change* (Los Altos, California: Hermes Publications, 1954), p. 274.

[2]Kenneth Burke, *A Grammar of Motives and a Rhetoric of Motives* (Cleveland: The World Publishing Company, 1962), p. xvii.

[3]*Ibid.*, pp. 127-320.

[man's] talk-about [his world]."[4]

A second conclusion that results from this analysis is that man's description of a situation reveals what he regards as the appropriate response to various human situations. For example, the speaker who views the agent as the cause of a problem, will reflect by his language not only what Burke would call an idealist philosophy, but he will be limited to proposing solutions that attempt to limit the actions of the agent or to remove the agent completely. The speaker who finds the agent to be the victim of the scene not only reflects a materialist philosophy but will propose solutions that attempt to limit the actions of the agent or to remove the agent completely. The speaker who finds the agent to be the victim of the scene not only reflects a materialistic philosophy but will propose solutions that would change the scene. Thus, an individual who describes the problem of slums as largely a matter of man's unwillingness to change his environment will propose self-help as the answer to the problem. The person who, looking at the same situation, describes man as a victim of his environment will propose that the slums be razed and its inhabitants be relocated into a more conducive environment. The way in which a speaker describes a situation reflects his perception of reality and indicates what choices of action are available to him.

The Pentad and Rhetorical Criticism

But what has all this to do with rhetoric? If persuasion is viewed as the attempt of one man to get another to accept his view of reality as the correct one, then the pentad can be used as a means of examining how the persuader has attempted to achieve the restructuring of the audience's view of reality. Burke suggests how such an analysis might take place when he says in *The Grammar:* "Indeed, though our concern here is with the Grammar of Motives, we may note a related resource of Rhetoric: one may deflect attention from scenic matters by situating the motives of an act in the agent (as were one to account for wars purely on the basis of a "warlike instinct" in people): or conversely, one may deflect attention from criticism of personal motives by deriving an act or attitude not from traits of the agent but from the nature of the situation."[5]

Thus beginning with the language of the stage, the Pentad, it is possible to examine a speaker's discourse to determine what view of the world he would have an audience accept. One may then make a judgment as to both the appropriateness and adequacy of the description the speaker has presented.

[4]*Ibid.*, p. 56.
[5]*Ibid.*, p. 17.

Edward Kennedy's July 25th Address

Having suggested the methodology we now turn to a consideration of Senator Edward Kennedy's address of July 25th to the people of Massachusetts. The analysis will attempt to establish two conclusions. First, the speech functioned to minimize Kennedy's responsibility for his actions after the death of Miss Kopechne. Second, the speech was also intended to place responsibility for Kennedy's future on the shoulders of the people of Massachusetts. These conclusions are the direct antithesis of statements made by Kennedy during the speech. Halfway through the presentation, Kennedy commented: "I do not seek to escape responsibility for my actions by placing blame either on the physical, emotional trauma brought on by the accident or on anyone else. I regard as indefensible the fact that I did not report the accident to the police immediately."[6] Late in the speech, in discussing the decision on whether or not to remain in the Senate, Kennedy stated that, "this is a decision that I will have finally to make on my own." These statements indicated that Kennedy accepted both the blame for the events of that evening and the responsibility for the decision regarding his future. However, the description of reality presented by Kennedy in this speech forced the audience to reject these two conclusions.

Edward Kennedy — Victim of the Scene

The speech can best be examined in two parts. The first is the narrative in which Kennedy explained what occurred on the evening of July 18th. The second part of the speech involved Kennedy's concern over remaining in the U.S. Senate.

In Kennedy's statement concerning the events of July 18th we can identify these elements:

> The scene (the events surrounding the death of Miss Kopechne)
>
> The agent (Kennedy)
>
> The act (Kennedy's failure to report immediately the accident)
>
> The agency (whatever methods were available to make such a report)
>
> The purpose (To fulfill his legal and moral responsibilities)

In describing this situation Kennedy ordered the elements of the situation in such a way that the scene became controlling. In Kennedy's description of the events of that evening, he began with statements that were, in essence, simple denials of any illicit relationship between Miss Kopechne and himself. "There is no truth, no truth whatever to the widely circulated

---

[6] This and all subsequent references to the text of Senator Edward Kennedy's speech of July 25, 1969 are taken from *The New York Times,* CXVII (July 26, 1969), p. 10.

suspicions of immoral conduct that have been leveled at my behavior and hers regarding that night. There has never been a private relationship between us of any kind.'' Kennedy further denied that he was ''driving under the influence of liquor.'' These statements function rhetorically to minimize his role as agent in this situation. That is, the statements suggest an agent whose actions were both moral and rational prior to the accident. Kennedy then turned to a description of the accident itself: ''Little over a mile away the car that I was driving on an *unlit* road went off a *narrow bridge* which had *no guard rails* and was built on a *left angle* to the road. The car overturned into a *deep pond* and immediately filled with water.'' (Emphasis mine) Such a statement placed Kennedy in the position of an agent caught in a situation not of his own making. It suggests the scene as the controlling element.

Even in Kennedy's description of his escape from the car, there is the implicit assumption that his survival was more a result of chance or fate than of his own actions. He commented: ''I remember thinking as the cold water rushed in around my head that I was for certain drowning. Then water entered my lungs and I actually felt the sensation of drowning. But somehow I struggled to the surface alive.'' The suggestion in Kennedy's statement was that he was in fact at the mercy of the situation, and that his survival was not the result of his own calculated actions. As an agent he was not in control of the scene, but rather its helpless victim.

After reaching the surface of the pond, Kennedy said that he ''made repeated efforts to save Mary Jo.'' However, the ''strong'' and ''murky'' tide not only prevented him from accomplishing the rescue, but only succeeded in ''increasing [his] state of utter exhaustion and alarm.'' The situation described is, then, one of an agent totally at the mercy of a scene that he cannot control. Added to this was Kennedy's statement that his physicians verified a cerebral concussion. If the audience accepted this entire description, it cannot conclude that Kennedy's actions during the next few hours were ''indefensible.'' The audience rather must conclude that Kennedy was the victim of a tragic set of circumstances.

At this point in the speech Senator Kennedy commented on the confused and irrational nature of his thoughts, thoughts which he ''would not have seriously entertained under normal circumstances.'' But, as Kennedy described them, these were not normal circumstances, and this was *not* a situation over which he had control.

Kennedy provided an even broader context for viewing him as the victim when he expressed the concern that ''some awful curse did actually hang over the Kennedys.'' What greater justification could be provided for concluding that an agent is not responsible for his acts than to suggest that the agent is, in fact, the victim of some tragic fate.

Thus, in spite of his conclusion that his actions were ''indefensible,'' the description of reality presented by Kennedy suggested that he, as agent, was the victim of a situation (the scene) over which he had no control.

Kennedy's Senate Seat: In the Hands of the People

In the second part and much shorter development of the speech, the situation changes. Here we can identify the following elements:

The scene (current reaction to the events of July 18th)

The agent (the people of Massachusetts)

The act (Kennedy's decision on whether to resign)

The agency (statement of resignation)

The purpose (to remove Kennedy from office)

Here, again, Kennedy described himself as having little control over the situation. However, it was not the scene that was controlling, but rather it was agents other than Kennedy. That is, Kennedy's decision on whether or not he will continue in the Senate was not to be based on the "whispers" and "innuendo" that constitute the scene. Rather his decision would be based on whether or not the people of Massachusetts believed those whispers.

Kennedy commented: "If at any time the citizens of Massachusetts should lack confidence in their senator's character or his ability, with or without justification, he could not, in my opinion, adequately perform his duties and should not continue in office." Thus, were Kennedy to decide not to remain in the Senate it would be because the people of Massachusetts had lost confidence in him; responsibility in the situation rests with agents other than Kennedy.

This analysis suggests that Kennedy presented descriptions of reality which, if accepted, would lead the audience to two conclusions:

1. Kennedy was a tragic victim of a scene he could not control.

2. His future depended, not on his own decision, but on whether or not the people of Massachusetts accepted the whispers and innuendo that constituted the immediate scene.

Acceptance of the first conclusion would, in essence, constitute a rejection of any real guilt on the part of Kennedy. Acceptance of the second conclusion meant that responsibility for Kennedy's future was dependent on whether or not the people of Massachusetts believed Kennedy's description of what happened on the evening of July 18th, or if they would believe "whispers and innuendo."

Rhetorical Choice and Audience Response

If this analysis is correct, then it suggests some tentative implications concerning the effect of the speech. First, the positive response of the people of Massachusetts was virtually assured. During the next few days thousands of letters of support poured into Kennedy's office. The overwhelming endorsement was as much an act of purification for the people of that state as it was of Kennedy. That is, the citizenry was saying "We choose not to believe whispers and innuendo. Therefore, there is no reason for Ted Kennedy to resign." Support also indicated that the audience accepted his description of reality rather than his conclusion that he was responsible for his actions. Guilt has, therefore, shifted from Kennedy to the people of Massachusetts. Having presented a description of the events of July 18th which restricts his responsibility for those events, Kennedy suggested that the real 'sin' would be for the people to believe that the "whispers and innuendoes" were true. As James Reston has commented, "What he [Kennedy] has really asked the people of Massachusetts is whether they want to kick a man when he is down, and clearly they are not going to do that to this doom-ridden and battered family."[7] The act of writing a letter of support becomes the means by which the people "absolve" themselves of guilt. The speech functioned to place responsibility for Kennedy's future as a Senator in the hands of the people and then provided a description that limited them to only one realistic alternative.

While the speech seemed to secure, at least temporarily, Kennedy's Senate seat, its effect on his national future appeared negligible, if not detrimental. There are three reasons for this conclusion. First, Kennedy's description of the events of July 18th presented him as a normal agent who was overcome by an extraordinary scene. However, the myth that has always surrounded the office of the President is that it must be held by an agent who can make clear, rational decisions in an extraordinary scene. Kennedy, in this speech was, at least in part, conceding that he may not be able to handle such situations. This may explain why 57 per cent of those who responded to a CBS poll were still favorably impressed by Kennedy after his speech, but 87 per cent thought his chances of becoming President had been hurt by the incident.[8]

A second reason why the speech may not have had a positive influence on Kennedy's national future was the way in which the speech was prepared. Prior to the presentation of Kennedy's speech important Kennedy advisers were summoned to Hyannis Port, among them Robert McNamara and Theodore Sorensen. It was common knowledge that these advisers played an important role in the preparation of that presentation. Such an approach to the formulation was rhetorically inconsistent with the description of reality Kennedy presented. If Kennedy was the simple victim of the scene he could not control, then, in the minds of the audience that should be a simple

---

[7] James Reston, "Senator Kennedy's Impossible Question," *The New York Times,* CXVII (July 27, 1969), section 4, p. 24.

[8] "C.B.S. Evening News," C.B.S. Telecast, July 31, 1969.

matter to convey. However, the vision of professionals "manipulating" the speech, suggested in the minds of his audience that Kennedy may have been hiding his true role as agent. Here was an instance of an agent trying to control the scene. But given Kennedy's description of what occurred on July 18th such "manipulation" appeared unnecessary and inappropriate. The result was a credibility gap between Kennedy and his audience.

A third factor that may have mitigated against the success of this speech was the lack of detail in Kennedy's description. A number of questions relating to the incident were left unanswered: Why the wrong turn? What was the purpose of the trip, etc.? These were questions that had been voiced in the media and by the general public during the week preceding Senator Kennedy's address. Kennedy's failure to mention these details raised the speculation in the minds of some columnists and citizens that Kennedy may, in fact, have been responsible for the situation having occurred: the agent may have determined the scene. If this was not the case, then Kennedy's lack of important detail may have been a mistake rhetorically. Thus, while Kennedy's speech resulted in the kind of immediate and overt response necessary to secure his seat in the Senate, the speech and the conditions under which it was prepared appear to have done little to enhance Kennedy's chances for the Presidency.

Conclusion

Much of the analysis of the effect of this speech has been speculative. Judging the response of an audience to a speech is a difficult matter; judging the reasons for that response is even more precarious. The methodology employed here has suggested two conclusions. First, in spite of his statements to the contrary, Kennedy's presentation portrayed him, in the first instance, as a victim of the scene and in the second, the possible victim of other agents. Second, the pentad, in suggesting that only five elements exist in the description of a situation, indicated what alternative descriptions were available to Kennedy. Given those choices, an attempt was made to suggest some of the possible implications of the choices Kennedy made.

Television News Coverage

Spiro Theodore Agnew

Spiro Agnew (November 9, 1918 -   ) was Governor of Maryland, 1967-69, and Vice-President, 1969-73. The speech was delivered at the Mid-west Regional Republican Committee, Des Moines, Iowa, November 13, 1969. Published version: Vital Speeches of the Day, *December 1, 1969, pp. 98-101.*

Tonight I want to discuss the importance of the television news medium to the American people. No nation depends more on the intelligent judgment of its citizens. No medium has a more profound influence over public opinion. Nowhere in our system are there fewer checks on vast power. So, nowhere should there be more conscientious responsibility exercised than by the news media. The question is, Are we demanding enough of our television news presentations? And are the men of this medium demanding enough of themselves?

Monday night a week ago, President Nixon delivered the most important address of his Administration, one of the most important of our decade. His subject was Vietnam. His hope was to rally the American people to see the conflict through to a lasting and just peace in the Pacific. For 32 minutes, he reasoned with a nation that has suffered almost a third of a million casualties in the longest war in its history.

When the President completed his address—an address, incidentally, that he spent weeks in the preparation of—his words and policies were subjected to instant analysis and querulous criticism. The audience of 70 million Americans gathered to hear the President of the United States was inherited by a small band of network commentators and self-appointed analysts, the majority of whom expressed in one way or another their hostility to what he had to say.

It was obvious that their minds were made up in advance. Those who recall the fumbling and groping that followed President Johnson's dramatic disclosure of his intention not to seek another term have seen these men in a genuine state of nonpreparedness. This was not it.

One commentator twice contradicted the President's statement about the exchange of correspondence with Ho Chi Minh. Another challenged the President's abilities as a politician. A third asserted that the President was following a Pentagon line. Others, by the expression on their faces, the tone of their questions and the sarcasm of their responses, made clear their sharp disapproval.

To guarantee in advance that the President's plea for national unity would be challenged, one network trotted out Averell Harriman for the occasion. Throughout the President's message, he waited in the wings. When the President concluded, Mr. Harriman recited perfectly. He attacked the Thieu Government as unrepresentative; he criticized the President's speech for various deficiencies; he twice isued a call to the Senate Foreign Relations Committee to debate Vietnam once again; he stated his belief that the Vietcong or North Vietnamese did not really want military take-over of South Vietnam; and he told a little anecdote about a "very, very responsible" fellow he had met in the North Vietnamese delegation.

All in all, Mr. Harriman offered a broad range of gratuitous advice challenging and contradicting the policies outlined by the President of the United States. Where the President had issued a call for unity, Mr. Harriman was encouraging the country not to listen to him.

A word about Mr. Harriman. For 10 months he was America's chief negotiator at the Paris peace talks—a period in which the United States swapped some of the greatest military concessions in the history of warfare for an enemy agreement on the shape of the bargaining table. Like Coleridge's Ancient Mariner, Mr. Harriman seems to be under some heavy compulsion to justify his failure to anyone who will listen. And the networks have shown themselves willing to give him all the air time he desires.

Now every American has a right to disagree with the President of the United States and to express publicly that disagreement. But the President of the United States has a right to communicate directly with the people who elected him, and the people of his country have the right to make up their own minds and form their own opinions about a Presidential address without having a President's words and thoughts characterized through the prejudices of hostile critics before they can even be digested.

When Winston Churchill rallied public opinion to stay the course against Hitler's Germany, he didn't have to contend with a gaggle of commentators raising doubts about whether he was reading public opinion right, or whether Britain had the stamina to see the war through.

When President Kennedy rallied the nation in the Cuban missile crisis, his address to the people was not chewed over by a roundtable of critics who disparaged the course of action he'd asked America to follow.

The purpose of my remarks tonight is to focus your attention on this little group of men who not only enjoy a right of instant rebuttal to every Presidential address, but, more importantly, wield a free hand in selecting, presenting and interpreting the great issues in our nation.

First, let's define that power. At least 40 million Americans every night, it's estimated, watch the network news. Seven million of them view A.B.C., the remainder being divided between N.B.C. and C.B.S.

According to Harris polls and other studies, for milions of Americans the networks are the sole source of national and world news. In Will Roger's observation, what you knew was what you read in the newspaper. Today for growing millions of Americans, it's what they see and hear on their television sets.

Now how is this network news determined? A small group of men, numbering perhaps no more than a dozen anchormen, commentators and executive producers, settle upon the 20 minutes or so of film and commentary that's to reach the public. This selection is made from the 90 to 180 minutes that may be available. Their powers of choice are broad.

They decide what 40 to 50 million Americans will learn of the day's events in the nation and in the world.

We cannot measure this power and influence by the traditional democratic standards, for these men can create national issues overnight.

They can make or break by their coverage and commentary a moratorium on the war.

They can elevate men from obscurity to national prominence within a week. They can reward some politicians with national exposure and ignore others.

For millions of Americans the network reporter who covers a continuing issue—like the ABM or civil rights—becomes, in effect, the presiding judge in a national trial by jury.

It must be recognized that the networks have made important contributions to the national knowledge—for news, documentaries and specials. They have often used their power constructively and creatively to awaken the public conscience to critical problems. The networks made hunger and black lung disease national issues overnight. The TV networks have done what no other medium could have done in terms of dramatizing the horrors of war. The networks have tackled our most difficult social problems with a directness and an immediacy that's the gift of their medium. They focus the nation's attention on its environmental abuses—on pollution in the Great Lakes and the threatened ecology of the Everglades.

But it was also the networks that elevated Stokely Carmichael and George Lincoln Rockwell from obscurity to national prominence.

Nor is their power confined to the substantive. A raised eyebrow, an inflection of the voice, a caustic remark dropped in the middle of a broadcast can raise doubts in a million minds about the veracity of a public official or the wisdom of a Government policy.

One Federal Communications Commissioner considers the powers of the networks equal to that of local state and Federal Governments all combined. Certainly it represents a concentration of power over American public opinion unknown in history.

Now what do Americans know of the men who wield this power? Of the men who produce and direct the network news, the nation knows practically nothing. Of the commentators, most Americans know little other than that they reflect an urbane and assured presence seemingly well-informed on every important matter.

We do know that to a man these commentators and producers live and work in the geographical and intellectual confines of Washington, D.C., or New York City, the latter of which James Reston terms the most unrepresentative community in the entire United States.

Both communities bask in their own provincialism, their own parochialism.

We can deduce that these men read the same newspapers. They draw their political and social views from the same sources. Worse, they talk constantly to one another, thereby providing artificial reinforcement to their shared viewpoints.

Do they allow their biases to influence the selection and presentation of the news? David Brinkley states objectivity is impossible to normal human behavior. Rather, he says, we should strive for fairness.

Another anchorman on a network news show contends, and I quote: "You can't expunge all your private convictions just because you sit in a seat like this and a camera starts to stare at you. I think your program has to reflect what your basic feelings are. I'll plead guilty to that."

Less than a week before the 1968 election, this same commentator charged that President Nixon's campaign commitments were no more durable than campaign balloons. He claimed that, were it not for the fear of hostile reaction, Richard Nixon would be giving into, and I quote him exactly, "his natural instinct to smash the enemy with a club or go after him with a meat axe."

Had this slander been made by one political candidate about another, it would have been dismissed by most commentators as a partisan attack. But this attack emanated from the privileged sanctuary of a network studio and therefore had the apparent dignity of an objective statement.

The American people would rightly not tolerate this concentration of power in Government.

Is it not fair and relevant to question its concentration in the hands of a tiny, enclosed fraternity of privileged men elected by no one and enjoying a monopoly sanctioned and licensed by Government?

The views of the majority of this fraternity do not—and I repeat, not—represent the views of America.

That is why such a great gulf existed between how the nation received the President's address and how the networks reviewed it.

Not only did the country receive the President's address more warmly than the networks, but so also did the Congress of the United States.

Yesterday, the President was notified that 300 individual Congressmen and 50 Senators of both parties had endorsed his efforts for peace.

As with other American institutions, perhaps it is time that the networks were made more responsive to the views of the nation and more responsible to the people they serve.

Now I want to make myself perfectly clear. I'm not asking for Government censorship or any other kind of censorship. I'm asking whether a form of censorship already exists when the news that 40 million Americans receive each night is determined by a handful of men responsible only to their corporate employers and is filtered through a handful of commentators who admit to their own set of biases.

The questions I'm raising here tonight should have been raised by others long ago. They should have been raised by those Americans who have traditionally considered the preservation of freedom of speech and freedom of the press their special provinces of responsibility.

They should have been raised by those Americans who share the view of the late Justice Learned Hand that right conclusions are more likely to be gathered out of a multitude of tongues than through any kind of authoritative selection.

Advocates for the networks have claimed a First Amendment right to the same unlimited freedoms held by the great newspapers of America.

(But the situations are not identical. Where *The New York Times* reaches 800,000 people, N.B.C. reaches 20 times that number on its evening news. [The average weekday circulation of the *Times* in October was 1,012,367; the average Sunday circulation was 1,523,558.] Nor can the tremendous impact of seeing television film and hearing commentary be compared with reading the printed page.)

A decade ago, before the network news acquired such dominance over public opinion, Walter Lippman spoke to the issue. He said there's an essential and radical difference between television and printing. The three or four competing television stations control virtually all that can be received over the air by ordinary television sets. But besides the mass circulation dailies, there are weeklies, monthlies, out-of-town newspapers and books. If a man doesn't like his newspaper, he can read another from out of town or wait for a weekly news magazine. It's not ideal, but it's infinitely better than the situation in television.

There if a man doesn't like what the networks are showing, all he can do is turn them off and listen to a phonograph. Networks he stated which are few in number had a virtual monopoly of a whole media of communications.

The newspapers of mass circulation have no monopoly on the medium of print.

Now a virtual monopoly of a whole medium of communication is not something that democratic people should blindly ignore. And we are not going to cut off our television sets and listen to the phonograph just because the airways belong to the networks. They don't. They belong to the people.

As Justice Byron wrote in his landmark opinion six months ago, it's the right of the viewers and listeners, not the right of the broadcasters, which is paramount.

Now it's argued that this power presents no danger in the hands of those who have used it responsibly. But, as to whether or not the networks have abused the power they enjoy, let us call as our first witness former Vice President Humphrey and the city of Chicago. According to Theodore White, television's intercutting of the film from the streets of Chicago with the current proceedings on the floor of the convention created the most striking and false political picture of 1968—the nomination of a man for the American Presidency by the brutality and violence of merciless police.

If we are to believe a recent report of the House of Representatives Commerce Committee, then television's presentation of the violence in the streets worked an injustice on the reputation of the Chicago police. According to the committee findings, one network in particular presented, and I quote, "a one-sided picture which in large measure exonerates the demonstrators and protesters." Film of provocations of police that was available never saw the light of day while the film of a police response which the protesters provoked was shown to millions.

Another network showed virtually the same scene of violence from three separate angles without making clear it was the same scene. And, while the full report is reticent in drawing conclusions, it is not a document to inspire confidence in the fairness of the network news.

Our knowledge of the impact of network news on the national mind is far from complete, but some early returns are available. Again, we have enough information to raise serious questions about its effect on a democratic society. Several years ago Fred Friendly, one of the pioneers of network news, wrote that its missing ingredients were conviction, controversy and a point of view. The networks have compensated with a vengeance.

And in the networks' endless pursuit of controversy, we should ask: What is the end value—to enlighten or to profit? What is the end result—to inform or to confuse? How does the ongoing exploration for more action, more excitement, more drama serve our national search for internal peace and stability.

Gresham's Law seems to be operating in the network news. Bad news drives out good news. The irrational is more controversial than the rational. Concurrence can no longer compete with dissent.

One minute of Eldridge Cleaver is worth 10 minutes of Roy Wilkins. The labor crisis settled at the negotiating table is nothing compared to the confrontation that results in a strike—or better yet, violence along the picket lines.

Normality has become the nemisis of the network news. Now the upshot of all this controversy is that a narrow and distorted picture of America often emerges from the televised news.

A single, dramatic piece of the mosaic becomes in the minds of millions the entire picture. And the American who relies upon television for his news might conclude that the majority of American students are embittered radicals. That the majority of black Americans feel no regard for their country. That violence and lawlessness are the rule rather than the exception on the American campus.

We know that none of these conclusions is true.

Perhaps the place to start looking for a credibility gap is not in the offices of the Government in Washington but in the studios of the networks in New York.

Television may have destroyed the old stereotypes, but has it not created new ones in their places?

What has this passionate pursuit of controversy done to the politics of progress through local compromise essential to the functioning of a democratic society?

The members of Congress or the Senate who follow their principles and philosophy quietly in a spirit of compromise are unknown to many Americans, while the loudest and most extreme dissenters on every issue are known to every man in the street.

How many marches and demonstrations would we have if the marchers did not know that the ever-faithful TV cameras would be there to record their antics for the next news show?

We've heard demands that Senators and Congressmen and judges make known all their financial connections so that the public will know who and what influences their decisions and their votes. Strong arguments can be made for that view.

But when a single commentator or producer, night after night, determines for millions of people how much of each side of a great issue they are going to see and hear, should he not first disclose his personal views on the issue as well?

In this search for excitement and controversy, has more than equal time gone to the minority of Americans who specialize in attacking the United

States — its institutions and its citizens?

Tonight I've raised questions. I've made no attempt to suggest the answers. The answers must come from the media men. They are challenged to turn their critical powers on themselves, to direct their energy, their talent and their conviction toward improving the quality and objectivity of news presentation.

They are challenged to structure their own civic ethics to relate to the great responsibilities they hold.

And the people of America are challenged, too, challenged to press for responsible news presentations. The people can let the networks know that they want their news straight and objective. The people can register their complaints on bias through mail to the networks and phone calls to local stations. This is one case where the people must defend themselves, where the citizen, not the Government, must be the reformer; where the consumer can be the most effective crusader.

By way of conclusion, let me say that every elected leader in the United States depends on these men of the media.

Whether what I've said to you tonight will be heard and seen at all by the nation is not my decision, it's not your decision, it's their decision.

In tomorrow's edition of The Des Moines Register, you'll be able to read a news story detailing what I've said tonight. Editorial comment will be reserved for the editorial page, where it belongs.

Should not the same wall of separation exist between news and comment on the nation's networks?

Now, my friends, we'd never trust such power, as I've described, over public opinion in the hands of an elected Government. It's time we questioned it in the hands of a small and unelected elite.

The great networks have dominated America's airwaves for decades. The people are entitled to a full accounting of their stewardship.

For the Equal Rights Amendment

Shirley Anita St. Hill Chisholm

*Shirley Chisholm (November 30, 1924 -   ) received her B.A.
from Brooklyn College and the M.A. from Columbia University; member of the New York State Assembly, 1964-68;
member of 91st-95th Congress. The speech was delivered to
the United States House of Representatives, August 10, 1970.
Published version:* Congressional Record, *91st Congress, 2nd
session, 116, pt. 21, pp. 28028-29.*

Mr. Speaker, House Joint Resolution 264, before us today, which provides for equality under the law for both men and women, represents one of
the most clear-cut opportunities we are likely to have to declare our faith in
the principles that shaped our Constitution. It provides a legal basis for
attack on the most subtle, most pervasive and most institutionalized form
of prejudice that exists. Discrimination against women, solely on the basis
of their sex, is so widespread that it seems to many persons normal, natural
and right. Legal expression of prejudice on the grounds of religious or
political belief has become a minor problem in our society. Prejudice on the
basis of race is, at least, under systematic attack. There is reason for
optimism that it will start to die with the present older generation. It is time
we act to assure full equality of opportunity to those citizens who, although
in a majority, suffer the restrictions that are commonly imposed on minorities, to women.

The argument that this amendment will not solve the problem of sex discrimination is not relevant. If the argument were used against a civil rights
bill — as it has been used in the past — the prejudice that lies behind it would
be embarrassing. Of course laws will not eliminate prejudice from the hearts
of human beings. But that is no reason to allow prejudice to continue to be

enshrined in our laws — to perpetuate injustice through inaction.

The amendment is necessary to clarify countless ambiguities and inconsistencies in our legal system. For instance, the Constitution guarantees due process of law, in the fifth and 14th amendments. But the applicability of due process of sex distinctions is not clear: Women are excluded from some State colleges and universities. In some States, restrictions are placed on a married woman who engages in an independent business. Women may not be chosen for some juries. Women even receive heavier criminal penalties than men who commit the same crime.

What would the legal effects of the equal rights amendment really be? The equal rights amendment would govern only the relationship between the State and its citizens — not relationships between private citizens.

The amendment would be largely self-executing, that is, any Federal or State laws in conflict would be ineffective one year after date of ratification without further action by the Congress or State legislatures.

Opponents of the amendment claim its ratification would throw the law into a state of confusion and would result in much litigation to establish its meaning. This objection overlooks the influence of legislative history in determining intent and the recent activities of many groups preparing for legislative changes in this direction.

State labor laws applying only to women, such as those limiting hours of work and weights to be lifted would become inoperative unless the legislature amended them to apply to men. As of early 1970 most States would have some laws that would be affected. However, changes are being made so rapidly as a result of title VII of the Civil Rights Act of 1964, it is likely that by the time the equal rights amendment would become effective, no conflicting State laws would remain.

In any event, there has for years been great controversy as to the usefulness to women of these State labor laws. There has never been any doubt that they worked a hardship on women who need or want to work overtime and on women who need or want better paying jobs, and there has been no persuasive evidence as to how many women benefit from the archaic policy of the laws. After the Delaware hours law was repealed in 1966, there were no complaints from women to any of the State agencies that might have been approached.

Jury service laws not making women equally liable for jury service would have to be revised.

The selective service law would have to include women, but women would not be required to serve in the Armed Forces where they are not fitted any more than men are required to serve. Military service, while a great responsibility, is not without benefits, particularly for young men with limited education or training. Since October 1966, 246,000 young men who did not meet the normal mental or physical requirements have been given opportunities for training and correcting physical problems. This opportunity is not open to their sisters. Only girls who have completed high school and meet high standards on the educational test can volunteer. Ratification of the amendment would not permit application of higher standards to women.

Survivorship benefits would be available to husbands of female workers on the same basis as to wives of male workers. The Social Security Act and the civil service and military service retirement acts are in conflict.

Public schools and universities could not be limited to one sex and could not apply different admission standards to men and women. Laws requiring longer prison sentences for women than men would be invalid, and equal opportunities for rehabilitation and vocational training would have to be provided in public correctional institutions.

Different ages of majority based on sex would have to be harmonized.

Federal, State, and other governmental bodies would be obligated to follow nondiscriminatory practices in all aspects of employment, including public school teachers and State university and college faculties.

What would be the economic effects of the equal rights amendment? Direct economic effects would be minor. If any labor laws applying only to women still remained, their amendment or repeal would provide opportunity for women in better-paying jobs in manufacturing. More opportunities in public vocational and graduate schools for women would also tend to open up opportunities in better jobs for women.

Indirect effects could be much greater. The focusing of public attention on the gross legal, economic, and social discrimination against women by hearings and debates in the Federal and State legislatures would result in changes in attitude of parents, educators, and employers that would bring about substantial economic changes in the long run.

Sex prejudice cuts both ways. Men are oppressed by the requirements of the Selective Service Act, by enforced legal guardianship of minors, and by alimony laws. Each sex, I believe, should be liable when necessary to serve and defend this country.

Each has a responsibility for the support of children.

There are objections raised to wiping out laws protecting women workers. No one would condone exploitation. But what does sex have to do with it? Working conditions and hours that are harmful to women are harmful to men; wages that are unfair for women are unfair for men. Laws setting employment limitations on the basis of sex are irrational, and the proof of this is their inconsistency from State to State. The physical characteristics of men and women are not fixed, but cover two wide spans that have a great deal of overlap. It is obvious, I think, that a robust woman could be more fit for physical labor than a weak man. The choice of occupation would be determined by individual capabilities, and the rewards for equal work should be equal.

This is what it comes down to: artificial distinctions between persons must be wiped out of the law. Legal discrimination between the sexes is, in almost every instance, founded on outmoded views of society and the pre-scientific beliefs about psychology and physiology. It is time to sweep away these relics of the past and set future generations free of them.

Federal agencies and institutions responsible for the enforcement of equal opportunity laws need the authority of a Constitutional amendment. The 1964 Civil Rights Act and the 1963 Equal Pay Act are not enough; they are limited in their coverage—for instance, one excludes teachers, and the other leaves out administrative and professional women. The Equal Employment Opportunity Commission has not proven to be an adequate device, with its powers limited to investigation, conciliation and recommendation to the Justice Department. In its cases involving sexual discrimination, it has failed in more than one-half. The Justice Department has been even less effective. It has intervened in only one case involving discrimination on the basis of sex, and this was on a procedural point. In a second case, in which both sexual and racial discrimination were alleged, the racial bias charge was given far greater weight.

Evidence of discrimination on the basis of sex should hardly have to be cited here. It is in the Labor Department's employment and salary figures for anyone who is still in doubt. Its elimination will involve so many changes in our State and Federal laws that, without the authority and impetus of this proposed amendment, it will perhaps take another 194 years. We cannot be parties to continuing a delay. The time is clearly now to put this House on record for the fullest expression of that equality of opportunity which our founding fathers professed.

They professed it, but they did not assure it to their daughters, as they tried to do for their sons.

The Constitution they wrote was designed to protect the rights of white, male citizens. As there were no black Founding Fathers, there were no founding mothers—a great pity, on both counts. It is not too late to complete the work they left undone. Today, here, we should start to do so.

In closing I would like to make one point. Social and psychological effects will be initially more important than legal or economic results. As Leo Kanowitz has pointed out:

> Rules of law that treat of the sexes per se inevitably produce far-reaching effects upon social, psychological and economic aspects of male-female relations beyond the limited confines of legislative chambers and courtrooms. As long as organized legal systems, at once the most respected and most feared of social institutions, continue to differentiate sharply, in treatment or in words, between men and women on the basis of irrelevant and artificially created distinctions, the likelihood of men and women com-

ing to regard one another primarily as fellow human beings and only secondarily as representatives of another sex will continue to be remote. When men and women are prevented from recognizing one another's essential humanity by sexual prejudices, nourished by legal as well as social institutions, society as a whole remains less than it could otherwise become.

Democratic Convention Keynote Address

Barbara C. Jordan

Barbara Jordan (February 21, 1936 -   ) graduated from Texas Southern University and received her law degree from Boston University in 1959; member of Texas Senate, 1966-72; member of 93rd-95th Congress; Lyndon Baines Johnson professor of public affairs, University of Texas at Austin since 1979. The speech was nationally broadcast from the Democratic National Convention, New York City, July 12, 1976. Published version: Vital Speeches of the Day, *August 15, 1976, pp. 645-46.*

One hundred and forty-four years ago, members of the Democratic Party first met in convention to select a Presidential candidate. Since that time, Democrats have continued to convene once every four years and draft a party platform and nominate a Presidential candidate. And our meeting this week is a continuation of that tradition.

But there is something different about tonight. There is something special about tonight. What is different? What is special? I, Barbara Jordan, am a keynote speaker.

A lot of years passed since 1832, and during that time it would have been most unusual for any national political party to ask that a Barbara Jordan deliver a keynote address...but tonight here I am. And I feel that notwithstanding the past that my presence here is one additional bit of evidence that the American Dream need not forever be deferred.

Now that I have this grand distinction what in the world am I supposed to say?

I could easily spend this time praising the accomplishments of this party and attacking the Republicans but I don't choose to do that.

I could list the many problems which Americans have. I could list the problems which cause people to feel cynical, angry, frustrated: problems which include lack of integrity in government; the feeling that the individual no longer counts; the reality of material and spiritual poverty; the feeling that the grand American experiment is falling or has failed. I could recite these problems and then I could sit down and offer no solutions. But I don't choose to do that either.

The citizens of America expect more. They deserve and they want more than a recital of problems.

We are a people in a quandry about the present. We are a people in search of our future. We are a people in search of a national community.

We are a people trying not only to solve the problems of the present: unemployment, inflation...but we are attempting on a larger scale to fulfill the promise of America. We are attempting to fulfill our national purpose; to create and sustain a society in which all of us are equal.

Throughout our history, when people have looked for new ways to solve their problems, and to uphold the principles of this nation, many times they have turned to political parties. They have often turned to the Democratic Party.

What is it, what is it about the Democratic Party that makes it the instrument that people use when they search for ways to shape their future? Well I believe the answer to that question lies in our concept of governing. Our concept of governing is derived from our view of people. It is a concept deeply rooted in a set of beliefs firmly etched in the national conscience, of all of us.

Now what are these beliefs?

First, we believe in equality for all and privileges for none. This is a belief that each American regardless of background has equal standing in the public forum, all of us. Because we believe this idea so firmly, we are an inclusive rather than an exclusive party. Let everybody come.

I think it no accident that most of those emigrating to America in the 19th century identified with the Democratic Party. We are a heterogeneous party made up of Americans of diverse backgrounds.

We believe that the people are the source of all governmental power; that the authority of the people is to be extended, not restricted. This can be accomplished only by providing each citizen with every opportunity to participate in the management of the government. They must have that.

We believe that the government which represents the authority of all the people, not just one interest group, but all the people, has an obligation to actively underscore, actively seek to remove those obstacles which would block individual achievement...obstacles emanating from race, sex, economic condition. The government must seek to remove them.

We are a party of innovation. We do not reject our traditions, but we are willing to adapt to changing circumstances, when change we must. We are willing to suffer the discomfort of change in order to achieve a better future.

We have a positive vision of the future founded on the belief that the gap between the promise and reality of America can one day be finally closed. We believe that.

This my friends, is the bedrock of our concept of governing. This is a part of the reason why Americans have turned to the Democratic Party. These are the foundations upon which a national community can be built.

Let's all understand that these guiding principles cannot be discarded for short-term political gains. They represent what this country is all about. They are indigenous to the American idea. And these are principles which are not negotiable.

In other times, I could stand here and give this kind of exposition on the beliefs of the Democratic Party and that would be enough. But today that is not enough. People want more. That is not sufficient reason for the majority of the people of this country to vote Democratic. We have made mistakes. In our haste to do all things for all people, we did not foresee the full consequences of our actions. And when the people raised their voices, we didn't hear. But our deafness was only a temporary condition, and not an irreversible condition.

Even as I stand here and admit that we have made mistakes I still believe that as the people of America sit in judgment on each party, they will recognize that our mistakes were mistakes of the heart. They'll recognize that.

And now we must look to the future. Let us heed the voice of the people and recognize their common sense. If we do not, we not only blaspheme our political heritage, we ignore the common ties that bind all Americans.

Many fear the future. Many are distrustful of their leaders, and believe that their voices are never heard. Many seek only to satisfy their private work wants. To satisfy private interests.

But this is the great danger America faces. That we will cease to be one nation and become instead a collection of interest groups: city against suburb, region against region, individual against individual. Each seeking to satisfy private wants.

If that happens, who then will speak for America?

Who then will speak for the common good?

This is the question which must be answered in 1976.

Are we to be one people bound together by common spirit sharing in a common endeavor or will we become a divided nation?

For all of its uncertainty, we cannot flee the future. We must not become the new puritans and reject our society. We must address and master the future together. It can be done if we restore the belief that we share a sense of national community, that we share a common national endeavor. It can be done.

There is no executive order; there is no law that can require the American people to form a national community. This we must do as individuals and if we do it as individuals, there is no President of the United States who can veto that decision.

As a first step, we must restore our belief in ourselves. We are a generous people so why can't we be generous with each other? We need to take to heart the words spoken by Thomas Jefferson:

Let us restore to social intercourse that harmony and that affection without which liberty and even life are but dreary things.

A nation is formed by the willingness of each of us to share in the responsibility for upholding the common good.

A government is invigorated when each of us is willing to participate in shaping the future of this nation.

In this election year we must define the common good and begin again to shape a common good and begin again to shape a common future. Let each person do his or her part. If one citizen is unwilling to participate, all of us are going to suffer. For the American idea, though it is shared by all of us, is realized in each one of us.

And now, what are those of us who are elected public officials supposed to do? We call ourselves public servants but I'll tell you this: we as public servants must set an example for the rest of the nation. It is hypocritical for the public official to admonish and exhort the people to uphold the common good if we are derelict in upholding the common good. More is required of public officials than slogans and handshakes and press releases. More is required. We must hold ourselves strictly accountable. We must provide the people with a vision of the future.

If we promise as public officials, we must deliver. If we as public officials propose, we must produce. If we say to the American people it is time for you to be sacrificial; sacrifice. If the public official says that, we (public officials) must be the first to give. We must be. And again, if we make mistakes, we must be willing to admit them. We have to do that. What we have to do is strike a balance between the idea that government should do everything and the idea, the belief, that government ought to do nothing. Strike a balance.

Let there be no illusions about the difficulty of forming this kind of a national community. It's tough, difficult, not easy. But a spirit of harmony will survive in America only if each of us remembers that we share a common destiny. If each of us remembers when self-interest and bitterness seem to prevail, that we share a common destiny.

I have confidence that we can form this kind of national community.

I have confidence that the democratic Party can lead the way. I have that confidence. We cannot improve on the system of government handed down to us by the founders of the Republic, there is no way to improve upon that.

But what we can do is to find new ways to implement that system and realize our destiny.

Now, I began this speech by commenting to you on the uniqueness of a Barbara Jordan making the keynote address. Well I am going to close my speech by quoting a Republican President and I ask you that as you listen to these words of Abraham Lincoln, relate them to the concept of a national community in which every last one of us participates: As I would not be a slave, so I would not be a master. This expresses my idea of Democracy. Whatever differs from this, to the extent of the difference is no Democracy.

Barbara Jordan's Keynote Address:
The Juxtaposition of Contradictory Values

Wayne N. Thompson

Dr. Thompson is Emeritus Professor, University of Houston, Texas. This article originally appeared in Southern Speech Communication Journal, *44 (1979), 223-32, and is reprinted with permission from the Southern Speech Communication Association.*

On July 12, 1976, Barbara Jordan delivered a keynote address to the National Democratic Convention that held unusually high attention for the circumstances and that delegates rewarded with their "most resoundingly heartfelt ovation" of the four-day program.[1] Two writers for the New York *Times* concurred in the opinion that the address was a great success. R.W. Apple, Jr., wrote, "The orator of the night and perhaps of the convention was the second keynoter, the eloquent black Representative from Houston, Barbara Jordan."[2] James M. Naughton in the same issue contrasted "the exuberant hoopla over Barbara Jordan" with the "impassive reaction to Senator John Glenn."[3]

The preceding statements are a combination of personal rhetorical judgments and of first-hand reporting of the reactions of those present in Madison Square Garden. Perhaps even more impressive are the data for the

---

[1] "A Happy Garden Party," *Time,* 108 (July 26, 1976), 16.
[2] "Democrats Meet...," New York *Times,* July 13, 1977, p. 1.
[3] "4 Days in a Sea of Good Will, Mostly," p. 24.

American people generally. A Harris Survey showed that fifty-four per cent of the respondents were positive toward the speech and that only nine per cent were negative. In contrast, the figures for the keynote address of Senator John Glenn were thirty-one per cent positive and twenty-five per cent negative.[4] Of the fourteen items that Harris studied for the convention, the address by Jordan elicited the smallest negative reaction and with a six-to-one margin ranked second in the ratio of positive to negative responses.[5] Only the judgment that the convention was marked by unity received a more favorable response.

The success of Jordan's address is especially noteworthy because of the rhetorical problems peculiar to keynoting as an oratorical genre. Whereas emotional partisans of a speaker's own party expect a vigorous attack on the opposition, neutrals and members of the other political party are likely to find strong attacks irritating and offensive.[6] Since scientific pollsters, such as Harris, construct samples that are microcosms of the population,[7] a nine percent figure strongly suggests that no major group found the address either unsatisfying or overdone.

Why did Barbara Jordan succeed so well at the difficult task of addressing both the partisan immediate crowd and the general American audience? The causes no doubt are multiple, and the present paper does not claim that its chosen point of analysis is the only one that would be fruitful. A preliminary examination of the address suggested to the writer, however, that a study of the value appeals might produce at least tentative conclusions concerning the reasons that the speech was a success with the dual audiences.

Individual Value Appeals

The best known taxonomy for the analysis of values is that of Milton Rokeach,[8] but to this writer the "fit" between the ideas in a political speech

---

[4]*Current Opinion,* 4 (Sept. 1976), 98.

[5]Pp. 97-98.

[6]For analyses of the special problems of the keynoter, see Robert L. Smith, "A Keynoter's Dilemma: A New Dimension," *Forensic,* 47 (March 1962), 9-11, 13; and Craig R. Smith, "The Republican Keynote Address of 1968: Adapative Rhetoric for the Multiple Audience," *Western Speech,* 39 (Winter 1975), 32-39.

[7]Statements on this feature of polling appear in many places. For example, see Bernard C. Hennesy, *Public Opinion,* 2nd ed. (Belmont, Cal.: Wadsworth, 1970), pp. 97-103; and Frederick F. Stephan and Philip J. McCarthy, "The Variety and Characteristics of Sampling Procedures," in Dan D. Nimmo and Charles M. Bonjean, eds., *Political Attitudes & Public Opinion* (New York: David McKay, 1972), pp. 81-100. Sample selection is a controversial topic, but comparisons of poll results and election balloting offer empirical evidence of accuracy. For example, Hennessy reports that the final Harris polls differed from the presidential election results by 2.6% in 1964 and by 3.4% in 1968; Gallup polls for the same elections were even more accurate (p. 97).

[8]Milton Rokeach, *Beliefs, Attitudes, and Values* (San Francisco: Jossey-Bass, 1968), p. 175.

and the available categories is clearer in a system created by Steele and Redding[9] than in an analysis based on Rokeach. That this superiority is more than personal preference seems likely because Steele and Redding developed their list in part through the analysis of speeches in presidential campaigns. Both systems, of course, are arbitrary, and the numerical data that follow are only general indicators of the significance of the respective appeals.

First in frequency as a value appeal, with twelve instances according to the writer's analysis, is patriotism, whose particular forms in the address were a repeated affirmation of the justness and nobility of the American Constitution and "System" and a repeated expression of faith in the present and future workability of these institutions. Barbara Jordan's own presence as keynoter, as she observed in the introduction, "[was] one additional bit of evidence that the American Dream need not forever be deferred." Shortly thereafter she deplored "the feeling that the grand American experiment is failing or has failed," and she praised the attempt "to fulfill the promise of America." In this same part of the speech she spoke of fulfilling "our national purpose" and "upholding the principles of this nation." In describing the Democratic Party, she said, "We do not reject our traditions."

As the speech progressed, the speaker's respect for her country's institutions continued to be prominent. She referred to "the American idea" at least twice, and in choosing to quote Jefferson she showed respect for the nation's heritage. Finally she said, "We cannot improve on the system of government handed down to us by the founders of the Republic, there is no way to improve upon that." Although the Congresswoman often acknowledged imperfections in the American system, her unswerving support of it was a value appeal that helps to explain why the speech succeeded with the general audience as well as with the cheering delegates.

Second, Jordan skillfully combined the appeals that Steele and Redding call "value of the individual" and "sociality." In some eight instances she asserted the former and in nine the latter, but as a rule she linked the two: the individual is important, but for effective, just government people must work together. Conversely, divisiveness and division are bad. The first appearance of praise for the individual was in her list of contemporary problems where she deplored "the feeling that the individual no longer counts." Additional statements on the importance of the individual appeared throughout, sometimes fully and sometimes briefly. One of the longer statements was this one: "We [the Democratic Party] believe that the people are the source of all governmental power; that the authority of the

---

[9]Edward D. Steele and W. Charles Redding, "The American Value System: Premises for Persuasion," *Western Speech,* 26 (Spring 1962), 83-91.

people is to be extended, not restricted. This can be accomplished only by providing each citizen with every opportunity to participate in the management of the government. They must have that.''

This statement, also, was significant for the flavor that it gave to the use of the value of the individual as an appeal. Whereas in some contexts support of this value would sound like special pleading by a black speaker for her own ethnic group, in this context it was an expression of political philosophy. Moreover, the stress on the importance of the individual did not appear to be special pleading because of the frequency with which such statements were combined with the seemingly contradictory emphasis on sociality. This value, too, assumed a special form in Jordan's address, for her remarks on this topic were an advocacy of an all-encompassing sociality at the national level. All Americans should work together; a united approach is good. A major section of the address began, ''Let us heed the voice of the people and recognize their common sense,'' but it closed with a plea that ''the American people...form a national community. This we must do as individuals.'' Shortly thereafter she again emphasized jointly the importance of the individual and the necessity for unity: ''A nation is formed by the willingness of each of us to share in the responsibility for upholding the common good.'' And soon after she asserted, ''If one citizen is unwilling to participate, all of us are going to suffer. For the American idea, though it is shared by all of us, is realized in each one of us.''

The next most important value appeal in the address was to what Steele and Redding label Puritan and pioneer morality. The affirmation of conventional morality began early in the speech when the Congresswoman deplored the lack of integrity in government and linked spiritual with material poverty as a national problem. The legitimate objective in governing, in the Puritan view, is serving the people, and Jordan affirmed this high principle: ''...these guiding principles cannot be discarded for short-term political gains....They are indigenous to the American idea. And these are principles which are not negotiable.'' Similar statements appeared later: ''...we as public servants,'' she affirmed, ''must set an example for the rest of the nation....We must hold ourselves strictly accountable.'' Immediately following she expressed support for such virtues as self-sacrifice, fair-mindedness, and moderation:

> If we promise as public officials, we must deliver. If we as public officials propose, we must produce. If we say to the American people it is time for you to sacrifice, if the public official says that, we must be the first to give. We must be. And again, if we make mistakes, we must be willing to admit them. We have to do that. What we have to do is strike a balance between the idea that government should do everything and the idea, the belief, that government ought to do nothing.

As a closing show of fairness Jordan quoted with approval a statement from a president of the opposing party, the Republican Abraham Lincoln. This rhetorical choice may have been helpful, also, as a linkage between the speaker and the congeries of positive qualities that references to Lincoln evoke.

Less frequent than the value appeals just cited but significant to the total effect of the speech, were change and progress (5 instances), ethical equality (4), equality of opportunity (4), and rejection of authority (3). Each of these is of interest, but the real importance lies in the clusters of values that are the topic for the following section.

Change and progress, as well as rejection of authority, are of special interest because of the central position that Jordan gave to her affirmation of the American Constitution and the related institutions. Despite that theme she said, "...when people have looked for new ways to solve their problems,...they have often turned to the Democratic Party." Later she stated, "We believe that the people are the source of all governmental power; that the authority of the people is to be extended, not restricted." In still another place she explicitly juxtaposed the value of change and progress with that of the patriotic support of American institutions: "We are a party of innovation. We do not reject our traditions, but we are willing to adapt to changing circumstances."

Ethical quality and equality of opportunity, the former an abstraction and the latter a practical affirmation, when combined were the final significant set of value appeals. The following examples indicate the moderate and high-minded form that they assumed in Jordan's address:

> We are attempting to fulfill our national purpose; to create and sustain a society in which all of us are equal.
>
> We believe in equality for all and privileges for none.
>
> "As I would not be a slave, so I would not be a master."[10]
>
> This can be accomplished only by providing each citizen with every opportunity to participate in the management of the government.
>
> We believe that the government...has an obligation to actively, underscore actively, seek to remove those obstacles which would block individual achievement....obstacles emanating from race, sex, economic condition.

Discussion

Why did the value appeals serve the rhetor's purpose so well? The answer to the question lies primarily in the perception that the eight principal value appeals formed two opposing clusters.

The first of the two clusters consists of the values called patriotism,

---

[10]Jordan credited Abraham Lincoln with this quotation.

sociality, and Puritan and pioneer morality. The dominant theme throughout the speech was the affirmation of America's historic traditions and institutions, the assertion of the importance of national unity, and the stand that the nation's political leaders must be responsible and responsive servants. The reason that this set of values is a plausible explanation of the very low percentage of respondents reporting negative reactions is clear: patriotism, sociality, and traditional morality, no matter whether the individual was conservative or liberal, Republican or Democrat, partisan or neutral, were not controversial. Whereas many potential materials and arguments for this keynote address would have been offensive to significant segments of the audience, these positions approached the universal acceptability of apple pie and motherhood.

Providing points that listeners of many backgrounds could approve was not, however, the only function that this first cluster served. A second outcome, arising from the prominence given to these three much-repeated values, may have been a lessening of the impact of the ideas that formed the second cluster. Endorsements of the value of the individual, change and progress, ethical equality, equality of opportunity, and rejection of authority—stands that Jordan probably had to take in order to please partisan supporters—have the potential for producing a class-conscious, race-conscious, polarizing speech. A possible explanation for the avoidance of this result was the juxtaposition of the values of the second cluster with those of the first. In the context that Jordan created, the second set of values became subaspects of an overall political philosophy.

Other reasons, however, also help to explain why the appeals worked so well—why the second cluster of values did not polarize the members of the audience into two hostile groups and why values such as patriotism and Puritan morality did not repel listeners as sentimental and banal. Five further points of analysis deserve brief paragraphs.

First, the appeals were set in harmless contexts that limited their applicability and that tempered their effects. The expressions of rejection of authority, for example, were in passages dealing with failures of those who govern to perform as they should. The use of rejection, thus, was not the mindless call of an agitator but reinforcement of the broader idea of Puritan morality as the proper standard for the conduct of public office. Also, as previously noted, statements of the value of the individual lacked agitative force because they were regularly combined with assertions of the importance of united efforts.

Second, the value appeals generally were in philosophic terms and unrelated to specific events and grievances. References to equality of sex and race, for example, were statements of a general viewpoint; as such, the ideas were neither controversial nor offensive. They might have become so if the speaker had berated the Republicans and had used statistics, examples, and/or loaded language to set forth specific injustices.

Third, praise for country and party was mixed with frank criticism—an unusual quality in a keynote address. The speech left no doubt that Barbara Jordan respected her country's institutions and believed steadfastly in her own party, but the support was considered, not thoughtless. In a probably unprecedented passage, she said, "That is not sufficient reason for the majority of the people of this country to vote Democratic. We have made mistakes. In our haste to do all things for all people, we did not foresee the full consequences of our actions. And when the people raised their voices, we didn't hear. But our deafness was only a temporary condition, and not an irreversible condition."

Fourth, the appeals were short, and the language was low in emotiveness. The word *Republican* appeared only twice, and in neither instance was the reference derogatory. The only member of the Republican Party named or even alluded to was Lincoln. Nor was there any strong attack on the opposition by innuendo. The parts of the speech that called for Americans to support the Democratic Party were affirmations of qualities ascribed to the Party. The language in such a sentence as "We are a party of innovation" was neutral and free of name calling or bitterness.

Fifth, the interactions of ethos and delivery with the message elements made the value appeals seem sincere. A detailed analysis of these two elements is beyond the purview of this paper, but briefly Jordan's imposing figure, earnestness, and deliberate, seemingly thoughtful manner contributed much to the total effect. Sincerity, according to at least some evidence, was actual as well as perceived. The support of America's traditions was consistent with statements made on other occasions. During the impeachment hearings for Nixon the Congresswoman had said, "My faith in the Constitution is whole...complete...total."[11] In an interview she had stated, "But the basic fundamental institutions of the country are durable. People still repeat those words 'liberty' and 'equality' and 'justice' with feeling, and somehow point them up as examples of what democracy can do and what masses of people can do when working together."[12]

For the preceding reasons, the value appeals were neither counter-productive nor overly obvious. Americans generally, including Republicans and/or conservatives viewing the speech on home television, saw much that they could affirm and little, if anything, that offended. At the same time they, the neutrals, and the partisan Democrats probably did not see the address as a pointless procession of platitudes. The speaker succeeded in retaining partisanship while transcending the partisan and in retaining a

[11]As cited in *Newsweek,* July 4, 1976, p. 70.
[12]*Newsweek,* July 4, 1976, p. 70.

liberal, humanitarian concern for the individual while transcending class consciousness.

But does a speech that satisfies the diverse elements in the seen and unseen audiences pose an ethical issue? Success in such an endeavor, so the writer believes, is not in itself unethical. As an analogy, one would not question the ethics of an arbitrator who persuaded both strikers and management that they should accept the arbitrator's proposed settlement. A speech that avoids divisiveness, it can be argued, meets the social utility test that some scholars consider important in the assessment of the ethics of a particular address.[13] Moreover, Jordan's address was without subterfuge. She was a keynote speaker whose role was obvious to both partisan and potential critic. That one set of values appealed to one audience and a second set to another would be reprehensible only if the purpose was bad or if the speaker was intellectually dishonest. The first possibility clearly was untrue, and the writer knows of no evidence to support the second. To the contrary, Jordan's positions in the keynote address seem consistent with her public stands on other occasions.

Summary

Barbara Jordan's speech at the Democratic Nominating Convention is an interesting study because she succeeded so well both in pleasing the immediate audience of cheering partisans and in avoiding offense to all but a few in the general audience. The explanation for this outcome, which is the topic of this paper, is the skillful use of appeals to values. The eight major appeals formed two clusters. The first of these, consisting of patriotism, sociality, and Puritan and pioneer morality, provides a plausible explanation for the success of the speech with the general audience. The second, comprised of appeals to the value of the individual, change and progress, ethical equality, equality of opportunity, and rejection of authority, is a possible reason that the delegates and spectators in Madison Square Garden were so enthusiastic. Managing successfully two opposing sets of values in a single speech is a rare rhetorical accomplishment.

[13]See Winston L. Brembeck and William S. Howell, *Persuasion: A Means of Social Influence* (Englewood Cliffs, N.J.: Prentice-Hall, 1976), p. 245.

The Panama Canal Treaties

Jimmy Carter

*Jimmy Carter (James Earl, Jr.) (October 1, 1924 -   )
graduated from the United States Naval Academy in 1947;
member of Georgia Senate, 1963-67; Governor of Georgia,
1971-75; President of the United States, 1977-81. Published
version:* Vital Speeches of the Day, *February 15, 1978, pp.
258-61. The televised address was delivered in Washington,
D.C., February 1, 1978.*

Good evening. Seventy-five years ago our nation signed a treaty which
gave us rights to build a canal across Panama—to take the historic step of
joining the Atlantic and Pacific Oceans. The results of the agreement have
been of great benefit to ourselves and to other nations throughout the world
who navigate the high seas. The building of the canal was one of the greatest
engineering feats of history.

Although massive in concept and construction, it's relatively simple in
design and has been reliable and efficient in operation. We Americans are
justly and deeply proud of this great achievement.

The canal has also been a source of pride and benefit to the people of
Panama, but a cause of some continuing discontent because we have
controlled a 10-mile-wide strip of land across the heart of their country.
And because they considered the original terms of the agreement to be
unfair, the people of Panama have been dissatisfied with the treaty.

It was drafted here in our country and was not signed by any
Panamanian. Our own Secretary of State, who did sign the original treaty,
said it was vastly advantageous to the United States and not so
advantageous to Panama.

In 1964, after consulting with former Presidents Truman and
Eisenhower, President Johnson committed our nation to work toward a

238

new treaty with the Republic of Panama. And last summer, after 14 years of negotiations under two Democratic Presidents and two Republican Presidents, we reached and signed an agreement that is fair and beneficial to both countries.

The United States Senate will soon be debating whether these treaties should be ratified. Throughout the negotiations we were determined that our national security interests would be protected; that the canal would always be open and neutral and available to ships of all nations; that in time of need or emergency our warships would have the right to go to the head of the line for priority passage through the canal, and that our military forces would have the permanent right to defend the canal if it should ever be in danger.

The new treaties meet all of these requirements.

Let me outline the terms of the agreement. There are two treaties, one covering the rest of this century and the other guaranteeing the safety, openness and neutrality of the canal after the year 1999 when Panama will be in charge of its operation. For the rest of this century we will operate the canal through a nine-person board of directors. Five members will be from the United States and four will be from Panama.

Within the area of the present Canal Zone we have the right to select whatever lands and waters our military and civilian forces need to maintain, to operate and to defend the canal. About 75 percent of those who now maintain and operate the canal are Panamanians. Over the next 22 years, as we manage the canal together, this percentage will increase.

The Americans who work on the canal will continue to have their right of employment, promotion and retirement carefully protected. We will share with Panama some of the fees paid by shippers who use the canal. As in the past the canal should continue to be self-supporting.

This is not a partisan issue. The treaties are strongly backed by President Gerald Ford and by former Secretaries of State Dean Rusk and Henry Kissinger. They're endorsed by our business and professional leaders, especially those who recognize the benefits of good will and trade with other nations in this Hemisphere. And they were endorsed overwhelmingly by the Senate Foreign Relations Committee, which this week moved closer to ratification by approving the treaties, although with some recommended changes which we do not feel are needed.

And the treaties are supported enthusiastically by every member of the Joint Chiefs of Staff: Gen. George Brown, the chairman; Gen. Bernard Rogers, Chief of Staff of the Army; Adm. James Holloway, Chief of Naval Operations; Gen. David Jones, Chief of Staff of the Air Force; and Gen. Louis Wilson, Commandant of the Marine Corps—responsible men whose profession is the defense of this nation and the preservation of our security.

The treaties also have been overwhelmingly supported throughout Latin

America; but predictably, they are opposed abroad by some who are unfriendly to the United States and who would like to see disorder in Panama, and a disruption of our political, economic and military ties with our friends in Central and South America and in the Caribbean.

I know that the treaties also have been opposed by many Americans. Much of that opposition is based on misunderstanding and misinformation. I've found that when the full terms of the agreement are known, most people are convinced that the national interest of our country will be served best by ratifying the treaties.

Tonight I want you to hear the facts. I want to answer the most serious questions and tell you why I feel the Panama Canal treaties should be approved.

The most important reason, the only reason, to ratify the treaties is that they are in the highest national interest of the United States and will strengthen our position in the world. Our security interest will be stronger; our trade opportunities will be improved. We will demonstrate that as a large and powerful country we are able to deal fairly and honorably with a proud but smaller sovereign nation.

We will honor our commitment to those engaged in world commerce that the Panama Canal will be open and available for use by their ships at a reasonable and competitive cost, both now and in the future.

Let me answer specifically the most common questions about the treaties. Will our nation have the right to protect and defend the canal against any armed attack or threat to the security of the canal or of ships going through it?

The answer is yes. And it's contained in both treaties and also in the Statement of Understanding between the leaders of our two nations. The first treaty says, and I quote, "The United States of America and the Republic of Panama commit themselves to protect and defend the Panama Canal. Each party shall act in accordance with its constitutional processes to meet the danger resulting from an armed attack or other action which threatens the security of the Panama Canal or ships transiting it."

The Neutrality Treaty says, and I quote again, "The United States of America and the Republic of Panama agree to maintain the regime of neutrality established in this treaty which shall be maintained in order that the canal shall remain permanently neutral."

And to explain exactly what that means, the Statement of Understanding says, and I quote again, "Under the Neutrality Treaty Panama and the United States have the responsibility to assure that the Panama Canal will remain open and secure to ships of all nations. And the correct interpretation of this principle is that each of the two countries shall in accordance with their respective constitutional processes defend the canal against any threat to the regime of neutrality and consequently will have the right to act against any aggression or threat directed against the canal or against the peaceful transit of vessels through the canal.''

It is obvious that we can take whatever military action is necessary to make sure that the canal always remains open and safe. Of course this does not give the United States any right to intervene in the internal affairs of Panama, nor would our military action ever be directed against the territorial integrity or the political independence of Panama.

Military experts agree that even with the Panamanian armed forces joined with us as brothers against a common enemy, it would take a large number of American troops to ward off a heavy attack. I, as President, would not hesitate to deploy whatever armed forces are necessary to defend the canal. And I have no doubt that even in a sustained combat we would be successful.

But there is a much better way than sending our sons and grandsons to fight in the jungles of Panama. We would serve our interests better by implementing the new treaties—an action that will help to avoid any attack on the Panama Canal.

What we want is a permanent right to use the canal, and we can defend this right through the treaties—through real cooperation with Panama. The citizens of Panama and their Government have already shown their support of the new partnership. And a protocol to the neutrality treaty will be signed by many other nations, thereby showing their strong approval.

The new treaties will naturally change Panama from a passive, and sometimes deeply resentful, bystander into an active and interested partner whose vital interests will be served by a well-operated canal. This agreement leads to cooperation and not confrontation between our country and Panama.

Another question is why should we give away the Panama Canal Zone? As many people say, we bought it, we paid for it, it's ours.

I must repeat a very important point: We do not own the Panama Canal Zone. We have never had sovereignty over it. We have only had the right to use it.

The Canal Zone cannot be compared with United States territory. We bought Alaska from the Russians, and no one has ever doubted that we own it. We bought the Louisiana Purchases—territories—from France, and that's an integral part of the United States.

From the beginning we have made an annual payment to Panama to use their land. You do not pay rent on your own land. The Panama Canal Zone has always been Panamanian territory.

The U.S. Supreme Court and previous American Presidents have repeatedly acknowledged the sovereignty of Panama over the Canal Zone. We've never needed to own the Panama Canal Zone, anymore than we need to own a 10-mile wide strip of land all the way through Canada from Alaska when we build an international gas pipeline.

The new treaties give us what we do need: not ownership of the canal, but the right to use it and to protect it.

As the chairman of the Joint Chiefs of Staff has said, "The strategic value of the canal lies in its use."

There's another question. Can our naval ships, our warships, in time of need or emergency get through the canal immediately instead of waiting in line? The treaties answer that clearly by guaranteeing that our ships will always have expeditious transit through the canal. To make sure that there could be no possible disagreement about what these words mean the joint statement says that expeditious transit—and I quote—is intended to assure the transit of such vessels through the canal as quickly as possible without any impediment with expedited treatment, and in case of need or emergency to go to the head of the line of vessels in order to transit the canal rapidly.

Will the treaties affect our standing in Latin America? Will they create a so-called power vacuum which our enemies might move in to fill? They will do just the opposite. The treaties will increase our nation's influence in this hemisphere, will help to reduce any mistrust and disagreement, and they will remove a major source of anti-American feeling. The new agreement has already provided vivid proof to the people of this hemisphere that a new era of friendship and cooperation is beginning, and that what they regard as a last remnant of alleged American colonialism is being removed.

Last fall I met individually with the leaders of 18 countries in this hemisphere. Between the United States and Latin America there is already a new sense of equality, a new sense of trust and mutual respect that exists because of the Panama Canal treaties. This opens up a fine opportunity for us in good will, trade, jobs, exports and political cooperation. If the treaties should be rejected, this would all be lost and disappointment and despair among our good neighbors and traditional friends would be severe.

In the peaceful struggle against alien ideologies, like Communism, these treaties are a step in the right direction. Nothing could strengthen our competitors and adversaries in this hemisphere more than for us to reject this agreement.

What if a new sea-level canal should be needed in the future? This question has been studied over and over throughout this century from before the time the canal was built up through the last few years. Every study has reached the same conclusion—that the best place to build a sea-level canal is in Panama. The treaties say that if we want to build such a canal, we will build it in Panama, and if any canal is to be built in Panama, that we, the United States, will have the right to participate in the project.

This is a clear benefit to us, for it insures that, say 10 or 20 years from now, no unfriendly but wealthy power will be able to purchase the right to build a sea-level canal to bypass the existing canal, perhaps leaving that other nation in control of the only usable waterway across the isthmus.

Are we paying Panama to take the canal? We are not. Under the new treaty, any payment to Panama will come from tolls paid by ships which use the canal.

What about the present and the future stability and the capability of the Panamanian Government? Do the people of Panama themselves support the agreement?

Well, as you know, Panama and her people have been our historical allies and friends. The present leader of Panama has been in office for more than nine years. And he heads a stable government which has encouraged the development of free enterprise in Panama. Democratic elections will be held this August to choose the members of the Panamanian Assembly, who will in turn elect a president and a vice president by majority vote.

In the past regimes have changed in Panama. But for 75 years no Panamanian government has ever wanted to close the canal.

Panama wants the canal open and neutral, perhaps even more than we do. The canal's continued operation is very important to us, but it is much more than that to Panama. To Panama it's crucial.

Much of her economy flows directly or indirectly from the canal. Panama would be no more likely to neglect or to close the canal than we would be to close the interstate highway system here in the United States.

In an open and free referendum last October which was monitored very carefully by the United Nations, the people of Panama gave the new treaties their support. The major threat to the canal comes not from any government of Panama but from misguided persons who may try to fan the flames of dissatisfaction with the terms of the old treaty.

There's a final question about the deeper meaning of the treaties themselves to us and to Panama.

Recently I discussed the treaties with David McCullough, author of *The Path Between the Seas*, the great history of the Panama Canal. He believes that the canal is something that we built and have looked at for these many years. It is "ours" in that sense, which is very different from just ownership.

So when we talk of the canal, whether we are old, young, for or against the treaties, we are talking about very deep and elemental feelings about our own strength.

Still, we Americans want a more humane and stable world. We believe in good will and fairness as well as strength. This agreement with Panama is something we want because we know it is right. This is not merely the surest way to protect and save the canal; it's a strong, positive act of a people who are still confident, still creative, still great.

This new partnership can become a source of national pride and self-respect in much the same way that building the canal was 75 years ago. It's the spirit in which we act that is so very important.

Theodore Roosevelt, who was President when America built the canal, saw history itself as a force. And the history of our own time and the changes it has brought would not be lost on him. He knew that change was inevitable and necessary. Change is growth. The true conservative, he once remarked, keeps his faith to the future.

But if Theodore Roosevelt were to endorse the treaties, as I'm quite sure he would, it would be mainly because he could see the decision as one by which we are demonstrating the kind of great power we wish to be.

We cannot avoid meeting great issues, Roosevelt said. All we can determine for ourselves is whether we shall meet them well or ill.

The Panama Canal is a vast heroic expression of that age-old desire to bridge a divide and to bring people closer together.

This is what the treaties are all about.

We can sense what Roosevelt called the lift toward nobler things which marks a great and generous people.

In this historic decision, he would join us in our pride for being a great and generous people with a national strength and wisdom to do what is right for us and what is fair to others.

Strengthening Families in the Nation

Jerry Falwell

Jerry Falwell (August 11, 1933 -   ) graduated from Baptist Bible College; he founded the Thomas Road Baptist Church, 1956, and Liberty Baptist College, 1971; founder of Moral Majority, Inc.; he broadcasts on the Old-Time Gospel Hour, a one-hour weekly television telecast over 392 stations, and a thirty-minute daily radio broadcast over 500 stations. The speech was delivered at the Southern Baptist Convention Christian Life Commission Annual Meeting in Atlanta, Georgia on March 23, 1982. It is reprinted with permission from Old-Time Gospel Hour. The text is transcribed from a recording of the speech.

Dr. Valentine, it's my great delight to be here. Dr. Allen, Dr. Mace, thank you for your messages. I learned much. We are just, first of all, brothers and sisters in Christ if we have trusted the same Saviour and I am so grateful. I see many of your faces whom I know and some whom I do not know, but we are happy to be with you. A mover and a shaker—I don't know about that. I was introduced in a Jewish group the other night as a fund-raiser. Maybe they left an offering if they didn't get in. My wife would agree with that. She received a letter the other day from a dear old gentleman in Pennsylvania, a widower who supports our college. He knows how to get the letter to me. He addressed it to my wife. They'll open my mail at the office, but they don't open hers. You're married. You understand that. The letter came to our house, and it had $1,000 check inside for the college. It said, "Dear Macel: Enclosed is $1,000 for Liberty Baptist College. This morning in my Bible reading time I found a verse that I want you to put on Jerry's tombstone. Luke 16:22, 'And it came to pass that the beggar died.'" So, to him I was a mover, shaker, fund-raiser.

245

Strengthening America's families, and I do not think that any emphasis more important than that has been assumed by any group anywhere, any place, any time, especially at this time in our national history. I'd like to read with you some verses from Deuteronomy, chapter 6, and then go over into Matthew, chapter 5. From the Old Testament, the New Testament gives sort of a preface to what I'll be talking about this evening. And that is returning to those traditional principles that have made, as Dr. Allen said, the family the basic unit. There's no question about that—the basic unit— in any successful and civilized society. In the sixth chapter of Deuteronomy, and reading just from verses four through nine, "Hear, O Israel: The Lord our God is one Lord: And thou shalt love the Lord thy God with all thine heart, and with all thy soul, and with all thy might. And these words, which I command thee this day, shall be in thine heart: And thou shalt teach them diligently unto thy children, and shalt talk of them when thou sittest in thine house, and when thou walkest by the way, and when thou liest down, and when thou risest up. And thou shalt bind them for a sign upon thine hand, and they shall be as frontlets between thine eyes. And thou shalt write them upon the posts of thy house, and on thy gates."

And then I'd like to skip down to verse twelve. The writer discusses the days of prosperity that will normally follow when families are solid and stable. And verse twelve, the warning. "Then after your barns are filled and your wells have all been digged," verse eleven, "and your vineyards and olive trees are flourishing, Then beware lest thou forget the Lord...."

In Matthew's Gospel, chapter 5, Jesus, in verses thirteen through sixteen said, "Ye are the salt of the earth: but if the salt have lost his savour, wherewith shall it be salted? It is thenceforth good for nothing, but to be cast out, and to be trodden under foot of men. Ye are the light of the world. A city that is set on a hill cannot be hid. Neither do men light a candle, and put it under a bushel, but on a candlestick; and it giveth light unto all that are in the house. Let your light so shine before men, that they may see your good works, and glorify your Father which is in heaven."

Let us pray.

Our heavenly Father, because we love you, because we love your church, because we love this nation and because with your love we love this world for whom Christ died, help us to understand the priority you have placed upon the home, the family, and help us, O God, to hear tonight and to gather what already has been said these days. Incorporate these truths and principles into our lives. Internalize them as a lifestyle for the future and not only build great homes and rebuild great homes, but translate the concepts to others. In Christ's name I pray, amen.

The fact that we are having a conference like this—and we're in many of them, as many of you pastors are—and finding it necessary to redefine the family is somewhat of an indictment against the real, spiritual dilemma in which our nation is found tonight. To even stop to define the family indicates that we've forgotten what the family is. We've forgotten basic, conceptual principles. That family in the Garden of Eden became a reality when God brought together a man and a woman — one man for one woman for one lifetime. And we in America have as a nation built upon the Judeo-Christian ethic. We have built great families. There's no question. In our 200 years of history, America has been great because we've had some great families inside. A nation is no greater than her families any more than a church is greater than its families. We've also, I think, Deuteronomy 6:12 — as a nation forgotten the Lord. Our families today are falling apart — outside and inside the churches. And the question simply is: what are the problems? What's causing this?

I'm sure you've discussed this week the economic pressures. There's no question we have economic pressures and both men and women working outside the home. My wife and I both worked in the early days of our marriage. She was a bank teller. Our first child was born and she felt, and I agreed, that it would just be great if she could be home with Jerry, Jr. He was born 19 years ago, and she never went back to work. But we have many families in our church where the mother cannot do that. I mean, there's just no way to eat unless both are working, and that is a tremendous problem. And we no doubt have talked this week about the moral permissiveness, the situational ethics of this generation — the do-your-own thing, if-it-feels-good-do-it philosophy. And not just our boys and girls, but our men and women are being captivated by that. And just before I left town today a politician that I've respected for a long time, the word came that he'd just informed his wife that he no longer loved her. Of course, that always means he's loving somebody else. And he'd asked her, "Could I live with you two days a week, and I will do that if you'll grant me the privilege of living with someone else the other five." A leader. And by the way, the man professes to be a Christian and may, indeed, be. But the moral permissiveness of our generation is permeating and touching everybody's. Dr. Allen said, and this is a third problem, that television set. Regardless of what you think about it, it's out there, it's dominant, it's the most powerful communication tool in history. And it is having an impact. And even if the impact is neither positive nor negative in your life as far as content, the less communication now in that home because of the hours concentrating on that content is having an effect upon the families in this country. And has been for many years. I personally think that the television set — and not so much the content as the time of communication robbed from families — has probably been one of the major contributors to the breakdown of families and our lack of discipline. And then just the plain busyness of our 20th century. We're all busy. We're all too busy. We're all traveling too many miles, getting up too early, going to bed too late. We're all doing too many things and we're caught on that merry-go-round and finding it difficult if not impossible to get off. I constantly must remind myself. My wife, if I don't. She reminds me. We have three children: Jerry, Jeannie, and Jonathan, 19, 17, and 15. What shall it profit a preacher if he saves the whole world and loses his own children? And no matter how great and glorious a ministry God may give to you and me, if we come down to the end of the road and have lost our children, it will be empty victory. Those thousands out there, those multitudes before whom we've preached, the glamour of all that disappears with one wayward son, with one broken daughter, with one child out there who one day has her marriage to fall apart. And you can't do a thing about it. And I would have to throw this in because I believe it's very dominant in today's society. The fact is that secular humanism is fast becoming the dominant religion of our society in America. As Dr. Schaeffer defines it, that which puts man at the center of everything and man as the measure of everything. That we got here by accident, and I personally believe that evolution is the cardinal doctrine of secular humanism, for if man, in fact, got here by accident, then there's no creator God, therefore, no God to whom one day we'll give an account and if we do not have a God on this end of life or a God on that end of life, if we happen to be an accident, it not only gives a low view of life, but it means that we can do our own thing, eat, drink, be merry. Tomorrow we die like the animals, cease to exist. Situational ethics. Today, there's no question about it, that's the religion of the media. And it's fast becoming the religion of the educational system of this nation. Then I suppose I would have to summarize by saying that with all of that being true, I really think the problem is not public schools or the television media. The problem with our families today cannot be laid at the doorsteps of the politicians, either the Democrats or the Republicans. I personally believe that the problems lie at the doorsteps of parents and pastors who have forgotten two things: (1) our Christian message (2) the Judeo-Christian values, the set of ethics on which this society was built. Dr. Allen mentioned salt and light. I just read from Matthew 5. Jesus said, "Ye are the light of the world, ye are the salt of the earth." And unless we are functioning effectively in both areas in our homes and in our churches, families cannot be cemented together. They cannot build. They cannot grow. They cannot succeed. The light of the world. We have a responsibility, pastors, in our churches to clearly enunciate the gospel. I was in a gorcery store the other night after church about 10:00. I go to grocery stores, too. And I was coming through and waiting to check out and the gentleman just in front of me was giving a gospel tract — that's what he said it was — to the fellow who was punching the cash register. And I could see the title. It had these words: "Fifty-seven Sins That Will Send You to Hell." I thought, "That's interesting." And so when I got there, I said, "Could I see that for a moment?" He was about to put it on a file there where he had two or three hundred of them stacked up. And I was flipping through while he was checking out groceries and finally handed it back to him and said, "Don't believe a word of it. There's not a sin on there that will send you to hell—adultery, pants suits, long hair, fifty-seven things.—The only sin that will send a man to hell is the rejection of Jesus Christ and his Gospel." And that gospel tract had no mention of the Gospel in it. I would challenge you the next time you read a gospel tract, see if you can find the Gospel in it. What is the Gospel? We've almost forgotten. Paul in Corinthians 15 said, "Wherefore I declare unto you the gospel." What is it? That Christ died for our sins, according to the Scripture. He was buried and on the third day he rose from the dead according to the Old Testament Scriptures. That's the full gospel, the half gospel, the whole gospel. That's all the gospel there is, the death, burial, and resurrection of Christ. And Paul said, "I'm not ashamed to preach, to declare that gospel of Christ, for it's the power of God unto salvation to everyone that believes." And he said further that it pleased God by the foolishness of preaching to save them that believe by preaching that gospel. We should never stand before an audience without sharing the gospel story, the death, the burial, the resurrection of Christ in our behalf, the atonement. That is the only means of salvation. And if we're going to write gospel tracts and gospel books, we ought to put the gospel in them. Or take "gospel" off the front. And we in our homes and in our churches need to maximize on the gospel. That's part of our light-of-the-world ministry. Under that light-of-the-world ministry we ought to teach and preach doctrine. In this world today togetherness is very important, but not at the exclusion or the expense of truth. What is the doctrine? What have Baptists always believed? We've always believed in the inerrancy of Scripture, the deity of Jesus Christ, the necessity of a new-birth experience for admission into the family of God. We've always believed in the Lord's return as the only hope for society—I mean ultimate hope. We've always believed in a real heaven where real people will spend a real and conscious eternity enjoying our inheritance. And we've always believed in a real hell where real people who have rejected Christ will spend a real eternity in conscious suffering. We've always believed there is fire in hell. It's not popular today, especially with the press. You'll get called a fire-and-brimstone preacher, which is what you ought to be. And I thought we were. We need to teach and preach doctrine in our churches and that's part of our light-of-the-world ministry. Then biblical righteousness—not the public schools, not government, but in our churches and in our homes, pastors and parents. We ought to from the Word of God, Deuteronomy 6, when the children get up in the morning, they walk through the house in the day, when they play in the field, when they come into the home at evening at dinner time, at bed time, by example and precept we ought to set forth what the Christian life is all about, what life is like when Jesus is in the center of that life. I was raised up in a home where my dad, as far as I know, never attended a church in his life, or his dad before him. I didn't own a Bible. I was a second-year student in college at the time. My mother was a godly woman, but she'd go off to church alone on Sunday mornings all during my high school days and my first two years of college. She'd leave the radio on, knowing full well no one would get up to cut if off, and I heard Dr. Charles E. Fuller, The Old Fashioned Revival Hour broadcast. I didn't know if he was a Baptist or a Catholic or a Jew. I didn't know the difference. But I heard the gospel, and I heard a voice that to me was compassionate, and I heard what I felt was sincerity coming through, and at age 18, planning to be a mechanical engineer, I trusted Christ as my Saviour. When I went church hunting, I was looking for a church that preached what I had been hearing Dr. Fuller preach. I didn't know what that was, really, but I thought I might recognize it if I heard it again somewhere. I didn't own a Bible and I happened to walk inside a little two-year-old fledgling congregation, no sign outside, and that, in fact, was what I had been hearing Dr. Fuller say. It happened to be a Baptist church. But I heard the gospel there and I heard biblical righteousness and my whole life had to be turned around. I had to have a spiritual brainwashing because I didn't have those values. I didn't know the things I'm talking about tonight. I had to start from ground zero. Sometimes I think it's better. Sometimes I think that a religious person has to come up to zero before he can really become a Christian person, for our religion is often a hindrance rather than a help when Christ is not the central personality in our religion. And so, biblical righteousness. And the first few months of my conversion, whatever the preacher said, whatever I heard preached, I began to read it like it was going out of style, this book, the Bible. And I didn't always maybe interpret it properly, but, whatever it said, that's what I started doing. And it changed my whole life, and by the time I was a married man six years later, I think I knew what a Christian home was. But, because someone had taught me those biblical standards. And then finally under that light-of-the-world ministry, I think we have an obligation to teach and preach judgment. God is a God of love, but he's also a consuming fire. God hates sin. Whatsoever a man soweth, that shall he also reap. And there is no fear of God in today's society. Do your own thing. We're not going to pay for it. And we don't realize that whatsoever a man soweth, that every thing will he also reap. I'm talking about believers now, not just the unredeemed. And we need to teach that to our children—that to violate the laws of God means also you activate divine retribution. He's a good God, he's a loving God, but sometimes he gets mad. And as far as God's dealings with society is concerned, I personally feel that America is in trouble. I think in serious trouble. I do not think America has any corner on God. There is not a verse in the Bible that gives America any preeiminence above the family of nations. None. I challenge you to rebut that. And the only reason God has blessed America is because we've had what I'll get to in just a few moments—a lot of salt sprinkled around, that preservative that prevents spoilage and God has honored this nation because people like you have been here for 206 years. That doesn't make you more valuable to God than others, but it's a principle, and you as the salt of the earth and millions like you through two centuries have brought the blessing of God upon the society and because you have followed divine principles which automatically invoke the blessings of heaven. I think an unredeemed person could get all the principles of the Scriptures of the Judeo-Christian ethic and live by them and enjoy all the blessings from living by them. Now he would go to hell a very disciplined person if he'd never accepted Christ, but he could enjoy the benefits of obedience to biblical principles on this earth if he lived by them because they're automatic. They're unalterable. This is the word of God—the light of the world.

Pastors, parents, you know I could spend a little time here and preach to myself along with you, but with the busyness of our schedules, do we have Bible reading and prayer with our families on a daily basis? Let's be honest about it. I mean, I know how busy you are. I do a few things myself and I know that coming and going, miles to travel, all kinds of ways to excuse it. Do we practice what we preach? Do we actually read the Bible with our families? I mean from infancy and until they leave the house and then with the wife alone after that? That is what Deuteronomy 6 teaches. That is what Ephesians 6:4 teaches. Train up a child in the way he should go and when he is old he will not depart from it. Rebuilding families is just coming back to the old biblical principle of getting them into the Word of God and by precept setting the example before them on a daily basis, letting them see Christ in Mom and Dad, and then that local church becomes the confirmation, the reinforcement center. Parents tell me all the time, "Pastor, you don't know what this church means to us because we try all week to do these things that you're talking about but when we bring our children to Sunday School on Sunday morning and place them out there in the Sunday School and we attend the preaching service or the adult classes and they get into the program and they get into all the recreational program, all that the church has to offer, it is just a ditto to all we are trying to say, and it's "In the mouth of two or three witnesses let everything be confirmed." Our children believe there's no other way because certainly our parents and church couldn't be wrong." And that is exactly what the church is all about. The light of the world.

Our three children were converted when two of them were five and one was six at the family altar. All three of them—now the church had played a role in the preaching of the Word and prayer and all, but the seed sowing, the watering, there came a time when each of them said, "Dad, I'm not saved and I'd like to be saved." Well, we all are concerned about little children being too young to understand. It's amazing how much a little child can understand. Many years have passed now and the evidence is in that they did know what they were doing. And they build upon that initial conversion experience—not perfect by any means. But I'll tell you, the evidence is there. They're bearing the fruit just as yours are.

Now let's talk about the salt of the earth. We'd like to ignore this side of it. As Dr. Allen said, this is the part we don't like. But just as Jesus said we are the light of the world, we're also the salt of the earth. We not only have the message of redemption to give to our family, to our church, to our city, to our nation, to the world, the Gospel of Christ, but we have a divine commission to be the salt of the earth—that which stings the open cut and produces tears in the eyes, thirst in the mouth, but that which kills the weeds and prevents spoilage. We're the salt of the earth. Salt has a negative connotation while light has a positive connotation. But you can't start a car with just a positive battery. You've got to have both poles and that is the way the Christian life is. That is the way the home is. That's the way the church is.

Let me talk to you about the salt-of-the-earth ministry. What's happened to our families? What's happened to our young people? I don't think young people are any worse today than they were 50 years ago. They just come from worse homes. That's all. And worse schools and sometimes worse churches. But kids are no different. They still respond and gravitate to authoritative and exemplary leadership. You can't say, "Do as I say." It's "You follow me, as I follow Christ. You do as I do." Kids are too smart today to fool. You never could fool them. You just thought you could. But today you don't even think you can. And we need, therefore, to teach them the principles that have made this such a great nation and that in every society has built great homes and great churches.

Our President said last January in his Inaugural Address what many presidents have said and what many members of Congress and the judiciary have said, that this is a nation under God. He didn't say it's a Christian nation. He didn't say it's a Jewish nation. He said it's a nation under God. A nation built upon the Judeo-Christian ethic. We hear a lot about the Judeo-Christian ethic. That just means in lay language principles out of the Old Testament—Judeo—and the New Testament—Christian And those Old and New Testament principles are the cornerstone upon which this great republic was built. Our founding fathers were by no means all godly men. But they were influenced by godly principles, by Pilgrims and Puritans and men and women of God insomuch that history supports the fact that we have a Constitution and a Declaration of Independence and a Bill of Rights that are definitely, strongly Judeo-Christian ethic in premise.

There are seven principles, in my opinion, in that ethic. The first is the dignity of human life. If we are going to strenthen our families, we've got to teach our children at home and in the church. Dr. Allen said that life is precious—that every kind of life is precious—not just the life of Americans, but the life of Russians is precious—that the life of Africans and Europeans and Asians is equally precious—that the life of the young and the life of the old is equally precious. One of the greatest men of our generation, in my estimate, is Dr. Francis Schaeffer. He's a man of courage, a great theologian, and his books as well as the books of his wife, Edith, have been to me a tremendous spiritual inspiration. I recommend them all to you. He's written recently a book entitled *A Christian Manifesto.* It's a masterpiece. The public wouldn't be surprised if I'd written it because I'm considered radical by many, but Dr. Schaeffer is not considered radical, and he advocates things there that I haven't quite yet come all the way full cycle to. But the principle of the dignity of human life is the cornerstone of any successful home, successful life, successful ministry, church and even nation.

And I agree as well with Dr. Allen that abortion on demand is not good. I might respectfully disagree and call it America's national sin. I might say that Adolph Hitler brought the wrath of God upon Germany for the destruction of 6 million Jewish lives and I would agree with the Roman Catholics and many of our friends nationwide that the 10 to 12 million little babies who have died in this country since *Roe* v. *Wade,* January, 1973 Supreme Court decision have brought the wrath of God upon this nation. And I do not believe that we can continue to devalue or ignore the lives of the unborn and expect God to smile upon this nation. Our little children at home, they can tell you all the dos and don'ts of abortion. I mean from the time they could talk they could tell you what abortion was. We had taught it to them medically. We had shown them films. We had taught it to them biblically all the way through. And they would say that abortion is wrong. It's the taking of human life. And I personally feel we need to teach that in our homes and teach that in our churches and teach that in our schools until the Christian doctrine, the Christian dogma has written right across the top "We value human life."

There's a second principle we need to teach to our children. That's the principle of the traditional monogamous family which I define as beginning and only beginning when a man legally marries a woman, period. While we want to reach out in love and compassion and with a saving gospel to homosexuals, there are no diverse family forms. There are polls taken quite often by those folk in our society who want a desired result, and they talk about the traditional family being 16 percent or 23 percent or 7 percent of the present American constituency. I always ask the question, "What's your definition of a traditional family?" Well, that's a man and a woman where the woman is at home, not working, and the man is outside working and they have two children. Some will say three children, some will say one. Well, of course, by taking that definition, you could add to it nine children and bring it down to 2 percent. I happen to believe that single-parent families are traditional families. One who is widowed doesn't cease to be a family, or someone who's been deserted doesn't cease to be a family, and if there are no children and just a mom and a dad, that's still a family. And if there are many children and a mom and a dad, that's a family. I don't think the demerits have anything to do with it, or the widowhood has anything to do with it. And the fact is that when properly asked—you know, you can make a poll say anything you want it to say—the fact is when properly asked, the American people have said that the only acceptable form is the husband-wife monogamous relationship. Our people haven't gone bad. I suspect that's about the percentage in 1776. In spite of Norman Lear, in spite of Hollywood, in spite of all the rest and Hugh Heffner, etc. we haven't changed. We still know right from wrong. It has not internalized into lifestyle as it needs to. And this is where parents and pastors have an obligation as the salt of the earth to make the family the priority in everything we do. I have one little girl. The only perfect child we have is our little daughter, Jeannie, who's graduating from high school this year as the valedictorian. I must tell you that. She just won the Bland Musical Festival as a concert pianist, and she's just everything. And my little daughter says she's going to be a medical doctor. And I hope she's a very successful one. But this precious little daughter has had quite a few dates, after I meet them, and it bothers her a little bit when she comes in at 11:00, and I just happen to be in the foyer and say, "How are you?" and turn the light on and just want to be sociable. And you know, I've done that with the boys. But the fact is I do not believe any of three—and none of them feel sheltered—my children are very normal. When I was preaching at the Indianapolis Convention Center some time ago when Jonathan was eight years old and the place was jammed with thousands of people and the fire trucks began coming and the firemen began coming in, I knew who'd pulled it. I looked around for Jonathan, my redhead. He's fifteen years old now, six feet two and a big ox. I asked him, "Son, why in the world did you pull that?" He said, "Dad, I just had to see what would happen." I'm not trying to tell you the kids are abnormally perfect. They are not. But I want to tell you this—that I don't think that any of the three of them would ever contemplate marriage without bringing Mom and Daddy into it. But that's not odd. That's normal. And I think it's healthy. You say, "Well, I believe in letting my children do their own thing." Some believe in just letting them be born, feed them, and watch them grow up. But I don't. And I think if we're going to teach our children to be successful, we need to teach them principles and this ethic of the traditional family is very important.

Common decency. The principle of common decency is principle number three. I could go to the Old Testament where God himself slew the animals and clothed the first parents. And go to the New Testament in Ephesians—

many of the passages where modesty is taught. We're living in a world today with very little shame. And you know there was a time when Christian people believed in modesty and still should. And we ought to teach that to our children and we ought to preach it in our churches. It isn't—you know I personally don't think that the framers of the First Amendment had Hugh Heffner in mind. I really don't. They don't like me and it's mutual. Pornography to me is poison. And it is destroying values in this country. You know when you walk into a convenience store at the eye level of a five-year-old child there is nudity. I resent that. I think it's damaging to our families. And I don't think one of our children has ever bought one of those kinds of magazines. You're sitting back there thinking "If old Jerry just knew." But Mama is at home and she's tougher than Daddy—much. But yet, we need to teach the principle of common decency.

I could go on talking about the work ethic. This country was built on hard work, not three-day weeks, not four-day weeks, not even five-day weeks, but six-day weeks. Not eight-hour days, but twelve-hour days. I'm not advocating a return to that, but I'm saying that there is a dignity to work. We have raised up—and it's not the fault of the young people—but we have raised up a generation, maybe two or three, who have been taught that the world, society, owes me a living because I've been born into the human race. And there's not a verse of Scripture to support that. Under the Judeo ethic God told Adam, "By the sweat of your brow you'll earn your bread," and Paul told the Thessolonians, "If a man will not work, neither shall he eat." Not that we're not trying to be uncompassionate. We should help those who cannot help themselves. We should help the aged. We should help those who would but cannot work. We have a generation of bums in this society who wouldn't work in a pie shop eating the holes out of donuts. And we raised many of them up that way. It's not their fault. It's our fault. And we need again. It's not government's place, it is the place of parents and pastors to teach our sons and daughters the importance and the value of work. The students who come to Liberty—many of them don't have to work. Most do, but many don't. They come from wealthy homes. But I speak in the first chapel every year and say, "In my opinion, all of you should find a job if you can, and you should work a number of hours a week whether you need the money or not and if you don't need it, help some needy student who does. But you ought to work because the idle time is not good for you and you need the discipline and you need to learn how to work so that once learning it you can pass that concept on to others." And you preachers out here who are building great churches, I can tell you what your secret is. You get up earlier than the others do and you go to bed later. That's the only difference. Not because you're a great preacher. They could hear better on television, and I'm not talking about the preachers on television. I'm talking about the prime-time shows. They don't come out to hear Jerry Falwell. They don't come out—Billy Graham will tell you that the day of just announcing a meeting and getting a crowd, it's all over. Boy, you work for a crowd today. Oh no, the churches that are bulging today are pastored by men who work harder than the other fellows do. And Monday, while you're out golfing, that guy who doubled you yesterday was knocking on doors. There's nothing wrong with golfing. If you can get around the course in thirty minutes, go ahead. But God knows we need to get back to work. You say, "Well, the doctor told me to slow down." If you do, you'll be in reverse, many of you. We don't need to slow down. We need to get with it. Nobody's ever killed themselves working. Now a lot of folks have killed themselves worrying, but nobody working. Work's good for you. Hard work's good for you and I've learned God can give you the strength. I'll guarantee you Dr. Allen can tell you there've been times when he got in the pulpit and didn't know what he was even going to talk about and didn't have the strength to get up and do it if he knew what he was going to talk about. He called on a strength beyond himself and probably preached his greatest sermon. Many of you preachers know what I'm talking about. God will give you that kind of strength. Everybody thinks you're really somebody. No, you're not. You're tired like the rest of us, but you refuse to admit it.

And beyond the principle of the work ethic, I call this one the Abrahamic covenant. I happen to believe that God deals with nations in relation to how those nations deal with Israel. I know I'll get some ohs and ahs here but I'll say it anyhow because I do not believe that America has been the protector of the Jews in these past many years and God has honored us because we have honored Abraham. God told Abraham, "I'll bless them that bless you and curse them that curse you." And if we could raise Adolph Hitler out of hell 30 seconds tonight, he'd say "Amen" to that because it's a matter of fact that God deals with nations in relation to how nations deal with Israel. And Russia is in trouble not because we're tough but because they're beginning to touch the apple of God's eye and persecute the Jews there and that's bad news anytime. A lot of reasons why I love Israel and support the State of Israel and Jewish people everywhere but one of them—and the basic one—is theological. I believe the Book teaches it and I am challenging America and I—you know, my children, they've loved Jews from the time they were old enough to talk. I remember introducing Jerry to a gentleman, a friend of mine. I said, "Jerry, this man's a Jew." "Oh!" He thought he was somebody special. I think he is, and I take that position in our church, and I preach that, and I try to get that out to the American public.

The sixth one is that of God-centered education. I didn't say Christ-centered, I said God-centered. You know when I grew up the only time I ever heard a hymn sung or entered into a hymn singing was in a public school. That was back before they were inhibited by anything. The old principal would have chapel — assembly they called it — when they'd have some-body lead a hymn, and I learned some of the old hymns that way. My respect for the Bible, for God, and prayer I got from a public schoolroom, so I'm for public schools. I'm for them being better. And I happen — I may disagree with some of you on this, but I certainly do it respectfully — I believe that we need a return of not mandated but voluntary prayer to our public schools in practice. We, 96 percent of all Americans,. do believe in God; 4 percent do not. We don't require the Jehovah's Witnesses to salute the flag, and we shouldn't want to make atheists silently bow their heads and pray to whomever they call god. Do their homework or write a letter to Madelyn or whatever, but this nation is a nation under God, and right now men and women who believe in God and children who believe in God are being discriminated against, in my opinion. And whether it's being done by the courts or by the school administrators or whoever, I want to challenge you teachers and administrators to change it. I believe that we ought to recognize that this is a nation under God and that there is a supreme being and that it shouldn't be embarrassing to acknowledge that we in fact do believe in God. I also happen to believe that evolution is the cardinal doctrine of secular humanism. And in the name of academic freedom, it's strange that 56 years ago the court battle at Dayton was the other way around. I would like to see in the name of academic freedom both of the predominant concepts of origin, both ''scientific'' creation and ''scientific'' evolution, taught in our public schools and the children with their parent's consultation be allowed to decide which they accept. To me, that is not dan-gerous. I think it takes a lot more — you know evolution is very religious — it takes a lot more faith to believe that this thing just happened. I believe a designer put it together, and it is not a violation of the Constitution. The Constitution nowhere separates God and state — just church and state. I don't want the state telling me what to do. They're not going to. And I don't want to tell them what to do. And I don't plan to. But I do want to believe that our children in America can be educated where there is an ac-knowledgment of a higher being — whatever the Jewish child or the Protestant child or the Moslem or Buddhist child may call God — in a silent, nonmandated way and that the two dominant philosophies in this country of origin — that is direct creation and evolution be taught as concepts — not facts — concepts only. That's academic freedom. I don't think it will hurt anybody. I think it would help a great deal.

And finally, divinely ordained institutions. We need, pastors and parents, teach our children, teach our churches that there are three institutions in God's society, clearly mandated in Scripture, and we ought to respect all three. One, of course, is the home. We've dealt with that. The second one, of course, is the state or civil government. The powers that be — the President, the members of Congress, the governors, the legislators, the powers that be are ordained of God in Romans 13. They are ministers of God, whether they know it or not, you're supposed to know it. And, therefore, we are to respect them and to obey them and the only time we have any right to disobey a law of man is when that law of man demands that we disobey a law of God and then we ought to obey God rather than man and pay the consequences. But in America that hasn't happened yet. In America you can obey God's laws without defying the laws of man, and I cannot off the top of my head think of any instance where you cannot do that, and I'm glad that's true in America.

And, finally, of course, the religious institution in the Old Testament, the tabernacle, the temple, the synagogue; the New Testament the church. And in order for a society to be healthy like the tripod supporting that camera, there must be three legs, and they must all be healthy—healthy homes, healthy government, free government, representative government, and healthy churches. And only the pastors and parents can ensure that. I think that the influence necessary for changing America is not in Washington. It's in this room. I think it's right here. And I think that every time the people of God come together there is the potential for guaranteeing if we do our thing right that our children and our children's children will grow up not in as good as, but a greater society than we've known. I think we have an obligation for that to happen.

I'd like to close by giving you a little story of a family devotional some years ago, seven or eight years when the children were that much younger. I was teaching the book of Revelation about a half a chapter at a time. Don't throw the whole bale of hay at once. Make it enjoyable, brief but enjoyable. And I was teaching Revelation and I made a statement. This was back in the early 70s when I'll have to admit I was pessimistic about America. I am not a pessimist about America today. I'm very optimistic. I think things are going the right direction. I'm not talking politics. I'm talking about I believe there's a spiritual movement in this country today that's real. There are things happening today that I think can be explained only that God is at work and people are praying and preachers are preaching and lives are being changed. But we were having family devotions and I made the statement, "Children, it's very doubtful that you will grow up to be as old as your parents in a free America. It's very doubtful you'll ever know what we've known and enjoyed." And Jonathan, who is the fireball in our family—he's broken at least one bone every year of his walking life and five last year—Jonathan said, "Daddy, why don't you do something about it?" Well, you know how little boys are. I said, "Son, I'm just one person in a very small town," and we closed. The next night apparently it had bothered the children for 24 hours, and little Jonathan before I'd finished the study said, "Daddy, why don't you do something about it?" Three or four times he did that, and a few weeks later in my private devotions I think

Somebody Else asked me that question, and I couldn't dismiss Him. I've never heard the voice of God, but I just felt the impression from the Lord, "You're one person, but you'd better do what you can." And it was in those early 70s when I really began to seek the face of God about rebuilding families, about building great churches. I am very much in favor of the public schools, but also I am in favor of Christian schools. There are 18,000 of them now in this country, four new ones starting every day. I think we need both. I began asking the Lord for directions, for guidance, and my time and talent and energy since that time have been spent in a direction that sometimes has brought the wrath of the press upon us. That shouldn't bother you. Zacchaeus couldn't get to Jesus for the press. Sometimes that's brought the wrath of my brethren against me. Many times I've deserved it; a few times I haven't. But I am determined that one day if, in fact, this country does fail, my children will never look me in the face and say, "Daddy, where were you the day freedom died?" I am determined if we go down, we'll go down swinging. We won't be called out. I think you are too, and I think that's why you're here. And if we win, it's going to be won at the family juncture first. If we put the families back together in this country—my associate pastor, Ed Hineson was looking out over the crowd Sunday morning, and he punched me and he said, "Jerry, I'm so excited. I see ten couples out there." He's a counselor. "I see ten couples out there in the last seven years that God's allowed me to put back together." Isn't that great. Heading for divorce courts. If we can rebuild the families of America, we'll be on our way to building—rebuilding—churches, our government, our society, and one day we can deliver to our children a greater America than we've known.

God bless you and thank you.

Women as Leaders

Anita Taylor

*Anita Taylor (September 24, 1935 -   ) graduated from
Kansas State University in 1957, and was awarded the Ph.D. in
1971 from the University of Missouri; president of the Speech
Communication Association, 1981; chair, department of
communication, George Mason University. The speech was
delivered to the GROW Conference, Eastern Kentucky
University, Richmond, Kentucky, February 23, 1984.
Published version:* Vital Speeches of the Day, *May 1, 1984,
pp. 445-48.*

"Now that I have this grand distinction, what in the world have I to
say?" Many of you will recognize this quotation from Barbara Jordan's
keynote address to the 1976 Democratic National Convention. Let me share
with you why I chose these words as a "text" for this speech. Barbara
Jordan, a powerful and moving speaker, has long been a role model for me.

My life has displayed a typically female pattern—or at least a pattern
typical for women of my generation. The second of three children (all girls)
in a home strongly imbued with the Protestant Ethic, I knew from earliest
childhood that I would attend college. My father insisted that we save ½ of
our meagre allowance ($.10 each week), so we could "go to college."

But I hadn't the foggiest idea what I was to study once there. I had no
clear or long range goals. The roles open to women were familiar and of
those that required college study, nursing and teaching school (which to me
meant elementary or high school), I wanted no part.

But, even though I had no clear goals, I was clearly driven. Described by
a college professor as "intense," by a student as "The Dragon Lady," by
an academic dean after a job interview as having a "killer instinct," I am
the type that today we describe as a "Type A" personality. Though never
very introspective, it's clear in retrospect that I was strongly motivated by a

very unfeminine "need" for power.

And though there have been other role models while climbing various ladders of success, I never really had a mentor. There was an exceptional and much loved graduate advisor at school who was much too ladylike to be a mentor for someone like me; there were two people, both men, who opened doors (pun intended) at critical career junctures; but there were no real mentors. What there were were heros, one of the most important, Barbara Jordan.

Barbara Jordan was and is a powerful woman who used the power of speech with consummate skill to achieve respected leadership roles. Her words are especially appropriate to introduce this speech about women as leaders.

Because my story is so typical of women, permit me a few more moments of personal reflection. Once a career found me, I moved rather rapidly, though in a haphazard course, upward. As part of a nationwide study by the Dept. of Health, Education and Welfare of female college graduates 10 years later, I learned that my salary placed me among the top 10 percent of all employed women—which speaks much more to the miserable earnings of women than to my income, which had just barely reached 5 figures by then.

During my early career, I was not active in the women's movement. Though I considered myself a feminist and had my own angry stories about salary and job discrimination, I never belonged to NOW and read no feminist literature. I was too busy "getting there." I made the excuse that I could best serve as a role model.

And in my own small world, I did that—never to the extent that Barbara Jordan was for me—but I did become a woman of modest influence who displayed many of the "right" characteristics: I was articulate, assertive, well-paid (by female standards) and, important because it legitimized me, married.

But in recent years—perhaps due to passing 40 and the mid-life crisis— I have begun to ask myself, What does it mean to be a female leader? What does it mean to be a woman who is motivated by a need for power? What can I say to the young women, who come to me so often now it is frightening, who are impressed with my position of quasi-power (students naively believe that a department chair is a position of real power), and ask me about leadership. Having made a passage into a more introspective personage, I flinch when I ask myself, What can I really say to young women about being female and aspiring to leadership? That is a question which many of you must ponder, if not now, later, like me.

What, after all, is leadership? It is behavior that influences people toward goals desired by the "leader." In a group—the setting in which most of us lead—leadership influences people toward the goals of the group. Thus, leadership heavily depends upon context, which for most women is in small groups, in interpersonal relationships and in organizations (be they as small and informal as the family or as large and formal as the business, agency or institution in which we work).

And what are the specific behaviors? It really doesn't matter which theorist you read, from Barnard and Bales through Bennis, Blake, Fiedler, Likert, March and Mouton (just to name a few) the same basic points emerge: goal setting, the organization and direction of resources (people, products, information) and motivation of people. Nor does it take much insight, intelligence or education to recognize that performing these roles effectively requires skills beyond the rational, analytical and mathematical. Certainly, such left-brain thinking is important, as is technical know-how. But without other skills, logic and technical expertise seldom result in leadership.

And, indeed, the theorists identify those needed skills. They fall into the constellation described as "people" skills: listening, empathizing, cooperating, encouraging, coordinating. These are characteristics at which women are uniquely skilled.

Why, then, have so few women achieved *recognized* leadership? Why, for instance, has there been no U.S. counterpart to Margaret Thatcher, Golda Meier, Indira Ghandi, Madame Chang Kai Chek? So few in the top ranks of corporate America?

There are several answers, probably. Among them would be:

Our nurturing nature—our tendency to give credit to others (note the emphasis above on *recognized* leadership.)

Discrimination.

Sex role socialization, which has led us to short-term, "I'll do a good job and someone will recognize my worth," thinking.

Capitalism—the competitive nature of U.S. society. While I abhor the label "Fear of Success" and much prefer the analysis of the data presented by Georgia Sassen, the studies by Matina Horner and many others have clearly demonstrated that many, if not most, women do not like competitive situations.

Doubtless the answers to the question involve all these and more. But my purpose here is not historical analysis. Instead, I wish to suggest that now, in the 1980s and beyond, women are uniquely qualified for leadership—if we acquire some specific skills and shed some attitudes that currently inhibit us.

Let's look ahead briefly, with a specific interest in what futurists say about leadership.

Among the 10 "megatrends" identified by John Naisbitt in his book by that title, for instance, are three which require skills that are demonstrably those at which women excel:

1. the movement to high tech will be accompanied by intensified need for touch;

2. the movement from representative democracy to direct democracy;

3. the movement from hierarchical frameworks to informal networks.

Women are more comfortable using touch than men; people (both men and women) are more willing to have women touch them than men. Defining that first trend more broadly as a movement to "keep in touch" even more strongly emphasizes a skill at which women have special skills. We have been socialized to be concerned for relationships, and to keep the group together, and, perhaps, as Carol Gilligan's research suggests, our concern for relationships is innate.

Moreover, small group research has consistently shown that women choose the cooperative leadership tasks, seeking to involve all members of the group, to keep the group together and harmonious. Women are uncomfortable with authority and hierarchy. Direct democracy and informal networks, whether at work or in the body politic, are contexts that increasingly will make cooperative skills more useful than skills at competing.

Moreover, Naisbitt's major trend—that the U.S. is becoming an information society—will eliminate the one major deficiency women have had in the workplace. Since leaders are usually expected to excel at whatever the group does, (even if the leadership role clearly precludes the leader performing the functions of the led), women were at a distinct disadvantage when the situations demanding leadership made physical strength important. In an information age, lack of brawn is no disadvantage. Manipulation of information requires few muscles!

My own favorite future thinker, Alvin Toffler, in *The Third Wave*, reinforces that point about the future, that information will be the basic raw material, again making clear that brawn will be of little value to leaders from now on.

Toffler makes other points in support of my argument. He notes the move from mass production to prosumption (producing for consumption), which will cause radical changes for most men, but is not at all new to women. We, who have cooked, sewed, raised children, gardens, etc., know what prosumption is. We have never quit doing it, not even those of us who also work outside our house each day.

But, most important for women, Toffler emphasizes the changed work setting in which prosumption will take place. He describes the electronic cottage, and points out how the megalith corporate structure will no longer dominate. As the work place changes, he believes, the family will re-emerge as a dominant institution in our lives, albeit a very different kind of family, and attitudes toward housework will change dramatically. Both trends will bring fundamental changes in the role of and the attitudes toward women.

Finally, Toffler speaks of major changes to come in corporate structure. Future managers must be able to "operate as capably in an open-door, free-flow style as in a hierarchical mode,... [to] work in organizations structured like an Egyptian pyramid as well as in those that look like a Calder mobile, with a few thin managerial strands holding a complex set of nearly autonomous modules that move in response to the gentlest breeze." Women, with their concern for relationships, and socialization to remain flexible in response to various dominant groups, are well prepared to manage in such an environment.

Nor is all of this far-off futures thinking. *In Search of Excellence,* by Thomas Peters and Robert Waterman, you will recall, cites the eight characteristics their research found in the seventy-five superior companies studied. All eight of these are fascinating, and none particularly gender biased, but one makes especially clear how women can fit especially well into leadership roles within even competitive system businesses. That is the characteristic of treating people (employees) as the root source of quality and productivity. Of course, no business*man*, would describe this as having a nurturant quality. But, I ask you, is it not exactly that?

Should I be more specific? Exactly what are the skills at which women are so uniquely qualified as I argue?

First, reviewing the work of Horner and the many who have followed her, as well as dozens of studies of small group leadership, we note that constellation of behaviors described as climate or group maintenance. Group maintenance functions are just as important as task leadership, even though often not thought of as leadership, and are functions at which women excel. In general (some notable exceptions among us aside), women dislike competition; they prefer and excel at cooperative situations. Women care about climate; they are concerned for others. They are—nurturant.

Indeed, what most of us have found so moving and reinforcing about the work of Carol Gilligan is her description of mature female morality. We reach that stage of development when we have learned to strike a balance between self and others. How reinforcing this means of describing our so-called "fear of success"! Women often do not fear, but rather reject, the individualistic value system required to be successful in so many settings.

Thus, I have explicated half my thesis: Leadership now and in the future will require many skills for which women are uniquely qualified.

There is another half. Women will be able to provide leadership only if they acquire some specific communication skills and shed some attitudes that currently inhibit them.

First, even in the future, women must become effective in the public forum. A recent Lou Harris poll noted that 4 of 10 people in this country stated that the situation they feared most was speaking in public. Now, I have difficulty believing people really thoughtfully answered that question.

I mean, really! Fear giving a speech more than cancer? Surely it is not thoughtful to say that!

As a speech teacher, however, I know that people do have an unreasonable fear of speaking in public, and while Harris' poll didn't distinguish between the sexes, my experience is that women fear public speaking more than do men. Even one of the most effective feminist spokespersons, Gloria Steinem, tells of her fear of the public platform and struggles to overcome it. Most women could tell similar tales.

Second, women must come to terms with their own aggressiveness. Women have two types of problems with aggressiveness—and they exist simultaneously in some of us! Many women share the drive for power, for control over others, to which I earlier confessed. But because aggressiveness has not been socially accepted or rewarded in women, the need has been sublimated. Be honest. Are any of you ever manipulative? Do you know any women who are? And what is that but sublimated aggression?

The other kind of problem women have with aggressiveness is that we deny it or don't have it. Women who wish to become leaders will have to quit being deferential, just as they will have to give up their manipulative skills.

What women need to learn is to be aggressively assertive. Let me define: Assertive people stand up for their own rights; aggressive people encroach upon the rights of others. Assertive people know their rights and insist upon them—not shrilly or loudly, but quietly, firmly and persistently, assertive people insist on their rights.

Of course, in a complex world, such distinctions are not simple. What one person perceives as assertive behavior, another is likely to view as aggressive. That is why I say we must be aggressively assertive. We must learn to assert our rights, insist on them, and not defer, back down, or manipulate when someone else perceives that what we believe is our right interferes with his/her rights. Employing our cooperative problem solving skills to resolve such impasses without giving in, without manipulative behavior, and without going beyond those rights which are indeed ours, that is being aggressively assertive.

Third, to do the first two things I have suggested, we must deal with perhaps the largest problem women have, weak self-esteem. We must reach that point of maturity described by Gilligan. We must learn to balance self and others. We must balance our desire to be liked/loved with our need to achieve self-actualization.

Pat Bradley, in a remarkable study of women in groups, discovered that women could perform leadership and be recognized for their achievements, but when they did so they paid a cost that men did not have to pay. Women who excelled at leadership were not as well liked as men who were leaders or women who were not leaders. Indeed, for men and women alike, it is lonely at the top; but it seems somewhat more lonely for women. Strong self-esteem is necessary to accept that burden of leadership.

Fourth, simply to be able to behave as leaders, women must assertively insist on certain rights. We must insist on social conditions that permit us to achieve our maximum potential. Specifically, that will involve at least three things.

1. *We must insist on equal pay for work of equal worth.* There is no equitable reason a secretary is paid less than a janitor. Nor that a librarian makes less than a carpenter, or... etc.

And we should quit waiting for others to provide these recognitions for us. We here are all university/college women. We work in institutions where routinely our clerical staffs—those departmental secretaries who in fact run many departments—are routinely paid less than the male janitors or groundskeepers. We work in institutions where the pay scale is not determined by level of skill and responsibility in the job, but by the hierarchy of the boss for whom the secretary works.

Yet, if the clerical staff were to remain home for a week, most universities would grind to a halt—as would most businesses and government agencies. Who have women to blame for secretarial salaries? Not totally, but in large part themselves for accepting them.

Far too few women will be in positions which permit them to move toward leadership roles unless this right is achieved. Equal pay for work of equal worth is a right we must insist upon.

2. *We must insist on equalizing the load at home.* With all our "liberation" these days, even among those of us who consider ourselves "professionals," who does the housework? Life has not changed significantly. Read the report from their massive study reported by Blumstein and Swartz in *Couples.* Women still assume that load *in addition* to full time work outside the home.

We cannot carry such baggage and reach our potential. I don't care what the song ("I Am Woman") says, we are not superwomen. We are human beings, with all the human frailties. We get tired. We have neither energy nor time to do it all.

If we choose to marry, as many of us will (and, I think, should), we must insist on equalizing the burden at home.

3. *We must insist on the rights of all men and women for safe and affordable child care.* The entire society has a stake in effective child raising. We all will pay when children do not receive effective parenting. We all will benefit when they get the nurturing they need and deserve. And this is not a responsibility of only the women in this world.

Our government, the companies and agencies and institutions for which we work, owe quality child care to the men and women who work for them. We need to be aggressively assertive about reminding those employing institutions that very important lesson from *Search For Excellence*: people are the source of productivity and quality.

This is, I hardly need to remind this audience, not an isolated nor decreasing problem. On the contrary, evidence reported recently by the United States House of Representatives Select Committee on Children, Youth and Families underlines how much the problem is likely to grow. Estimates provided by the Congressional Budget Office indicate that by 1990 over half of all mothers with children under 6 will be working as will nearly three-fourths of mothers with children 7 to 17. And while it is established that most families can afford to devote 10 percent of their budget on child care, the actual cost for families with more than 1 child is more likely to be 25-50 percent. Such costs are unconscionable.

Women should not have to choose between being childless and career success. Families should not have to choose between two careers and having children. Yet at the moment, if we care about the quality of parenting our children receive, we virtually have to make that choice. That should end; it can be ended if we insist upon it.

Finally, we need to guard against three dangers: *apathy, anger,* and *lethargy*. These were highlighted strongly for me in a recent speech by Stephanie Bennett, Dean of Westhampton College, University of Richmond.

The first danger is apathy, frighteningly widespread among young women today. Many of us who teach in colleges and universities find great apathy toward the "women's movement." Our young women students believe, oh so naively, that the battles have all been won. They have lived with relatively enlightened parents, studied in relatively nondiscriminatory schools, and expect to find the same situations when they leave our ivory towers. We must find a way to prepare these young women for the shock they will face when they leave us.

The second danger is anger. There are among us many who have encountered significant instances of discrimination and who have responded with anger, hard, rigid, debilitating anger. These women, however justified their feelings—as they usually are—are not effective either for themselves or for other women. Their anger disarms them and hardens its targets. Anger is exhausting and, unless controlled, not effective as a weapon to eliminate the factors causing it.

Please note, this message is not that the anger is unjustified, nor that it should be avoided. Anger is often a reasonable response to unreasonable conditions, and it *can* be used effectively to achieve goals. But it must be reasonable, controlled and not all consuming if it is not to destroy.

The final danger is lethargy. Lethargy is different from apathy. It is found in the woman who has battled, battled, and battled again. She has become exhausted. It is not that she no longer cares. It is that she no longer can exert the energy.

The women's movement periodically encounters times during which many of its best soldiers (how's that for competitive imagery?) have dropped out due to exhaustion. We must learn to cope with stress so that does not happen to those of us who haven't reached that point yet; and we must find ways to revitalize those thousands we have lost due to lethargy.

When George Allen came to Washington to coach the Redskins, he proclaimed, "The future is now." For those of us interested in equal opportunity for all people, regardless of their sex, Allen's prescription applies. Indeed, for women, the future is now. They are uniquely qualified to meet its challenges.

Keynote Address

Mario Cuomo

Mario Mathew Cuomo (June 15, 1932 -   ) graduated from St. John's College summa cum laude *in 1953 and received his law degree,* cum laude, *from St. John's University in 1956; secretary of state of New York, 1975-79; Lieutenant-Governor, 1979-82, and Governor of New York, 1983 - . Published version:* Vital Speeches of the Day, *August 15, 1984, pp. 646-49. The speech was the keynote address at the Democratic National Convention, San Francisco, California, July 17, 1984.*

On behalf of the Empire State and the family of New York, I thank you for the great privilege of being allowed to address this convention.

Please allow me to skip the stories and the poetry and the temptation to deal in nice but vague rhetoric.

Let me instead use this valuable opportunity to deal with the questions that should determine this election and that are vital to the American people.

Ten days ago, President Reagan admitted that although some people in this country seemed to be doing well nowadays, others were unhappy, and even worried, about themselves, their families and their futures.

The President said he didn't understand that fear. He said, "Why, this country is a shining city on a hill."

The President is right. In many ways we are "a shining city on a hill."

But the hard truth is that not everyone is sharing in this city's splendor and glory.

A shining city is perhaps all the President sees from the portico of the White House and the veranda of his ranch, where everyone seems to be doing well.

But there's another part of the city, the part where some people can't pay their mortgages and most young people can't afford one, where students can't afford the education they need and middle-class parents watch the dreams they hold for their children evaporate.

In this part of the city there are more poor than ever, more families in trouble. More and more people who need help but can't find it.

Even worse: There are elderly people who tremble in the basements of the houses there.

There are people who sleep in the city's streets, in the gutter, where the glitter doesn't show.

There are ghettos where thousands of young people, without an education or a job, give their lives away to drug dealers every day.

There is despair, Mr. President, in faces you never see, in the places you never visit in your shining city.

In fact, Mr. President, this nation is more a "Tale of Two Cities" than it is a "Shining City on a Hill."

Maybe if you visited more places, Mr. President, you'd understand.

Maybe if you went to Appalachia where some people still live in sheds and to Lackawanna where thousands of unemployed steel workers wonder why we subsidized foreign steel while we surrender their dignity to unemployment and to welfare checks; maybe if you stepped into a shelter in Chicago and talked with some of the homeless there; maybe, Mr. President if you asked a woman who'd been denied the help she needs to feed her children because you say we need the money to give a tax break to a millionaire or to build a missile we can't even afford to use—maybe then you'd understand.

Maybe, Mr. President.

But I'm afraid not.

Because, the truth is, this is how we were warned it would be.

President Reagan told us from the beginning that he believes in a kind of social Darwinism. Survival of the fittest. "Government can't do everything," we were told. "So it should settle for taking care of the strong and hope that economic ambition and charity will do the rest. Make the rich richer and what falls from their table will be enough for the middle class and those trying to make it into the middle class."

The Republicans called it trickle-down when Hoover tried it. Now they call it supply side. It is the same shining city for those relative few who are lucky enough to live in its good neighborhoods.

But for the people who are excluded—locked out—all they can do is to stare from a distance at that city's glimmering towers.

It's an old story. As old as our history.

The difference between Democrats and Republicans has always been measured in courage and confidence. The Republicans believe the wagon train will not make it to the frontier unless some of our old, some of our young and some of our weak are left behind by the side of the trail.

The strong will inherit the land!

We Democrats believe that we can make it all the way with the whole family intact.

We have. More than once.

Ever since Franklin Roosevelt lifted himself from his wheelchair to lift this nation from its knees. Wagon train after wagon train. To new frontier of education, housing, peace. The whole family aboard. Constantly reaching out to extend and enlarge that family. Lifting them up into the wagon on the way. Blacks and Hispanics, people of every ethnic group, and Native Americans — all those struggling to build their families claim some small share of America.

For nearly 50 years we carried them to new levels of comfort, security, dignity, even affluence.

Some of us are in this room today only because this nation had that confidence.

It would be wrong to forget that.

So, we are at this convention to remind ourselves where we come from and to claim the future for ourselves and for our children.

Today, our great Democratic Party, which has saved this nation from depression, from fascism, from racism, from corruption, is called upon to do it again — this time to save the nation from confusion and division, most of all from a fear of a nuclear holocaust.

In order to succeed, we must answer our opponent's polished and appealing rhetoric with a more telling reasonableness and rationality.

We must win this case on the merits.

We must get the American public to look past the glitter, beyond the showmanship — to reality, to the hard substance of things. And we will do that not so much with speeches that sound good as with speeches that are good and sound.

Not so much with speeches that bring people to their feet as with speeches that bring people to their senses.

We must make the American people hear our "tale of two cities."

We must convince them that we don't have to settle for two cities, that we can have one city, indivisible, shining for all its people.

We will have no chance to do that if what comes out of this convention, what is heard throughout the campaign, is a babel of arguing voices.

To succeed we will have to surrender small parts of our individual interests, to build a platform we can all stand on, at once, comfortably, proudly singing out the truth for the nation to hear, in chorus, its logic so clear and commanding that no slick commercial, no amount of geniality, no martial music will be able to muffle it.

We Democrats must unite so that the entire nation can. Surely the Republicans won't bring the convention together. Their policies divide the nation: into the lucky and the left-out, the royalty and the rabble.

The Republicans are willing to treat that division as victory. They would cut this nation in half, into those temporarily better off and those worse off than before, and call it recovery.

We should not be embarrassed or dismayed if the process of unifying is difficult, even at times wrenching.

Unlike any other party, we embrace men and women of every color, every creed, every orientation, every economic class. In our family are gathered everyone from the abject poor of Essex County in New York to the enlightened affluent of the gold coasts of both ends of our nation. And in between is the heart of our constituency. The middle class, the people not rich enough to be worry-free but not poor enough to be on welfare, those who work for a living because they have to. White collar and blue collar. Young professionals. Men and women in small business desperate for the capital and contracts they need to prove their worth.

We speak for the minorities who have not yet entered the mainstream.

For ethnics who want to add their culture to the mosaic that is America.

For women indignant that we refuse to etch into our governmental commandments the simple rule "thou shalt not sin against equality," a commandment so obvious it can be spelled in three letters: E.R.A.!

For young people demanding an education and a future.

For senior citizens terrorized by the idea that their only security, their Social Security, is being threatened.

For millions of reasoning people fighting to preserve our environment from greed and stupidity. And fighting to preserve our very existence from a macho intransigence that refuses to make intelligent attempts to discuss the possibility of nuclear holocaust with our enemy. Refusing because they believe we can pile missiles so high that they will pierce the clouds and the sight of them will frighten our enemies into submission.

We're proud of this diversity. Grateful we don't have to manufacture its appearance the way the Republicans will next month in Dallas, by propping up mannequin delegates on the convention floor.

But we pay a price for it.

The different people we represent have many points of view. Sometimes they compete and then we have debates, even arguments. That's what our primaries were.

But now the primaries are over, and it is time to lock arms and move into this campaign together.

If we need any inspiration to make the effort to put aside our small differences, all we need to do is to reflect on the Republican policy of divide and cajole and how it has injured our land since 1980.

The President has asked us to judge him on whether or not he's fulfilled the promises he made four years ago. I accept that. Just consider what he said and what he's done.

Inflation is down since 1980. But not because of the supply-side miracle promised by the President. Inflation was reduced the old-fashioned way, with a recession, the worst since 1932. More than 55,000 bankruptcies. Two years of massive unemployment. Two-hundred-thousand farmers and ranchers forced off the land. More homeless than at any time since the Great Depression. More hungry, more poor—mostly women—and a nearly $200 billion deficit threatening our future.

The President's deficit is a direct and dramatic repudiation of his promise to balance our budget by 1983.

That deficit is the largest in the history of this universe; more than three times larger than the deficit in President Carter's last year.

It is a deficit that, according to the President's own fiscal advisor, could grow as high as $300 billion a year, stretching "as far as the eye can see."

It is a debt so large that as much as one-half of our revenue from the income tax goes to pay the interest on it each year.

It is a mortgage on our children's futures that can only be paid in pain and that could eventually bring this nation to its knees.

Don't take my word for it—I'm a Democrat.

Ask the Republican investment bankers on Wall Street what they think the chances are this recovery will be permanent. If they're not too embarrassed to tell you the truth, they'll say they are appalled and frightened by the President's deficit. Ask them what they think of our economy, now that it has been driven by the distorted value of the dollar back to its colonial condition, exporting agricultural products and importing manufactured ones.

Ask those Republican investment bankers what they expect the interest rate to be a year from now. And ask them what they predict for the inflation rate then.

How important is this question of the deficit?

Think about it: What chance would the Republican candidate have had in 1980 if he had told the American people that he intended to pay for his so-called economic recovery with bankruptcies, unemployment and the largest Government debt known to humankind? Would American voters have signed the loan certificate for him on Election Day? Of course not! It was an election won with smoke and mirrors, with illusions. It is a recovery made of the same stuff.

And what about foreign policy?

They said they would make us and the whole world safer. They say they have.

By creating the largest defense budget in history, one even they now admit is excessive, failed to discuss peace with our enemies. By the loss of 279 young Americans in Lebanon in pursuit of a plan and a policy no one can find or describe.

We give monies to Latin American governments that murder nuns, and then lie about it.

We have been less than zealous in our support of the only real friend we have in the Middle East, the one democracy there, our flesh and blood ally, the state of Israel.

Our policy drifts with no real direction, other than an hysterical commitment to an arms race that leads nowhere, if we're lucky. If we're not — it could lead us to bankruptcy or war.

Of course we must have a strong defense!

Of course Democrats believe that there are times when we must stand and fight. And we have. Thousands of us have paid for freedom with our lives. But always, when we've been at our best, our purposes were clear.

Now they're not. Now our allies are as confused as our enemies.

Now we have no real commitment to our friends or our ideals to human rights, to the refusenicks, to Sakharov, to Bishop Tutu and the others struggling for freedom in South Africa.

We have spent more than we can afford. We have pounded our chest and made bold speeches. But we lost 279 young Americans in Lebanon and we are forced to live behind sand bags in Washington.

How can anyone believe that we are stronger, safer or better?

That's the Republican record.

That its disastrous quality is not more fully understood by the American people is attributable, I think, to the President's amiability and the failure by some to separate the salesman from the product.

It's now up to us to make the case to America.

And to remind Americans that if they are not happy with all the President has done so far, they should consider how much worse it will be if he is left to his radical proclivities for another four years unrestrained by the need once again to come before the American people.

If July brings back Anne Gorsuch Burford, what can we expect of December?

Where would another four years take us?

How much larger will the deficit be?

How much deeper the cuts in programs for the struggling middle class and the poor to limit that deficit? How high the interest rates? How much more acid rain killing our forests and fouling our lakes?

What kind of Supreme Court? What kind of court and country will be fashioned by the man who believes in having government mandate people's religion and morality?

The man who believes that trees pollute the environment, that the laws against discrimination go too far. The man who threatens Social Security and Medicaid and help for the disabled.

How high will we pile the missiles?

How much deeper will be the gulf between us and our enemies?

Will we make meaner the spirit of our people?

This election will measure the record of the past four years. But more than that, it will answer the question of what kind of people we want to be.

We Democrats still have a dream. We still believe in this nation's future.

And this is our answer — our credo:

We believe in only the government we need, but we insist on all the government we need.

We believe in a government characterized by fairness and reasonableness, a reasonableness that goes beyond labels, that doesn't distort or promise to do what it knows it can't do.

A government strong enough to use the words "love" and "compassion" and smart enough to convert our noblest aspirations.

We believe in encouraging the talented, but we believe that while survival of the fittest may be a good working description of the process of evolution, a government of humans should elevate itself to a higher order, one which fills the gaps left by chance or a wisdom we don't understand.

We would rather have laws written by the patron of this great city, the man called the "world's most sincere Democrat," St. Francis of Assisi, than laws written by Darwin.

We believe, as Democrats, that a society as blessed as ours, the most affluent democracy in the world's history, that can spend trillions on instruments of destruction, ought to be able to help the middle class in its struggle, ought to be able to find work for all who can do it, room at the table, shelter for the homeless, care for the elderly and infirm, hope for the destitute.

We proclaim as loudly as we can the utter insanity of nuclear proliferation and the need for a nuclear freeze, if only to affirm the simple truth that peace is better than war because life is better than death.

We believe in firm but fair law and order, in the union movement, in privacy for people, openness by government, civil rights, and human rights.

We believe in a single fundamental idea that describes better than most textbooks and any speech what a proper government should be. The idea of family. Mutuality. The sharing of benefits and burdens for the good of all. Feeling one another's pain. Sharing one another's blessings. Reasonably, honestly, fairly, without respect to race, or sex, or geography or political affiliation.

We believe we must be the family of America, recognizing that at the heart of the matter we are bound one to another, that the problems of a retired school teacher in Duluth are our problems. That the future of the child in Buffalo is our future. The struggle of a disabled man in Boston to survive, to live decently is our struggle. The hunger of a woman in Little Rock, our hunger. The failure anywhere to provide what reasonably we might, to avoid pain, is our failure.

For 50 years we Democrats created a better future for our children, using traditional democratic principles as a fixed beacon, giving us direction and purpose, but constantly innovating, adapting to new realities; Roosevelt's alphabet programs; Truman's NATO and the GI Bill of Rights; Kennedy's intelligent tax incentives and the Alliance For Progress; Johnson's civil rights; Carter's human rights and the nearly miraculous Camp David peace accord.

Democrats did it — and Democrats can do it again.

We can build a future that deals with our deficit.

Remember, 50 years of progress never cost us what the last four years of stagnation have. We can deal with that deficit intelligently, by shared sacrifice, with all parts of the nation's family contributing, building partnerships with the private sector, providing a sound defense without depriving ourselves of what we need to feed our children and care for our people.

We can have a future that provides for all the young of the present by marrying common sense and compassion.

We know we can, because we did it for nearly 50 years before 1980.

We can do it again. If we do not forget. Forget that this entire nation has profited by these progressive principles. That they helped lift up generations to the middle class and higher: gave us a chance to work, to go to college, to raise a family, to own a house, to be secure in our old age and, before that, to reach heights that our own parents would not have dared dream of.

That struggle to live with dignity is the real story of the shining city. It's a story I didn't read in a book, or learn in a classroom. I saw it, and lived it. Like many of you.

I watched a small man with thick calluses on both hands work 15 and 16 hours a day. I saw him once literally bleed from the bottoms of his feet, a man who came here uneducated, alone, unable to speak the language, who taught me all I needed to know about faith and hard work by the simple eloquence of his example. I learned about our kind of democracy from my father. I learned about our obligation to each other from him and from my mother. They asked only for a chance to work and to make the world better for their children and to be protected in those moments when they would not be able to protect themselves. This nation and its government did that for them.

And that they were able to build a family and live in dignity and see one of their children go from behind their little grocery store on the other side of the tracks in south Jamaica where he was born, to occupy the highest seat in the greatest state of the greatest nation in the only world we know, is an ineffably beautiful tribute to the democratic process.

And on Jan. 20, 1985, it will happen again. Only on a much grander scale. We will have a new President of the United States, a Democrat born not to the blood of kings but to the blood of immigrants and pioneers.

We will have America's first woman Vice President, the child of immigrants, a New Yorker, opening with one magnificent stroke a whole new frontier for the United States.

It will happen, if we make it happen.

I ask you, ladies and gentlemen, brothers and sisters—for the good of all of us, for the love of this great nation, for the family of America, for the love of God. Please make this nation remember how futures are built.

The Rainbow Coalition

Jesse Jackson

Jesse Louis Jackson (October 8, 1941 -) graduated from Agricultural and Technical College of North Carolina in 1964; ordained in the ministry, 1968; Operation Breadbasket, 1966; PUSH (People United to Serve Humanity), 1971; candidate for Democratic nomination for president, 1984. The speech was delivered at the Democratic National Convention, San Francisco, California, July 17, 1984. Published version: Vital Speeches of the Day, *November 15, 1984, pp. 77-81.*

Tonight we come together bound by our faith in a mighty God, with genuine respect for our country, and inheriting the legacy of a great party—a Democratic Party—which is the best hope for redirecting our nation on a more humane, just and peaceful course.

This is not a perfect party. We are not a perfect people. Yet, we are called to a perfect mission: our mission, to feed the hungry, to clothe the naked, to house the homeless, to teach the illiterate, to provide jobs for the jobless, and to choose the human race over the nuclear race.

We are gathered here this week to nominate a candidate and write a platform which will expand, unify, direct and inspire our party and the nation to fulfill this mission.

My constituency is the damned, disinherited, disrespected and the despised.

They are restless and seek relief. They've voted in record numbers. They have invested the faith, hope and trust that they have in us. The Democratic Party must send them a signal that we care. I pledge my best not to let them down.

There is the call of conscience: redemption, expansion, healing and unity. Leadership must heed the call of conscience, redemption, expansion, healing and unity, for they are the key to achieving our mission.

Time is neutral and does not change things.

With courage and initiative leaders change things. No generation can choose the age or circumstances in which it is born, but through leadership it can choose to make the age in which it is born an age of enlightenment — an age of jobs, and peace, and justice.

Only leadership — that intangible combination of gifts, discipline, information, circumstance, courage, timing, will and divine inspiration — can lead us out of the crisis in which we find ourselves.

Leadership can mitigate the misery of our nation. Leadership can part the waters and lead our nation in the direction of the Promised Land. Leadership can lift the boats stuck at the bottom.

I have had the rare opportunity to watch seven men, and then two, pour out their souls, offer their service and heed the call of duty to direct the course of our nation.

There is a proper season for everything. There is a time to sow and a time to reap. There is a time to compete, and a time to cooperate.

I ask for your vote on the ballot as a vote for a new direction for this party and this nation; a vote for conviction, a vote for conscience.

But I will be proud to support the nominee of this convention for the president of the United States of America.

I have watched the leadership of our party develop and grow. My respect for both Mr. Mondale and Mr. Hart is great.

I have watched them struggle with the cross-winds and cross-fires of being public servants, and I believe that they will both continue to try to serve us faithfully. I am elated by the knowledge that for the first time in our history a woman, Geraldine Ferraro, will be recommended to share our ticket.

Throughout this campaign, I have tried to offer leadership to the Democratic Party and the nation.

If in my high moments, I have done some good, offered some service, shed some light, healed some wounds, rekindled some hope or stirred someone from apathy and indifference, or in any way along the way helped somebody, then this campaign has not been in vain.

For friends who loved and cared for me, and for a God who spared me, and for a family who understood, I am eternally grateful.

If in my low moments, in word, deed or attitude, through some error of temper, taste or tone, I have caused anyone discomfort, created pain, or revived someone's fears, that was not my truest self.

If there were occasions when my grape turned into a raisin and my joy bell lost its resonance, please forgive me. Charge it to my head and not to my heart. My head is so limited in its finitude; my heart is boundless in its love for the human family. I am not a perfect servant. I am a public servant.

I'm doing my best against the odds. As I develop and serve, be patient. God is not finished with me yet.

This campaign has taught me much: that leaders must be tough enough to fight, tender enough to cry, human enough to make mistakes, humble enough to admit them, strong enough to absorb the pain, and resilient enough to bounce back and keep on moving. For leaders, the pain is often intense. But you must smile through your tears and keep moving with the faith that there is a brighter side somewhere.

I went to see Hubert Humphrey three days before he died. He had just called Richard Nixon from his dying bed, and many people wondered why. And, I asked him.

He said, "Jesse, from this vantage point, with the sun setting in my life, all of the speeches, the political conventions, the crowds and the great fights are behind me now. At a time like this you are forced to deal with your irreducible essence, forced to grapple with that which is really important to you. And what I have concluded about life," Hubert Humphrey said, "when all is said and done, we must forgive each other, and redeem each other, and move on."

Our party is emerging from one of its most hard-fought battles for the Democratic Party's presidential nomination in our history. But our healthy competition should make us better, not bitter. We must use the insight, wisdom and experience of the late Hubert Humphrey as a balm for the wounds in our party, this nation and the world. We must forgive each other, redeem each other, regroup and move on.

Our flag is red, white and blue, but our nation is rainbow—red, yellow, brown, black and white—we're all precious in God's sight. America is not like a blanket—one piece of unbroken cloth, the same color, the same texture, the same size. America is more like a quilt—many patches, many pieces, many colors, many sizes, all woven and held together by a common thread.

The white, the Hispanic, the black, the Arab, the Jew, the woman, the Native American, the small farmer, the businessperson, the environmentalist, the peace activist, the young, the old, the lesbian, the gay and the disabled make up the American quilt.

Even in our fractured state, all of us count and fit somewhere. We have proven that we can survive without each other. But we have not proven that we can win or make progress without each other. We must come together.

From Fannie Lee Hamer in Atlantic City in 1964 to the Rainbow Coalition in San Francisco today; from the Atlantic to the Pacific, we have experienced pain but progress as we ended American apartheid laws; we got public accommodations; we secured voting rights; we obtained open housing; as young people got the right to vote; we lost Malcolm, Martin, Medgar, Bobby and John and Viola.

The team that got us here must be expanded, not abandoned. Twenty years ago, tears welled up in our eyes as the bodies of Schwerner, Goodman and Chaney were dredged from the depths of a river in Mississippi. Twenty years later, our communities, black and Jewish, are in anguish, anger and pain.

Feelings have been hurt on both sides. There is a crisis in communications. Confusion is in the air. We cannot afford to lose our way. We may agree to agree, or agree to disagree on issues; we must bring back civility to these tensions.

We are co-partners in a long and rich religious history—the Judeo-Christian traditions. Many blacks and Jews have a shared passion for social justice at home and peace abroad. We must seek a revival of the spirit, inspired by a new vision and new possibilities. We must return to higher ground. We are bound by Moses and Jesus, but also connected to Islam and Mohammed.

These three great religions—Judaism, Christianity and Islam—were all born in the revered and holy city of Jerusalem. We are bound by Dr. Martin Luther King Jr. and Rabbi Abraham Heschel, crying out from their graves for us to reach common ground. We are bound by shared blood and shared sacrifices. We are much too intelligent; much too bound by our Judeo-Christian heritage; much too victimized by racism, sexism, militarism and anti-Semitism; much too threatened as historical scapegoats to go on divided one from another. We must turn from finger-pointing to clasped hands. We must share our burdens and our joys with each other once again. We must turn to each other and not on each other and choose higher ground.

Twenty years later, we cannot be satisfied by just restoring the old coalition. Old wine skins must make room for new wine. We must heal and expand. The Rainbow Coalition is making room for Arab-Americans. They too know the pain and hurt of racial and religious rejection. They must not continue to be made pariahs. The Rainbow Coalition is making room for Hispanic-Americans who this very night are living under the threat of the Simpson-Mazzoli bill, and farm workers from Ohio who are fighting the Campbell Soup Company with a boycott to achieve legitimate workers rights.

The Rainbow is making room for the Native Americans, the most exploited people of all, a people with the greatest moral claim amongst us. We support them as they seek the restoration of their ancient land and claim amongst us. We support them as they seek the restoration of land and water rights, as they seek to preserve their ancestral homelands and the beauty of a land that was once all theirs. They can never receive a fair share for all that they have given us, but they must finally have a fair chance to develop their great resources and to preserve their people and their culture.

The Rainbow Coalition includes Asian-Americans, now being killed in our streets—scapegoats for the failures of corporate, industrial and economic policies. The Rainbow is making room for the young Americans. Twenty years ago, our young people were dying in a war for which they could not even vote. But 20 years later, Young America has the power to stop a war in Central America and the responsibility to vote in great numbers. Young America must be politically active in 1984. The choice is war or peace. We must make room for Young America.

The Rainbow includes disabled veterans. The color scheme fits in the Rainbow. The disabled have their handicap revealed and their genius concealed; while the able-bodied have their genius revealed and their disability concealed. But ultimately we must judge people by their values and their contribution. Don't leave anybody out. I would rather have Roosevelt in a wheelchair than Reagan on a horse.

The Rainbow is making room for small farmers. They have suffered tremendously under the Reagan regime. They will either receive 90 percent parity or 100 percent charity. We must address their concerns and make room for them. The Rainbow includes lesbians and gays. No American citizen ought be denied equal protection under the law.

We must be unusually committed and caring as we expand our family to include new members. All of us must be tolerant and understanding as the fears and anxieties of the rejected and of the party leadership express themselves in many different ways. Too often what we call hate—as if it were deeply rooted in some philosophy or strategy—is simply ignorance, anxiety, paranoia, fear and insecurity. To be strong leaders, we must be long-suffering as we seek to right the wrongs of our party and our nation. We must expand our party, heal our party and unify our party. That is our mission in 1984.

We are often reminded that we live in a great nation—and we do. But it can be greater still. The Rainbow is mandating a new definition of greatness. We must not measure greatness from the mansion down, but the manger up.

Jesus said that we should not be judged by the bark we wear but by the fruit that we bear. Jesus said that we must measure greatness by how we treat the least of these.

President Reagan says the nation is in recovery. Those 90,000 corporations that made a profit last year but paid no federal taxes are recovering. The 37,000 military contractors who have benefited from Reagan's more than doubling the military budget in peacetime, surely they are recovering. The big corporations and rich individuals who received the bulk of the three-year, multibillion tax cut from Mr. Reagan are recovering. But no such recovery is under way for the least of these. Rising tides don't lift all boats, particularly those stuck on the bottom.

For the boats stuck at the bottom there is a misery index. This administration has made life more miserable for the poor. Its attitude has been contemptuous. Its policies and programs have been cruel and unfair to working people. They must be held accountable in November for increasing infant mortality among the poor. In Detroit, one of the great cities of the Western world, babies are dying at the same rate as Honduras, the most underdeveloped nation in our hemisphere.

This administration must be held accountable for policies that contribute to the growing poverty in America. Under President Reagan, there are now 34 million people in poverty, 15 percent of our nation. Twenty-three million are white, 11 million black, Hispanic, Asian and others. Mostly women and children. By the end of this year, there will be 41 million people in poverty. We cannot stand idly by. We must fight for change, now.

Under this regime we look at Social Security. The 1981 budget cuts included nine permanent Social Security benefits cuts totaling $20 billion over five years.

Small businesses have suffered under Reagan tax cuts. Only 18 percent of total business tax cuts went to them—82 percent to big business.

Health care under Mr. Reagan has been sharply cut.

Education under Mr. Reagan has been cut 25 percent.

Under Mr. Reagan there are now 9.7 million female-head families. They represent 16 percent of all families, half of all of them are poor. Seventy percent of all poor children live in a house headed by a woman, where there is no man.

Under Mr. Reagan, the administration has cleaned up only 6 of 546 priority toxic waste dumps.

Farmers' real net income was only about half its level in 1979.

Many say that the race in November will be decided in the South. President Reagan is depending on the conservative South to return him to office. But the South, I tell you, is unnaturally conservative. The South is the poorest region in our nation and, therefore, has the least to conserve. In his appeal to the South, Mr. Reagan is trying to substitute flags and prayer cloths for food, and clothing, and education, health care and housing. But President Reagan who asks us to pray, and I believe in prayer—I've come this way by the power of prayer. But, we must watch false prophecy.

He cuts energy assistance to the poor, cuts breakfast programs from children, cuts lunch programs from children, cuts job training from children and then says, when at the table, "let us pray." Apparently he is not familiar with the structure of a prayer. You thank the Lord for the food that you are about to receive, not the food that just left.

I think that we should pray. But don't pray for the food that left, pray for the man that took the food to leave. We need a change. We need a change in November.

Under President Reagan, the misery index has risen for the poor, but the danger index has risen for everybody.

Under this administration we've lost the lives of our boys in Central America, in Honduras, in Grenada, in Lebanon.

A nuclear standoff in Europe. Under this administration, one-third of our children believe they will die in a nuclear war. The danger index is increasing in this world.

With all the talk about defense against Russia, the Russian submarines are closer and their missiles are more accurate. We live in a world tonight more miserable and a world more dangerous.

While Reaganomics and Reaganism is talked about often, so often we miss the real meaning. Reaganism is a spirit. Reaganomics represents the real economic facts of life.

In 1980, Mr. George Bush, a man with reasonable access to Mr. Reagan, did an analysis of Mr. Reagan's economic plan. Mr. Bush concluded Reagan's plan was "voodoo economics." He was right. Third-party candidate John Anderson said that the combination of military spending, tax cuts and a balanced budget by '84 could be accomplished with blue smoke and mirrors. They were both right.

Mr. Reagan talks about a dynamic recovery. There is some measure of recovery, three and a half years later. Unemployment has inched just below where it was when he took office in 1981. But there are still 8.1 million people officially unemployed, 11 million working only part-time jobs. Inflation has come down, but let's analyze for a moment who has paid the price for this superficial economic recovery.

Mr. Reagan curbed inflation by cutting consumer demand. He cut consumer demand with conscious and callous fiscal and monetary policy. He used the federal budget to deliberately induce unemployment and curb social spending. He then waged and supported tight monetary policies of the Federal Reserve Board to deliberately drive up interest rates—again to curb consumer demand created through borrowing.

Unemployment reached 10.7 percent; we experienced skyrocketing interest rates; our dollar inflated abroad; there were record bank failures; record farm foreclosures; record business bankruptcies; record budget deficits; record trade deficits. Mr Reagan brought inflation down by destabilizing our economy and disrupting family life.

He promised in 1980 a balanced budget, but instead we now have a record $200 billion budget deficit. Under President Reagan, the cumulative budget deficit for his four years is more than the sum total of deficits from George Washington to Jimmy Carter combined. I tell you, we need a change.

How is he paying for these short-term jobs? Reagan's economic recovery is being financed by deficit spending—$200 billion a year. Military spending, a major cause of this deficit, is projected over the next five years to be nearly $2 trillion, and will cost about $40,000 for every taxpaying family.

When the government borrows $200 billion annually to finance the deficit, this encourages the private sector to make its money off of interest rates as opposed to development and economic growth. Even money abroad—we don't have enough money domestically to finance the debt, so we are now borrowing money abroad, from foreign banks, government and financial institutions—$40 billion in 1983; $70 to $80 billion in 1984 (40 percent of our total); over $100 billion (50 percent of our total) in 1985.

By 1989, it is projected that 50 percent of all individual income taxes will be going to pay just for the interest on that debt. The U.S. used to be the largest exporter of capital, but under Mr. Reagan we will quite likely become the largest debtor nation. About two weeks ago, on July 4, we celebrated our Declaration of Independence. Yet every day, supply-side economics is making our nation more economically dependent and less economically free. Five to six percent of our gross national product is now being eaten up with President Reagan's budget deficit.

To depend on foreign military powers to protect our national security would be foolish, making us dependent and less secure. Yet Reaganomics has us increasingly dependent on foreign economic sources. This consumer-led but deficit-financed recovery is unbalanced and artificial.

We have a challenge as Democrats: support a way out. Democracy guarantees opportunity, not success. Democracy guarantees the right to participate, not a license for either the majority or a minority to dominate. The victory for the rainbow coalition in the platform debates today was not whether we won or lost; but that we raised the right issues. We can afford to lose the vote; issues are negotiable. We cannot afford to avoid raising the right questions. Our self respect and our moral integrity were at stake. Our heads are perhaps bloodied but not bowed. Our backs are straight. We can go home and face our people. Our vision is clear. When we think, on this journey from slaveship to championship, we've gone from the planks of the boardwalk in Atlantic City in 1964 to fighting to have the right planks in the platform in San Francisco in '84. There is a deep and abiding sense of joy in our soul, despite the tears in our eyes. For while there are missing planks, there is a solid foundation upon which to build. Our party can win. But we must provide hope that will inspire people to struggle and achieve; provide a plan to show the way out of our dilemma, and then lead the way.

In 1984, my heart is made to feel glad because I know there is a way out. Justice. The requirement for rebuilding America is justice. The linchpin of progressive politics in our nation will not come from the North; they in fact will come from the South. That is why I argue over and over again— from Lynchburg, Va., down to Texas, there is only one black congressperson out of 115. Nineteen years later, we're locked out of the Congress, the Senate and the governor's mansion. What does this large black vote mean? Why do I fight to end second primaries and fight gerrymandering and *(unintelligible)* and at large. Why do we fight over that? Because I tell you, you cannot hold someone in the ditch and linger there with them. If we want a change in this nation, reinforce that Voting Rights Act—we'll get 12 to 20 black, Hispanic, female and progressive congresspersons from the South. We can save the cotton, but we've got to fight the boll weevil—we've got to make a judgment.

It's not enough to hope ERA will pass; how can we pass ERA? If blacks vote in great numbers, progressive whites win. It's the only way progressive whites win. If blacks vote in great numbers, Hispanics win. If blacks, Hispanics and progressive whites vote, women win. When women win, children win. When women and children win, workers win. We must all come up together. We must come up together.

I tell you, with all of our joy and excitement, we must not save the world and lose our souls; we should never short-circuit enforcement of the Voting Rights Act at every level. If one of us rises, all of us must rise. Justice is the way out. Peace is a way out. We should not act as if nuclear weaponry is negotiable and debatable. In this world in which we live, we dropped the bomb on Japan and felt guilty. But in 1984, other folks also got bombs. This time, if we drop the bomb, six minutes later, we, too, will be destroyed. It's not about dropping the bomb on somebody; it's about dropping the bomb on everybody. We must choose developed minds over guided missiles, and think it out and not fight it out. It's time for a change.

Our foreign policy must be characterized by mutual respect, not by gunboat diplomacy, big stick diplomacy and threats. Our nation at its best feeds the hungry. Our nation at its worst will mine the harbors of Nicaragua; at its worst, will try to overthrow that government; at its worst, will cut aid to American education and increase aid to El Salvador; at its worst our nation will have partnership with South Africa. That's a moral disgrace. It's a moral disgrace. It's a moral disgrace.

When we look at Africa, we cannot just focus on apartheid in southern Africa. We must fight for trade with Africa, and not just aid to Africa. We cannot stand idly by and say we will not relate to Nicaragua unless they have elections there and then embrace military regimes in Africa, overthrowing Democratic governments in Nigeria and Liberia and Ghana. We must fight for democracy all around the world, and play the game by one set of rules.

Peace in this world. Our present formula for peace in the Middle East is inadequate; it will not work. There are 22 nations in the Middle East. Our nation must be able to talk and act and influence all of them. We must build upon Camp David and measure human rights by one yardstick and as we *(unintelligible)* too many interests and too few friends.

There is a way out. Jobs. Put Americans back to work. When I was a child growing up in Greenville, S.C., the Rev. (*unintelligible*) who used to preach every so often a sermon about Jesus. He said, if I be lifted up, I'll draw all men unto me. I didn't quite understand what he meant as a child growing up. But I understand a little better now. If you raise up truth, it's magnetic. It has a way of drawing people. With all this confusion in this convention—there is bright lights and parties and big fun—we must raise up the simple proposition: if we lift up a program to feed the hungry, they'll come running. If we lift up a program to study war no more, our youth will come running. If we lift up a program to put American (*sic*) back to work, an alternative to welfare and despair, they will come working. If we cut that military budget without cutting our defense, and use that money to rebuild bridges and put steelworkers back to work, and use that money, and provide jobs for our citizens, and use that money to build schools and train teachers and educate our children, and build hospitals and train doctors and train nurses, the whole nation will come running to us.

As I leave you now, vote in this convention and get ready to go back across this nation in a couple of days, in this campaign, I'll try to be faithful by my promise. I'll live in the old barrios, and ghettos and reservations, and housing projects. I have a message for our youth. I challenge them to put hope in their brains, and not dope in their veins. I told them like Jesus, I, too, was born in a slum, but just because you're born in a slum, does not mean the slum is born in you, and you can rise above it if your mind is made up. I told them in every slum, there are two sides. When I see a broken window, that's the slummy side. Train that youth to be a glazier, that's the sunny side. When I see a missing brick, that's the slummy side. Let that child in the union, and become a brickmason, and build, that's the sunny side. When I see a missing door, that's the slummy side. Train some youth to become a carpenter, that's the sunny side. When I see the vulgar words and hieroglyphics of destitution on the walls, that's the slummy side. Train some youth to be a painter, an artist—that's the sunny side. We need this place looking for the sunny side because there's a brighter side somewhere. I am more convinced than ever that we can win. We'll vault up the rough side of the mountain; we can win. I just want young America to do me one favor.

Exercise the right to dream. You must face reality—that which is. But then dream of the reality that ought to be, that must be. Live beyond the pain of reality with the dream of a bright tomorrow. Use hope and imagination as weapons of survival and progress. Use love to motivate you and obligate you to serve the human family.

Young America, dream. Choose the human race over the nuclear race. Bury the weapons and don't burn the people. Dream of a new value system. Teachers, who teach for life, and not just for a living, teach because they can't help it. Dream of lawyers more concerned with justice than a judgeship. Dream of doctors more concerned with public health than personal wealth. Dream (*sic*) preachers and priests who will prophesy and not just profiteer. Preach and dream. Our time has come.

Our time has come. Suffering breeds character. Character breeds faith. And in the end, faith will not disappoint.

Our time has come. Our faith, hope and dreams will prevail. Our time has come. Weeping has endured for the night. And, now joy cometh in the morning.

Our time has come. No graves can hold our body down.

Our time has come. No lie can live forever.

Our time has come. We must leave racial battleground and come to economic common ground and moral higher ground. America, our time has come.

We've come from disgrace to Amazing Grace, our time has come.

Give me your tired, give me your poor, your huddled masses who yearn to breathe free and come November, there will be a change because our time has come.

Thank you and God bless you.

Free Enterprise

Ronald Reagan

Ronald Reagan (February 6, 1911 -   ) graduated from Eureka College in 1932; he was a sports announcer, 1932-37; actor 1937-66; Governor of California, 1967-74; 40th President of the United States, 1981 -   . The speech was delivered before the Annual Dinner, 77th Congress of American Industry, National Association of Manufacturers, New York City, December 8, 1972. Published version: Vital Speeches of the Day, *January 15, 1973,* pp. 196-201.

I thank you very much for very briefly honoring me more than I think I deserve. President Gullander, incoming President Kenna, Chairman Burt Raynes, distinguished gentlemen here on the board, and you, ladies and gentlemen:

I am delighted to be here and very honored to express my concern over the plight of the distinguished minority that you represent.

If you are a born worrier, you were born at the right time.

Of course, I am bathed, myself, in the warm glow of nostalgia, thanks to our good, kind musicians, who played a great many favorites, winding up with my own alma mater — and the fact that Cornell University stole it before we got it does not change my love for it.

This is an honor. I am honored. I am also a little timorous, because collectively you represent so much solid achievement. You are responsible for so much of the material blessings that we call the American standard of living.

When I think of my own position here in addressing you, there is a story that I think would explain my role and how I see it better than I could put it into words.

There was a football game being played between the teams from two little country towns up in the hills, and late in the game — and a very bruising game it was—the home team had the ball on the 35-yard line. They went into the huddle, and the voice out of the distance says "Give the ball to Alexander." The quarterback gave the ball to somebody else and he got clobbered and they carried him off the field. Again the same voice said, "Give the ball to Alexander," and they gave it to someone else, who lost eleven yards and was roughed up. They went into huddle again, and the same voice cried, "Give the ball to Alexander," and the quarterback straightened up and said, "Alexander says he don't want it."

Communication is a very important thing today. Someone has said we are not worlds apart, we are only words apart, and that is true. Words can separate us as well as bring us together. The meaning of words—you take the two words "fact" and "faith." It is a fact that I am here addressing you; it is faith that makes me think you will listen.

When you come to communicating, Reverend, I hope you will forgive me—I am not being sacrilegious—but this story about the need to listen as well as to speak in communicating was told to me by a clergyman, so I assume it is all right. He told me the story of a man named Joseph who lived in a little village near Jerusalem. Joseph was a carpenter, and he had a wife named Mary, and Joseph and Mary had a little son. And one day the son came running in to the father and said, "Father, did you call?" and his father said, "No, I just hit my thumb with the hammer."

But, you know, in these post-election days, in the news media and wherever people gather, there is speculation about the course the President will take and what the government will do in the days ahead. Personally, I think the President is moving toward a solid recovery and a stable economy based on productivity and not the exotic nostrums of the new economics. But I doubt that he will have very much help from Congress or from that great, permanent structure of government that is so often referred to as the bureaucracy. They will fight to preserve and continue the massive social programs which were enacted without concern to cost, and without any regard as to whether they offered any solution to the problems of human misery that prompted their adoption in the first place. But they did contribute mightily to the fiscal problems that have plagued us in this last decade.

Those individuals today, who prescribe more spending and higher taxes as an answer to our problem make about as much sense as the fellow that tells you another drink will cure your hangover. A noted philosopher once wrote, "Whenever businessmen spend money, they can be trusted to get value for it. When a politician spends money, value leaves the marketplace."

Everyone is talking about where is the government going. May I ask where are you going?

For the second time in this century the idea of free enterprise is under attack. You are being blamed on a daily basis for many things you have not done, and you are given very little credit for things you have done and done very well. Under the guise of consumerism or environmental protection or just that old bromide "big business and big labor require big government," an assortment of activists for one cause or another are attempting to take from you the prerogatives of management without accepting any of the responsibilities that drive you on occasion to a Milltown. Little Sir Ralph has become a folk hero taking whacks at you with his wooden sword, and all of a sudden in too many minds, you are the dragon that must be slain. Don't get me wrong—Little Ralph isn't really the enemy; he is just a symptom.

There is an appalling lack of understanding regarding the workings of the marketplace and the simple business of making something people want and need and getting it to them at a reasonable price. Typical of this economic and political mythology that exists today is a story that is given wide credence—or the mythology is given wide credence by many people who should know better. The story is one that appeared in a newspaper column not too long ago.

The columnist wrote of a welfare recipient who borrowed a country ham on the farm where he had part-time work. He didn't tell the farmer he'd borrowed it. He sold it to a grocer for $27, and then the man used 20 of the 27 dollars to buy $80 worth of food stamps for which he was eligible because of his welfare status. The man then bought $51 worth of groceries and bought the ham back for $29 worth of food stamps. He returned the ham to the smokehouse; the grocer made a profit, the farmer got his ham back, the welfare recipient wound up with $7 in cash and $51 in groceries. And the columnist concluded with this line: "with no one being the loser." No one—unless you ask who paid for the food stamps.

Just recently in one of our western states, the state superintendent of education decided wisely that hereafter high school graduates of that state must have taken a course in free enterprise and capitalism. He went to their three state universities, to the economics department, and asked the professors of those departments to help in constructing this course in free enterprise, and only two out of forty economics professors were willing to say that they believed in free enterprise and would help design such a course.

There was a student at a university in one of our Middle Atlantic states who cancelled the course in history after he had registered for it and bought the textbook. The first line of the textbook, a book entitled "Up Against the America Myth," read "Capitalism stinks. We can only solve our social problems by doing away with capitalism and the institutions that support it." There were 458 pages of that kind of talk. On page 439, for example, it said, "It is only through developing an expanding socialist rationality that the advanced industrial countries can hope to overcome the ills of society."

When the young professor of the course was asked if he intended to assign a second text defining capitalism, he said he knew of no such text.

Our young people complain of big impersonal government; they are determined to live their own lives, and yet the mythology is so prevalent today that they pay heed to and follow political demagogues who offer government as the only proper protection against you.

Two days ago I attended a Governors conference where I heard a panel of pollsters and political experts analyze the recent campaign, and they were agreed on one thing over-all: the fact that American people in overwhelming numbers have a deep mistrust of America's institutions. And why shouldn't they? Because for many years prior to this and capped by the long months of the campaign, they have heard not so much a discussion of policy and philosophy and honest disagreement of the viewpoints, but they have been subjected to an attack on the integrity of the so-called establishment.

In this last campaign over and over again, we were told that 40 per cent of the corporations in America paid no corporate income tax last year, and you heard also that there were three unnamed individuals in this country who last year managed to earn one million dollars or more each, and they paid no personal income tax; that the businessman's lunch was tax-free and the workingman's was not. Thus they appealed to the envy and selfishness that is inherent in all human nature, and this new but shabby populism ended up dividing the people, with mistrust and resentment for each other.

Of course, the clear inference was not so much that the individual or the business firm was cheating, but the government and business and those with affluent earnings had an unholy alliance whereby the working men and women, by the very structure of our tax system, are made to bear an unfair share of the tax burden. They simply were repeating and adding to the economy mythology which replaced understanding of the free enterprise system.

Like all myths, however, there is a kernel of truth in what they said, and truth should be your weapon, because truth will keep you free.

Forty per cent of America's corporations—actually, it was 38 per cent last year—*did* avoid the payment of any corporate income tax, for the simple reason that 40 per cent of them did not make any profit and therefore they owed no tax. And if you want to go back through the last 20 or 25 years, you will find that in every one of those years roughly four out of ten corporations in America made no profit.

Free enterprise is a rough and competitive game. It is a hell of a lot better than a government monopoly. And, as for those three who earned a million dollars or more, that too, is true, but why didn't they add that there were 624 people in the United States last year who earned one million dollars or more and that 621 of them paid an average income tax of $935,000?

Now, it is asking an awful lot of us to think that the tax structure, if it is so riddled with dishonest loopholes that 60 per cent of the most successful businesses and 621 individuals smart enough to earn one million dollars a year, were all too stupid to avoid finding the loopholes that those other few found.

It is time for business to start presenting the facts, because the facts are on your side. But, for heaven's sake, don't just repeat them to each other by way of your trade journals. Tell the people, and especially your customers and your employees—and usually they are one and the same—and tell our sons and daughters.

Item one of the mythology: Some years ago a poll was taken. An overwhelming majority of the American people revealed that they believe the average rate of margin of profit for business is 21 per cent, and they thought that was too high. Not too long ago the same pollsters went back to the same people and took the poll again, and they no longer believe the profit is 21 per cent; they now think it is 28 per cent. So they were asked what did they think a fair margin of profit would be, and they said they thought that business ought to be happy with 10 per cent.

Well, business would be ecstatic, I know, with 10 per cent, because for the last 20 years it has never been higher than 5½ per cent and right now it is down to 4.3 per cent.

But why not level with the people? Why shouldn't business tell the people of this country, who are in danger of being victimized all the time by the demagogues, that business does not really pay taxes at all, that business collects taxes for government and does it very efficiently, and the taxes become part of the cost of production and are passed on in the price of the product, and if government makes you collect too many taxes, you price yourself out of the market and a great many people become unemployed when you have to close your doors.

Right now one of the greatest threats to the American worker's job comes from the lower-priced foreign imports.

The other day in the rush hour in Sacramento I saw a fellow on his way home from work. He had a bumper sticker that looked like it was right out of the past on his car, "Buy America." He was driving a Toyota.

Some of the hierarchy of organized labor are demanding that government provide protection against these foreign imports, but the same hierarchy is also protesting, because government a couple of years ago gave you a 7 per cent accelerated depreciation allowance on new plant and equipment, and they fear foreign competition. In West Germany they get a 17 per cent accelerated depreciation allowance. Japan and France can deduct a full one-third of the cost of new machinery and equipment in the first year. The nations of European Common Market average a tax burden that, in relation to the gross national product, is less than half of what yours is, and possibly this explains why our balance of trade is at the lowest point it has been since 1893.

More than 100 years ago, the French economist and philosopher, Frederic Bastiat, said, "When a nation is burdened with taxes, nothing is more difficult or impossible than to levy them equally. The state can have an abundance of money only by taking from everyone, especially the masses."

In the economic and political mythology, the sales tax employed by some states is known to be regressive, falling heaviest on those who are least able to pay, and yet those who subscribe to the myth and those who promote the myth invariably advocate as an alternative tax another tax on business. What they really are saying is they want the sales tax but they want it kept invisible, and thus, when they want to raise the tax, the merchant gets the blame for raising the price of the product; it does not fall on government's shoulders.

There are 116 taxes in a suit of clothes each one of us is wearing, 151 on the bread we had for dinner tonight. There are 100 taxes on an egg and I don't think the chicken put them there; some place between the hen and the table they crept in.

The plain truth is, when they start talking about taxes, government costs too much, and most proposals to close loopholes, or to shift the cost to someone else, are in reality efforts by someone in politics to get more money for government, not to equalize the tax burden or correct an inequity.

The average citizen works from January 1st into the first week of June to pay his taxes, federal, state and local. This is longer than he has to work to buy food, shelter and clothing for his family. Taxes take 43.1 per cent of the total income of the people in the United States.

Where is the breaking point beyond which a free economy can no longer exist? And you have to ask yourselves at 43.1 per cent — does government's track record justify this?

Just recently, Secretary Romney told a Congressional committee that under the present statutes of Congress and the regulations of the bureaus, as a result of those statutes, private industry can build low-cost housing 20 per cent cheaper than the government can provide it.

Not many years ago, you will remember that the government was going to save the family farmer in America. They spent a lot of money. Now there are only a third as many family farmers as when they set out to save them, but there are three times as many Department of Agriculture employees. There's one for every 22 farms in the United States.

They tell a story in Washington about one of those bureaus, one of those great big buildings, with the acres and acres of floor space and the rows and rows of desks, and the hundreds of employees, and one morning one fellow in the corner had his head on his desk and was sobbing as if his heart would break. They finally persuaded him to tell them what was wrong. It was the Bureau of Indian Affairs. He said, "My Indian died."

We spent billions of dollars to keep the wheat farmers some time ago and succeeded in cutting the price of wheat in half and doubling the price of bread.

For 50 years the railroads have been getting deeper into trouble and they have been complaining that their trouble is caused by unrealistic and illogical regulations. Finally, their situation became so desperate that the government took over the passenger service, and apparently the government is running it with great success — and why not? The first thing government did was exempt itself from obeying the regulations the railroads have been complaining about for 50 years.

In this land of the free and home of the brave, we are getting less free perhaps because we have been less brave.

I have told a number of business groups on occasions that some years ago, eight or ten years ago, you will remember, the Department of Internal revenue decided to change the rules of the game with regard to business tax deductions. It was not an Act of Congress; it was not brought about by our elected representatives; the bureaucrats just changed the rules.

They decided to get into the business of whether on a business trip you could deduct for tax purposes as an expense a filet mignon or whether you had to eat in a one-arm joint and get the blue plate special. And then they moved into the area of gifts you could give a customer or to your employees.

The trouble was when this happened business abdicated. Business sat down and negotiated with government whether they would be allowed 25 or 35 dollars. Why in heaven's name didn't business say to government at that point, "As long as we spend the money with the legitimate expectation of making a profit, it is none of your business how much we spend."

What has happened since? The same government that subsidizes the growing of tobacco has ruled that cigarettes cannot be advertised on television. Here is a product which can be legally sold providing it bears the government's tax stamp. It can advertise on other media, but not on television. Why is there no protest about this, and what product will be next?

Is it any wonder that serious consideration is now being given under the name of consumerism to allowing what they call counter-advertising, which is a delightful euphemism for the fact that they will now allow anyone to go on the air and demand equal time to dispute your advertising claims for the product you manufacture.

I know that no one would ever think of putting up Berkeley, California, as an example of good old Main Street America, but, even though it happened in Berkeley, it should be disturbing to all of us that they have under consideration an ordinance that would reduce the work week for the municipal employees to 30 hours but retain 40 hours' pay, and the same rule would be applied to all businesses and industries employing more than nine people. And an excess business license tax would be applied against business to cover the cost of increasing the number of municipal employees.

"Profit" is a dirty word only when you use it or when.you make it. On the bookshelves right now in many of our campuses there is a book which extols a kind of 1984 socialism. It condemns the competitive system and attacks the profit motive. The price of the book is $12.95.

So I ask: When are you going to tell your story? And sometimes, if you will forgive me for being presumptuous, I have to wonder, do you know the story that you have to tell?

For example, I have lived ten years longer than my life expectancy when I was born thanks to medical research financed largely by free enterprise profits. Ninety per cent of the people at the time of my birth lived below what is now considered the poverty line; more than two-thirds of us lived in substandard housing; today, thanks to free enterprise, both of those figures in our single lifetime are less than 10 per cent.

Hardly a week passes without some television program sponsored by some of you, but what portrays the horrors of poverty and hunger in the United States — and yet 99 per cent of the homes in America have electricity and the basic appliances such as refrigerator and range and 96 per cent of the homes have television and telephones; 80 per cent have automobiles.

If our sons and daughters, in their very real and sincere idealism, say this is proof that we have a materialistic society, maybe we should tell them over the next three years you will spend $18 billion on environmental projects, that this generation of young Americans, a greater number of them will go to college and get a higher education in this country than the young people in all the rest of the world, because of scholarships and college endowments that you support, that this generation of Americans is bigger and healthier, will live longer and travel more and be exposed to more cultural refinements than any generation that ever lived, that there are more books published in America and more symphony orchestras and community theaters and operas maintained by voluntary subscription than in all the rest of the world put together.

Perhaps I have told you this next little experience before.

Some of you, I know, but if so, you will have to remember that life not only begins at 40 but so does lumbago, arthritis and a tendency to tell the same story three or four times to the same people. I was meeting with a group of university student body presidents in California, back when things were not as quiet as they are now on the campus. Finally, one slouched in the chair, in jeans and tee shirt, and challenged me and said, "You have to realize you cannot understand our generation; you don't understand your own sons and daughters." I tried to pass it off and said, "We know more about being young than being old." He said, "I am serious. When you were our age and going to school, you didn't live in a world and grow up in a world that had instant electronic communication, jet travel, nuclear power, space travel to the moon, cybernetics, computers that could compute in seconds what it used to take months and even years for men to figure out."

And that is true. When we were growing up we didn't have those things. We invented them.

More than a half of the economic activity in the entire history of man has taken place under American auspices, and most of that in this century.

Journalists who accompanied the President on his trip to China came home with tales of getting a very tasty lunch in Peking for only 15 cents. They didn't bother to add that the average daily wage there is only 27 cents, which is not enough to afford two meals a day.

To those who are impressed today—and there are many particularly in some of the salons that are peopled by certain of our intellectual element— the Soviet Union, the workers' paradise, is held in high esteem. I don't think that you should feel bad about that, because I think if you put your minds to it you could match the Soviet Union's achievements. You would only have to cut all the paychecks 75 per cent, send 60 million people back to the farm, tear down almost three-fourths of the houses in America, destroy 60 per cent of the steel-making capacity, rip up fourteen out of fifteen miles of road, two-thirds of the railroad track, junk 85 per cent of the autos, and tear out nine out of ten telephones.

Resist the nitpicking and the harassment by the multitudinous agencies that interfere with the free rhythm of the market place. Repudiate what Cicero called the arrogance of officialdom. I don't mean you should return to some sort of dog-eat-dog attitude, that might have characterized an earlier day in the industrial revolution, nor do I mean that you should reject what has become modern-day corporate citizenship, some of the experience that I have just mentioned.

Government does have legitimate functions, and I think that government performs a number of those very well when it sticks to its own last. It does them better when it has participation by the citizenry. And participation that is more than just a campaign contribution or the activity of a lobby in your behalf. The simple fact is that politics is too important to be left to politicians. I am suggesting what in an older world the aristocracy recognized as a responsibility which accompanied the privilege, and that was noblesse oblige. In America our aristocracy is not by accident of birth or royal favor but by virtue of accomplishment. And noblesse oblige is not unknown to us —we may not have used the term—but in times of emergency and danger our people have risen to the occasion. We have won our wars with citizen soldiers and dollar-a-year men. No government can match or afford the genius and the talent that is available in the private sector, and our nation cannot afford to have that manpower uninvolved.

When democracy in ancient Athens was becoming "mobocracy,"

Pericles warned, "The man who takes no interest in public affairs is not a man who minds his own business; we say he has no business being here at all."

If you will permit me, I would like to tell you of a personal experience that illustrates what can be done if business and government work together to help free enterprise stay free. For more years than I care to count I have been expressing publicly a concern lest government should grow beyond the consent of the governed, and I have been, over these years, and continue to be rather harsh in my criticism of the permanent structure of government. Then, six years ago, a funny thing happened to me on my way to the theater. I became a part of government myself. And this has not lessened my concern about the way government, in recent decades, has increased its size in cost and power.

Dr. Parkinson said, "Government hires a rat catcher, and the first thing you know he has become a rodent control officer, and he has no intention of getting rid of the rats; they have become his constituency."

Six years ago I came out of the woods an innocent, and inherited a California government that was adding several thousand employees each year and had been adding that many for more than a decade. It was increasing its size two and a half times as fast as our increase in population. Our budget was second only to the Federal budget. We were spending a million dollars a day more than we were taking in. The great water project that was being built to supply the southern part of the state was under-funded by $300 million and the kids were burning down the schools. I was shuffling through the papers on my desk one day, I thought there had to be a letter of resignation there some place and one of the fellows said, "Cheer up, things could be worse." So I cheered up and sure enough things got worse.

But I had an abiding faith in common-sense business practices that you use every day and a belief that they would also work for government. I also believed that people are eager to help if only someone would give them a chance. And I might tell you that the first time you mention common sense in connection with government, you cause something of a traumatic shock in the marble halls. But I asked some public-spirited citizens — members of the business and industrial community in California — to form a committee, not to screen applicants for jobs, but to recruit. I had the kind of men in that committee who know where the bodies and talent were in California, and I was interested in the kind of men and women who were not interested in government careers. I wanted the kind who would be willing to give a year or 2 years or more, but who would be the first to tell me if their job was unnecessary. Then I asked an additional favor of the business and industrial leadership of California. I asked them to provide the best experts and the best talent they could produce in a variety of fields, free of charge, to form task forces based on their particular expertise and skill. And that these task forces would go into every agency and department of state government to see how modern business practices could be employed to make government more efficient and more economical.

There are men in this room and at this head table who participated in that task force undertaking in California. Some 250 top people in our state gave an average of 117 days, full time, to bring us more than 1,800 recommendations. So far we have implemented 1560 of them; 29 boards and commissions have been eliminated. The new government buildings that had been approved for construction have been canceled, because it was found they were unnecessary. We adopted new warehousing and purchasing procedures. We built more than 1,000 miles of highway with money that was formerly spent on administrative overhead. We have a rehabilitation program that has enabled us to close half a dozen penal institutions, and the big house, San Quentin, is being phased out.

We have a new approach to the treatment of the mentally ill that has reduced the number of patients sentenced to a hopeless lifetime in our asylums from 26,500 to 7,000. We had a retirement plan with an unfunded liability of $400,000,000 that has been put on a sound actuarial basis. We are completing that water program without adding $300 million to make up for the deficit but within the funds that were available.

Our growth in population has given us a work load increase of as much as 30 percent in many of our departments, but we have fewer employees than we had 6 years ago when we started. Our budget is now fourth in the nation, not second. As a matter of fact, the budget for our host city here is about $2 billion bigger than the budget for the whole state of California, and they have more than four times as many employees as we do. And he did all that while he was a Republican; what do you think is going to happen now that he is a Democrat?

We have returned more than $2 billion over these 6 years to the taxpayers in rebates of one kind or another, and in January I intend to ask the legislature for a cut in the income tax. You will know when I do it because I am sure the wind from the West will bring the scream of outrage from the legislature.

But three years ago we realized that all our gains were being eaten up by one thing; one thing that had resisted our every effort. Welfare was increasing at a cost that was almost 4 times as much as the annual increase in revenues. California was adding 40,000 people, new people, to the welfare rolls each and every month.

And again we turned to the private sector for a task force to check the regulations against the original intent of Congress when the laws were passed, and to suggest practical ways that we might be responsible to the truly needy at the same time that we curbed abuses. We found that the multitude, namely Federal regulations, made it impossible to prevent people from being on welfare several times under several different names. We found one county that had 600 of its own full-time county employees legally drawing welfare. Welfare employees sitting at adjoining desks where the welfare employee for the recipient at the next desk and they did it for each other.

We found another county where they were mailing checks to people living abroad, one in Russia. When we brought before the legislature, they refused to give us the statutory reforms that we were requesting, and again the business community came to our rescue. They loaned men and women, full time, to form a state-wide movement, a grass-roots people movement, and they didn't make the legislature see the light, but they sure made them feel the heat. And a year ago this last October our reforms were fully implemented.

The welfare case load in California is no longer increasing at 40,000 a month, and there are, today, 246,000 fewer people on welfare in our state than there were when we started a year ago in October.

We have increased the grants to the truly needy, the aged, the blind, and the disabled by 30 per cent and the taxpayers are saving $708 million a year. None of what had been done could have been accomplished without the practice of noblesse oblige by the business and industrial community of California.

I hope that what I have told you in just this experience will be some encouragement for you to carry on the fight that should have begun yesterday, but should begin now.

Karl Marx had a theory of inevitability. He was confident that you would give up and just feed the crocodile, hoping that he would eat you last. If about 90 per cent of the laws that are passed by Congress and the state legislatures each year were lost on the way to the printer, and if all the people in the bureaus went fishing, I don't think they would be missed for quite a while. But realize your strength, because if you did not go to work, I am sure the country would feel it and grind to a halt in about 24 hours.

Resist the nitpicking and the paper shuffling that adds tens of billions of dollars of cost and hence adds to the price of your product, but at the same time offer your expertise to ease the problems of human misery that still plague us. Don't let the doctors fight socialized medicine by themselves, because you cannot socialize the doctor without socializing the patient. Don't let the President, in these next four years, stand alone in his fight against a Congress that has already declared they are not going to let him cancel these great social reforms which have been such costly failures. Don't let him fight alone against the bureaucracy that is going to see executive order after executive order, if they have their way, flow like water out into the sands and never heard from again.

You can make your weight felt with Congressmen and state legislators. You can impress upon them once and for all that you want something done and that you believe that the President's idea of reducing the size and power of government and returning freedom to the people is a pretty good idea after all. Choose some of the great problems that government thinks are so much its own province; come up with a plan of your own, a suggestion for their solution.

Take for example the biggest sacred cow in all of the United States; social security. I have to say that if you couldn't come up with a better idea than that, you wouldn't still be in business. But above all, tell your story. If you have to on the campuses take out ads in the college papers to tell some of the facts about tax structure and economics and profit margins, what free enterprise does.

My daughter came home from her class in college one day and she was all thrilled with the idea that if all of us would quit buying an automobile for just one year, and everybody would just drive their cars for another year, we would have enough money to build hospitals and schools and take care of all the problems. And I agreed with her and said, "That's just great. We would save billions. But we are going to have to find some money for all those fellows unemployed in the automobile factories and those fellows in the steel mills, and Firestone and Goodyear with the tires and the fellows when you go in to have your car serviced — because she has to have a car to drive to school. And she began to get the idea that maybe there was something in economics she had not learned.

You have a story to tell. Tell your story again and again and don't risk having some day to face your children or your children's children when they ask you where you were and what you were doing on the day that freedom was lost. Thank you.

Lebanon and Grenada

Ronald Reagan

The speech was delivered to the nation, Washington D.C., on October 27, 1983. Published version: Vital Speeches of the Day, *November 15, 1983, pp. 66-69.*

My fellow Americans, some two months ago we were shocked by the brutal massacre of 269 men, women and children, in the shooting down of a Korean airliner. Now, in these past several days, violence has erupted again, in Lebanon and Grenada.

In Lebanon we have some 1,600 marines, part of a multinational force that's trying to help the people of Lebanon restore order and stability to that troubled land. Our marines are assigned to the south of the city of Beirut near the only airport operating in Lebanon. Just a mile or so to the north is the Italian contingent and not far from them the French and a company of British soldiers.

This past Sunday, at 22 minutes after 6, Beirut time, with dawn just breaking, a truck looking like a lot of other vehicles in the city approached the airport on a busy main road. There was nothing in its appearance to suggest it was any different than the trucks or cars that were normally seen on and around the airport. But this one was different.

At the wheel was a young man on a suicide mission. The truck carried some 2,000 pounds of explosives, but there was no way our marine guards could know this. Their first warning that something was wrong came when the truck crashed through a series of barriers, including a chain link fence and barbed wire entanglements. The guards opened fire but it was too late.

The truck smashed through the doors of the headquarters building in which our marines were sleeping and instantly exploded. The four-story concrete building collapsed in a pile of rubble.

More than 200 of the sleeping men were killed in that one hideous insane attack. Many others suffered injury and are hospitalized here or in Europe. This was not the end of the horror.

At almost the same instant another vehicle on a suicide and murder mission crashed into the headquarters of the French peacekeeping force, an eight-story building, destroying and killing more than 50 French soldiers.

Prior to this day of horror there had been several tragedies for our men in the multinational force; attacks by snipers and mortar fire had taken their toll. I called the bereaved parents and/or widows of the victims to express on behalf of all of us our sorrow and sympathy. Sometimes there were questions. And now many of you are asking: Why should our young men be dying in Lebanon? Why is Lebanon important to us?

Well, it's true Lebanon is a small country more than five and a half thousand miles from our shores, on the edge of what we call the Middle East. But every President who has occupied this office in recent years has recognized that peace in the Middle East is of vital concern to our nation and, indeed, to our allies in Western Europe and Japan. We've been concerned because the Middle East is a powder keg. Four times in the last 30 years the Arabs and Israelis have gone to war and each time the world has teetered near the edge of catastrophe. The area is key to the economic and political life of the West. Its strategic importance, its energy resources, the Suez Canal, the well-being of the nearly 200 million people living there; all are vital to us and to world peace.

If that key should fall into the hands of a power or powers hostile to the free world, there would be a direct threat to the United States and to our allies.

We have another reason to be involved. Since 1948, our nation has recognized and accepted a moral obligation to assure the continued existence of Israel as a nation. Israel shares our democratic values and is a formidable force an invader of the Middle East would have to reckon with. For several years, Lebanon has been torn by internal strife. Once a prosperous, peaceful nation, its Government had become ineffective in controlling the militias that warred on each other.

Sixteen months ago we were watching on our TV screens the shelling and bombing of Beirut, which was being used as a fortress by P.L.O. bands. Hundreds and hundreds of civilians were being killed and wounded in the daily battles. Syria, which makes no secret of its claim that Lebanon should be part of a greater Syria, was occupying a large part of Lebanon. Today, Syria has become a home for 7,000 Soviet advisers and technicians who man a massive amount of Soviet weaponry, including SS-21 ground-to-ground missiles capable of reaching vital areas of Israel.

A little over a year ago, hoping to build on the Camp David accords, which have led to peace between Israel and Egypt, I proposed a peace plan for the Middle East to end the wars between the Arab states and Israel. It was based on U.N. Resolution 242 and 338 and called for a fair and just solution to the Palestinian problem, as well as a fair and just settlement of issues between the Arab states and Israel.

Before the necessary negotiations could begin, it was essential to get all foreign forces out of Lebanon and to end the fighting there. So why are we there? Well, the answer is straight-forward: to help bring peace to Lebanon and stability to the vital Middle East. To that end the multinational force was created to help stabilize the situation in Lebanon until a government could be established and the Lebanese Army mobilized to restore Lebanese sovereignty over its own soil as the foreign forces withdrew.

Israel agreed to withdraw as did Syria. But Syria then reneged on its promise. Over 10,000 Palestinians who had been bringing ruin down on Beirut, however, did leave the country. Lebanon has formed a Government under the leadership of President Gemayel and that Government, with our assistance and training, has set up its own army. In only a year's time that army has been rebuilt. It's a good army composed of Lebanese of all factions.

A few weeks ago the Israeli Army pulled back to the Awali River in southern Lebanon. Despite fierce resistance by Syrian-backed forces the Lebanese Army was able to hold the lines and maintain the defensive perimeter around Beirut. In the year that our marines have been there Lebanon has made important steps toward stability and order. The physical presence of the marines lends support to both the Lebanese Government and its army. It allows the hard work of diplomacy to go forward. Indeed without the peacekeepers from the U.S., France, Italy and Britain, the efforts to find a peaceful solution in Lebanon would collapse.

As for that narrower question, what exactly is the operational mission of the marines, the answer is to secure a piece of Beirut; to keep order in their sector and to prevent the area from becoming a battlefield. Our Marines are not just sitting in an airport. Part of their task is to guard that airport. Because of their presence the airport has remained operational. In addition they patrol the surrounding area. This is their part — a limited but essential part — in a larger effort that I described.

If our marines must be there, I'm asked, why can't we make them safer? Who committed this latest atrocity against them and why? Well, we'll do everything we can to insure that our men are as safe as possible. We ordered the battleship New Jersey to join our naval forces offshore. Without even firing them, the threat of its 16-inch guns silenced those who once fired down on our marines from the hills. And they're a good part of the reason we suddenly had a cease-fire. We're doing our best to make our forces less vulnerable to those who want to snipe at them or send in future suicide missions.

Secretary Schultz called me today from Europe, where he was meeting with the foreign ministers of our allies and the multinational force. They remain committed to our task, and plans were made to share information as to how we can improve security for all our men.

We have strong circumstantial evidence that the attack on the marines was directed by terrorists who used the same method to destroy our embassy in Beirut. Those who directed this atrocity must be dealt justice, and they will be. The obvious purpose behind the sniping and now this attack was to weaken American will and force the withdrawal of U.S. and French forces from Lebanon.

The clear intent of the terrorists was to limit our support of the Lebanese Government and to destroy the ability of the Lebanese people to determine their own destiny. To answer those who ask if we're serving any purpose in being there, let me answer a question with a question: would the terrorists have launched their suicide attacks against the multinational force if it were not doing its job?

The multinational force was attacked precisely because it is doing the job it was sent to do in Beirut. It is accomplishing its mission.

Now then, where do we go from here?

What can we do now to help Lebanon gain greater stability so that our marines can come home? I believe we can take three steps now that will make a difference.

First, we will accelerate the search for peace and stability in that region. Little attention is being paid to the fact that we have had special envoys there working literally around the clock to bring the warring factions together. This coming Monday in Geneva President Gemayel of Lebanon will sit down with other factions from his country to see if national reconciliation can be achieved. He has our firm support.

I will soon be announcing a replacement for Bud McFarlane who was preceded by Phil Habib. Both worked tirelessly and must be credited for much, if not, most, of the progress we've made.

Second, we'll work even more closely with our allies in providing support for the Government of Lebanon and for the rebuilding of a national consensus.

Third, we will insure that the multinational peacekeeping forces, our Marines, are given the greatest possible protection. Our Commandant of the Marine Corps, General Kelley, returned from Lebanon today and will be advising us on steps we can take to improve security.

Vice President Bush returned just last night from Beirut and gave me a full report of his brief visit.

Beyond our progress in Lebanon let us remember that our main goal and purpose is to achieve a broader peace in all of the Middle East. The factions and bitterness that we see in Lebanon are just a microcosm of the difficulties that are spread across much of that region. A peace initiative for

the entire Middle East, consistent with the Camp David accord, and U.N.
Resolutions 242 and 338, still offers the best hope for bringing peace to the
region.

Let me ask those who say we should get out of Lebanon: If we were to
leave Lebanon now, what message would that send to those who foment
instability and terrorism? If Americans were to walk away from Lebanon,
what chance would there be for a negotiated settlement producing the
unified, democratic Lebanon? If we turned our backs on Lebanon now,
what would be the future of Israel? At stake is the fate of only the second
Arab country to negotiate a major agreement with Israel. That's another
accomplishment of this past year, the May 17 accord signed by Lebanon
and Israel.

If terrorism and intimidation succeed, it'll be a devastating blow to the
peace process and to Israel's search for genuine security. It won't just be
Lebanon sentenced to a future of chaos. Can the United States, or the free
world, for that matter, stand by and see the Middle East incorporated into
the Soviet bloc? What of Western Europe and Japan's dependence on
Middle East oil for the energy to fuel their industries? The Middle East is, as
I said, vital to our national security and economic well-being.

Brave young men have been taken from us. Many others have been
grievously wounded. Are we to tell them their sacrifice was wasted or that
they gave their lives in defense of our national security every bit as much as
any man who ever died fighting in a war?

We must not strip every ounce of meaning and purpose from their
courageous sacrifice. We are a nation with global responsibilities, we're not
somewhere else in the world protecting someone else's interest. We're there
protecting our own.

I received a message from the father of a marine in Lebanon. He told me:
"In a world where we speak of human rights, there is a sad lack of
acceptance of responsibility. My son has chosen the acceptance of
responsibility for the privilege of living in this country."

Certainly in this country one does not inherently have rights unless the
responsibility for these rights is accepted.

Dr. Kenneth Morrison said that while he was waiting to learn if his son
was one of the dead. I was thrilled for him to learn today that his son, Ross,
is alive and well and carrying on his duties in Lebanon.

Let us meet our responsibilities. For longer than any of us can remember,
the people of the Middle East have lived from war to war with no prospect
for any other future. That dreadful cycle must be broken.

Why are we there? When a Lebanese mother told one of our ambassadors
that her little girl had only attended school two of the last eight years. Now,
because of our presence there, she said her daughter could live a normal life.
With patience and firmness we can help bring peace to that strife-torn

region and make our own lives more secure.

Our role is to help the Lebanese put their country together, not to do it for them.

Now I know another part of the world is very much on our minds. A place much closer to our shores. Grenada. The island is only twice the size of the District of Columbia with a total population of about 110,000 people. Grenada and a half-dozen other Caribbean islands here were, until recently, British colonies. They are now independent states and members of the British Commonwealth.

While they respect each other's independence they also feel a kinship with each other and think of themselves as one people. In 1979 trouble came to Grenada. Maurice Bishop, a protégé of Fidel Castro, staged a military coup and overthrew the government which had been elected under the constitution left to the people by the British.

He sought the help of Cuba in building an airport, which he claimed was for tourist trade, but which looked suspiciously suitable for military aircraft, including Soviet-built long-range bombers. The six sovereign countries and one remaining colony are joined together in what they call the Organization of Eastern Caribbean States. The six became increasingly alarmed as Bishop built an army greater than all of theirs combined.

Obviously it was not purely for defense. In this last year or so, Prime Minister Bishop gave indications that he might like better relations with the United States. He even made a trip to our country and met with senior officials at the White House and the State Department. Whether he was serious or not we'll never know.

On Oct. 12, a small group in his militia seized him and put him under arrest. They were, if anything, even more radical and more devoted to Castro's Cuba than he had been. Several days later, a crowd of citizens appeared before Bishop's home, freed him and escorted him toward the headquarters of the Military Council. They were fired upon. A number, including some children, were killed and Bishop was seized. He and several members of his Cabinet were subsequently executed and a 24-hour shoot-to-kill curfew was put in effect. Grenada was without a government, its only authority exercised by a self-proclaimed band of military men.

There were then about 1,000 of our citizens on Grenada, 800 of them students in St. George's University Medical School. Concern that they'd be harmed or held as hostages, I ordered a flotilla of ships then on its way to Lebanon with Marines—part of our regular rotation program—to circle south on a course that would put them somewhere in the vicinity of Grenada in case there should be a need to evacuate our people.

Last weekend I was awakened in the early morning hours and told that six members of the Organization of Eastern Caribbean States joined by Jamaica and Barbados had sent an urgent request that we join them in a military operation to restore order and democracy to Grenada.

They were proposing this action under the terms of a treaty, a mutual assistance pact that existed among them. These small peaceful nations needed our help. Three of them don't have armies at all and the others have very limited forces.

The legitimacy of their request plus my own concern for our citizens dictated my decision. I believe our Government has a responsibility to go to the aid of its citizens if their right to life and liberty is threatened. The nightmare of our hostages in Iran must never be repeated.

We knew we had little time and that complete secrecy was vital to insure both the safety of the young men who would undertake this mission and the Americans they were about to rescue.

The joint chiefs worked around the clock to come up with a plan. They had little intelligence information about conditions on the island. We had to assume that several hundred Cubans working on the airport could be military reserves. As it turned out the number was much larger and they were a military force. Six hundred of them have been taken prisoner and we have discovered a complete base with weapons and communications equipment which makes it clear a Cuban occupation of the island had been planned.

Two hours ago we released the first photos from Grenada. They included pictures of a warehouse of military equipment, one of three we've uncovered so far. This warehouse contained weapons and ammunition stacked almost to the ceiling, enough to supply thousands of terrorists.

Grenada, we were told, was a friendly island paradise for tourism. Well it wasn't. It was a Soviet-Cuban colony being readied as a major military bastion to export terror and undermine democracy.

We got there just in time.

I can't say enough in praise of our military. Army Rangers and paratroopers, Navy Marine and Air Force personnel, those who planned a brilliant campaign and those who carried it out.

Almost instantly our military seized the two airports, secured the campus where most of our students were and they're now in the mopping-up phase.

It should be noted that in all the planning, a top priority was to minimize risk, to avoid casualties to our own men and also the Grenadian forces as much as humanly possible. But there were casualties. And we all owe a debt to those who lost their lives or were wounded. They were few in number but even one is a tragic price to pay.

It's our intention to get our men out as soon as possible.

Prime Minister Eugenia Charles of Dominica—I called that wrong, she pronounces it Dom-in-EE-kuh—she is chairman of O.E.C.S. She's calling for help from Commonwealth nations in giving the people their right to establish a constitutional government on Grenada. We anticipate that the

Governor General, a Grenadian, will participate in setting up a provisional government in the interim.

The events in Lebanon and Grenada, though oceans apart, are closely related. Not only has Moscow assisted and encouraged the violence in both countries, but it provides direct support through a network of surrogates and terrorists. It is no coincidence that when the thugs tried to wrest control of Grenada, there were 30 Soviet advisers and hundreds of Cuban military and paramilitary forces on the island. At the moment of our landing we communicated with the governments of Cuba and the Soviet Union and told them we would offer shelter and security to their people on Grenada. Regrettably, Castro ordered his men to fight to the death and some did. The others will be sent to their homelands.

Now there was a time when our national security was based on a standing army here within our own borders and shore batteries of artillery along our coast, and of course, a navy to keep the sea lanes open for the shipping of things necessary to our well being. The world has changed. Today our national security can be threatened in far-away places. It's up to all of us to be aware of the strategic importance of such places and to be able to identify them.

Sam Rayburn once said that freedom is not something a nation can work for once and win forever. He said it's like an insurance policy, its premiums must be kept up to date. In order to keep it we have to keep working for it and sacrificing for it just as long as we live. If we do not, our children may not know the pleasure of working to keep it for it may not be theirs to keep.

In these last few days, I've been more sure than I've ever been that we Americans of today will keep freedom and maintain peace. I've been made to feel that by the magnificent spirit of our young men and women in uniform, and by something here in our nation's capital.

In this city, where political strife is so much a part of our lives, I've seen Democratic leaders in the Congress join their Republican colleagues, send a message to the world that we're all Americans before we're anything else, and when our country is threatened, we stand shoulder to shoulder in support of men and women in the armed forces.

May I share something with you I think you'd like to know? It's something that happened to the Commandant of our Marine Corps, Gen. Paul Kelley, while he was visiting our critically injured marines in an Air Force hospital. It says more than any of us could ever hope to say about the gallantry and heroism of these young men, young men who served so willingly so that others might have a chance at peace and freedom in their own lives and in the life of their country.

I'll let General Kelley's words describe the incident. He spoke of a "young marine with more tubes going in and out of his body than I have ever seen in one body. He couldn't see very well. He reached up and grabbed my four stars just to make sure I was who I said I was. He held my hand with a firm grip. He was making signals and we realized he wanted to tell me something. We put a pad of paper in his hand and he wrote: 'semper fi.' "

Well, if you've been a marine, or if, like myself, you're an admirer of the Marines, you know those words are a battle cry, a greeting and a legend in the Marine Corps. They're Marine shorthand for the motto of the Corps: Semper Fidelis. Always Faithful.

General Kelley has a reputation for being a very sophisticated general and a very tough marine, but he cried when he saw those words, and who can blame him. That marine, and all those others like him living and dead, have been faithful to their ideals. They've given willingly of themselves so that a nearly defenseless people in a region of great strategic importance to the free world will have a chance someday to live lives free of murder and mayhem and terrorism. I think that young marine and all of his comrades have given every one of us something to live up to.

They were not afraid to stand up for their country or no matter how difficult and slow the journey might be, to give to others that last best hope of a better future.

We cannot and will not dishonor them now and the sacrifices they made by failing to remain as faithful to the cause of freedom and the pursuit of peace as they have been.

I will not ask you to pray for the dead because they are safe in God's loving arms and beyond need of our prayers.

I would like to ask you all, where ever you may be in this blessed land, to pray for these wounded young men and to pray for the bereaved families of those who gave their lives for our freedom.

God bless you and God bless America.

The Fight Against Terrorism

Ronald Reagan

*The speech was delivered to the nation, Washington, D.C., on
April 14, 1986. Published version:* Vital Speeches of the Day,
May 1, 1986, pp. 418-19.

My fellow Americans, at 7 o'clock this evening Eastern time, air and
naval forces of the United States launched a series of strikes against the
headquarters, terrorist facilities and military assets that support Muammar
Qaddafi's subversive activities.

The attacks were concentrated and carefully targeted to minimize
casualties among the Libyan people, with whom we have no quarrel.

From initial reports, our forces have succeeded in their mission. Several
weeks ago, in New Orleans, I warned Colonel Qaddafi we would hold his
regime accountable for any new terrorist attacks launched against American
citizens. More recently, I made it clear we would respond as soon as we
determined conclusively who was responsible for such attacks.

On April 5 in West Berlin a terrorist bomb exploded in a nightclub
frequented by American servicemen. Sgt. Kenneth Ford and a young
Turkish woman were killed and 230 others were wounded, among them
some 50 American military personnel.

This monstrous brutality is but the latest act in Colonel Qaddafi's reign
of terror. The evidence is now conclusive that the terrorist bombing of La
Belle discotheque was planned and executed under the direct orders of the
Libyan regime.

On March 25, more than a week before the attack, orders were sent from
Tripoli to the Libyan People's Bureau in East Berlin to conduct a terrorist
attack against Americans, to cause maximum and indiscriminate casualties.
Libya's agents then planted the bomb.

On April 4, the People's Bureau alerted Tripoli that the attack would be carried out the following morning. The next day they reported back to Tripoli on the great success of their mission.

Our evidence is direct, it is precise, it is irrefutable. We have solid evidence about other attacks Qaddafi has planned against the United States' installations and diplomats and even American tourists.

Thanks to close cooperation with our friends, some of these have been prevented. With the help of French authorities, we recently aborted one such attack: a planned massacre using grenades and small arms of civilians waiting in lines for visas at an American Embassy.

Colonel Qaddafi is not only an enemy of the United States. His record of subversion and aggression against the neighboring states in Africa is well documented and well known. He has ordered the murder of fellow Libyans in countless countries. He has sanctioned acts of terror in Africa, Europe and the Middle East, as well as the Western Hemisphere. Today we have done what we had to do. If necessary, we shall do it again.

It gives me no pleasure to say that, and I wish it were otherwise. Before Qaddafi seized power in 1969, the people of Libya had been friends of the United States, and I'm sure that today most Libyans are ashamed and disgusted that this man has made their country a synonym for barbarism around the world.

The Libyan people are a decent people caught in the grip of a tyrant.

To our friends and allies in Europe who cooperated in today's mission, I would only say you have the primary gratitude of the American people. Europeans who remember history understand better than most that there is no security, no safety, in the appeasement of evil. It must be the core of Western policy that there be no sanctuary for terror, and to sustain such a policy, free men and free nations must unite and work together.

Sometimes it is said that by imposing sanctions against Colonel Qaddafi or by striking at his terrorist installations, we only magnify the man's importance—that the proper way to deal with him is to ignore him. I do not agree. Long before I came into this office, Colonel Qaddafi had engaged in acts of international terror—acts that put him outside the company of civilized men. For years, however, he suffered no economic, or political or military sanction, and the atrocities mounted in number, as did the innocent dead and wounded.

And for us to ignore, by inaction, the slaughter of American civilians and American soldiers, whether in nightclubs or airline terminals, is simply not in the American tradition. When our citizens are abused or attacked anywhere in the world, on the direct orders of a hostile regime, we will respond, so long as I'm in this Oval Office. Self-defense is not only our right, it is our duty. It is the purpose behind the mission undertaken tonight—a mission fully consistent with Article 51 of the United Nations Charter.

We believe that this pre-emptive action against his terrorist installations will not only diminish Colonel Qaddafi's capacity to export terror—it will provide him with incentives and reasons to alter his criminal behavior. I have no illusion that tonight's action will bring down the curtain on Qaddafi's reign of terror, but this mission, violent though it was, can bring closer a safer and more secure world for decent men and women. We will persevere.

This afternoon we consulted with the leaders of Congress regarding what we were about to do and why. Tonight, I salute the skill and professionalism of the men and women of our armed forces who carried out this mission. It's an honor to be your Commander-in-Chief.

We Americans are slow to anger. We always seek peaceful avenues before resorting to the use of force, and we did. We tried quiet diplomacy, public condemnation, economic sanctions and demonstrations of military force—none succeeded. Despite our repeated warnings, Qaddafi continued his reckless policy of intimidation, his relentless pursuit of terror.

He counted on America to be passive. He counted wrong. I warned that there should be no place on earth where terrorists can rest and train and practice their deadly skills. I meant it. I said that we would act with others if possible and alone if necessary to insure that terrorists have no sanctuary anywhere.

Tonight we have. Thank you and God bless you.

Apologia *on Iranian Arms Sales*

Ronald Reagan

The speech was delivered to the nation from the White House, Washington, D.C., November 13, 1986. Published version: The New York Times, November 14, 1986, p. A8.

Good evening. I know you've been reading, seeing and hearing a lot of stories the past several days attributed to Danish sailors, unnamed observers at Italian ports and Spanish harbors, and especially unnamed Government officials of my Administration. Well, now you're going to hear the facts from a White House source, and you know my name.

I wanted this time to talk with you about an extremely sensitive and profoundly important matter of foreign policy.

For 18 months now, we have had under way a secret diplomatic initiative to Iran. That initiative was undertaken for the simplest and best of reasons:

- To renew a relationship with the nation of Iran;
- To bring an honorable end to the bloody six-year war between Iran and Iraq;
- To eliminate state-sponsored terrorism and subversion, and
- To effect the safe return of all hostages.

Without Iran's cooperation, we cannot bring an end to the Persian Gulf war; without Iran's concurrence, there can be no enduring peace in the Middle East.

For 10 days now, the American and world press have been full of reports and rumors about this initiative and these objectives.

Now, my fellow Americans, there is an old saying that nothing spreads so quickly as a rumor. So I thought it was time to speak with you directly—to tell you first-hand about our dealings with Iran. As Will Rogers once said,

"Rumor travels faster, but it don't stay put as long as truth." So let's get to the facts.

The charge has been made that the United States has shipped weapons to Iran as ransom payment for the release of American hostages in Lebanon, that the United States undercut its allies and secretly violated American policy against trafficking with terrorists.

Those charges are utterly false. The United States has not made concessions to those who hold our people captive in Lebanon. And we will not. The United States has not swapped boatloads or planeloads of American weapons for the return of American hostages. And we will not.

Other reports have surfaced alleging U.S. involvement. Reports of a sealift to Iran using Danish ships to carry American arms. Of vessels in Spanish ports being employed in secret U.S. arms shipments. Of Italian ports being used. Of the U.S. spending—or sending spare parts and weapons for combat aircraft. All these reports are quite exciting; but as far as we are concerned, not one of them is true.

During the course of our secret discussions, I authorized the transfer of small amounts of defensive weapons and spare parts for defensive systems to Iran. My purpose was to convince Teheran that our negotiators were acting with my authority to send a signal that the United States was prepared to replace the animosity between us with a new relationship. These modest deliveries, taken together, could easily fit into a single cargo plane. They could not, taken together, affect the outcome of the six-year war between Iran and Iraq—nor could they affect in any way the military balance between the two countries.

Those with whom we were in contact took considerable risks and needed a signal of our serious intent if they were to carry on and broaden the dialogue.

At the same time we undertook this initiative, we made clear that Iran must oppose all forms of international terrorism as a condition of progress in our relationship. The most significant step which Iran could take, we indicated, would be to use its influence in Lebanon to secure the release of all hostages held there.

Some progress has already been made. Since U.S. Government contact began with Iran, there's been no evidence of Iranian Government complicity in acts of terrorism against the United States. Hostages have come home—and we welcome the efforts that the Government of Iran has taken in the past and is currently undertaking.

But why, you might ask, is any relationship with Iran important to the United States?

Iran encompasses some of the most critical geography in the world. It lies between the Soviet Union and access to the warm waters of the Indian Ocean. Geography explains why the Soviet Union has sent an army into

Afghanistan to dominate that country and, if they could, Iran and Pakistan.

Iran's geography gives it a critical position from which adversaries could interfere with oil flows from the Arab states that border the Persian Gulf. Apart from geography, Iran's oil deposits are important to the long-term health of the world economy.

For these reasons, it is in our national interest to watch for changes within Iran that might offer hope for an improved relationship. Until last year, there was little to justify that hope.

Indeed, we have bitter and enduring disagreements that persist today. At the heart of our quarrel has been Iran's past sponsorship of international terrorism. Iranian policy has been devoted to expelling all Western influence from the Middle East. We cannot abide that because our interests in the Middle East are vital. At the same time, we seek no territory or special position in Iran. The Iranian revolution is a fact of history; but between American and Iranian basic national interests there need be no permanent conflict.

Since 1983, various countries have made overtures to stimulate direct contact between the U.S. and Iran. European, Near East and Far East countries have attempted to serve as intermediaries. Despite a U.S. willingness to proceed, none of these overtures bore fruit.

With this history in mind, we were receptive last year, when we were alerted to the possibility of establishing a direct dialogue with Iranian officials.

Now, let me repeat, America's longstanding goals in the region have been to help preserve Iran's independence from Soviet domination; to bring an honorable end to the bloody Iran-Iraq War; to halt the export of subversion and terrorism in the region. A major impediment to those goals has been an absence of dialogue, a cut-off in communication between us.

It's because of Iran's strategic importance and its influence in the Islamic world that we chose to probe for a better relationship between our countries.

Our discussions continued into the spring of this year. Based upon the progress we felt we had made, we sought to raise the diplomatic level of contacts. A meeting was arranged in Teheran. I then asked my former national security adviser, Robert McFarlane, to undertake a secret mission and gave him explicit instructions. I asked him to go to Iran to open a dialogue, making stark and clear our basic objectives and disagreements.

The four days of talks were conducted in a civil fashion, and American personnel were not mistreated. Since then, the dialogue has continued and step-by-step progress continues to be made.

Let me repeat: our interests are clearly served by opening a dialogue with Iran and thereby helping to end the Iran-Iraq war. That war has dragged on for more than six years, with no prospect of a negotiated settlement. The slaughter on both sides has been enormous, and the adverse economic and political consequences for that vital region of the world have been growing. We sought to establish communication with both sides in that senseless struggle, so that we could assist in bringing about a cease-fire and, eventually, a settlement. We have sought to be even-handed by working with both sides and with other interested nations to prevent a widening of the war.

This sensitive undertaking has entailed great risk for those involved. There is no question but that we could never have begun or continued this dialogue had the initiative been disclosed earlier. Due to the publicity of the past week, the entire initiative is very much at risk today.

There is ample precedent in our history for this kind of secret diplomacy. In 1971, then-President Nixon sent his national security adviser on a secret mission to China. In that case, as today, there was a basic requirement for discretion and for a sensitivity to the situation in the nation we were attempting to engage.

Since the welcome return of former hostage David Jacobsen, there has been unprecedented speculation and countless reports that have not only been wrong, but have been potentially dangerous to the hostages and destructive of the opportunity before us. The efforts of courageous people like Terry Waite have been jeopardized. So extensive have been the false rumors and erroneous reports that the risks of remaining silent now exceed the risks of speaking out. And that's why I decided to address you tonight.

It's been widely reported, for example, that the Congress, as well as top executive branch officials, were circumvented. Although the efforts we undertook were highly sensitive and involvement of Government officials was limited to those with a strict need to know, all appropriate Cabinet officers were fully consulted. The actions I authorized were and continue to be in full compliance with Federal law, and the relevant committees of Congress are being and will be fully informed.

Another charge is that we have tilted toward Iran in the Gulf War. This, too, is unfounded. We have consistently condemned the violence on both sides. We have consistently sought a negotiated settlement that preserves the territorial integrity of both nations. The overtures we've made to the Government of Iran have not been a shift to supporting one side over the other. Rather, it has been a diplomatic initiative to gain some degree of access and influence within Iran—as well as Iraq—and to bring about an honorable end to that bloody conflict. It is in the interests of all parties in the Gulf region to end that war as soon as possible.

To summarize, our Government has a firm policy not to capitulate to terrorist demands. That "no concessions" policy remains in force, in spite of the wildly speculative and false stories about arms for hostages and alleged ransom payments. We did not—repeat—did not trade weapons or anything else for hostages—nor will we. Those who think that we have "gone soft" on terrorism should take up the question with Colonel Qaddafi.

We have not, nor will we, capitulate to terrorists. We will, however, get on with advancing the vital interests of our great nation, in spite of terrorists and radicals who seek to sabotage our efforts and immobilize the United States.

Our goals have been, and remain:

To restore a relationship with Iran, to bring an honorable end to the war in the Gulf, to bring a halt to state-supported terror in the Middle East; and, finally, to effect the safe return of all hostages from Lebanon.

As President I have always operated on the belief that, given the facts, the American people will make the right decision. I believe that to be true now.

I cannot guarantee the outcome. But, as in the past, I ask for your support because I believe you share the hope for peace in the Middle East, for freedom for all hostages and for a world free of terrorism. Certainly there are risks in this pursuit but there are greater risks if we do not persevere.

It will take patience and understanding; it will take continued resistance to those who commit terrorist acts, and it will take cooperation with all who seek to rid the world of this scourge.

Thank you and God bless you.

Ronald Reagan and "The Speech"

The Rhetoric of Public Relations Politics

Kurt W. Ritter

Dr. Ritter is Associate Professor and Director of the Speech Communication Program in the Department of English, Texas A & M University, College Station, Texas. This article origin- ally appeared in Western Journal of Speech Communication, *32 (1968), 50-58, and is reprinted with permission of the the Western Speech Communication Association.*

On Tuesday evening, October 27, 1964, less than a week before the presi- dential election, actor Ronald Reagan, co-chairman of the California Citi- zens for Goldwater-Miller Committee, delivered a thirty-minute Republican appeal on a nationwide television broadcast.[1] Reagan called for a defense of "the freedoms intended for us by the Founding Fathers," and urged a rejec- tion of government by a "little intellectual elite in a far-distant capital."[2] According to Stephen Shadegg, Senator Barry Goldwater's long-time campaign manager, "thousands of Republicans...classified this as the most effective program of the Goldwater campaign." Republican commit- tees in most states rebroadcast the speech under local sponsorship during the next week, and the Republican National Committee quickly published the text in a special pamphlet.[3] Reagan's address brought an estimated

---

[1]Los Angeles *Times,* October 27, 1964, part IV, p. 11, and November 2, 1964, part I, p. 31; Louisville *Courier-Journal,* January 9, 1966, p. A-3.

[2]Ronald Reagan, "A Time for Choosing," p. 1, mimeographed copies distributed by Friends of Ronald Reagan, Southern California office of Spencer-Roberts and Haffner, 1300 W. Olympic Blvd., Suite 300, Los Angeles, Calif., hereafter cited as Reagan, "A Time."

[3]Stephen Shadegg, *What Happened to Goldwater?* (New York, 1965), p. 252.

$750,000 in campaign contributions, of which $100,000 came in even after Goldwater had lost.[4] William F. Buckley, Jr.'s conservative *National Review* described it as "probably the most successful single political broadcast since Mr. Nixon's Checkers speech" in 1952.[5] With this speech, Reagan rose out of a disastrous Republican defeat to establish himself as a potential candidate for Governor of California, and the "hottest new product on the Republican horizon."[6]

Early in 1965, a group of conservative southern California businessmen,[7] impressed by Reagan's Goldwater address, urged the actor to run for governor and engaged the public relations firm of Spencer-Roberts and Haffner to manage his campaign.[8] On March 27, 1965, Reagan "made it abundantly clear" that he would run for governor if he was convinced that all major factions of California's Republican Party supported him. Under the guidance of his public relations firm, Reagan immediately launched a statewide "survey," ostensibly to determine whether he commanded public support. He opened his unannounced campaign for governor with an expansion of his Goldwater television address, which Reagan called simply "The Speech," delivered at the annual convention of the conservative California Republican Assembly in San Diego. The convention "went wild" over the movie and television personality, contributing a standing ovation before and after his forty-five-minute speech.[9] During the remaining nine months of 1965 his public relations firm scheduled 150 more speaking engagements. Reagan traveled 10,000 miles to deliver his speech throughout California and across the nation before officially announcing his candidacy for the Republican gubernatorial nomination on January 4, 1966.[10] The thirty-minute announcement address, a retooled version of

---

[4]*Time,* LXXXVI (July 30, 1965), 14; Walter Pincus, "The Fight Over Money," *Atlantic Monthly,* CCXVII (April 1966), 73.

[5]*National Review,* XVII (December 1, 1964), 1039.

[6]Stewart Alsop, "The Good Guy," *Saturday Evening Post,* CCXXXVIII (November 20, 1965), 18.

[7]Henry Salvatori, a Los Angeles banker; Holmes Tuttle, an auto distributor; and A.C. (Cy) Rubel of the Union Oil Company of California headed this group. See Richard Oulahan and William Lambert, "The Real Ronald Reagan Stands Up," *Life,* LX (January 21, 1966), 82; James Phelan, "Can Reagan Win California?" *Saturday Evening Post,* CCXXXIX (June 4, 1966), 91; and New York *Times,* June 6, 1965, p. L-54.

[8]The firm's past political clients include liberal Republican Senator Thomas H. Kuchel of California; the John Birch Society's national public relations director, John Roussellot, in his successful 1960 campaign for Congress; New York Governor Nelson A. Rockefeller in his unsuccessful 1964 California presidential primary election battle against Senator Barry Goldwater of Arizona.

[9]Los Angeles *Times,* March 28, 1965, sec. A, p. B.

[10]Louisville *Courier-Journal,* January 9, 1966, p. A-3; *Time,* LXXXVII (January 14, 1966), 28.

"The Speech," was carried on fifteen television stations throughout the state.[11]

Through his sudden rise from a recent Republican convert[12] who had never held a public office to an important political figure, Reagan provides a contemporary case study in the rhetoric of public relations politics. Although public relations firms have been active in California politics since 1930, Reagan's lack of reputation as a political leader placed an extra burden of persuasion on Spencer-Roberts and Haffner and increased the significance of his nine-month unannounced campaign.[13] This study focuses on Reagan's speaking as an unannounced candidate from March, 1965, to January, 1966, and suggests a rhetorical strategy of "The Speech."

Reagan started to form his speech in 1954, ten years before his Goldwater address. In conjunction with his duties as host of the television program *G.E. Theatre,* he contributed to General Electric's public relations program by speaking to hundreds of "routine weekly luncheon clubs," state Chamber of Commerce banquets, and national business conventions. Reagan became an increasingly popular "nonpartisan" speaker during his eight-year association with General Electric; when *G.E. Theatre* was canceled in 1962, he had speaking tours booked as far ahead as 1966. This speech, entitled "Encroaching Government Controls," warned of Communist subversion in the United States and decried the "swiftly rising tide of collectivism" in America. As Reagan spoke in the Republican campaigns of 1962 and 1964, his speech "underwent a kind of evolution," and the attack on big government became his major theme.[14]

In various versions of "The Speech," Reagan spelled out the dangers of

[11]Los Angeles *Times,* January 5, 1966, part I, p. 3.

[12]Reagan (born February 6, 1911) was a Democrat and avid New Dealer; he organized the Labor League of Hollywood Voters to support President Truman in 1948 and campaigned for the liberal Helen Gahagan Douglas against Richard Nixon in their 1950 senatorial race in California. He did not change his voting registration to Republican until 1962.

[13]Robert C. Jeffrey most recently touched upon the influence of public relations firms on political rhetoric in his paper, "The Congressional Primary: An Exercise in Deception," read at the 1966 Convention of the Central States Speech Association, Chicago, April 16, 1966. The most thorough study of public relations firms in California politics is Robert J. Pitchell, "The Influence of Professional Campaign Management Firms in Partisan Elections in California," *Western Political Quarterly,* XI (June 1958), 278-300. Stanley Kelley, Jr., *Professional Public Relations and Political Power* (Baltimore, 1956) provides the best treatment of public relations in our national politics and its implications to American government.

[14]Ronald Reagan with Richard G. Hubler, *Where's the Rest of Me?* (New York, 1965), pp. 266-267, 297, 273; hereafter cited as Reagan, *Where.* For a text of the General Electric speech see Ronald Reagan, "Encroaching Control: Keep Government Poor and Remain Free," *Vital Speeches of the Day,* XXVII (September 1, 1961), 677-681.

"a Big Brother or paternalistic government."[15] He attacked the "planners" who have uprooted "our limited government" philosophy and the economists "who breathe too deeply of the mists off the Potomac." The actor-politician often asserted a simple, all-or-nothing relationship between freedom and private property: "You can't be a little bit Socialist and you can't be partly free." Freedom, Reagan claimed, comes only under a system of capitalism. He warned that the farm subsidy program, the National Labor Relations Board, and the Area Redevelopment Administration erode our freedoms, while federal aid to education and Medicare present a harmful centralization of America's traditionally local institutions. Reagan condemned rising taxes and the growing federal budget; with a vivid analogy, he dismissed the Democratic administration's tax cuts as "bookkeeping tricks that would jail a private citizen." Appealing to an audience unfamiliar with Keynesian economic theory, Reagan insisted that "to pretend" taxes can be reduced without a cut in government spending "is to perpetuate a fraud upon the people." He admonished economists for paying only "lip service" to the "ancient truths" while they advocated "managed money" and "planning in the market place." Throughout his attack on big government, Reagan did not categorically oppose aid to education and adequate medical care for all citizens. Instead, he asserted that these "problems would all be solved if the Federal Government would return to the states and communities some of the sources of taxation the Federal Government has usurped for itself." Reagan concluded with a sober warning that freedom might be lost "in our lifetime," with its failure being recorded in "a book not yet written: *The Rise and Fall of the United States of America.*" Amid an appeal for Republican unity and Democratic converts, he proclaimed: "You and I have reached our moment of truth, our rendezvous with destiny. You and you alone must make the decision as to whether freedom will perish from the earth."[16]

[15]Ronald Reagan, *A Plan for Action: An Address by Ronald Reagan, January 4, 1966,* p. 10, distributed by Friends of Ronald Reagan, Northern California office of Spencer-Roberts and Haffner, 47 Kearny St., Suite 800, San Francisco, Calif., hereafter cited as Reagan, *A Plan.* A comparison of this pamphlet with a tape recording of Reagan's announcement address verified it as an accurate transcript.

[16]Ronald Reagan, "California Republican Assembly Address," San Diego, Calif., March 27, 1965, hereafter cited as Reagan, "C.R.A. Address"; all quotations from this address are from a tape recording in the possession of the author. Ronald Reagan, "A Moment of Truth: Our Rendezvous with Destiny," *Vital Speeches of the Day,* XXXI (September 1, 1965), 681-686, hereafter cited as Reagan, "Moment." This speech was delivered at a testimonial dinner for U.S. Rep. John M. Ashbrook in Granville, Ohio, June 8, 1965, and was published in pamphlet form under the title *The Granville Rally,* distributed by Friends of Ronald Reagan, Southern California office.

From March through December, 1965, the various versions of Reagan's speech followed the same general theme. Specific examples often changed from speech to speech, but Reagan did not find such rewriting difficult, since he could "reach out blindfolded and grab a hundred examples of over-grown government."[17] The actor-politician admitted that while his lyrics changed, the tune remained the same. When accused of having only one speech, however, Reagan replied, a little angrily, that he varied his speeches from day to day, "taking an introduction from one, the middle from another and the conclusion from a third."[18] Running through all the speeches was a series of commonplace jokes and "big government" jabs that balanced Reagan's grim economic warnings and unfailingly drew laughter and newspaper attention. "Government," he explained, "is like a baby. It's an alimentary canal with an appetite at one end and no sense of responsibility at the other." "The *status quo*" he defined as "Latin for the mess we're in."[19]

In Reagan's unannounced campaign, "The Speech" served a two-fold rhetorical strategy: the identification of the actor with diverse political factions, and the manipulation of his reputation to present the "reasonable picture of a candidate" that his public relations firm desired.[20] By adapting "The Speech" to his different audiences, Reagan attempted to retain the confidence of the Republican right wing, while publicly modifying his recent position as a political conservative. The televised and published speeches addressed to the general public did not dwell on the Communist menace to America, but rather on Reagan's eagerness to solve the problems of age, health, poverty, and housing "without compulsion and without fiscal irresponsibility."[21] By emphasizing a positive program in his announcement address, Reagan appeared "no more farout than a Rotarian," and moved closer to what his public relations firm called "Nixon types" and Rockefeller supporters.[22]

In contrast to his publicized speeches, Reagan's unpublished talks to conservative groups stressed the dangers of Communistic collectivism and the "yeast-like growth" of government.[23] The California Republican Assembly, which favors repeal of the income tax and wants a "complete

[17]Reagan, *Where,* p. 270.

[18]San Francisco *Chronicle,* September 25, 1965, p. 6; San Jose (Calif.) *News,* December 21, 1965, p. 3.

[19]*Reagan,* "Moment," pp. 685, 682; Reagan, "C.R.A. Address."

[20]William E. Roberts of Spencer-Roberts and Haffner quoted in *Newsweek,* LXV (June 7, 1965), 19.

[21]Reagan, "Moment," p. 685.

[22]*Newsweek,* LXVII (January 17, 1966), 32; Fred J. Haffner of Spencer-Roberts and Haffner quoted in the New York *Times,* June 6, 1965, p. L-54.

[23]Reagan, "C.R.A. Address."

investigation" of the United Nations,[24] heard Reagan warn that our nation is engaged in a contest, "a war between philosophies: Communism versus Capitalism," which will determine whether the "nation and way of life" our forefathers created can endure. In the face of the "all embraced, all blood-soaked reality of the Communist program," he argued, "we must do everything we can to strengthen capitalism" and "repudiate everything that weakens it." The right-wing version of "The Speech" differed from the moderate version by explicitly citing Communism as an exterior enemy to whose philosophy our nation might unwittingly succumb through "voluntary slavery" to a "controlled economy" and a "proliferation of bureaucratic agencies."[25] By carrying on Barry Goldwater's rhetoric of limited government,[26] Reagan inherited the Goldwater supporters and financial contributors. The right-wing version reflected the political reality expressed by one John Birch Society section leader, that "a lot of conservatives aren't going to contribute if they don't have someone of Barry Goldwater's philosophy."[27] Whenever newspaper reporters asked Reagan about the Birch Society, he read his "500-word statement" denouncing the Society's president, Robert Welch, but "The Speech" did not mention extremism or the Birch Society.[28]

In appealing to Democrats, Reagan often referred to his own switch to the Republican Party in a search for the old Democratic "principles of Jefferson, Jackson and Cleveland."[29] He attempted to win a hearing from liberals by stressing that he attacked neither their sincerity nor their humanitarian motives, but only their measures. He shrewdly called out to the voter bloc "that crosses party lines" and to the "unsung heroes" who "pay their bills, contribute to their church and their charity and their community." Reagan's rhetoric was geared to picture him as the leader of these "forgotten Americans" who "believe in God as the Creator of all our rights and freedoms" and are "disturbed because their children can't ask His blessing on a lunch in the school cafeteria."[30]

[24]Los Angeles *Times,* March 29, 1965, part I, pp. 3, 24.

[25]Reagan, "C.R.A. Address."

[26]John Hammerback, "The Rhetorical Effectiveness of Barry Goldwater from 1960-1963," unpublished M.A. Thesis, University of Oklahoma, 1965, pp. 45, 48-52. The right-wing version of Reagan's speech reflects a point of view strikingly similar to "The Little World of Barry Goldwater," described by Ernest J. Wrage in *Western Speech,* XXVII (Fall 1963), 207-215.

[27]San Jose *News,* December 21, 1965, p. 44Z.

[28]San Francisco *Examiner,* October 2, 1965, p. 5; *Christian Science Monitor,* Western Edition, January 6, 1966, p. 3.

[29]Reagan, "Moment," p. 685; Reagan, "A Time," p. 1; Reagan, *A Plan,* p. 18.

[30]Reagan, "Moment," pp. 683, 685; Reagan, "C.R.A. Address"; Ronald Reagan, "The Republican Party and the Conservative Movement." *National Review,* XVII (December 1, 1964), 1055.

The second objective of Spencer-Roberts and Haffner's rhetorical strategy was to make Reagan appear as "a sensible, reasonable guy" who had the "intellectual capacity" to be a state governor. This public relations firm hoped to "prove, symbolically" that Reagan was "a good administrator."[31] By speaking from three-by-five inch cards, rather than from a manuscript or a memorized text, Reagan gave the impression of a well-informed "citizen politician," not of an actor reading his lines.[32] Reagan's well-publicized claim that he "has always written his own speeches and done his own research work" helped counteract the charge that he knew only what his public relations firm told him.[33] The actor-politician gained academic respectability from frequent references to Professor Alexander Frazer Tytler, Lord Atkin, Alexis de Tocqueville, Thomas Wolfe, and, of course, Abraham Lincoln.[34] More important to Reagan's speaker credibility were "the facts." He lamented that it required 520 pages to list all the executive agencies of the federal government. A federal ruling on cabbage, Reagan pointed out, took 29,911 words, while the Declaration of Independence used only 300. One federal questionnaire, he testified, "was 428 pages long, weighed ten pounds, and each page was twenty-four inches long." Interspersed with such statistics, Reagan offered unrelated and unsupported generalizations: Federal loans to college students have "an extremely high rate of default"; and the United States is taxing a "higher percentage from the free, productive economy than any society has ever taken without ruin."[35]

Reagan carefully denied ever attending "dramatic school," but often mentioned his college degree in economics.[36] Such appeals to personal authority presumably lent weight to his economic analysis. Reagan has stated, however, that he chose economics and sociology as his major subjects "because they afforded him more free time for the things he liked better—dramatics, football and [student] politics."[37]

In addition to presenting Reagan as a plausible gubernatorial candidate, "The Speech" provided his campaign with a fighting spirit. California political management firms consider this spirit vital in appealing to an

[31]William E. Roberts quoted in *Newsweek,* LXV (June 7, 1965), 19.
[32]A teleprompter was used in the announcement speech. San Francisco *Examiner,* January 9, 1966, sec. II, p. 2; Louisville *Courier-Journal,* January 9, 1966, p. A-3; Reagan, *A Plan,* p. 20.
[33]Correspondence from William E. Roberts, January 12, 1966; Los Angeles *Times,* October 26, 1965, part II, p. 4.
[34]Reagan, "C.R.A. Address"; Reagan, "Moment," pp. 682, 685-686.
[35]Reagan, "Moment," pp. 682-683; Reagan, "C.R.A. Address"; Reagan, "A Time," p. 1.
[36]Reagan, *A Plan,* p. 21; Reagan, "C.R.A. Address"; San Francisco *Examiner,* October 21, 1965, p. 6.
[37]"Ronald Reagan," *Current Biography: Who's News and Why, 1949,* ed. Anna Rothe (New York, 1950), p. 503.

American audience that enjoys a contest.[38] Here Reagan's acting career, which he minimized in his addresses, played a significant but silent role. The dark-haired, six-foot one-inch, smiling politician projected a crusading image by attacking "encroaching government" and defending individual rights against "federal control." Reagan's audiences knew him as the handsome host and actor in the television series, *Death Valley Days*; when he spoke, he carried this rugged western image with him. Before Reagan arrived at a rally, the public address system would blare out the Notre Dame fight song, subtly reminding the waiting crowd of Reagan's aggressive acting roles, including his movie portrayal of the Notre Dame football hero, George Gripp.[39]

Spencer-Roberts and Haffner manipulated Reagan's personal appeal by using "The Speech" to create the impression of Ronald Reagan as a national Republican spokesman. Although Reagan was preparing for a California state office, he spoke on national issues. The actor-politician admitted that "by deliberate intent" California was only mentioned incidentally during his unannounced campaign. Less than a tenth of Reagan's opening speech to the California Republican Assembly dealt with state issues. Reagan indicated he would discuss California "if and when" he became a candidate;[40] yet, much of his announcement address was devoted to topics "beyond the scope of purely state issues." By transferring his attack from federal bureaucracy to the "dangerously top-heavy" executive branch of California's state government, Reagan placed California issues within the ideological framework of "The Speech."[41] California Democratic leaders, who had ignored Reagan's earlier speaking on national issues, promptly charged that he was "simply wrong" on state issues.[42]

Since "The Speech" did not center on California topics, Reagan could deliver it across the nation. In June, 1965, he spoke at a series of Ohio Republican rallies, which concluded with a Cincinnati banquet that placed him on a state-wide program with nine major Republican leaders, including former President Eisenhower, former Vice President Nixon, and California's Senator Murphy. Reagan and Murphy "drew the lion's share of the applause."[43] In October, 1965, Reagan attracted the attention of the national news media by taking up a year-old invitation to speak in New

[38]Pitchell, "Campaign Management Firms in California," p. 288.

[39]"GOP 'Fight Song' Cheers Ex-Film Gridder Reagan," San Jose *News,* December 21, 1965, p. 3; Reagan, *Where,* pp. 90-95.

[40]San Jose *News,* December 21, 1965, p. 3.

[41]Reagan, *A Plan,* pp. 13, 10-12, 18-20.

[42]Rebuttals to Reagan's comments on national issues were published only after he announced his candidacy; see Oulahan, "The Real Ronald Reagan Stands Up," pp. 72, 74. Los Angeles *Times,* January 5, 1966, part I, p. 3; San Francisco *Examiner,* January 4, 1966, p. 8.

[43]Cincinnati, *Enquirer,* June 10, 1965, p. 1; New York *Times,* June 10, 1965, p. L-21.

England, where he addressed the National Federation of Republican Women in Boston and the "right-wing" Connecticut Republican Citizens Committee in New Haven.[44] The strategy of "The Speech" was so effective that before Regan declared himself a candidate, he was ahead of California's Democratic Governor Edmund G. (Pat) Brown in public opinion polls and had received nearly $140,000 in campaign contributions.[45] Ironically, Reagan managed to condemn such "false-image making" while announcing his candidacy from "a homey setting" in a Hollywood movie studio.[46]

Ronald Reagan's all-purpose speech and unannounced campaign suggest that in today's public relations politics a state candidate's pre-campaign oragory can effectively promote a planned rhetorical strategy of identifying the candidate with diverse political factions and manipulating his image. With this strategy, the state candidate can create a national reputation as a political spokesman, take advantage of national news media, and later discuss the specific state campaign issues in terms of his national posture.

[44]San Francisco *Examiner,* October 6, 1965, p. 38; *Newsweek,* LXVI (October 11, 1965), 42.

[45]These polls, of course, were taken too far in advance of the November 1966 election to be a necessarily valid prediction of the final result. *Time,* LXXXVI (November 5, 1965), 38; Louisville *Courier-Journal,* January 9, 1966, p. A-3.

[46]Reagan, *A Plan,* p. 21; Los Angeles *Times,* January 6, 1966, part I, p. 3; San Francisco *Examiner,* January 9, sec. II, p. 2.

Checklist of Sources in American Public Address

Presidential Rhetoric

Voice recordings of presidents' speeches may be obtained from the appropriate presidential libraries. Additionally, the libraries have revisions of speech texts, memoranda, position papers, etc., that contributed to the Final Reading Copy. Information about grants for research in the libraries may be obtained by writing to the appropriate library director.

Audio Materials

For voice recordings of some of the speeches in this anthology, see *Great American Speeches*, ed. John Graham, Caedmon Records, Vol. Three, 1931-1947, TC 2033, and Vol. Four, 1950-1963, TC 2035.

Video Materials

Video tapes for some of the speeches herein are available from The Educational Video Group. Motion picture newsreels, containing samples of famous orators' speeches, are available in the National Archives, Washington, D.C. The Museum of Broadcasting, New York City, may be helpful.

Research Materials

The following scholarly journals publish critical essays on American rhetoric:

- *Quarterly Journal of Speech*
- *Southern Speech Communication Journal*
- *Central States Speech Journal*
- *Western Journal of Speech Communication*
- *Communication Quarterly*
- *Presidential Studies Quarterly*
- *Speaker and Gavel*

Reference

American Orators of the Twentieth Century: Critical Studies and Sources, ed. by Bernard K. Duffy and Halford R. Ryan (Westport, CT: Greenwood Press, 1987).
Oratorical Encounters: Selected Studies and Sources of Twentieth-Century Political Accusations and Apologies, ed. by Halford R. Ryan (Westport, CT: Greenwood Press, 1987).